Microsoft® Exchange Server 2007:
A Beginner's Guide

ABOUT THE AUTHOR

Nick Cavalancia, MCSE, MCT, MCNE, MCNI, is an accomplished consultant, trainer, author, columnist, and speaker and has been in the IT industry for over 15 years, having designed Exchange environments for some of the most well-known companies today. He has contributed to over a dozen books on topics such as Windows, Active Directory, SQL Server, and Exchange, and is the coauthor of *Exchange 2000 Server Administration: A Beginner's Guide* and *Exchange 2000 Server: The Complete Reference*. Nick currently serves as Vice President of Product Marketing for ScriptLogic Corporation, where he assists in driving innovation and leads the evangelism of ScriptLogic solutions.

About the Contributing Authors

Sarbjit Singh Gill has 18 years' worth of experience in the IT world. He is currently an Independent Microsoft Certified Trainer (MCT) and Principal Consultant for Gill Technologies, a solutions consulting company he started. Gill Technologies provides consulting services to system integrators, independant software vendors, and customers who seek specialist advice and consulting on Microsoft technologies. He has presented at technical workshops and Microsoft events like TechEd Asia/South East Asia, TechNet, MSDN Connection, product launches, Microsoft Partner and customer briefings, community/user group event, and even pre-sales technical presentations for Microsoft directly for their customers. In his professional life in the IT industry, he has progressed from HP 3000 MPE/XL minicomputers to VMS, NetWare, IBM systems to Microsoft technologies. He is currently also a Microsoft MVP for Windows Management (MOM). His Exchange experience started with a senior technology executive role for a top financial Multinational Company (MNC) with 50,000 seats on Exchange 5.5.

He can be contacted at ssgill@gilltechnologies.com. His MVP profile is at https://mvp .support.microsoft.com/profile=88820A30-4B1D-48D7-BF42-3CD5F46081AA).

Richard Luckett is the president, chairman of the board of directors, and one of the founding partners of SYSTMS of NY, Inc. Prior to becoming president, he was president of American Messaging, Inc. Richard is an IT professional with over 15 years of experience in delivery, configuration, Microsoft consulting, network engineering, and security for both the public and private sectors. He has a wealth of field experience and real-world knowledge of Microsoft systems, specializing in Microsoft Active Directory services and Exchange messaging. Richard is a Microsoft Certified Systems Engineer (+Messaging +Security) and received the Exchange MVP award from Microsoft. He is the co-author of *Administering Exchange 2000 Server*, published by McGraw Hill, and is the course director and author of several Exchange courses, Introduction to Exchange 2000 and Exchange Server 2003, Ultimate Exchange Server 2003, and Exchange Server 2003 Administrator Boot Camp for Global Knowledge, Inc. Richard leads SYSTMS of NY, Inc.'s Microsoft Practice.

About the Technical Editor

Henrik Walther is a Microsoft Exchange MVP, MCTS in Exchange 2007, and MCSE Security/Messaging who works as a system specialist for Interprise Consulting A/S, a Microsoft Gold Partner based in Denmark. Interprise Consulting designs, migrates, implements, and supports Microsoft Server solutions (such as ISA Server, MOM, Exchange, SharePoint, etc.) for relatively large organizations. Henrik has been in the IT industry for more than 12 years (primarily working with MS Servers), but has over the years become a Microsoft Exchange Messaging Specialist. Henrik is also a frequent contributor to MSExchange.org.

Microsoft® Exchange Server 2007: A Beginner's Guide

NICK **CAVALANCIA**

New York Chicago San Francisco
Lisbon London Madrid Mexico City Milan
New Delhi San Juan Seoul Singapore Sydney Toronto

The McGraw·Hill Companies

Cataloging-in-Publication Data is on file with the Library of Congress

Microsoft® Exchange Server 2007: A Beginner's Guide

1234567890 DOC DOC 01987

ISBN: 978-0-07-148639-2
MHID: 0-07-148639-9

Sponsoring Editor Jane Brownlow	**Technical Editor** Henrik Walther	**Production Supervisor** George Anderson
Editorial Supervisor Patty Mon	**Copy Editor** Lisa McCoy	**Composition** International Typesetting and Composition
Project Manager Madhu Bhardwaj (International Typesetting and Composition)	**Proofreader** Nigel Peter O'Brien **Indexer** Kevin Broccoli	**Illustration** International Typesetting and Composition
Acquisitions Coordinator Jennifer Housh		**Art Director, Cover** Jeff Weeks

To my wife Jenay and my four children Colin,
Nicholas, Ryan, and Maggie, without
whom my life would have no joy.

AT A GLANCE

CONTENTS

Part I
Migration and Deployment

Part II

Administration

Part IV

Advanced Administration

ACKNOWLEDGMENTS

By the time you're reading this very sentence, the content of this book has passed through many inboxes, been edited, reviewed, corrected, tweaked, updated, etc. So many people contribute to the success of this book, each doing their part to ensure technical accuracy, grammatical accuracy, proper presentation, correct order, and more, striving to make the book the highest quality possible.

I'd like to recognize them, as they, too, should be proud of the work they've done. Let me first start with Jane Brownlow, my acquisitions editor at Mc-Graw-Hill; without her, this book would have never gotten off the ground. Jane, thank you for your professionalism and patience during the writing of the book (I checked with the folks at Webster, and they've agreed to put your picture next to the word *patient*!).

Next, I'd like to thank Sarbjit Singh Gill and Richard Luckett for their author-ing skills that helped keep this book on track. Sarbjit took on part of the monitor-ing chapter and Richard the scripting chapter. The expertise you both brought to the table helped make this an even better book.

Jenni Housh, Megg Morin, Patty Mon, George Anderson, and David Zielonka at McGraw-Hill did the really tough part: keeping the book moving with all the various stages each chapter passes through (I had to devise a spreadsheet just to keep it straight myself). You all are a fantastic team to work with—thank you for hounding me when I needed it and giving me time when that was needed as well.

Madhu Bhardwaj and the folks at International Typesetting and Composition worked hard to make the final presentation of the book fit the story I wanted to tell and went the extra mile to help me get as close as possible to what I envisioned. Thanks go to my agent Neil Salkind and the folks at Studio B, who have done their part to ensure the business end of the book was in line (no, it's not all fun and games! <g>).

I want to add an expression of thanks to Paul Robichaux, who answered a ton of questions for me on everything from trying to get the initial private Beta 1 of Exchange to pointing me to resources during the writing of this book. Paul, thank you for taking time out of your *extremely* busy schedule to help a fellow lover of Exchange without asking for anything in return.

I want to especially thank my wife Jenay, who put up with many, many, many late nights writing after 11-hour work days. Raising four kids is hard enough, but try it when your husband is working double-time. J – you're simply the best. Proverbs 31:27-28!

Since authoring this book didn't exist in a vacuum (I have a full-time job as well), I want to thank Jason Judge and Andy Langsam at ScriptLogic who put up with my schedule and gave me the time necessary to complete this project.

Lastly and most importantly, I want to thank Jesus Christ for giving me the desire, opportunity, and ability to write this book. Without you, life has no meaning.

INTRODUCTION

After four years in the making, Exchange Server 2007 has finally arrived. It is not only a robust messaging platform that meets the needs of today's Internet-savvy users, but also is one that has been architecturally improved to provide faster performance, better scalability, and an enhanced user experience.

Exchange 2007 doesn't exist as an island; Microsoft has worked diligently to improve the ability to collaborate with other Microsoft solutions by integrating tightly with Microsoft Office SharePoint Server 2007 for sharing information, InfoPath for creating electronic forms, and ISA Server for improving the security of Exchange.

More clients than ever before can now access Exchange information beyond that of traditional Windows clients; mobile devices, more Web browsers, even a standard phone can now access messages and attachments, making this version of Exchange a truly "anytime, anywhere, any device" messaging platform.

I'm excited that you've chosen to implement Exchange 2007 in your environment. It is a decision you won't regret.

WHO SHOULD READ THIS BOOK

Because Exchange 2007 has undergone so many changes, this book is for both those completely new to Exchange and those running previous versions of it. In either case, a primer on all the new technologies, methods of administration, and client capabilities is definitely in order, making this book the perfect choice. If you're an absolute Exchange expert, you will find this book to be a quick read, allowing you to cover a majority of Exchange in a compact, easy-to-understand format.

WHAT THIS BOOK COVERS

While I cover in detail the content of this book in Chapter 1, I do want to give you a high-level overview of the book here. The basic stream of consciousness is: installation, configuration, clients, and advanced administration.

Part I, "Migration and Deployment"

This part of the book introduces you to Exchange; discusses some new administrative concepts; and covers the what, when, how, and why of installing Exchange.

Part II, "Administration"

This part of the book breaks down Exchange into its various roles and addresses the administration necessary to properly configure Exchange for your environment.

Part III, "Administering Clients"

This part addresses standard clients, such as Outlook 2007 and Outlook Web Access, but also digs a bit deeper and discusses newer clients, such as Outlook Voice Access and the latest Windows Mobile client.

Part IV, "Advanced Administration"

This part addresses many topics, such as backup and restore, security, scripting, monitoring, performance, and compliance.

You can find more detail on what is new with Exchange and what is covered in the book in Chapter 1.

HOW TO READ THIS BOOK

You don't necessarily need to read this book front to back. I would recommend you read at least the first two chapters and then wander off from there. Most of the chapters have been designed to work on their own, with references to other chapters when necessary. So if you're more inclined to use this book as a "when needed" reference or are looking to read it cover to cover, it will work in either case. I would like to point out that the order of the chapters and the organization of the material was designed for front-to-back reading but, again, you can read the various chapters as needed.

PART I

Migration and Deployment

CHAPTER 1

Introduction to Exchange Server 2007

Welcome to the world of Exchange Server 2007! Microsoft has taken great strides to create a comprehensive messaging platform that provides "anytime, anywhere, any client" access to your e-mail and voice mail. In this book, I'll expose you to a broad range of new technologies and features Microsoft has incorporated into Exchange to make it the "anytime, anywhere, any device" messaging platform.

IS THIS BOOK FOR YOU?

While this book covers nearly every aspect of Exchange Server 2007 (which I often simply refer to as "Exchange" or "Exchange 2007" in this book), it is intended for an audience that is either completely new to Exchange (and I'll add those of you running Exchange 5.5 in this category) or for those who are familiar with previous versions of Exchange (such as 2000 or 2003) but need a broad overview of the new platform. If you are familiar with Exchange 2000 or 2003, administering it daily and are running, say, a multiple-site Exchange environment, this book is probably a bit too general for you, as you will be looking for more detailed information. You may still get quite a bit out of it, but please keep in mind that it was intended for an audience of Exchange "beginners."

The book provides a number of screenshots throughout the chapters to walk you through the various processes, dialog boxes, configuration options, and the like to ensure you don't just read about what I'm talking about, but also see it. There are tips and reminders throughout to point out key facts, security issues, and more. I've also sprinkled tips on the use of the new Exchange Management Shell throughout the book (as well as devoted a chapter on the subject) to show you how powerful this tool really can be. Let me break out each chapter's importance based on the audience.

Those Completely New to Exchange

If you are migrating to Exchange from some other platform, or are perhaps still on Exchange 5.5 (don't laugh—some are!), this entire book is for you. While I don't go into too much detail on migrating from either Exchange 5.5 (which is not supported; it requires first upgrading to either Exchange 2000 or 2003) or a foreign messaging system (in which case, your migration will focus on moving pertinent messaging data), I do cover all you need to know to get your Exchange environment up and running and configured properly. While all chapters will be relevant for you, let me outline a few groups of chapters:

Chapters 2-5 will cover the installation of Exchange, the basic configuration of recipients and the management of Exchange storage. The installation and daily management of Exchange has completely changed from previous versions, but will have similar concepts to any messaging platform you may be currently on.

▼ Chapters 6-9 cover the new server roles that each Exchange server can take on, providing detail and insight into the proper use and configuration of those roles.

■ Chapters 10 and 11 focus on the Exchange clients, giving you a starting point to both deploy and configure any of the supported clients.

▲   Chapters 12-17 are all on advanced topics that are still needed for even a beginner to Exchange, but just won't be utilized on a daily basis. These topics include securing your servers, use of the new Exchange Management Shell to manage Exchange from a command prompt, monitoring troubleshooting and viewing Exchange performance, backing up and restoring Exchange, and applying Exchange to compliance standards.

Overall, this book will provide a solid foundation for you to begin your ownership of an Exchange Server 2007–based environment.

Those Familiar with Exchange

For those of you currently working with either Exchange 2000 or 2003, a lot has changed from both of those versions to now. (I group these two together, as the administration is almost identical and 2003 was nothing more than a features upgrade to 2000, as indicated by the version numbers of each product—Exchange 2000 was version 6.0, and 2003 was 6.5.) When I first planned this book out with the editors at Osborne, I thought that a lot of the administration content (such as creating a mailbox, etc.) would be the same—boy was I wrong! Nearly every last detail of Exchange has changed. I would suggest that you view each of the chapters as a great overview of how things have changed, either in the context of "where," as in how Exchange administration is now organized within the Exchange Management Console, as well as the context of "how," as some management tasks have completely changed. While I believe all the chapters in this book will still be relevant for you (although not as much as for someone who hasn't touched Exchange before), let me outline what you should focus on within the book:

▼   Chapter 2 is a must, as the migration will not be what you are thinking (it's not a "slap in the DVD and upgrade"). I'll cover a primer on the Exchange server roles and the process of transitioning to Exchange 2007.

■   Chapters 3-4, which are on managing recipients and public folders, while conceptually are not new to you, the "how" and "where" will be different, and you should give them a quick read.

■   Chapter 5 (storage) is relatively the same architecturally, with a few changes you'll grasp quickly. You should still read this chapter to see the changes in storage (such as the number of storage groups, the database changes, etc.), as well as the "how" and "where" that have changed.

■   Chapters 6-9 show how all the administration you performed (outside of managing recipients) in the Exchange System Manager has been simplified into four roles.

■   Chapters 10-11, covering clients, will give you insight into the latest Exchange-related features of Outlook 2007, Outlook Web Access, and mobile devices.

■   Chapter 12 (on securing Exchange) is always a good refresher to ensure that you have your environment properly locked down.

■   Chapter 13 will be completely new, covering the use of the new Exchange Management Shell to manage Exchange.

- ■ Chapters 15 and 16 will be a review, but will cover some new (or enhanced) tools you can use to accomplish needed tasks.

- ▲ Chapter 17 (on compliance and Exchange) may be a new topic for you. It covers a number of new technologies that did not previously exist to help make your Exchange environment compliant with any imposed standards.

In summary, while I know those of you fitting into this category of reader *are* familiar with Exchange, this book will still provide you with plenty of good information on how to continue your administration with Exchange 2007.

EXCHANGE: A BRIEF PRIMER

Because this is a beginner's book, I feel I should cover some of the basics on Exchange—what it is, where it came from, and how we got to where we are today (of course, if you are simply new to Exchange 2007 but have experience with Exchange 2000 or 2003, you can feel free to skip this section). Exchange represents not only Microsoft's messaging platform, but also a building block in creating a true collaborative environment using Microsoft solutions. Exchange Server 2007 provides the messaging connectivity both within and outside of the organization, while other Microsoft solutions, such as SharePoint Server 2007, Live Communication Server 2005, Groove Server 2007, and others add more collaborative value.

Previous Versions

Exchange had its beginnings in Microsoft Mail, a messaging-only platform (even calendaring wasn't a part of Microsoft Mail; you needed Microsoft's Schedule+ to keep track of your schedule). Microsoft Mail provided messaging within the organization, public folders, had the capability of multiple locations, connectivity to the Internet (it was painful to support, but it worked), routing, and more. However, at the time, the concept of collaboration via e-mail simply was not a reality in most people's minds. Microsoft Mail was replaced by Exchange Server version 4.0 (the last version of Microsoft Mail was 3.5, so Exchange got a version of 4.0). Exchange Server 4.0 was a complete rewrite of the messaging platform (although many of the concepts from Microsoft Mail were retained in one form or another). Messaging over the Internet via Simple Mail Transfer Protocol (SMTP) was an integrated part of the product, instead of as a purchased add-on (as was the case for Microsoft Mail) in the form of the Internet Mail Service.

Exchange 5.x

Exchange 5.0 added Outlook Web Access (OWA) to provide remote users access to their messages via a Web browser. Version 5.5 added support for Internet-standard messaging protocols, such as Post Office Protocol version 3 (POP3) and Internet Message Access Protocol version 4 (IMAP4), and became the version of Exchange that seemed to really make Exchange the messaging platform of choice. If anyone remembers, Exchange 5.x also had a built-in chat server: Comic Chat—you could pick a character, choose a facial expression, and chat with the other person in the form of what appeared to be a comic strip!

Exchange 2000/2003

Exchange 2000 was an amazing update to the product. The directory containing the list of mailboxes, recipients, etc. moved to Active Directory, and SMTP became the primary protocol used to communicate, both within Exchange and between Exchange and other messaging systems. Significant improvements to OWA were Microsoft's first attempt at making it a viable primary client (although, in my experience, it wasn't until Exchange 2003 that OWA was really looked at as a real messaging client). Exchange 2000 continued to support the chat service, but also had a new instant messaging (IM) service that has since moved out of Exchange into Live Communication Server. Exchange 2000 was supposed to be the "anytime, anywhere, any client" messaging platform, but beyond OWA, Outlook 2000, and any standard POP3/IMAP4 client, if you wanted to access Exchange from a mobile device, you needed a separate product called Mobile Information Server (MIS). So Exchange wasn't completely there just yet. Exchange 2000 also had a separate version, Exchange 2000 Conferencing Server, which provided data, voice, and video conferencing, and has since moved to Live Communication Server.

Exchange 2003 was a features upgrade to 2000, but was not a truly new version (in fact, Exchange 2000 was considered to be Exchange version 6.0, and Exchange 2003 was version 6.5). Exchange 2003 added features such as advanced recovery features, the Intelligent Message Filter (IMF) to block spam, Outlook Mobile Access to get your e-mail from your cell phone's browser, access to Exchange over the Internet using Outlook 2003 and integration with Microsoft Operations Manager, and a much-improved OWA client. This was indeed an improvement upon Exchange 2000. So the question loomed "How can Microsoft improve on a fantastic messaging platform?"

EXCHANGE 2007: WHAT TO EXPECT

Because Exchange 2007 is not another "features upgrade" to Exchange 2003, but a completely new version of the platform, I want to cover some highlights of what you will find when exploring it.

Simplified Administration

Microsoft has taken great strides in making every aspect of managing Exchange easier. From installation to the management interface to configuration of every aspect of Exchange, one of the overall goals was to make administration easier to accomplish. Here are a few highlights of what you will see with Exchange 2007.

A Newly Organized Management Console

The first thing I noticed when both installing and using Exchange 2007 was the simplified administrative environment. Figure 1-1 shows the new Exchange Management Console. If you were to compare this with the completely expanded hierarchy of either Exchange 2000 or 2003 (for those of you not familiar with those versions, we're talking a long and deep hierarchy that would mirror a small file system), you would agree that

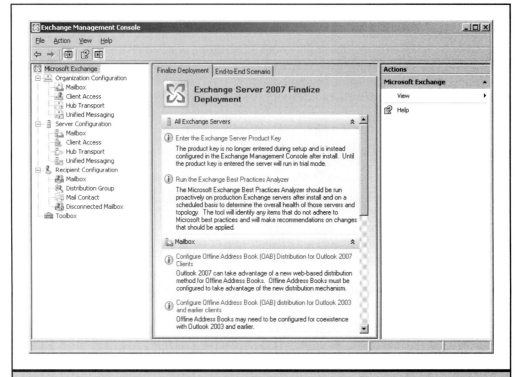

Figure 1-1.   The Exchange Management Console has undergone a complete revision.

this is a far more simplified environment—so much so, that you may begin to wonder "Is everything actually in here?"

All of your Exchange management has been broken down into server role work centers at the organization and server levels, with the recipients hosted in their own node.

Integrated Access to Troubleshooting Tools

Instead of searching the file system for troubleshooting tools (as was the case in all the previous versions of Exchange), the Toolbox node of the Exchange Management Console hosts a myriad of tools for various functions (which I cover a bit more in this chapter and then in depth throughout the book), as shown in Figure 1-2.

Improved Wizards

Microsoft has enhanced the concept of using wizards to automate tasks by making them more intuitive and more informative as to where you are in the process and the steps left to accomplish. They continue these goals by also being more dynamic in terms of modifying the wizard mid-stream based on choices made. Figure 1-3 shows an example of a wizard called from within the Exchange Management Console. Notice the steps

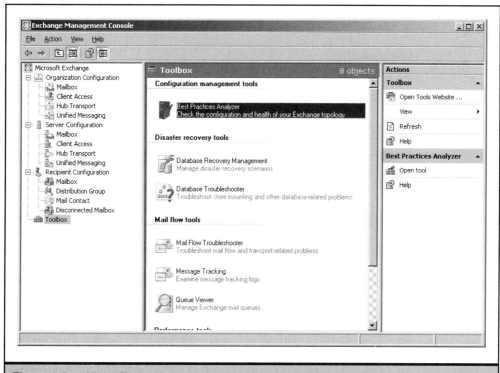

Figure 1-2.   All the Exchange tools you need...in one place!

on the left that outline where in the wizard process you are. Also, as an example of the dynamic ability of the wizards, the Master Account pane of the wizard you see in the figure was not shown when the wizard initially started.

In addition, at the end of each wizard, Exchange shows you the Exchange Management Shell code that was used to perform the task(s).

Customized Administration

Even the best graphical interface won't meet every need possible on the planet. So in Exchange 2007, Microsoft introduces the Exchange Management Shell, which is based on its Windows PowerShell technology. In the Exchange Management Shell, you can script your own management tasks, from the simple to the extremely complex. This means that whatever you can dream (and script), you can accomplish.

Enhanced Security

This version of Exchange continues to make messaging more secure in both how it is administered and the security of the messages and recipients using it. I have a chapter devoted to covering all the security features Exchange has to offer. You'll also find some

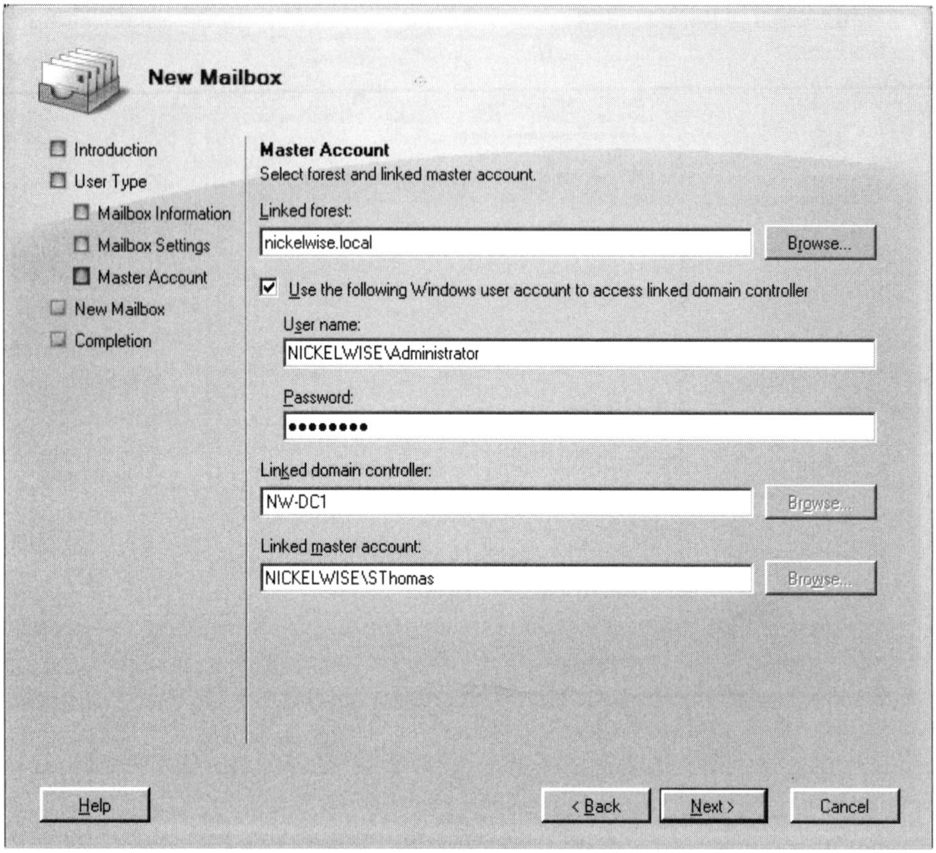

Figure 1-3. An example of a wizard in Exchange 2007.

security measures discussed throughout the book. Here are a few examples of the security features you'll find in Exchange 2007.

Administrative Security

Securing the administration of Exchange has been enhanced to meet the varying administrative needs related to managing recipients, servers, or the entire environment, all the while simplifying the process of delegating appropriate permissions. Figure 1-4 shows an example of how Microsoft has revamped permissions to reflect the actual administrative levels of access organizations will use to manage Exchange. I'll cover this in more detail in Chapter 2.

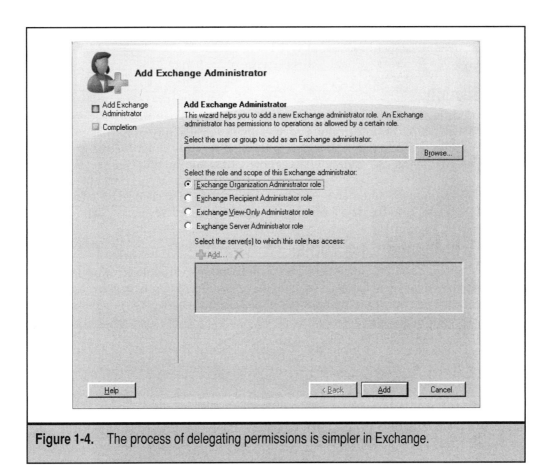

Figure 1-4. The process of delegating permissions is simpler in Exchange.

Message Security

For every piece of viable e-mail you receive, there are plenty of undesirable messages you won't want to see. Spam has become such a part of life that Microsoft first included their Intelligent Message Filter (IMF) in Exchange 2003. This has been greatly improved in Exchange 2007 to not just block undesirable messages, but to also block undesirable content, such as embedded viruses and spyware, and is now appropriately renamed the Content Filter. The Content Filter filters based on connection (IP address or via a block list provider), sender and recipient address, the reputation of the sender, the new Sender ID technology, and the new Outlook 2007 e-mail postmark validation.

In addition, to address the issue of viruses and spyware that do enter your environment, Microsoft has improved Exchange's virus-scanning application programming interface (VSAPI) by introducing the concept of transport agents to allow custom actions to be taken as a function of transporting messages.

Lastly, Microsoft has introduced Forefront Security for Exchange Server, an on-premise additional layer of scanner-based security. It is available as a separate product, but is also included with an Enterprise Client Access License of Exchange 2007.

Client Security

Microsoft has ensured client security by integrating technology from ISA Server 2006 with Exchange 2007. This integration provides higher availability of Exchange services via load-balancing services, secure access to internal services by hiding the translation of internal server names to externally accessible URLs, and by bridging secure sockets layer (SSL) connections, where ISA acts as the SSL endpoint, decrypts the data stream to inspect the data content, and then re-encrypts the session to the client. This ensures that prying eyes cannot read the data stream from the Exchange server to the client.

Improved Troubleshooting Tools

As I have already pointed out, Microsoft has incorporated troubleshooting tools into the Exchange Management Console so that you can quickly identify problems. Some of these tools have existed as command-line utilities since Exchange 4.x; others have been around and improved upon since Exchange 2003. Table 1-1 lists the tools and describes why you may want to utilize them.

Extensive Client Access

I started this book by claiming that this version of Exchange could provide "anytime, anywhere, any device" access to e-mail. As you will see in the relevant chapters, Microsoft has implemented technologies that will allow the highest possible number of varying client types to access Exchange.

Outlook Clients

Outlook 2007 is not just a new prettier interface for an age-old product; it was updated to take advantage of several new feature sets of Exchange 2007 that increase productivity of the support professional as well as the end user, and to enhance the security of the end user. For example, Outlook 2007 now includes the ability to auto-configure the user profile, partially shown in Figure 1-5. This enhances the productivity of the support professional in that very little time (if any) is required to configure (or reconfigure) an Outlook profile. In addition, the end-user has productivity gains from this one feature in situations such as when a disaster occurs and a user's mailbox is moved to an alternate server—the Outlook profile will automatically update. That means no calls to the help desk (or at least fewer calls) and happily working users who are unaware any kind of Outlook connectivity issue even occurred.

The management of external Outlook clients accessing Exchange has been enhanced. Outlook Anywhere (formerly known as RPC over HTTP) allows remote Outlook 2007 users to access Exchange via a secure Web connection. The setup and configuration has been greatly improved to reduce administrative overhead.

Exchange Tool	Description
Exchange Best Practices Analyzer	Performs various tests, including health checks, connectivity tests, permissions tests; collects performance baselines for later comparison and Exchange 2007 readiness checks, all in the interest of ensuring your Exchange environment follows the best practices Microsoft has established for Exchange. More on this tool can be found in Chapter 14.
Database Recovery Management	Provides two major functions: You can validate databases and their related log files, analyze disk space usage, repair failing databases, and view database-related event log entries. You can also manage the process of restoring databases using the Recovery Storage Group, as well as merge or copy the contents of a mailbox to another server. More on this tool can be found in Chapter 15.
Database Troubleshooter	Same as the event log capabilities of the Database Recovery Management tool.
Mail Flow Troubleshooter	Uses symptom-based troubleshooting to determine the root cause of mail flow issues. More on this tool can be found in Chapters 6 and 9.
Message Tracking	Use this tool to find messages based on a number of criteria, such as sender, recipient, subject, time/date, and more. I'll cover this in Chapter 6.
Queue Viewer	Provides a window into the queues Exchange dynamically maintains when sending and receiving messages. More on this in Chapter 6.
Performance Monitor	Runs System Monitor, but with default Exchange-specific counters already added in. This is covered in Chapter 16.
Performance Troubleshooter	Uses symptom-based troubleshooting to determine what is causing performance issues. More on this in Chapter 16.

Table 1-1. Troubleshooting Tools Included with Exchange 2007

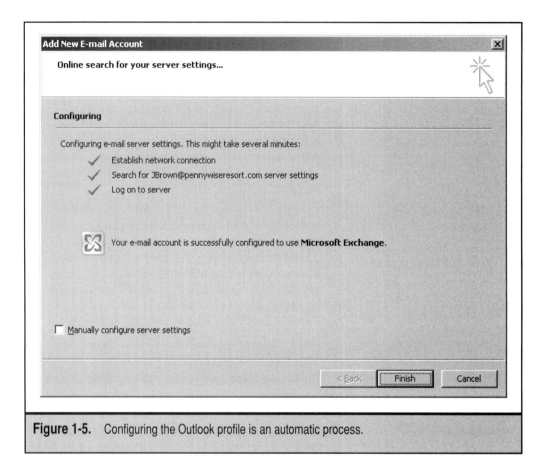

Figure 1-5. Configuring the Outlook profile is an automatic process.

Microsoft officially supports Outlook clients back to version 2002 (which was a part of Office XP), but admits that basic functionality (while not supported) is available all the way back to Outlook 97. This means that you have a wide variety of clients available to you while you are moving to Outlook 2007.

Outlook Web Access

It has been a long-time desire of many that Outlook Web Access (OWA) be "as good" as Outlook itself. The latest version of OWA provides the closest experience to the full Outlook client as Microsoft has ever come before. OWA, as shown in Figure 1-6, is a much richer client in both functionality and user experience. The OWA client supports access to nearly every folder in Outlook (with exceptions such as the Journal folder), drag-and-drop management of messages, extensive option configurations, and even access to documents on both Windows servers and SharePoint Server 2007. OWA is accessible from nearly every Web browser on the market today.

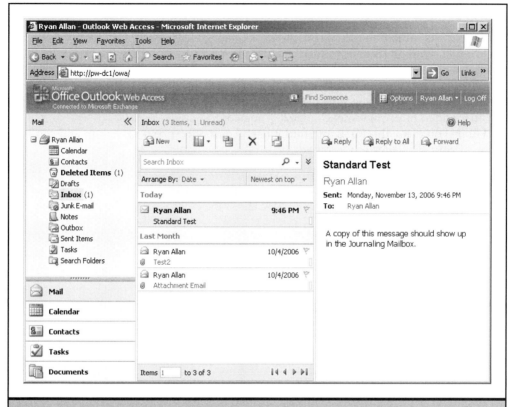

Figure 1-6. The Outlook Web Access client provides a richer client experience.

Mobile Clients

Microsoft has enhanced their ActiveSync technology, which provides access to Exchange via a handheld mobile device. Features such as over-the-air provisioning, automatic discovery of configuration, and access to files on Windows and SharePoint servers all aligned with the new version of Windows Mobile 6.0 (along with traditional access to messages, calendar, address lists, etc.), making mobile clients truly viable.

Unified Messaging

This is completely new to Exchange (but was previously available via third-party vendors) and provides access to voice mail, faxes, and e-mail from a single mailbox. Messages are accessible from Outlook 2007, mobile clients, and a new client, Outlook Voice Access, where you can access email messages and faxes via a phone-based client.

FINAL NOTES

This book was initially written against the beta and release candidate (RC) versions of the product, with all chapters edited against the final version of Exchange Server 2007, which was released in December 2006, and the beta version of Service Pack 1. Should you wish to communicate with me about the content of this book, I can be reached via e-mail at e2k7abg@exchangeconsultants.com, as well as on the blog for this book which can be found at http://www.exchange2007abg.com.

I hope you enjoy this book and find it useful as a reference in the setup and configuration of your Exchange environment.

CHAPTER 2

Installing Exchange Server 2007

I would think you would expect to see a migration chapter before an installation chapter, as most readers are probably already running an earlier version of Exchange. As I will explain in more detail later in this chapter, there is no true in-place "upgrade" from previous versions of Exchange to Exchange 2007. Even in the case of migrations from Exchange 5.5, 2000, and 2003, the installations of Exchange 2007 will be on brand-new servers. So you should use this chapter as a guide for installation during new installs as well as for migrations.

In this chapter, I'll discuss how to install Exchange Server 2007 by focusing on the practical steps and actions you'll need to perform before, during, and after in order to install it. I'll also focus on the new server roles employed by Exchange Server 2007 that you will need to specify during installation. Then I'll cover the process of moving your existing Exchange organization to Exchange 2007. Last, I'll briefly discuss the migration options you have when moving from a foreign messaging system.

Let's first take a look at what Exchange Server 2007 requires before it can be installed and then look at how to perform a manual installation. Then I'll show you what is involved in performing an unattended-mode installation.

REQUIREMENTS TO INSTALL
EXCHANGE SERVER 2007

Like Exchange 2000 and 2003, you need to be certain that your Active Directory environment is in proper shape before you can begin installing Exchange 2007. While Microsoft still assists with determining the state of your Active Directory pre-installation, it is still worthwhile for me to cover the basics.

Active Directory Requirements

Here's what your Windows environment must look like to install Exchange Server 2007:

▼ An available Active Directory forest running a domain functional level of at least Windows 2000 Server native. The Schema Master role must be running Windows Server 2003 Service Pack 1 (SP1). As already required by the presence of Active Directory, you need to have Domain Name Service (DNS) installed and configured properly.

■ At least one global catalog server running at least Windows Server 2003 SP1 in each Active Directory site on which you plan on running Exchange 2007.

▲ If an Exchange organization already exists, there cannot be any Exchange 5.5 servers, and the organization must be running in either Exchange 2000 or Exchange 2003 native mode.

Server Requirements

If your Active Directory environment is aligned with these requirements, your Exchange server must meet the following minimums:

▼ x64 Intel Xeon or Pentium processor supporting the Intel Extended Memory 64 Technology (Itanium IA64 processors are not supported by Windows Server 2003).

■ x64 AMD processor supporting the AMD64 platform.

■ A 64-bit version of Windows Server 2003 running with at least Service Pack 1, with New Technology File System (NTFS) as the file system on both the operating system partition and all partitions containing Exchange binaries, databases, transaction logs, etc.

■ A minimum of 1 gigabyte (GB) of random access memory (RAM) for the operating system, plus 7 megabytes (MB) per mailbox you plan on hosting. Microsoft recommends 2 GB of RAM and 10 MB per mailbox.

■ A minimum of 200 MB of available disk space on the system partition.

■ A minimum of 1.2 GB of available disk space on the partition where you will install Exchange.

■ An additional 500 MB of available disk space per unified messaging language pack you plan on installing.

■ A DVD drive (which can be located either locally on the Exchange server or on a remote computer).

■ Microsoft .NET Framework 2.0.

■ Windows PowerShell.

▲ Microsoft Management Console (MMC) 3.0.

TIP Microsoft ships Exchange 2007 in both 32-bit and 64-bit versions. However, only the 64-bit version of Exchange running on a 64-bit version of Windows Server 2003 is supported by Microsoft in production environments.

Normally, at this point in the chapter, you'd expect to see some silly minimum requirement, like a Pentium 500 MHz with 512 MB or RAM (not even your *kids* are running a computer *that* slow!), at which point, I would write a few paragraphs on what the really *real* minimums are. In this case, Microsoft is taking a bold move forward and making the basic requirement to install Exchange 2007 be that you are running state-of-the-art hardware. The move to recommend 64-bit hardware for Exchange and Active Directory is to increase the performance of both in larger environments. Table 2-1 lists the processor and memory requirements recommended by Microsoft.

Exchange Server Role	Processor Cores			Memory (in GB)		
	Minimum	Recommended	Recommended Maximum	Minimum	Recommended	Recommended Maximum
Edge Transport	1	2	4	2	1 per core (2 GB min.)	16
Hub Transport	1	4	8	2	1 per core (2 GB min.)	16
Mailbox	1	4	8	2	2 GB plus 2–5 MB per mailbox	32
Client Access	1	4	4	2	1 per core (2 GB min.)	8
Unified Messaging	1	4	4	2	1 per core (2 GB min.)	4
Multiple Roles on a Single Server	1 core	4 cores	4 cores	2	4 GB plus 2–5 MB per mailbox	8

Table 2-1. Processor and Memory Requirements

Mailbox Role Memory Recommendations

Deciphering the "2–5 MB per mailbox" statement in Table 2-1 can be tricky. Since Microsoft cannot guess how heavily your Mailbox role servers will be utilized, they make their memory recommendations (above the default recommendation of 4 GB) in somewhat subjective terms. The only clarity I can provide is that you should add 2 MB per "light" user, 3.5 MB for "average" users, and 5 MB for "heavy" users. Sorry this is so vague, but that is as good as Microsoft is going to give you. In addition, Microsoft also recommends that you have 2 GB of RAM for every one to four storage groups (more on storage groups can be found in Chapter 5). That is, for one to four storage groups, you should have at least 2 GB of RAM, five to eight storage groups would require 4 GB, nine to twelve need 6 GBs, and so on, but even so, with one to four storage groups, keep with the minimum recommendation of 4 GB of RAM.

Pre-Installation Steps

So you thought you were ready, right? Not so fast—there are still a few steps you must perform before you can get to the good stuff. Depending on whether your install will be done to an existing Exchange organization or a new one, you will need to do the following:

▼ Prepare the legacy exchange permissions

■ Prepare the Active Directory schema

■ Prepare Active Directory

▲ Prepare the domain

Preparing the Legacy Exchange Permissions

If you are installing Exchange 2007 into an existing Exchange 2000 or 2003 organization, certain permissions need to be modified to allow Exchange 2007 and previous versions to function together. The command you need to run is:

```
setup /PrepareLegacyExchangePermissions
```

This command allows the Recipient Update Service of the legacy Exchange servers to continue to modify recipient attributes. I'll explain more about this in Chapter 3.

Preparing the Active Directory Schema

This step updates the Active Directory schema with Exchange 2007–specific attributes. You must be a member of the Schema Admins group to perform this step. The command you will need to run is:

```
setup /PrepareSchema
```

You will need to run this command from a computer that is in the same Active Directory domain and site as the Schema Master (just run it from the Schema Master if you can). You'll only need to run this command in environments where those admins controlling the schema are not the same as those that will control Exchange. If, in your case, you are in ownership of both, you can safely skip this step, as the next step will prepare the schema.

Preparing the Active Directory

If you forget the first two steps I just mentioned, this step will perform them both, as well as a few more tasks. This step configures the Exchange-related objects in Active Directory that are required in both the root domain and the domain you will be installing Exchange 2007 into. The command you will need to run is:

```
setup /PrepareAD
```

You will need to be a member of the Enterprise Admins group and, if you have a legacy Exchange organization, the Exchange Admins group.

NOTE You can verify this step by looking for the Microsoft Exchange Security Groups organizational unit (OU) in the root domain, as well as in the following Exchange Universal Security Groups (USGs):

Exchange Organization Administrators

Exchange Recipient Administrators

Exchange View-Only Administrators

Exchange Servers

Exchange2003Interop

Preparing the Domain

This last step is only required if you are installing Exchange 2007 into domains other than the one you ran one or more of the previous three steps. Table 2-2 lists the commands you can run at this step.

Command	Purpose	Requirement
`setup /PrepareDomain`	Prepares the current domain	Member of the Domain Admins group in the current domain
`setup /PrepareDomain: <FQDN of domain>`	Prepares the specified domain	Member of the Domain Admins group in the specified domain
`setup /PrepareAllDomains`	Prepares all domains in the forest	Member of the Enterprise Admins group

Table 2-2. Domain Setup Commands

NOTE   The reason the 32-bit version of Exchange remains available is to allow for any of the previously mentioned preparation steps to be run, even if you have no 64-bit servers yet.

EXCHANGE SERVER ROLES

The installation of Exchange 2007 has changed drastically. In previous versions, it was as simple as starting the install of Exchange, adding on a few extra components, and you were done. With Exchange 2007, Microsoft introduces role-based deployments of Exchange. Each of the five roles breaks up the services and functionalities you may have seen in a single installation with previous versions of Exchange. While many of the roles can coexist on a single server, certain roles don't play well with others. I need to briefly cover these roles before we get into the install steps, as you will need to select server roles during the process. I'll summarize each role first and then show you how they interact within an organization.

The five roles an Exchange 2007 server can take on are:

▼   Edge Transport Server role

■   Hub Transport Server role

■   Mailbox Server role

■   Client Access Server role

▲   Unified Messaging Server role

Edge Transport Server Role

The Edge Transport server sits on the edge of your network, presumably in the perimeter network (previously known as a DMZ—demilitarized zone). It is responsible for protecting the internal Exchange environment using a number of agents:

▼   Antispam and antivirus

■   Connection, content, and recipient filtering

■   SenderID and sender/IP reputation

■   Edge transport rules

▲   Address rewriting

All inbound and outbound messages from and to the Internet travel through the Edge Transport role. Think of this role like the Internet Mail Connector in Exchange 5.5 and a Simple Mail Transfer Protocol (SMTP) Connector in Exchange 2000/2003. In the case of Exchange 2007, the connector is running on overdrive, focusing on the security of the Exchange organization.

NOTE   Keep in mind that the Edge Transport role is completely optional. If you choose not to use it, you'll need to configure the Exchange environment to accept mail for your domain.

The Edge Transport server is not installed as a member of your Active Directory, as it sits in the perimeter network. Because there is a need for the server to perform recipient lookups, this server runs the Active Directory Application Mode (ADAM) services, which synchronizes recipient and configuration information stored in Active Directory to the Edge Transport server.

TIP   More than one Edge Transport server can be used in the perimeter network to provide redundancy for your SMTP communications via either multiple Mail Exchanger (MX) records using increasing priority values or by using a *round-robin* DNS configuration, where two or more servers are assigned the same host name within DNS so that when a fully qualified domain name (FQDN) is queried in order to connect to the Edge Transport servers, DNS will return one server this time and another server next time. The end result in both the case of the multiple MX records or the round-robin DNS is redundancy for inbound communications.

Hub Transport Role

Hub Transport servers handle all mail flow within the Exchange organization. In Exchange 2000/2003, this role would be considered the same as a Bridgehead server. The Hub Transport role houses the *categorizer*, which is responsible for tasks like retrieving recipient information from Active Directory, expanding distribution lists, applying any policies, converting content, and finally routing the message. The Hub Transport role can also have both antispyware and antivirus agents installed on it. It must be installed on a server that is a domain member.

Mailbox Role

This role performs the tasks most people associate with Exchange. The Mailbox server hosts users' mailboxes and public folders. Outlook clients will connect directly to the Mailbox server to retrieve their e-mail. The Mailbox server role must be installed on a server that is a domain member.

Client Access Role

The Client Access server manages clients other than traditional Outlook clients within your network. Post Office Protocol version 3 (POP3), Internet Messaging Access Protocol 4 (IMAP4), Outlook Web Access (OWA), and ActiveSync clients all interact with Exchange via the Client Access role. In addition, Outlook Anywhere clients (utilizing RPC traffic over a secure Web connection) access Exchange via the Client Access server role. The Client Access server role must be installed on a server that is a domain member.

Unified Messaging Server Role

This is a brand-new function for Exchange. The Unified Messaging server takes voice mail, faxes, and traditional e-mail and makes all three accessible via both an Exchange client, such as Outlook or OWA, and a telephone. The Unified Messaging server role must be installed on a server that is a domain member.

TIP When you install the Unified Messaging server role into the Exchange organization, Setup will look for the Hub Transport, Mailbox, and Client Access roles to already be installed within the organization, whether they exist on the same server on which you are installing the Unified Messaging server role or on separate servers.

Putting the Roles Together

It may seem like you now have five different Exchange servers to plan for. Not so; Microsoft has simply added these roles as a way of streamlining Exchange duties. In a larger Exchange environment, where multiple Exchange servers are utilized, in previous versions of Exchange, each server hosted nearly every service, whether it needed to or not. With the server roles, each Exchange server need only host the services appropriate for that Exchange server's purpose within the organization. To demonstrate how these roles fit together in an Exchange installation, let's look at a single-server implementation and a few multiple-server implementation scenarios.

Single-Server Environment

I bet you think you're already ahead of me and have put all five roles on one server, right? If so, you forgot that the Edge Transport role is deployed outside of Active Directory in a perimeter network. The following illustration shows how all the roles except the Edge Transport server, along with the Global Catalog/Domain Controller services, will exist on a single server. While it makes sense that you may still want all the features of the Edge Transport server in your environment, if you have a single server, you're out of luck.

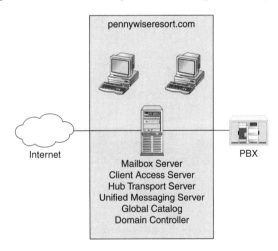

TIP In a single-server environment, you can install the antispam agents using the Install-AntispamAgents.ps1 script found in the Scripts folder within your Exchange installation. This script can be run on any Exchange server running the Hub Transport role.

Multiple-Server Environments

Here's where things can get complicated. The following illustration shows a simple two-server environment where an Edge Transport server has been added but everything else remains the same. The next illustration shows how a larger organization might split out the services to have different servers handling client access, message storage, message routing, message security, and unified messaging.

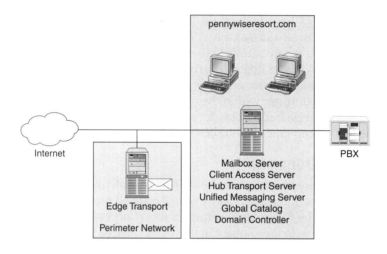

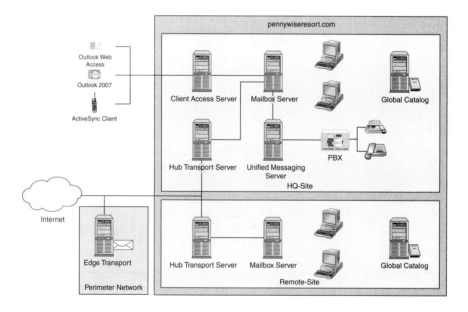

Now that I've covered the various roles that you will see during the installation of Exchange, let's dive into the install itself.

INSTALLING EXCHANGE SERVER 2007

There are three ways to install Exchange Server 2007. The most common, straightforward method is to perform a typical installation of the program. This would be appropriate for a single-server Exchange organization. The second method is a custom installation, which would be utilized when installing the various server roles on separate servers in a custom configuration. A third method of installing Exchange Server 2007 is to perform an unattended installation (see "Performing an Unattended-Mode Installation" later in this chapter).

For the purposes of this book, I'll be using the fictitious company, *Pennywise Resort*, a luxury vacation property that focuses on providing its customers with the most value for their vacation dollar.

Performing a New Installation of Exchange Server 2007

There are several decision points that you need to plan for during the installation:

▼ The name of the Exchange organization

■ Placement of the various server roles

■ Whether you'll be performing a typical or custom installation

■ Location of your Exchange files and databases

▲ Whether you'll be supporting versions of Outlook earlier than 2007

These are rather important points to plan ahead for. For example, once you have named the Exchange organization, it will be extremely difficult (and will most likely involve a call to Microsoft Technical Support) to remove and rename it.

To start the installation, run setup.exe from the root folder on your Exchange Server 2007 DVD, or you can just insert the DVD into the DVD drive and it will automatically start and display the Exchange Server 2007 splash screen. Choose to install Exchange Server 2007, and you'll see the Welcome screen for the installation program, shown in Figure 2-1.

The first thing you should notice is that installing Exchange is step four; the first three steps are all prerequisites to getting Exchange installed. The first step, to install .NET Framework 2.0, opens an Internet Explorer window to allow you to download the .NET Framework redistributable package, as shown in Figure 2-2.

Once the .NET Framework is installed, you will continue with the MMC 3.0 and Microsoft Windows PowerShell installs. As you complete each installation, the Welcome screen updates appropriately, as shown in Figure 2-3.

Once all the prerequisites are met, you can finally start the Exchange setup by selecting Step 4: Install Microsoft Exchange. After copying the needed files, the setup begins initializing, leaving you at the Introduction page of the Exchange Server 2007 Setup Wizard, shown in Figure 2-4.

After clicking Next, you are shown the license agreement (which, of course, you are going to read in its entirety!). If you agree, select the I Accept The Terms In The License Agreement option, and click Next. The Error Reporting page is something new to Exchange. If you are considering participating in the Error Reporting Service and are concerned about what information Microsoft will collect, you should click the Read More About Error Reports hyperlink, shown in Figure 2-5.

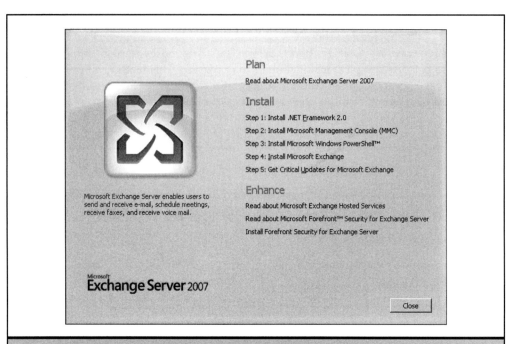

Figure 2-1.   The Exchange Server 2007 installation Welcome screen.

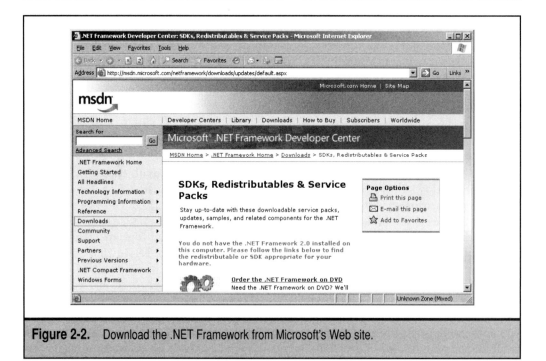

Figure 2-2.   Download the .NET Framework from Microsoft's Web site.

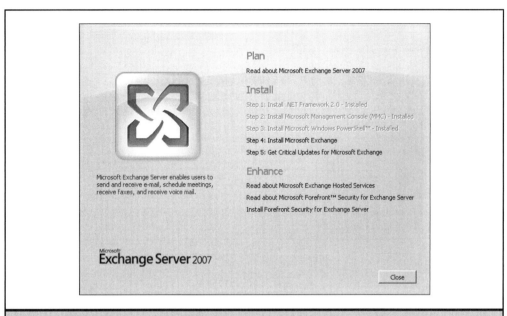

Figure 2-3.   The updated Exchange Server 2007 installation Welcome screen.

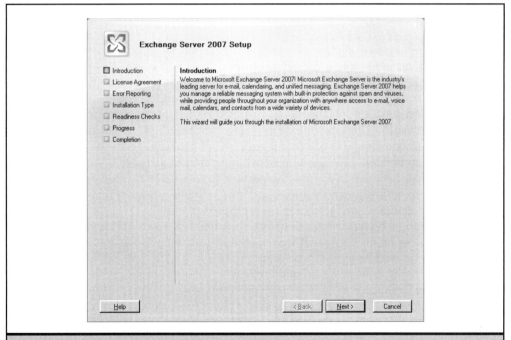

Figure 2-4.   The Exchange Server 2007 Installation Wizard starts at the Introduction page.

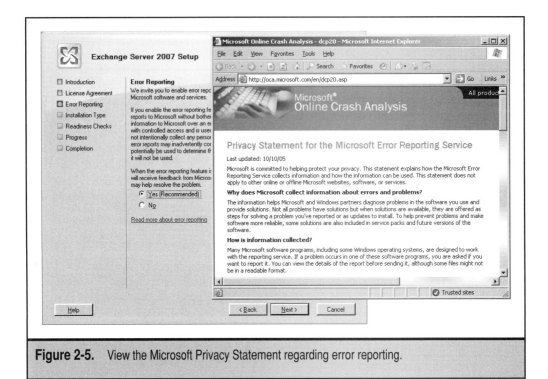

Figure 2-5.   View the Microsoft Privacy Statement regarding error reporting.

Once you've decided whether to report errors to Microsoft or not and have clicked Next, we *finally* get to some real Exchange options. The Installation Type page, shown in Figure 2-6, gives you the option to select either a typical or custom installation. Notice how the focus of each installation is on the placement of server roles.

The typical installation installs the Hub Transport, Client Access, and Mailbox roles on a single server (the Unified Messaging role is not installed by default, as you may not have your phone system ready to integrate with Exchange). The custom installation gives you a bit of flexibility in choosing which roles will be installed on the Server Roles page of the wizard, shown in Figure 2-7. As you choose various roles, any unavailable options will automatically appear dim. Choose a custom installation if you are planning on installing specific Exchange services on multiple servers.

Upon selecting a typical installation, or after you have selected a custom installation and chosen your server roles, you will need to specify the name of the Exchange organization if this is the first Exchange server in the organization (see Figure 2-8). I would recommend that you use a name that means something to you (other than the extremely unhelpful default of "First Organization").

After giving your Exchange organization a name, you are asked whether there will be versions of Outlook earlier than Outlook 2007 running in the organization, as shown in Figure 2-9.

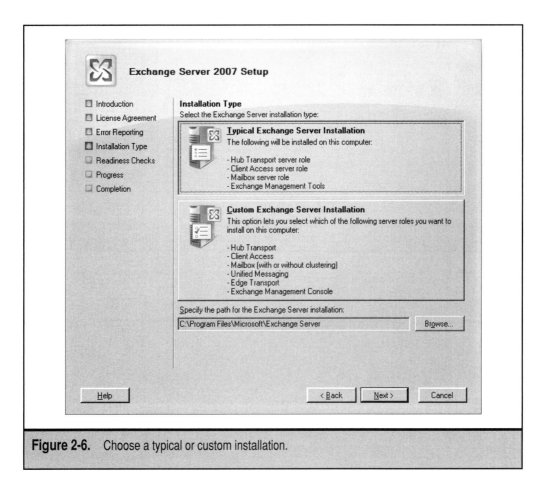

Figure 2-6.   Choose a typical or custom installation.

Your answer determines if Exchange should create a public folder store on the mailbox server. Outlook 2003 and earlier versions require public folders, not just for the purpose of sharing data, but also as the location to find the offline address book, free/busy lookups, Outlook security settings, and organizational forms. Outlook 2007 does not require public folders for the following reasons:

▼   The offline address book is available to Outlook 2007 clients via an https connection to a Client Access server.

■   Free/busy information is accessed by Outlook 2007 clients via the new Availability service. Outlook 2007 will use the traditional public folder method should it be configured to access a mailbox residing on an Exchange 2000/2003 server.

▲   Outlook security settings (which were introduced to block attachments with certain extensions) are deployed via Group Policy.

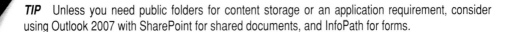

TIP   Unless you need public folders for content storage or an application requirement, consider using Outlook 2007 with SharePoint for shared documents, and InfoPath for forms.

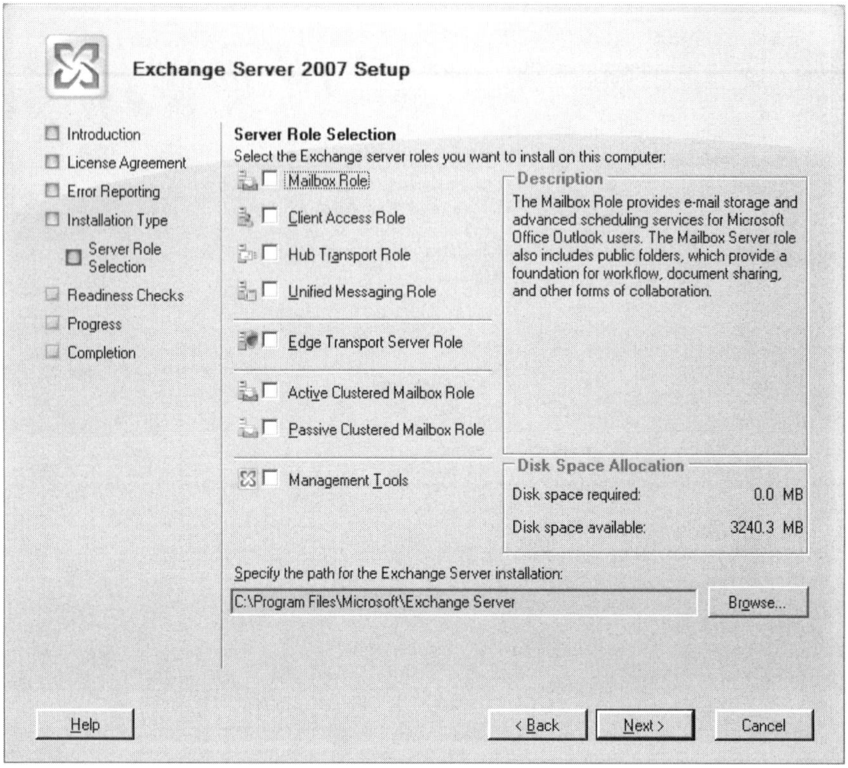

Figure 2-7.   Custom installation options.

Because this is supposed to be a typical installation of a new Exchange organization, I'm going to continue this example assuming you'll be using just Outlook 2007, so you'd select No and click Next.

Exchange performs a set of readiness checks and reports any issues with the state of (or lack thereof) an Exchange organization and the server roles, as shown in Figure 2-10. A perfect example of how this is helpful is that I had the .NET Framework installed on my server such that the setup splash screen (shown previously in Figure 2-3) showed that I had it installed; yet, when I hit this screen during my install of the release-to-market (RTM) version of Exchange, I needed a .NET Framework hotfix update. This readiness check will definitely ensure that your server is up to date.

The new progress screen, shown in Figure 2-11, is far better than previous versions, which made you rely on a single simple progress bar. You can tell exactly where you are in the install.

Once the installation is complete, the Completion screen of the wizard, shown in Figure 2-12, shows the status of the installation, steps that were completed, and any errors that may have occurred during the install.

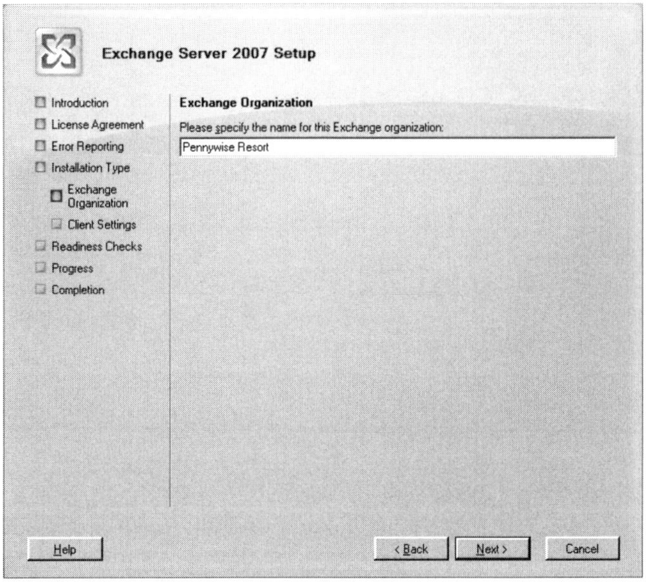

Figure 2-8.   Specify an Exchange organization name.

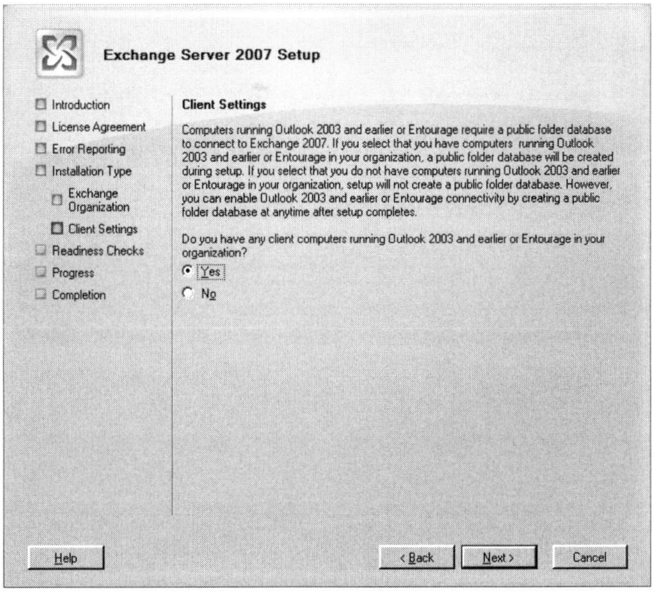

Figure 2-9.   Choose whether you will run earlier versions of Outlook.

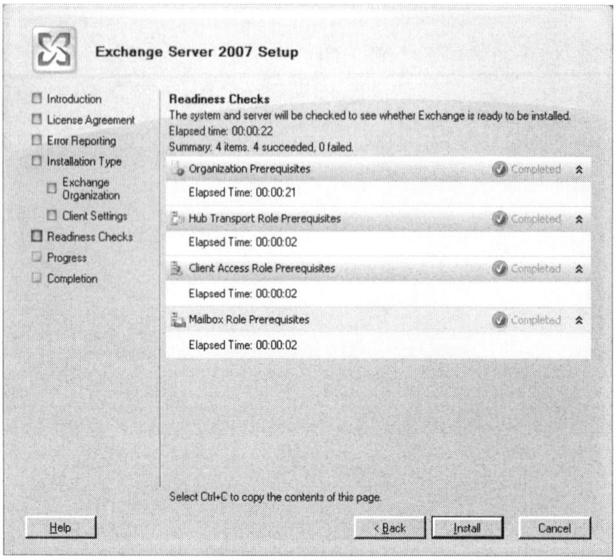

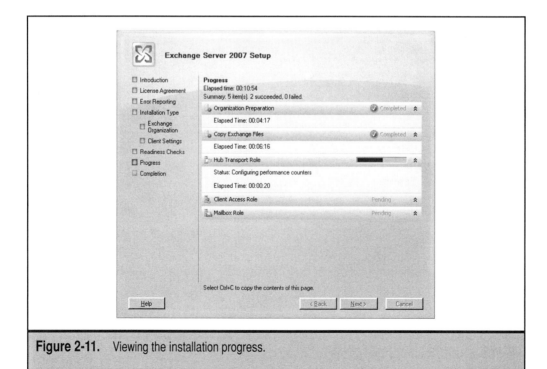

Figure 2-10. Exchange performs a readiness check before starting the install.

Figure 2-11. Viewing the installation progress.

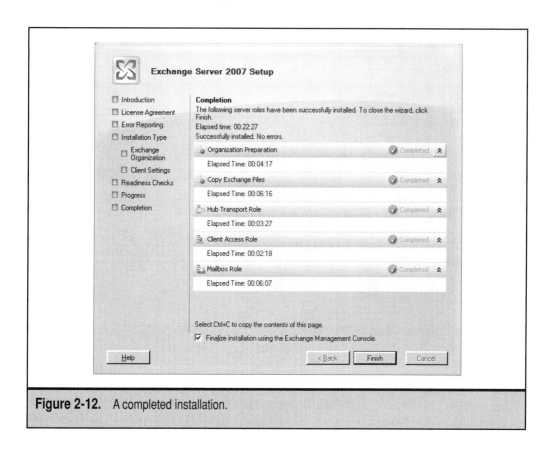

Figure 2-12.   A completed installation.

Upon clicking Next, Setup opens the new Exchange System Manager, which I'll cover in more detail later in the chapter. You should have noticed by now that nowhere during the install did you put in a product key. Microsoft has moved this step to the first time the Exchange Management Console is opened. This is helpful in a multiple-server environment, where you may need different people performing installs but do not want to distribute the product key to all participants. When running the Exchange Management Console, the dialog box shown in Figure 2-13 is automatically displayed. I'll cover the process of licensing your installation later in the chapter.

Performing an Unattended-Mode Installation

Performing an unattended, or silent, installation means that, without manual intervention, you supply the answers that Setup needs in order to complete. Unlike previous versions of Exchange, which used a text file called an *unattend file*, Exchange 2007 performs an unattended installation from a single, command prompt–based command.

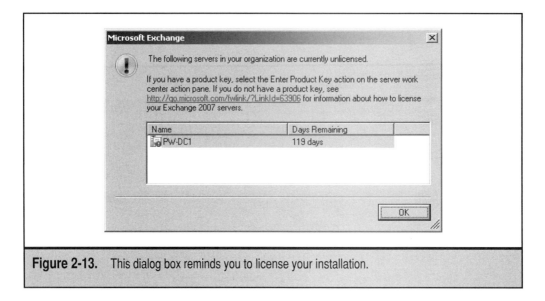

Figure 2-13.   This dialog box reminds you to license your installation.

You can only run an unattended-mode installation on a server that has no Exchange roles currently on it (that is, you cannot use the unattended-mode install to add roles to an existing Exchange server). The command is as follows:

```
Setup /mode:<setup mode> /roles:<server roles to install>
[/TargetDir:<destination folder>] [SourceDir:<source folder>]
[/DomainControler <FQDN of domain controller>] [/AnswerFile <file>]
[/DisableErrorReporting] [/NoSelfSignedCertificates]
[/AdamLdapPort <port>] [/AdamSslPort <port>] [/NewProvisionedServer]
[/RemoveProvisionedServer] [/ForeignForestFQDN]
[/ServerAdmin <user or group>] [/?]
```

Table 2-3 explains each of the command parameters.

POST-INSTALLATION TASKS

However you have installed your Exchange server, until you become familiar with the installation process and all its nuances, you should validate your installs to be sure that everything completed successfully. In this section I'll first look at the steps you can take to verify an Exchange installation in general and then focus on the tasks you perform for each type of server role install.

Validating an Exchange Install

There are two simple steps you can take to verify that you have successfully installed Exchange. The first is to look at the event logs for event IDs 1003 and 1004, with an event source of MSExchangeSetup, to see the outcome of your Exchange install. The next step

Parameter	Description
/mode: or /m:	Specifies the type of setup: Install, Upgrade, Uninstall, RecoverServer.
/roles: or /r:	Specifies the roles to be installed on the server: ClientAccess/CA/C, EdgeTransport/ET/ E, HubTransport/HT/H, Mailbox/MB/M, UnifiedMessaging/UM/U, ManagementTools/ MT/M.
/TargetDir or /t	Specifies the destination folder. The default is %programfiles%\Microsoft\Exchange.
/SourceDir or /s	Specifies the location of the Exchange DVD.
/DomainController or /dc	Specifies the domain controller used during setup to communicate with Active Directory.
/AnswerFile or /a	Specifies the location of the answer file used for advanced settings.
/DisableErrorReporting	Disables the Error Reporting service.
/NoSelfSignedCertificates	Specifies whether the Client Access and Unified Messaging roles should use self-signed certificates when establishing Transport Layer Security (TLS) or Secure Socket Layer (SSL) sessions.
/AdamLdapPort	Specifies the Lightweight Directory Access Protocol (LDAP) port the ADAM services should use on an Edge Transport server.
/AdamSslPort	Specifies the SSL port the ADAM service should use on an Edge Transport server.
/NewProvisionedServer or /nprs	Creates a placeholder server object within Active Directory so the setup of that server can be delegated.
/RemoveProvisioned Server or /rprs	Removes the placeholder server specified in a setup that used the /NewProvisionedServer parameter.
/ForeignForestFQDN	Creates Exchange USGs in a separate forest.
/ServerAdmin	Specifies an account that will be delegated permissions to a provisioned server.
/?	Display command help.

Table 2-3.   Unattended Mode Setup Parameters

is to take your first look at the Exchange Management Shell (see Figure 2-14) and run the command `get-ExchangeServer | format-list`. This command shows the Exchange server roles that are installed on the server. You can find the Exchange Management Shell in the newly created Microsoft Exchange Server 2007 program group.

Viewing the Setup Logs

You can validate various parts of the install by reviewing the setup logs. Unlike previous versions of Exchange, where there was a single setup log file, Exchange 2007 has a number of log files you can view. The logs can all be found in the <system drive>\Exchange-SetupLogs folder. Table 2-4 lists the various logs files and their purpose.

Viewing the Folder Structure

Another way to validate the installation of Exchange is to look at the folder structure created during install. Table 2-5 shows the folder structure Exchange creates, the server roles that will utilize each of the folders, and the general purpose of the folder content. The default installation folder is *C:\Program Files\Microsoft\Exchange Server*.

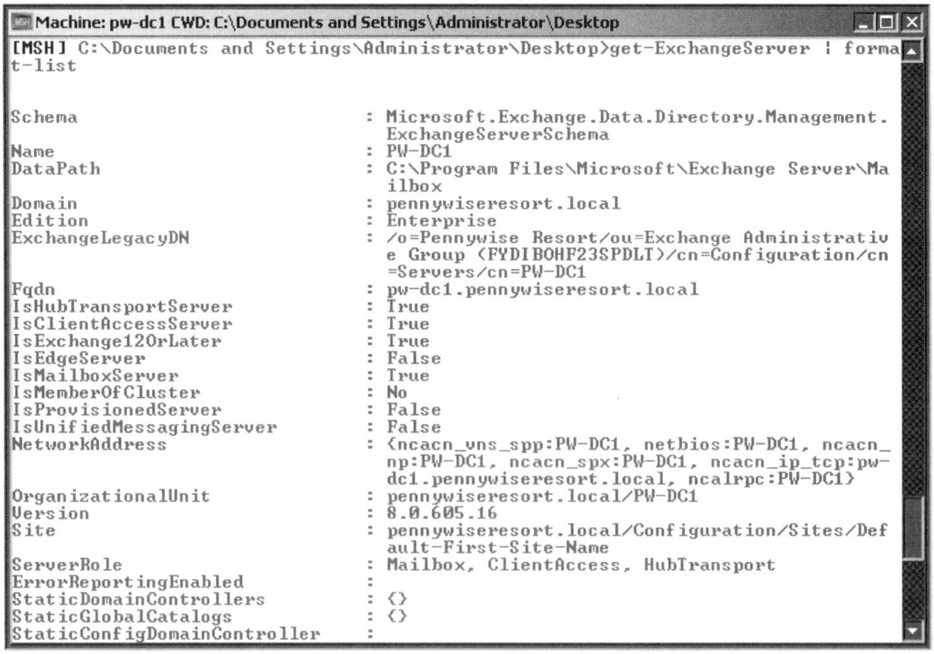

Figure 2-14. Verify the installed Exchange server roles.

Setup Log	Purpose
ExchangeSetup.log	Contains prerequisite system check information, as well as information about the installation of each of the server roles.
ExchangeSetup.msilog	Contains details about the extraction of files from the installer file.
Exchange Server Setup Progress.log	Details the changes made to the operating system during the installation.
Install-*ServerRole-yyyymmdd-hhmmss*.msh	Details the tasks performed during the installation of each server role. The date and time specifiers in the file name are used to document when each server role was installed. A log file will be created for each server role installed.
Install-ExchangeOrganization-InternalTaskLog*yymmddhh mmss*.txt	Details the changes made to the Exchange organization, such as permission changes. The date and time specifiers in the file name are used to document when the installation occurred.
\SetupLogs\ldif.log	Used by the Edge Transport server role to detail the schema changes during the ADAM installation.

Table 2-4.   Setup Log File List

Viewing the Installed Services

If you're going so far as to validate the installation by checking the logs and folder structures, you will also be interested in seeing if the proper services have been installed. Table 2-6 lists the services you will find post-installation, along with the applicable server roles, service purpose, and startup type.

Finalizing the Deployment

The last step you should take once you have Exchange installed is to launch the Exchange Management Console and complete the steps to finalize deployment.

For each server role you have installed, the Exchange Management Console lists the steps you'll need to take to complete the installation, as shown in Figure 2-15. This is a major help in comparison to previous versions. For example, in Exchange 2000/2003, if it was your first time installing Exchange, no one told you that you had to first establish the e-mail domain for your Exchange organization. With Exchange 2007, these final steps are listed for you to complete.

A Brief Primer on Exchange Management Console

The Exchange Management Console replaces the Exchange System Manager console in Exchange 2000/2003. It is an MMC 3.0 snap-in that is based on Windows PowerShell, and it is where you will perform nearly all your Exchange-related management tasks. There are four basic parts to the new console, shown in Figure 2-16.

The *console tree* is used to navigate to the various parts of the Exchange console. For each console node you select, the *result pane* lists the tabs you will manage. The *work pane* is the lower subset of the results pane where you can select objects to manage. The *action pane* lists the tasks you can perform. The console tree is broken into four basic areas: *Organization Configuration*, where you will manage global settings; *Server Organization*, where you will manage the configuration of your servers based on server role; *Recipient Configuration*, where you will manage your recipients; and *Toolbox*, where you will find various analysis and diagnostic tools.

Folder	Roles	Contents
Bin	Mailbox, Hub Transport, Edge Transport, Client Access, Unified Messaging	Exchange server management applications
Client Access	Client Access	Client Access configuration files
ExchangeOAB	Client Access	Exchange offline address book data
Logging	Mailbox, Hub Transport, Edge Transport, Client Access, Unified Messaging	Log files
Mailbox	Mailbox	Addressing DLLs, schema files, databases and log files for the mailbox and public folder databases
Public	Edge Transport, Hub Transport	Address-looking and header-processing files
Scripts	Mailbox, Hub Transport, Edge Transport, Client Access, Unified Messaging	Antispam scripts for the Exchange Management Shell
Transport Roles	Hub Transport, Edge Transport	Binaries, message storage, logs, and configuration files
UnifiedMessaging	Unified Messaging	Configuration files, message storage, administrative scripts, and log files for unified messaging

Table 2-5. Folders Created During the Exchange 2007 Install

Service Name	Roles	Purpose	Startup Type
Microsoft Exchange Active Directory Topology	Hub Transport, Mailbox, Client Access, Unified Messaging	Provides Active Directory topology into Exchange	Automatic
Microsoft Exchange Credential	Edge Transport	Handles credentials between ADAM and a Hub Transport server	Automatic
Microsoft Exchange EdgeSync	Hub Transport	Performs a one-way replication of recipient and configuration information from Active Directory to ADAM on an Edge Transport server	Automatic
Microsoft Exchange File Distribution	Client Access, Unified Messaging	Distributes offline address books	Automatic
Microsoft Exchange IMAP4	Client Access	Services IMAP4 messaging clients	Manual
Microsoft Exchange Information Store	Mailbox	Manages the mailbox and public folder stores	Automatic
Microsoft Exchange Mail Submission	Mailbox	Submits messages from Mailbox servers to Hub Transport servers	Automatic
Microsoft Exchange Mailbox Attendants	Mailbox	Manages mailbox assistants responsible for calendar updates	Automatic
Microsoft Exchange Mail Submission Service	Mailbox	Submits mail from Mailbox servers to Hub Transport servers	Automatic

Table 2-6.   Services Created During the Exchange 2007 Install

Service Name	Roles	Purpose	Startup Type
Microsoft Exchange Monitoring	All	Allows applications to call diagnostic cmdlets	Manual
Microsoft Exchange POP3	Client Access	Supports POP3 messaging clients	Manual
Microsoft Exchange Replication	Mailbox	Used by local continuous backup and cluster replication	Automatic
Microsoft Exchange Service Host	Mailbox, Client Access	Provides a host for several services	Automatic
Microsoft Exchange Speech Engine	Unified Messaging	Speech service	Automatic
Microsoft Exchange System Attendant	Mailbox, Client Access	Provides maintenance, Active Directory lookups, and monitoring	Automatic
Microsoft Exchange Transport	Hub Transport, Edge Transport	Provides SMTP services	Automatic
Microsoft Exchange Transport Log Search	Hub Transport, Edge Transport	Allows remote search of transport logs	Automatic
Microsoft Exchange Unified Messaging	Unified Messaging	Provides unified messaging services	Automatic
IIS Admin	Client Access	Allows management of Web services	Automatic
HTTP SSL	Client Access	Enables SSL over the Hypertext Transfer Protocol (HTTP)	Manual
World Wide Web Publishing	Client Access	Provides Web services	Automatic
Microsoft Search (Exchange)	Mailbox	Provides search services	Automatic

Table 2-6.   Services Created During the Exchange 2007 Install (*Continued*)

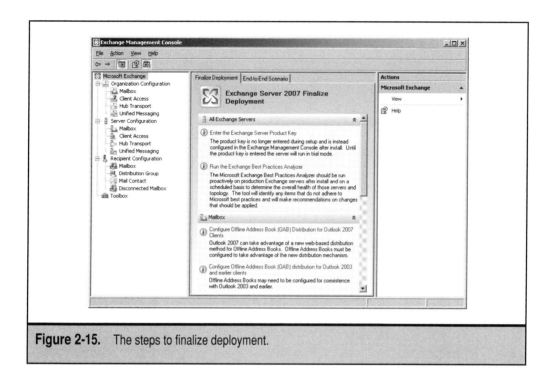

Figure 2-15.   The steps to finalize deployment.

You should first license the installation. The steps are spelled out and are easy enough, so I'll skip them here. Microsoft also recommends that you run the Exchange Best Practices Analyzer. I cover this tool in Chapter 16. Let's look at the tasks necessary for each of the server roles.

Final Steps for the Hub Transport Role

You'll need to first establish the SMTP domains your Exchange organization will support. By clicking the Configure Domains For Which You Will Accept Mail link, you are given a small Help window, explaining the step and providing a Go To Accepted Domain Management link to complete the task. By clicking this link, you are taken within the Exchange Management Console to the Accepted Domains tab of the Hub Transport node, shown in Figure 2-17.

By default, Exchange supports the same domain names as that of Active Directory. If you, like most, do not have Active Directory configured with a domain name that exists on the Internet (such as my example of *pennywiseresort.local*), initially, you will want to add the SMTP domain your organization needs to use on the Internet. You can do this by clicking New Accepted Domain in the action pane, which starts the New Accepted Domain Wizard. Tip: You cannot modify the domain value of an existing supported domain, so you will need to add the domain name(s) you want to support.

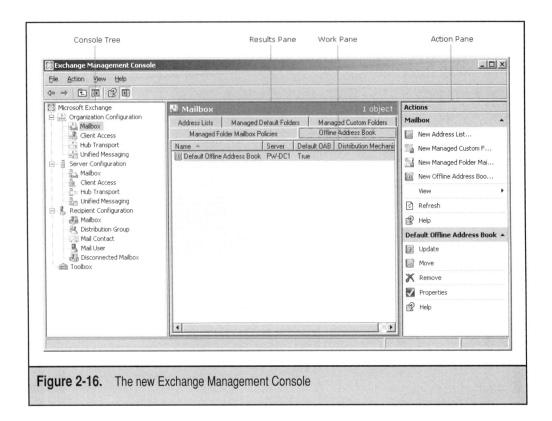

Figure 2-16. The new Exchange Management Console

The New Accepted Domain Wizard, shown in Figure 2-18, first asks for a name for the domain object and the accepted domain, which is the SMTP domain for which you will receive e-mail on the Internet. You can also select whether Exchange is authoritative for the domain specified; whether the domain exists within the organization but in another Active Directory forest and, therefore, messages to this domain should be relayed; or whether the domain is external to Exchange and messages should be relayed. At this point in the installation process, you want to configure Exchange to be responsible for this domain, so select Authoritative Domain and click New. The Completion page of the wizard tells you the outcome and any errors that may have occurred. Click Finish to close the wizard.

Now that the proper domain name is supported, we'll return to the steps to finalize deployment. The next step for a Hub Transport role involves the Edge Transport server. I'm going to cover the implementation of an Edge Transport server in the next chapter, so for now, I'm going to skip this step. The final step is to establish the postmaster mailbox, which will receive e-mail sent to the postmaster. By clicking the Create A Postmaster

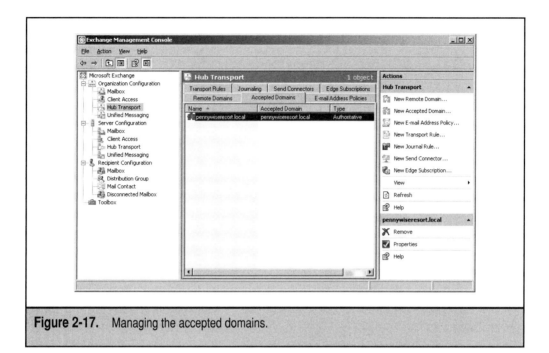

Figure 2-17. Managing the accepted domains.

Mailbox link, instructions are provided to perform this task using the Exchange Management Shell, shown in Figure 2-19.

To establish the postmaster mailbox, run the command `Get-TransportServer` to see the ExternalPostmasterAddress value. By default, the entry will be *postmaster@<original domain name>*. To change this value to use the new domain name you configured your Exchange environment to support, run the command `Set-TransportServer [servername] -ExternalPostmasterAddress [postmaster e-mail address]`. I'd also suggest you re-run the `Get-TransportServer` command to verify that the postmaster address is correctly established, shown in Figure 2-20.

If necessary, create a user mailbox for the e-mail address specified (you can find out how to do this in Chapter 3).

Final Steps for the Client Access Role

You'll need to configure ActiveSync to facilitate mobile access to Exchange. I'll cover this process in Chapter 8.

Final Steps for the Mailbox Role

You need to configure the offline address books (OABs) for both Outlook 2007 and legacy Outlook clients so that cached and offline-mode clients have access to the global address

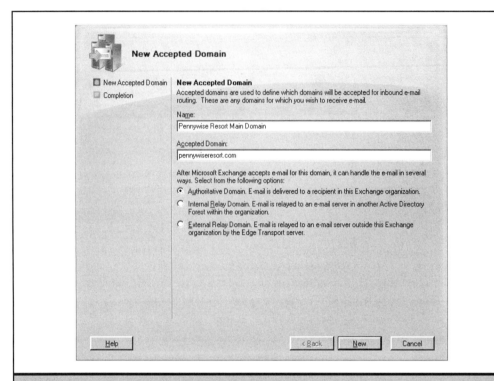

Figure 2-18. Starting the Add New Accepted Domain Wizard.

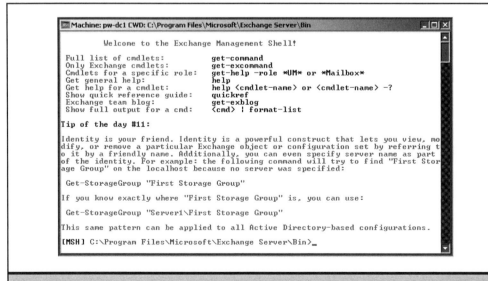

Figure 2-19. A newly opened Exchange Management Shell window.

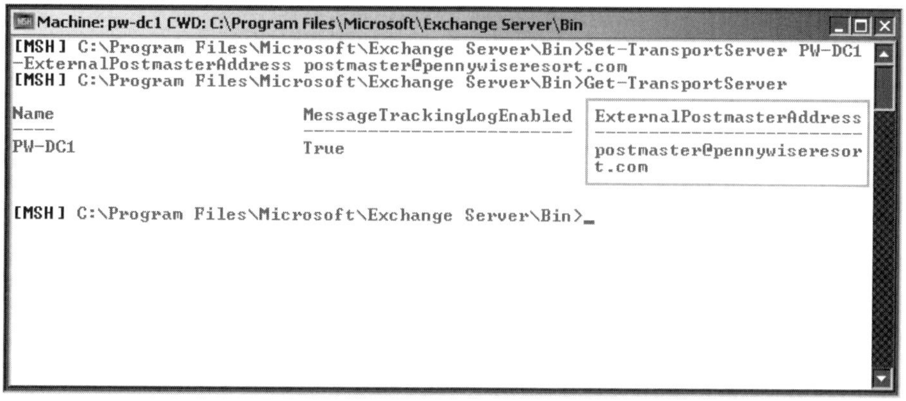

Figure 2-20. Change the postmaster e-mail address.

book and any custom address books. Let's start by configuring the OAB for Outlook 2007. By clicking the Configure Offline Address Book (OAB) Distribution For Outlook 2007 Clients link, the Help window opens, explaining the steps to accomplish this task. By clicking the Go To Offline Address Book Management link, you are taken to the Offline Address Book tab of the Mailbox node under Organization Configuration, shown in Figure 2-21.

Select the desired offline address book in the work pane, and select Properties from the action pane. On the Distribution tab, shown in Figure 2-22, select the Enable Web-Based Distribution check box, click the Add button, select an OAB virtual directory, and click OK to save the updated properties. You must publish the OAB within an Internet Information Services (IIS) virtual directory in order for Outlook 2007 to access and download the OAB.

The previous step only tells Exchange where Outlook 2007 clients should look for the OAB. This next step actually gives an external uniform resource locator (URL) for the OAB virtual directory previously selected. Clicking the Go To OAB Virtual Directory Management link takes you to the Offline Address Book Distribution tab on the Client Access node under Server Configuration in the console tree. Select the default OAB virtual directory, and in the action pane, select Properties. On the URLs tab, shown in Figure 2-23, enter an external URL, and click OK.

If you plan on supporting Outlook 2003 clients (and you probably will initially), you will need to configure a separate OAB. Outlook 2003 clients do not get their OAB via Web services; they still download from a public folder specifically created by Exchange to house the OAB (remember, this was discussed during the setup of Exchange when asked if you will be supporting older Outlook clients). You will need to establish which public folder database (previously known as a public folder store) will host the OAB. To do this, click the

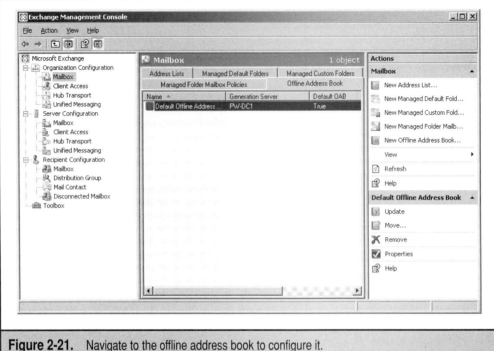

Figure 2-21. Navigate to the offline address book to configure it.

Configure Offline Address Book (OAB) Distribution For Outlook 2003 And Earlier Clients link from the Finalize Deployment task list. Click the Go To Database Management link from within the Help window, which will take you to the Database Management tab on the Mailbox node under Server Configuration, shown in Figure 2-24. During the setup of Exchange, I chose not to support older Outlook clients, and this is the repercussion of that action: no public folders exist. If I had chosen to support older Outlook clients, I would not have to perform the next step of creating the public folder database. Select the First Storage group, and click New Public Folder Database on the action pane.

On the New pane of the New Public Folder Database Wizard, enter a name for the public folder database and modify, if desired, the path to the database files, as shown in Figure 2-25. Click New to create the database. The completion pane will show the results of the public folder database creation. Once this is done, the Help window takes you back to the Offline Address Book tab on the Mailbox node under Organization Configuration. Select the OAB and click Properties in the action pane. Select the Enable Public Folder Distribution check box to complete configuration of OAB distribution for Outlook 2003, previously shown in Figure 2-22.

Now that you have validated the installation using the post-installation tasks and completed the final deployment tasks, your Exchange server install is complete. Let's take a look at what is involved in delegating responsibility within the Exchange organization.

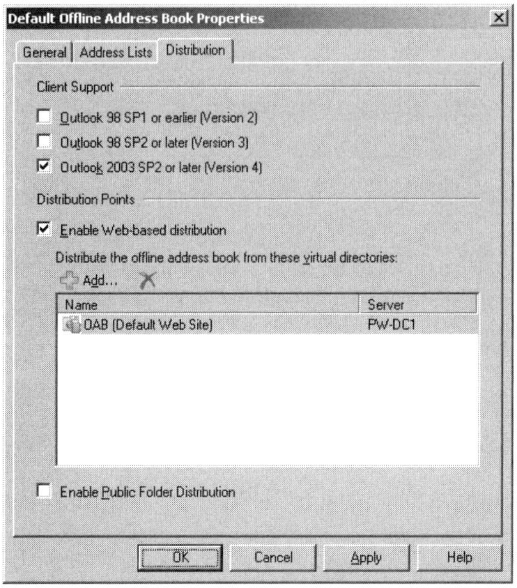

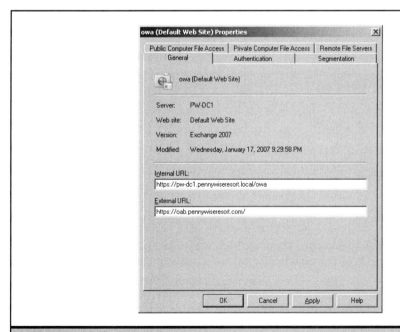

Figure 2-22.   Configure client support for the offline address book.

Figure 2-23.   Configure an external URL for the OAB virtual directory.

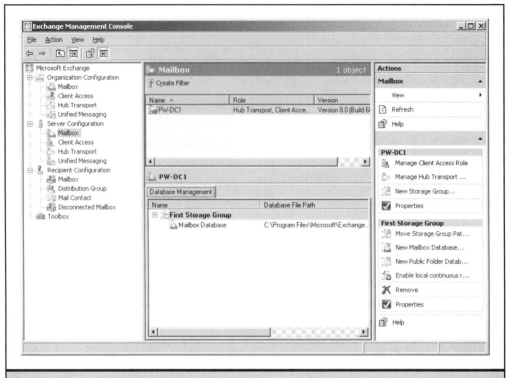

Figure 2-24.   Begin creating the public folder database.

Establishing Permissions to Administer Exchange

Once you have your Exchange environment set up, you may need to delegate responsibility to others within your organization. Microsoft has moved away from the three levels of delegation found in Exchange 2000/2003 and moved to a model that more closely reflects the functions members of each role will perform. Table 2-7 lists the new roles and the abilities they each have.

Delegating Permissions

Delegating each of the roles is accomplished at the Organizational level within the Exchange Management Console by selecting the Exchange Organization node within the console tree and selecting Add Exchange Administrator in the Actions pane. When selected, the Add Exchange Administrator wizard starts, as shown in Figure 2-26.

As you can see in Figure 2-26, if you choose the Exchange Organization Administrator role, the Exchange Recipient Administrator role, or the Exchange View-Only Administrator role, Exchange will apply the delegation at the organization level, whereas the Exchange

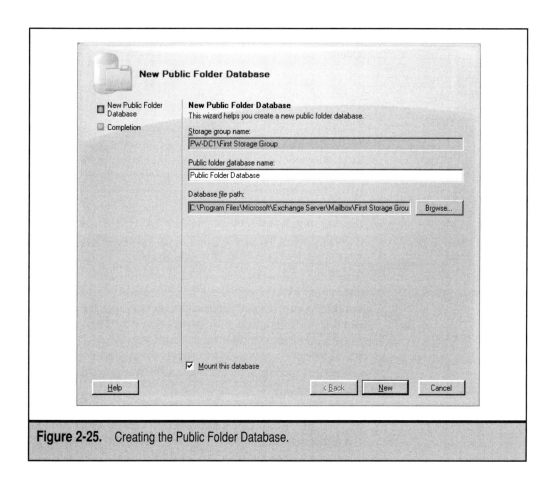

Figure 2-25. Creating the Public Folder Database.

Server Administrator role will apply to only the server designated, as shown in Figure 2-27.

TIP You can also use the Exchange Management Shell to delegate responsibility using the Add-ExchangeAdministrator cmdlet. More on the Exchange Management Shell can be found in Chapter 13.

MIGRATING FROM PREVIOUS VERSIONS OF EXCHANGE

Earlier in this chapter, I covered the process of installing Exchange 2007. You'll utilize that knowledge in this section as well, as the installation process is the same. If you are not moving to Exchange 2007 from an earlier version of Exchange, the remainder of the chapter is not intended for you; you can move on to the next chapter if you wish to begin reading about administering Exchange 2007.

Role	Abilities
Exchange Organization Administrator	This group has full control over the Exchange organization within the configuration container in Active Directory, read access to all domain user containers in Active Directory, and write access to all Exchange-specific properties of objects within the domain user containers in Active Directory. These permissions are established during setup when using the /PrepareAD switch by creating a group with the same name as the role and assigning it the permissions listed previously. This group is a member of both the Exchange Recipient Administrators and Exchange Server Administrators groups.
Exchange Recipient Administrator	This group has read access to all domain user containers in Active Directory and write access to all Exchange-specific properties of objects within the domain user containers in Active Directory. These permissions are established during setup when using the /PrepareAD switch by creating a group with the same name as the role and assigning it the permissions listed previously.
Exchange Server Administrator	This group has rights to manage specific Exchange servers, but not to make changes that would affect the entire organization. This group is made the local administrator of the specified server, and is a member of the Exchange View-Only Administrators role.
Exchange View-Only Administrator	This group has read-only access to the entire Exchange organization and read-only access to all domain user containers within Active Directory.

Table 2-7. Exchange Delegation Roles

Let me start by covering some basics. As I hinted at the beginning of this chapter, there is no *in-place* upgrade of earlier versions of Exchange to Exchange 2007; that is, you will not be performing installs of Exchange 2007 on existing servers running Exchange 5.5, 2000, or 2003. Instead, you will be performing what is referred to as a *transition*. Microsoft uses the term to refer to the upgrade path from a previous version of Exchange in which you install Exchange 2007 into the same organization and move the mailbox

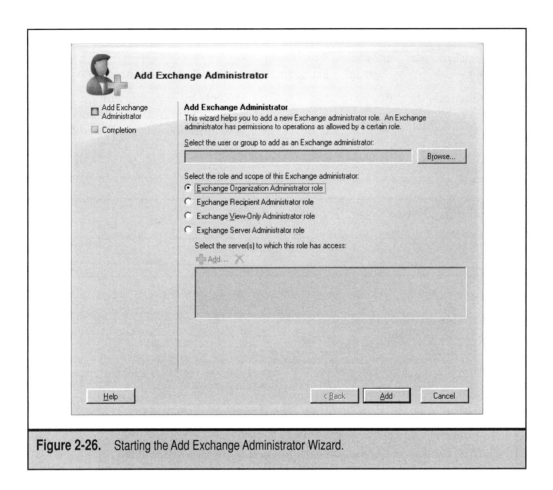

Figure 2-26.   Starting the Add Exchange Administrator Wizard.

and public folder data onto Exchange 2007. One of the key reasons you cannot perform in-place upgrades to Exchange 2007 is the new hardware requirements of a 64-bit processor; existing servers are most likely running on 32-bit hardware. In addition, those of you who have performed upgrades from NT to Windows 2000 know that in-place upgrading is not always clean or easy. Using a clean install provides you with a fresh server on which to build your new Exchange environment.

The term *migration* is used in this chapter to refer to moving messaging data from any non-Exchange platform or to moving messages from one Exchange organization to a completely new Exchange–based organization. Since the only data you'd be moving from a foreign e-mail system or a foreign Exchange organization would be message and public folder data, a migration is really not much more than a transition, without Exchange 2007 installed into the original environment.

Table 2-8 shows the possible transition and migration paths you can take with previous versions of Exchange.

Previous Exchange Version	In Place Upgrade?	Transition to Exchange 2007?	Migration to Exchange 2007?
Exchange 5.5	No	No	Only by upgrading to Exchange 2000 or 2003 and transitioning to Exchange 2007
Exchange 2000	No	Yes	Yes
Exchange 2003	No	Yes	Yes

Table 2-8.   Transition and Migration Paths to Exchange 2007

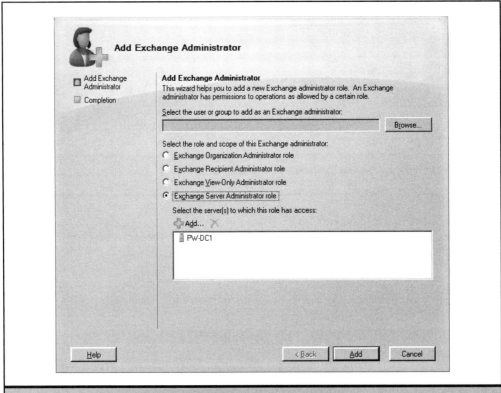

Figure 2-27.   Delegating the Exchange Server Administrator role.

Migrating from Exchange 5.5

Because the focus of this book is to move you to Exchange 2007, I won't be covering how to migrate Exchange 5.5 to either Exchange 2000 or 2003. You can get information on how to perform this migration on Microsoft's Web site at http://www.microsoft.com/technet/prodtechnol/exchange/2003/upgrade.mspx.

Once you have successfully upgraded to Exchange 2000 or 2003, the remainder of this chapter will apply.

Migrating from Exchange 2000/2003

If you are running an Exchange 2000 or 2003 organization, you are well on your way to transitioning to Exchange Server 2007. The first step is for you to plan your server roles. In Exchange 2000 and 2003, every server, despite its purpose within the organization, ran pretty much a full version of Exchange. This meant that your servers were not as optimized as they could be with Exchange 2007. For example, if you have a server running Exchange 2000 that is acting as a messaging bridgehead (which would be the Hub Transport role in Exchange 2007), it is still also hosting mailbox and public folder stores (the equivalent of the Mailbox Server role), an SMTP service (which could be considered part of the Edge Transport role), and supporting POP3 and IMAP4 (which are now part of the Client Access role). So you see that the server that you had designated as only a messaging bridgehead was undesirably so much more. Please review the section "Exchange Server Roles" earlier in this chapter for more information on the roles to assist in your planning.

The next issue to address is those features that are no longer utilized within Exchange 2007. Some are simply not supported, while others have been moved to various Microsoft products. Table 2-9 lists the Exchange 2000 and 2003 features no longer supported and, if applicable, where you can now find equivalent functionality.

Let's discuss the most common scenario you may find yourself in when transitioning to Exchange 2007. This is a transition within a single Exchange organization. I'll cover the basic steps required to accomplish a successful transition. Should you have a more advanced environment, such as moving between two Exchange organizations, please refer to the Deployment section in the Exchange 2007 Online Help at http://www.microsoft .com/technet/prodtechnol/exchange/E2k7Help.

Transitioning Within a Single Exchange Organization

The steps to transition to Exchange 2007 within a single organization are rather simple. (I'm assuming you are familiar with Exchange 2000 administration.)

1. Install Exchange 2007 into the existing Exchange organization on a new server. At a minimum, you'll need to install the Client Access, Mailbox, and Hub Transport roles on either a single server or separate servers. The server will be installed into the Routing Group DWBGZMFD01QNBJR within the Administrative Group FYDIBOHF23SPDLT. *Do not* move Exchange 2007 servers out of these groups or rename them with a low-level directory editor (such as ADSIEDIT.MSC). Exchange 2007 uses these specific names when coexisting with earlier versions.

Feature	Last Exchange Version	Where to Find It in Exchange 2007
cc:Mail connector	2000	No longer supported
Microsoft Mail connector	2000	No longer supported
Novell GroupWise connector	2003	No longer supported
Instant Messaging	2000	Moved to Live Communication Server (www.microsoft.com/lcs)
Chat Service	2000	No longer supported
Key Management Service	2000	Utilize Certificate Services
Exchange 2000 Conferencing Server	2000	Moved to Microsoft Office Live Meeting (www.microsoft.com/livemeeting)
Mobile Information Server	n/a	Integrated into Exchange as of Exchange 2003

Table 2-9. Legacy Exchange 2000 Services in Exchange 2007

2. Create a routing group connector between the existing routing groups and the newly created one housing the Exchange 2007 servers.

3. Move mailboxes from the existing Exchange servers to your Exchange 2007 server(s) running the Mailbox role. You can find out how to move mailboxes in the next chapter.

4. If you intend on keeping your public folders, create replicas of them using the Exchange System Manager on an Exchange 2000/2003 server.

TIP Unlike moving from Exchange 2000 to 2003, when transitioning to Exchange 2007, you do not need to establish replicas of the free/busy information or the offline address book. This happens automatically when you install the first Exchange 2007 server into the organization.

5. You then need to move your routing group connectors from the existing Exchange 2000/2003 servers to the Exchange 2007 servers installed with the Hub Transport role. Because Exchange 2007 does not use the link-state routing information utilized by Exchange 2000/2003, you first need to disable the propagation of this information to avoid routing loops as you make routing changes. You can do this by adding the following REG_DWORD entry with a value of one to the Exchange 2000/2003 servers and restarting the server(s): `HKLM\System\CurrentCon-trolSet\Services\RESvc\Parameters\ SuppressStateChanges`.

6. Create new or adjust existing routing group connectors utilizing the Hub Transport servers with a lower cost than that of their Exchange 2000/2003 counterparts. You can find out more information on how to do this in the *Administration Guide for Exchange 2003* at www.microsoft.com/technet/prodtechnol/exchange/2003/library/admingde.mspx.

7. Once the existing Exchange servers are no longer needed, remove the Exchange 2000/2003 connectors. Again, refer to the *Administration Guide for Exchange 2003* for more information.

8. Remove your existing Exchange servers by performing a proper uninstall. You can also find out how to do this in the *Administration Guide for Exchange 2003.*

MIGRATING FROM NON-EXCHANGE MESSAGING SYSTEMS

Microsoft officially only supports migrations from Lotus Notes versions 5.x, 6.x, and 7.x. However, many third-party solutions exist that can either move mailbox data to Exchange or at least to a PST file (which you can then use to import to an Exchange mailbox.) In addition, datasets, such as personal address books and the equivalent of Exchange's public folders, can often be moved. More information on migrating to Exchange 2007 from Lotus Notes can be found at http://go.microsoft.com/fwlink/?LinkId=58466.

SUMMARY

In this chapter, I covered the Exchange Server 2007 pre-installation considerations, discussed the steps to install Exchange Server 2007, explained how to perform an unattended installation, and described some of the post-installation tasks. I also covered the basic steps needed to move an existing Exchange 5.5, 2000, or 2003 environment to Exchange 2007 to get you pointed in the right direction. In the next chapter, I'll begin to cover the steps needed to manage recipients in Exchange 2007.

PART II

Administration

CHAPTER 3

Creating and Managing Recipients

Once Exchange Server 2007 is installed and any transitions have occurred from previous versions of Exchange, it's time to get down to the business of managing your Exchange 2007 environment.

One of the main functions in managing an Exchange 2007 environment is the creation and configuration of recipient objects. Now, let's not be fooled here—this involves much more than just mail-enabling a user account or public folder. Once enabled, there are a host of configuration parameters that need to be considered. In addition, the types of recipients have drastically changed from Exchange 5.5 and have somewhat changed from that of Exchange 2000/2003. As well as using graphical tools to accomplish administrative tasks, Microsoft now enables nearly everything you can normally do via the graphical user interface (GUI) through the new Exchange Management Shell (EMS).

In this chapter, I'll illustrate how to create and configure each of these recipient types, both through the primary graphical tool, the Exchange Management Console, as well as the Exchange Management Shell. Then we'll look at how to create and manage customized address lists for your users.

CREATING AND MANAGING RECIPIENTS

Let's start out by covering the various types of recipients. You would naturally figure a mailbox is the first type, but with Exchange 2007, there are *four* types of mailboxes you can create. A *user mailbox* is an Exchange 2007–based mailbox associated with an Active Directory user. A *room mailbox* is a mailbox that is associated with a disabled user for the purpose of room scheduling. An *equipment mailbox*, like a room mailbox, is associated with a disabled user, but is used for the purpose of scheduling equipment within your organization. Last, a *linked mailbox* is a mailbox that is accessible by a security principle (such as a user account) in a separate forest that exists across a trust.

The next set of contacts are used to represent external recipients without Exchange mailboxes. The first is a *mail contact,* which is an Active Directory object representing a person external to your organization who has an associated e-mail address pointing to an external messaging system. You could use mail contact objects, for example, to ensure that important clients are in the global address list. The second type of external recipient is a *mail user*, which is an Active Directory user that has no Exchange mailbox, but instead uses an external messaging system. This object is perfect for situations when you have a contractor on site who needs to log on to Active Directory to access resources, but has his or her own messaging system at his or her office.

A *distribution group* is an Active Directory group that is mail-enabled, having an e-mail address on the Exchange system. Messages sent to a distribution group will be sent to each of the members of that group. Lastly, *public folders* are automatically assigned e-mail addresses. Table 3-1 compares the various recipient types.

While you have been using Active Directory Users And Computers on a server that has the Exchange management tools installed to manage your recipients for years, in order to manage Exchange 2007 recipients, you'll need to focus your attention on the Exchange 2007 management tools.

Recipient Type	Associated Object Type in Active Directory	Accessed By	Internal or External Recipient?	Example of Usage
User mailbox	User	Associated user account	Internal	Internal user
Room mailbox	User	Other users	Internal	Conference room
Equipment mailbox	User	Other users	Internal	Video projector
Linked mailbox	User	User account in a trusted domain in a separate forest	Internal	Centralized company e-mail mailbox accessed by a user in a business unit using a separate (but trusted) Active Directory forest
Mail contact	Contact	n/a	External	External person commonly sent e-mail
Mail user	User	Associated user account	External	Contractor with temporary internal user account but external e-mail
Distribution group	Group	n/a	Can include internal and external recipients	Combines multiple recipients into a single destination
Public folder	Public folder	n/a	Internal	Receives messages needed to be viewed by multiple users

Table 3-1.   Comparison of Exchange 2007 Recipients

TIP   If you have a mixed Exchange 2007/Exchange 2000 or 2003 environment, you can use the Active Directory Users And Computers MMC snap-in to manage Exchange 2000/2003 recipients.

In this chapter, I'm going to focus on how to manage recipients using the Exchange Management Console and the Exchange Management Shell. I'll cover managing public folders in the next chapter. If you would like a refresher on managing recipients using Active Directory Users And Computers while you are still running a mix of Exchange 2000/2003 and 2007, please refer to the *Exchange Server 2003 Administration Guide* at http://www.microsoft.com/technet/prodtechnol/exchange/2003/library/admingde.mspx.

Let's start by looking at how to create and manage the four mailbox types.

Creating and Configuring New Mailboxes

Unlike previous versions of Exchange, where the focus was on creating a user and then associating a mailbox to it, think of this version as reversing the two. Since you'll be working within the Exchange Management Console, the focus is the mailbox; the user is somewhat secondary. Begin managing mailboxes by selecting the Mailbox node in the console tree, just under Recipient Configuration, shown in Figure 3-1. The results pane

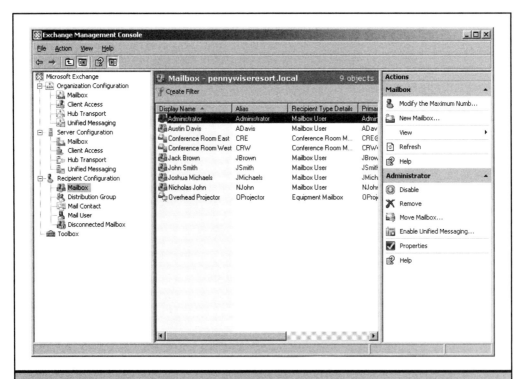

Figure 3-1.   You manage recipients within the Exchange Management Console.

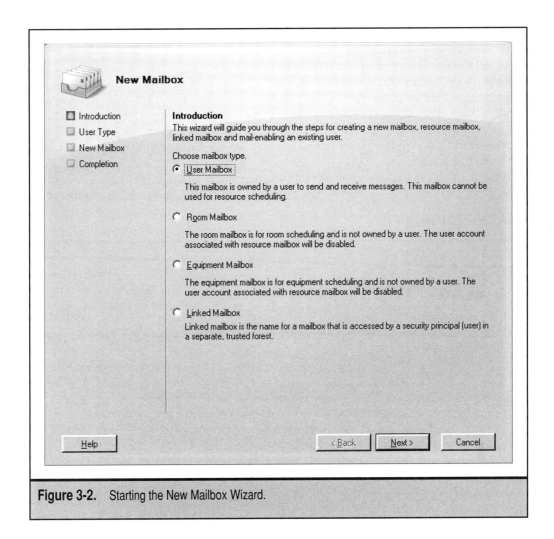

Figure 3-2.   Starting the New Mailbox Wizard.

shows any mailboxes that exist within the organization. Even though you may have many more user accounts in Active Directory, this list is specific to those users that have a mailbox. To begin creating a mailbox, select New Mailbox from the action pane. The New Mailbox Wizard starts, giving you the option to create one of the four mailbox types described earlier, as shown in Figure 3-2.

Let's walk through creating each of the four types of mailboxes, starting with the user mailbox.

Creating a User, Room, or Equipment Mailbox

While the purposes for each mailbox type are different, the process is exactly the same, with one caveat—the user account either selected or created during the creation of the room or equipment mailbox is disabled at the end of the wizard. I'll walk through the creation of a user mailbox to demonstrate creating all three mailbox types.

Select the User Mailbox option, and click Next. On the User Type page of the wizard, you can choose to either create a new user as part of creating the user mailbox or select an existing user that currently does not have a mailbox associated with it, shown in Figure 3-3. Should you need to create a user, you would select New User and click Next, which would display the User Information pane, shown in Figure 3-4. Otherwise, you select Existing User on the User Type page and click the Browse button to select a user, as shown in Figure 3-5.

Whether you create a new user and provide user information or select an existing user, the next page in the wizard is the Mailbox Settings page, shown in Figure 3-6. On this page,

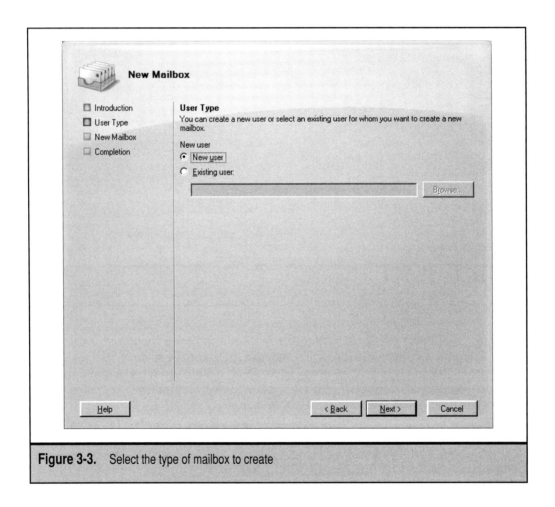

Figure 3-3. Select the type of mailbox to create

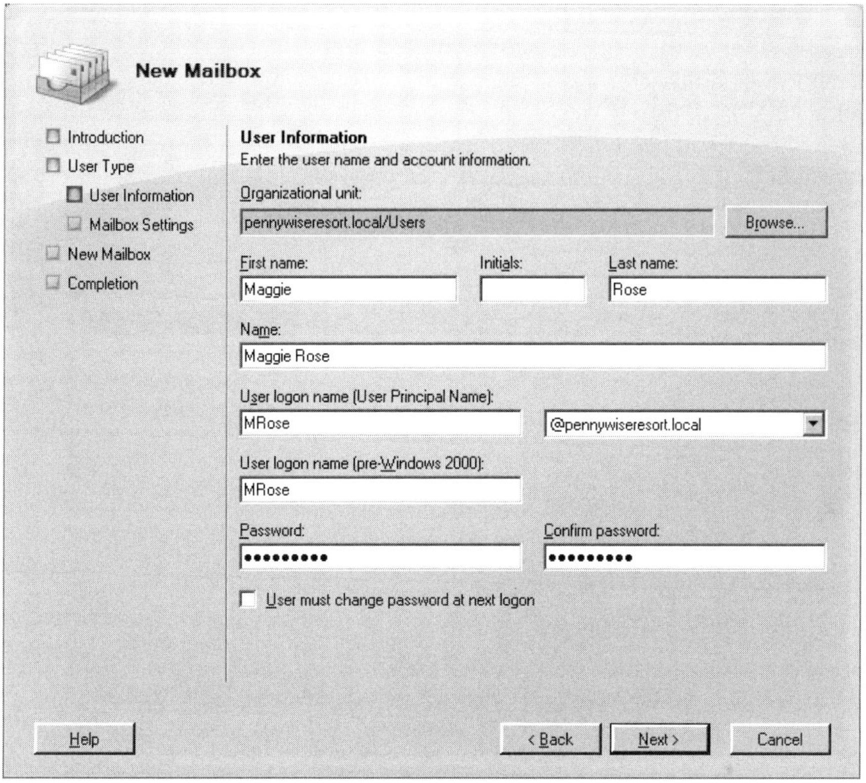

New Mailbox

- Introduction
- User Type
  - User Information
  - Mailbox Settings
- New Mailbox
- Completion

User Information
Enter the user name and account information.

Organizational unit:

pennywiseresort.local/Users   Browse...

First name: Initials: Last name:
Maggie   Rose

Name:
Maggie Rose

User logon name (User Principal Name):
MRose   @pennywiseresort.local

User logon name (pre-Windows 2000):
MRose

Password: Confirm password:
●●●●●●●●●   ●●●●●●●●●

☐ User must change password at next logon

Help   < Back   Next >   Cancel

Figure 3-4. Create a user within the New Mailbox Wizard.

you need to specify the alias for the mailbox (which defaults to the user name), the server and mailbox location, and two advanced parameters for establishing mailbox policies (which establish mailbox retention settings, for example) and a policy for ActiveSync (which configures settings for Pocket PC clients that utilize ActiveSync to retrieve messages).

Once you have configured the mailbox settings, click Next, review the configuration summary (shown in Figure 3-7), and click New to complete the wizard.

Creating a Linked Mailbox

As you recall from earlier in this chapter, a linked mailbox is a mailbox in your Exchange organization that is associated with a user in another Active Directory forest.

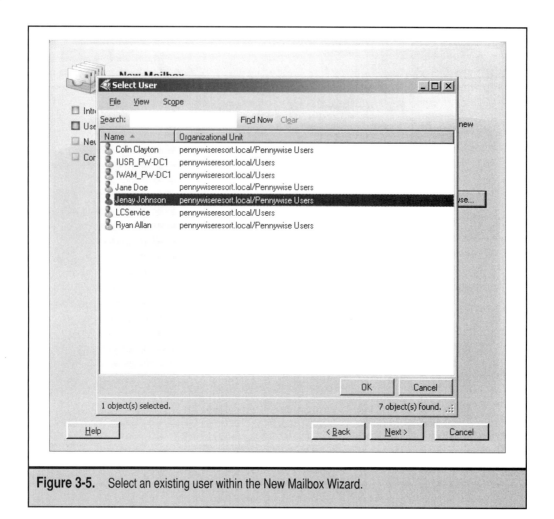

Figure 3-5. Select an existing user within the New Mailbox Wizard.

So the process in your organization is essentially the same as with the previous three mailbox types, with the user account specified from your organization disabled, but specifying another Active Directory forest, domain controller in that forest, and user account that will be granted access to the mailbox in your organization, shown in Figure 3-8.

Configuring Mailboxes

Now that you know how to create a new mailbox and associate a user with it, it's time to configure the mailbox. To start the configuration process, navigate within the Exchange

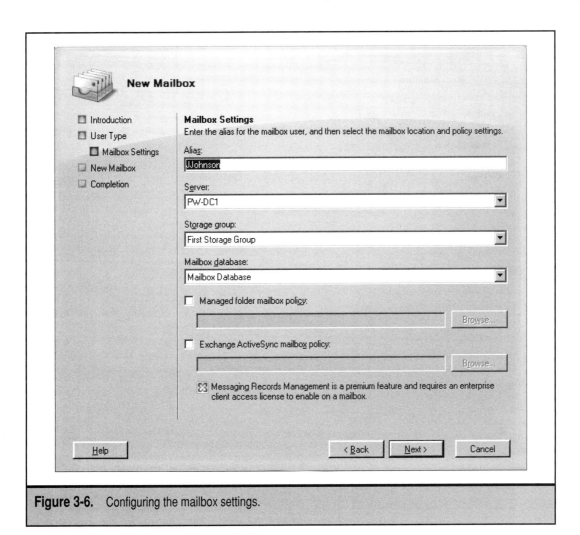

Figure 3-6.   Configuring the mailbox settings.

Management Console to the Mailbox node under Recipient Configuration in the console tree. Select the desired mailbox from the results pane, and click the Properties link in the action pane, as shown in Figure 3-9.

Of the ten tabs that are available by default, there are five tabs of interest for our discussions: General, E-mail Addresses, Mailbox Settings, Mail Flow Settings, and Mailbox Features. On the General tab (Figure 3-10), you can learn where the user's mailbox is presently stored, the mailbox size, the associated user account, the user's location in Active Directory, and what alias the mailbox is using, The Custom Attributes button displays the 15 custom attributes supported by Exchange 2007.

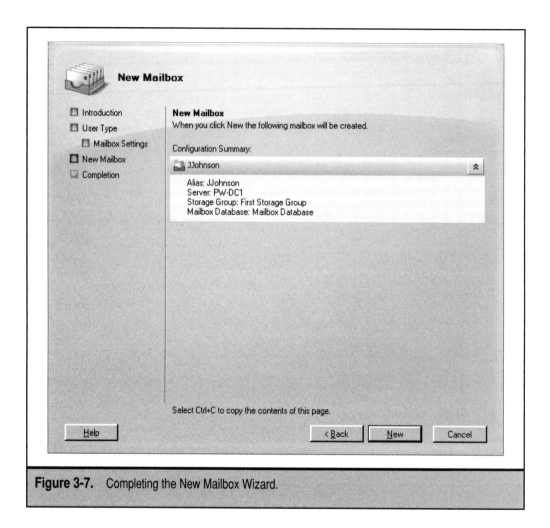

Figure 3-7. Completing the New Mailbox Wizard.

Moving to the E-mail Addresses tab (Figure 3-11), we find the various addresses that have been created for this user account and mailbox. You'll notice that there is only a Simple Mail Transfer Protocol (SMTP) address. X.400 addresses are only needed if you plan on connecting to a foreign messaging system via X.400. You should also note that by leaving the Automatically Update E-mail Addresses Based On Recipient Policy check box selected, you can have these e-mail addresses updated without ever having to physically visit each user account.

Management Shell Corner

Throughout this book, when appropriate, I will cover how to accomplish a task from within the Exchange Management Shell using an example command. You should consider the commands presented as examples; you will need to provide your own parameters specific to your organization, servers, storage, etc. To create a new mailbox from the Exchange Management Shell, run the following command (I've added parameters matching the previous GUI-based creation example to show you the equivalent command):

```
New-Mailbox -alias JJohnson -database 'First Storage Group\Mailbox
Database' -Name JJohnson -OrganizationalUnit Users -password $password
-FirstName Jenay -LastName Johnson -DisplayName 'Jenay Johnson'
```

Note that the $password value is established by first entering the following command so that the user will be prompted for the password:

```
$password = Read-Host "Enter password" -AsSecureString
```

If you are creating a new mailbox for an existing user, the command would be:

```
Enable-Mailbox -Identity:'pennywiseresort.local/Pennywise Users/Jenay
Johnson' -Alias:'JJohnson' -Database: 'First Storage Group\Mailbox
Database'
```

In addition to using the Management Shell Corner throughout this book, you can find more information on how to work with the Exchange Management Shell in Chapter 14. Note that after you run any wizard-driven process within the Exchange Management Console, you will also see the Exchange Management Shell cmdlet and appropriate switches used to perform the command.

Management Shell Corner

To create a linked mailbox from the Exchange Management Shell, perform the following command:

```
New-Mailbox -Database "First Storage Group\Mailbox Database" -Name "Shelly
Thomas" -LinkedDomainController "NW-DC1" -LinkedMasterAccount NICKELWISE\
SThomas -LinkedCredentials NICKELWISE\Administrator -OrganizationalUnit Users
```

Custom Attribute Display Names

You can modify the custom attribute display names by modifying the Active Directory schema with a tool like ADSIEdit. By editing the lDAPDisplayName attribute of the ms-Exch-Extension-Attribute-x object (where x is the number of the attribute) within the Schema container, shown in Figure 3-12, you will modify the appearance of your custom attributes, shown in Figure 3-13 from within the Active Directory Users And Computers MMC snap-in.

The attribute names don't change within the Exchange Management Console, because the field names are hard-coded into the interface rather than being pulled from the Lightweight Directory Access Protocol (LDAP) display name within Active Directory, as is the case with Active Directory Users And Computers.

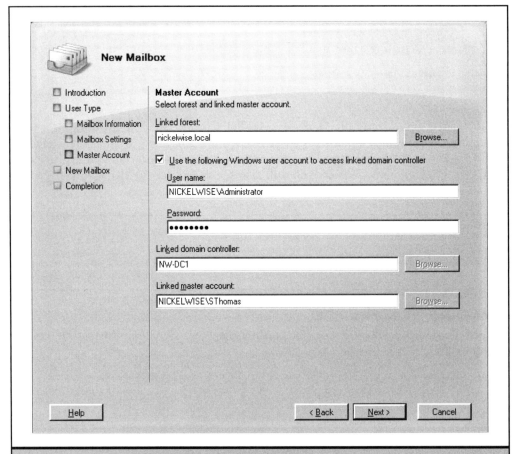

Figure 3-8. Specifying the user account to be linked to a mailbox.

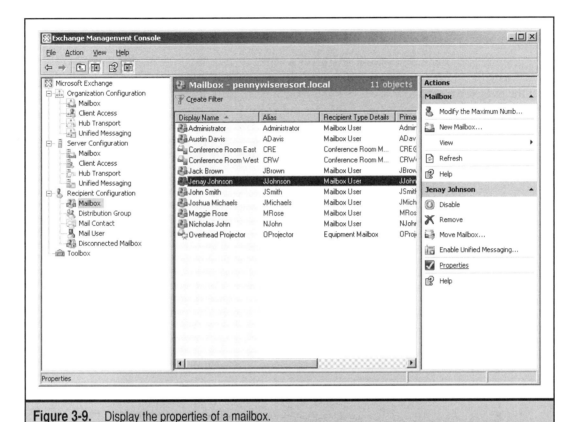

Figure 3-9. Display the properties of a mailbox.

Each user account can have multiple SMTP addresses, which comes in handy if you want mail addressed to more than one recipient to appear in the same mailbox. For example, if you are the administrator for your Web site, you'll have one internal SMTP address that coworkers will use to send you mail. But you could also have the postmaster and Webmaster e-mail addresses assigned to your mailbox so that visitors on the Internet who send mail to the Webmaster will have their messages routed to your inbox.

This feature can also be used if some of your users have names that are difficult to spell. For example, a female user named "Gale" could have her first name misspelled as "Gayle" or "Gail." Adding SMTP addresses to Gale's account that include the various misspellings of her name will reduce the number of non-delivery reports (NDRs) returned to the message originators and will increase her chances that she will receive messages sent to her, even if her name is misspelled.

TIP Remember that even though you can type just about anything as an alternative SMTP address, even with a different domain name, only those domain names that are supported by your Exchange organization will be routed to the recipient.

Managing Your Recipient Policies

If you need to see what default addresses are being generated for mailbox recipients in your forest, navigate to the Hub Transport node under Organization Configuration within the console tree in the Exchange Management Console. Click the E-mail Addresses Policy tab, and select the default policy (Figure 3-14).

Select Edit from the action pane to launch the Edit E-mail Address Policy Wizard. Since there are no editable values on the Introduction page (because you are editing the default policy—if you create a new policy, the grayed-out options will be available for selection), press Next to see the Conditions page, where you can review the recipients this policy will affect. Again, because this is the default policy, you cannot modify these values. Clicking the Preview button will show all the recipients (regardless of their type) affected by this policy. Clicking Next takes you to the E-mail Address page (Figure 3-15) which is the very reason we came here in the first place.

You should first notice that with a new installation of Exchange 2007, the default SMTP address matches that of the Active Directory domain name. Depending on your organization, this may not be a viable public address. If this is your case, you need to first add the domain to be supported, which I discussed in Chapter 2, and then modify the SMTP address value by selecting it and clicking the Edit button. You'll want to select the appropriate domain (.com, .net, etc.), like I've done in Figure 3-16, and click OK.

If your company supports more than one e-mail domain and you want the additional e-mail domain to apply to everyone within the organization, you'll need to add it to the list of supported domains (I discussed this in Chapter 2), and then you can add the extra SMTP address by clicking the Add button (there is also a drop-down list where you can select a custom e-mail address) and selecting the to-be-added domain from the E-mail Address Domain drop-down list.

The E-mail Address Local Part value facilitates the customization of the individual user's alias before the domain name. The default is to have the e-mail alias match the user's alias in Active Directory. If your company has a standard when it comes to naming user accounts that will not match the standard when naming e-mail addresses, you should consider using one of the possible alias-naming values. Once you have the appropriate e-mail addresses listed, click Next to see the Schedule page (Figure 3-17). Here, you can choose when to have the addressing changes applied.

Clicking Next takes you to the Edit E-mail Address Policy page (which is just a summary of changes to take place). Click Edit to complete the wizard.

If you have more than one address of a given type, such as multiple SMTP addresses, you'll need to select one to be the *primary* address, which will act as the reply-to address when e-mail is originated using this account. To select such an address, highlight the desired address in the user's properties, and then click the Set As Reply button, as shown in Figure 3-18.

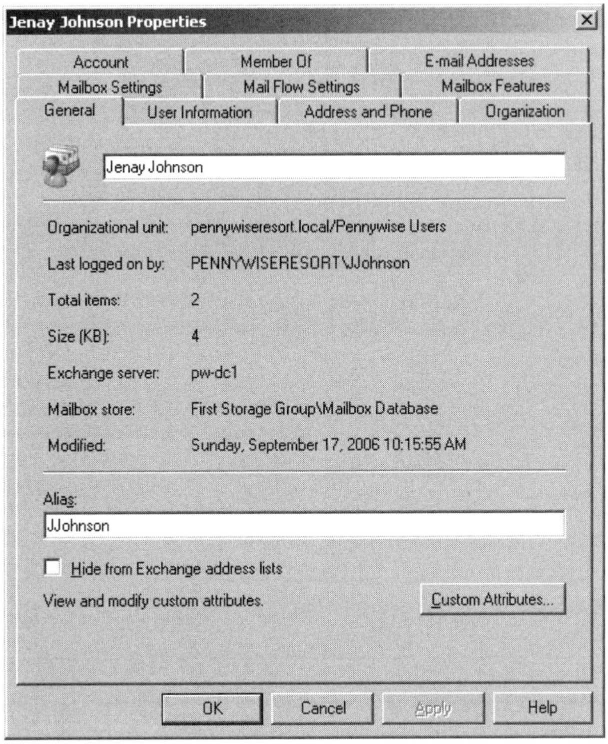

Figure 3-10. The general properties of a mailbox.

Getting back to the e-mail addresses properties of the mailbox, you can clear the Automatically Update E-mail Addresses Based On Recipient Policy check box to keep the e-mail addresses from being affected by a recipient policy. You may want to do this, for example, if a user's e-mail alias before the domain name does not conform to the corporate standard (e.g. JohnS versus the corporate standard of JSmith). Like the recipient policy, if you have multiple addresses of the same type, you can choose one to be the reply-to address by choosing one of the addresses and clicking the Set As Reply button. Keep in mind that if the Automatically Update E-mail Addresses Based On Recipient Policy check box is selected, your choice of reply-to addresses may be overridden by the settings in a recipient policy.

Moving on to the Mailbox Settings tab (Figure 3-19), you can manage messaging records management (MRM), where you can specify retention hold times and managed content settings (more on this topic in Chapter 17), as well as storage limits and deleted

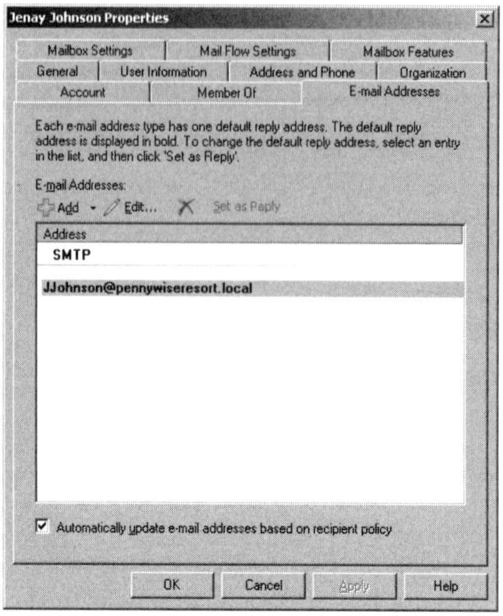

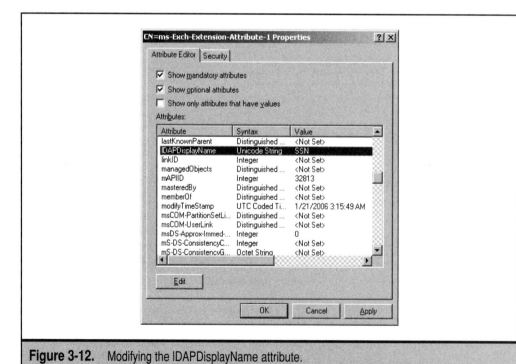

Figure 3-11. View the e-mail addresses associated with the mailbox.

Figure 3-12. Modifying the IDAPDisplayName attribute.

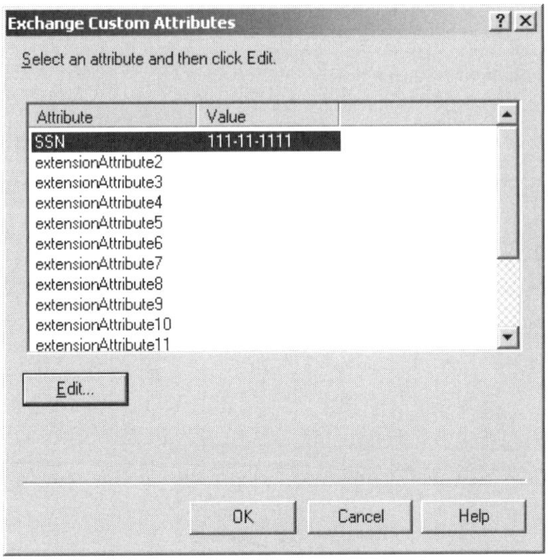

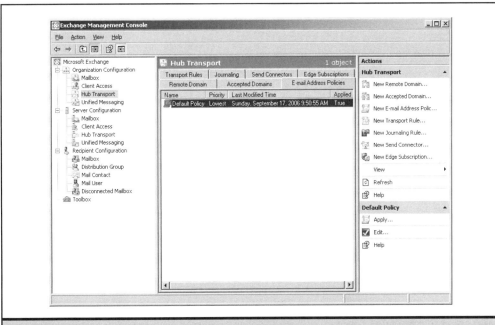

Figure 3-13.   The result of modifying the IDAPDisplayName attribute.

Figure 3-14.   Navigating to the default e-mail address policy.

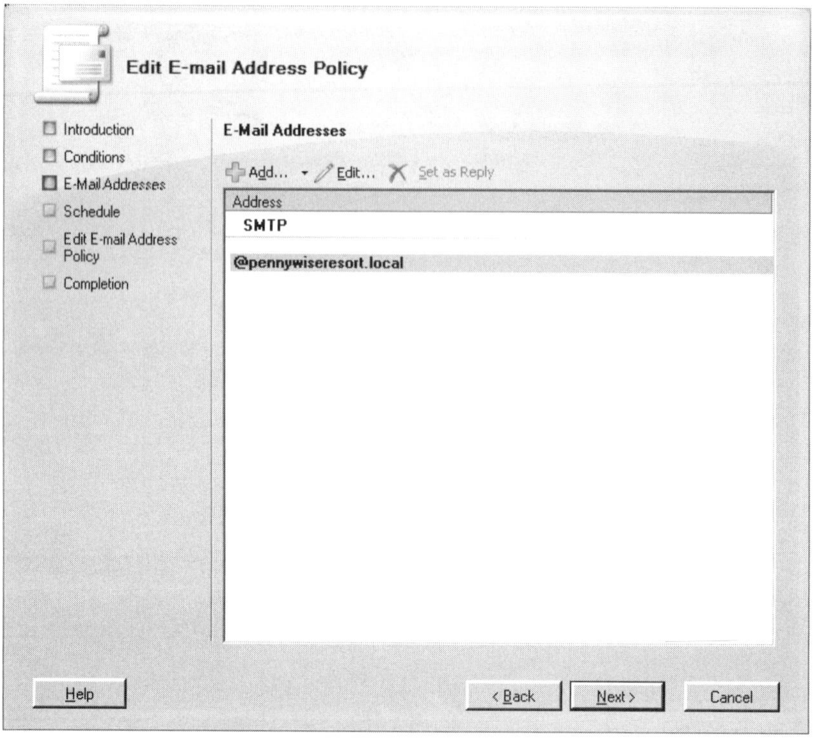

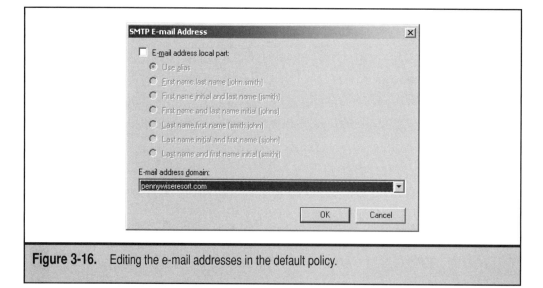

Figure 3-15. View the e-mail addresses in the default policy.

Figure 3-16. Editing the e-mail addresses in the default policy.

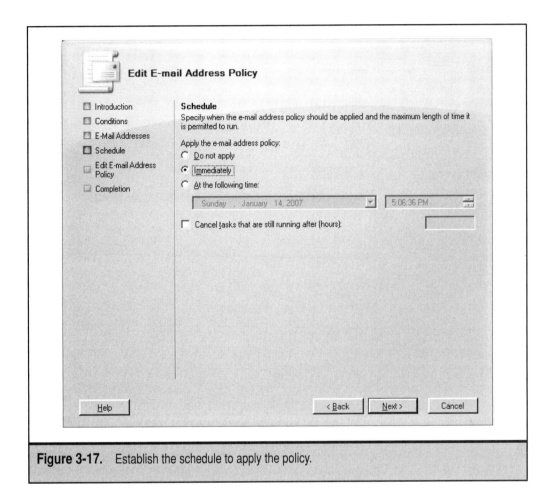

Figure 3-17. Establish the schedule to apply the policy.

item retention times. These latter two settings, shown in Figure 3-20, default to utilizing values from the mailbox database where the mailbox resides.

Should you need to have values specific to a single mailbox, you can clear the Use Mailbox Database Defaults check box for either set of parameters and establish either storage quota values or define how long to retain "deleted" items before permanently removing them from the mailbox database. Storage quota values can, when storage limits are exceeded, warn the user, limit the user to only receive mail but not send, or even restrict both sending and receiving of messages.

TIP If you are going to establish storage quota values at either an individual mailbox or mailbox database level, I highly recommend establishing settings that warn the user of excessive storage and even settings that restrict the user's ability to send messages. However, I typically do not recommend restricting the user's ability to receive. The reason is that while it does motivate the user to clean his or her mailbox more quickly, the only loser is the sender of a message, who receives an NDR. This may affect your company's ability to interact with customers, vendors, or even other internal users.

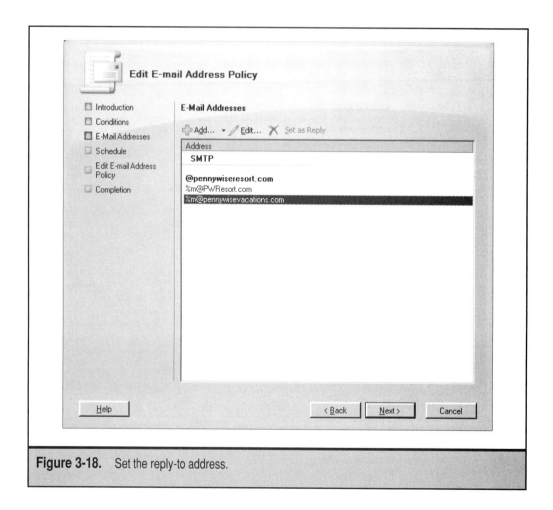

Figure 3-18. Set the reply-to address.

The Mail Flow Settings tab (Figure 3-21) establishes restrictions related to whether messages can come in to the mailbox, go out, and who messages should be delivered to.

To see the Delivery Options dialog box, shown in Figure 3-22, select Delivery Options and click the Properties button. The Send On Behalf area displays relevant permissions (which allow other users to send messages marked as being from them, but send on your behalf), forwarding settings (which can be used to make a copy of all received messages in another mailbox or to forward messages to an outside account), and recipient limits (which specify the number of recipients an individual message can have from a given mailbox.)

To see the message size restrictions, select the same named property from the Mail Flow Settings tab, and click Properties (Figure 3-23). Here, you can restrict the size of incoming and outgoing messages.

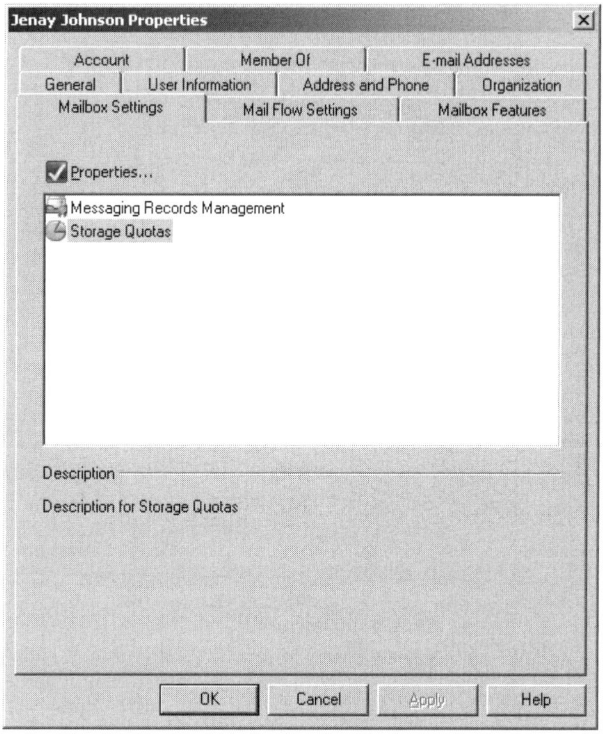

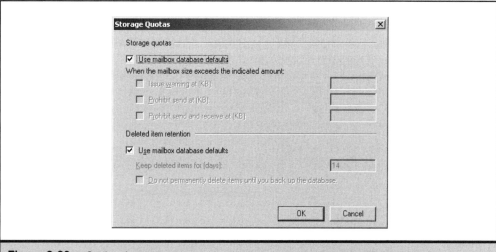

Figure 3-19.   The properties associated with a mailbox.

Figure 3-20.   Setting the storage quotas.

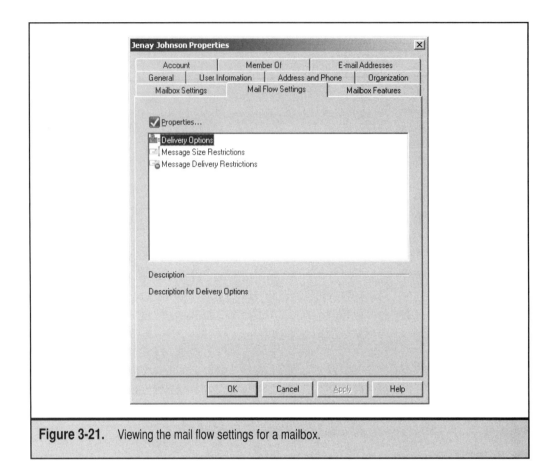

Figure 3-21. Viewing the mail flow settings for a mailbox.

The Message Delivery Restrictions dialog box, shown in Figure 3-24, restricts who can send messages to a given mailbox.

The last tab we will look at is the Mailbox Features tab, shown in Figure 3-25. It lists the various Exchange features available to users of mailboxes. For most settings on this tab, the most you can do is disable or enable a given feature, which you may want to do for various reasons. For example, you may want to restrict usage of Outlook Web Access by certain users whom you do not want accessing e-mail from outside the organization. Or you may have a licensing issue with your phone system provider that integrates with Exchange's unified messaging, so you need to limit the number of mailboxes with this feature turned on. This list may be potentially extended by third-party products.

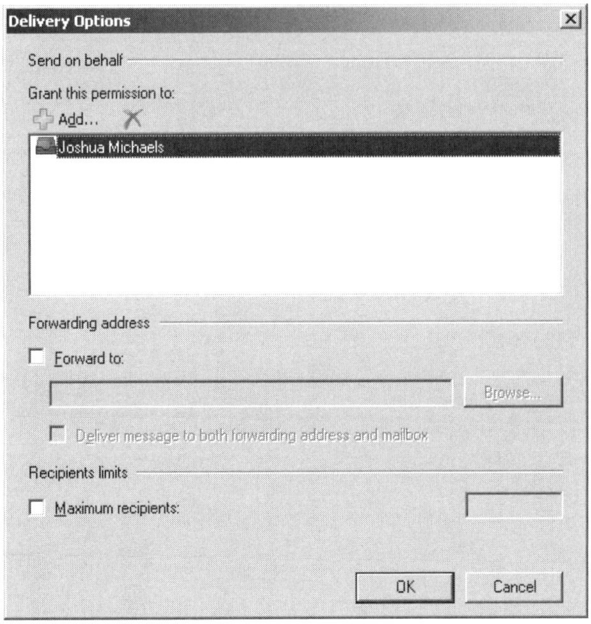

Figure 3-22.   Modifying the delivery options.

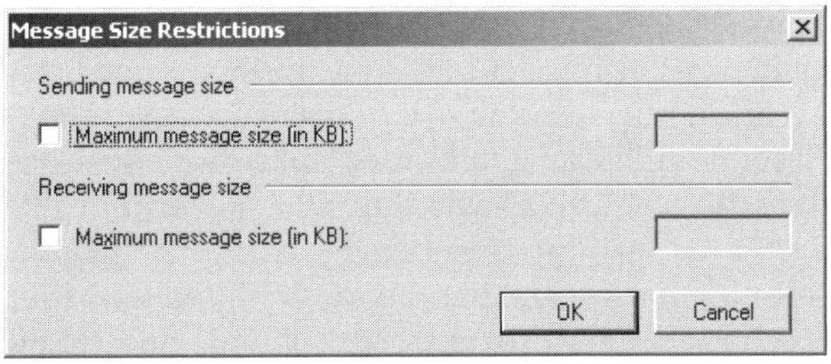

Figure 3-23.   Modifying the message size restrictions.

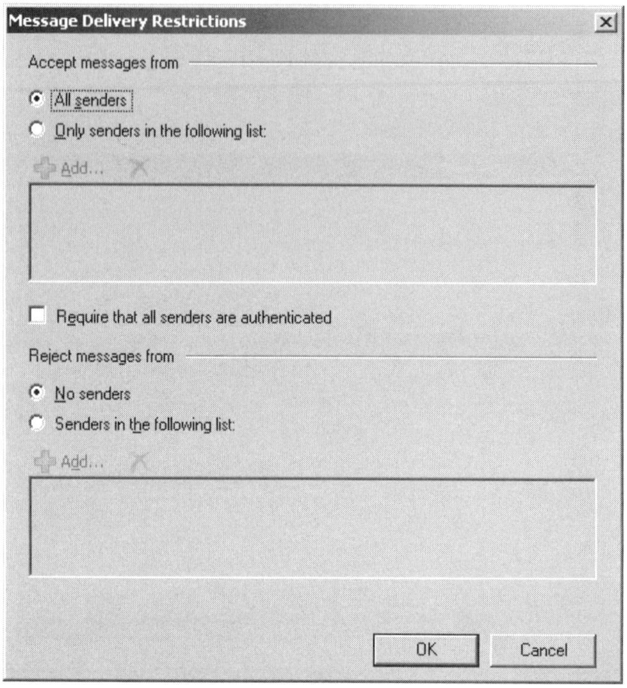

Figure 3-24. Modifying the message delivery restrictions.

Deleting and Reconnecting Mailboxes

Deleting a mailbox is a rather simple task in Exchange 2007: choose the mailbox, select Remove from the action pane, and it's gone. The opportunity exists, though, to reassociate the "deleted" mailbox (which is actually in a "disconnected" state and won't be deleted immediately) with another existing user account in Active Directory. First, the issue of deleted versus disconnected: Each mailbox database has its own settings on how long to retain deleted mailboxes, as well as a setting on whether to wait for a backup before deleting mailboxes. You can read more on this in Chapter 5. The process of recovering a mailbox involves selecting the "deleted" mailbox (I put deleted in quotes, as it isn't really deleted until Exchange deems it so) and connecting it to an existing Active Directory user account that currently does not have a mailbox. Figure 3-26 shows the disconnected mailbox object in the Exchange Management Console.

Selecting the mailbox and choosing Connect from the action pane starts the Connect Mailbox Wizard, shown in Figure 3-27. You can choose the type of mailbox the reconnected

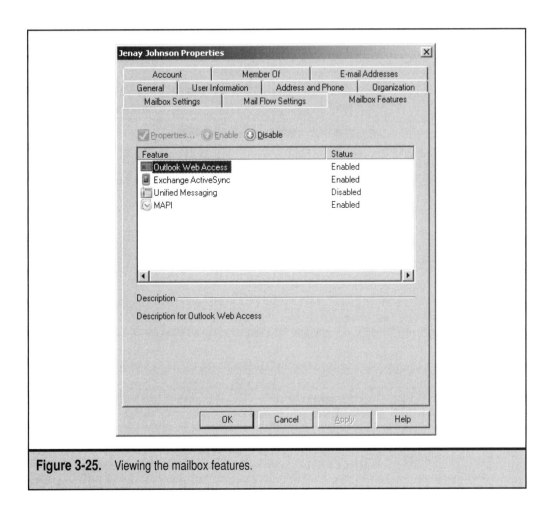

Figure 3-25. Viewing the mailbox features.

mailbox will be. The process is similar to creating a new mailbox, with the only difference being that the mailbox dataset already exists and you need to select the existing user or match it to an alias, as shown in Figure 3-28.

Creating and Configuring Contacts

A contact is an account that is created in Active Directory that has two main features. First, it can neither be used to authenticate a user on the network nor to assign permissions to objects in the directory, so creating these accounts doesn't represent a security threat. Second, the account is created to send messages to a foreign e-mail account, usually an SMTP account, and does not represent a human user on your network.

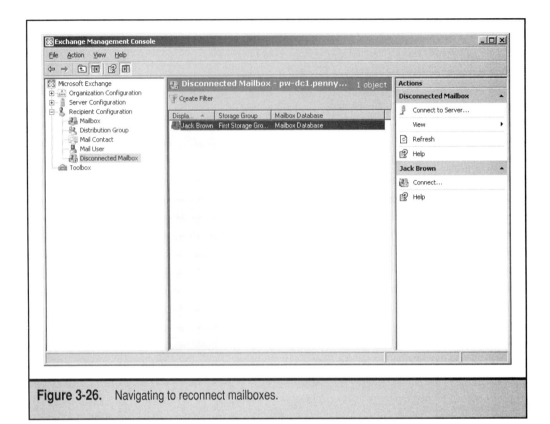

Figure 3-26. Navigating to reconnect mailboxes.

Generally speaking, it is a good idea to create a different organizational unit in which to house your contacts, especially if you're going to have more than a few of them. In some companies, where contractors are used on a regular basis, this becomes even more important. So consider creating an organizational unit (OU) for your contacts.

To create a contact in the Exchange Management Console, begin by navigating to the Mail Contact node under Recipient Configuration in the console tree. In the action pane, click the New Mail Contact link (Figure 3-29) to start the New Mail Contact Wizard (Figure 3-30).

On the Introduction page of the wizard, you can choose to create a new contact or, by selecting an existing contact, you mail-enable it and associate an e-mail address with it. In this chapter, we'll focus on creating a new contact, so you'd select New Contact and click Next. On the Contact Information page (Figure 3-31), provide contact information and specifically add information to the External E-mail Address field by clicking the Edit button and entering an SMTP address. Once complete, click Next.

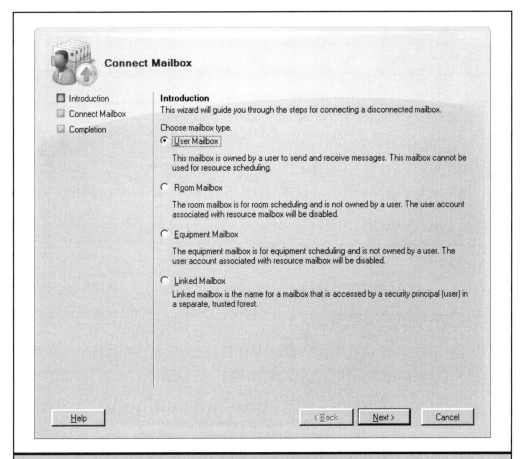

Figure 3-27. Reconnecting via the Connect Mailbox Wizard.

Management Shell Corner

To create a new mail contact, run the following command:

```
New-MailContact -ExternalEmailAddress:'SMTP:bthomas@outsidecompanyaddress
.com' -Name:'Brandi Thomas' -Alias:'Brandi_Thomas' -OrganizationalUnit:
'pennywiseresort.local/Users' -DisplayName:'Brandi Thomas' -FirstName:'Brandi'
-Initials:'' -LastName:'Thomas'
```

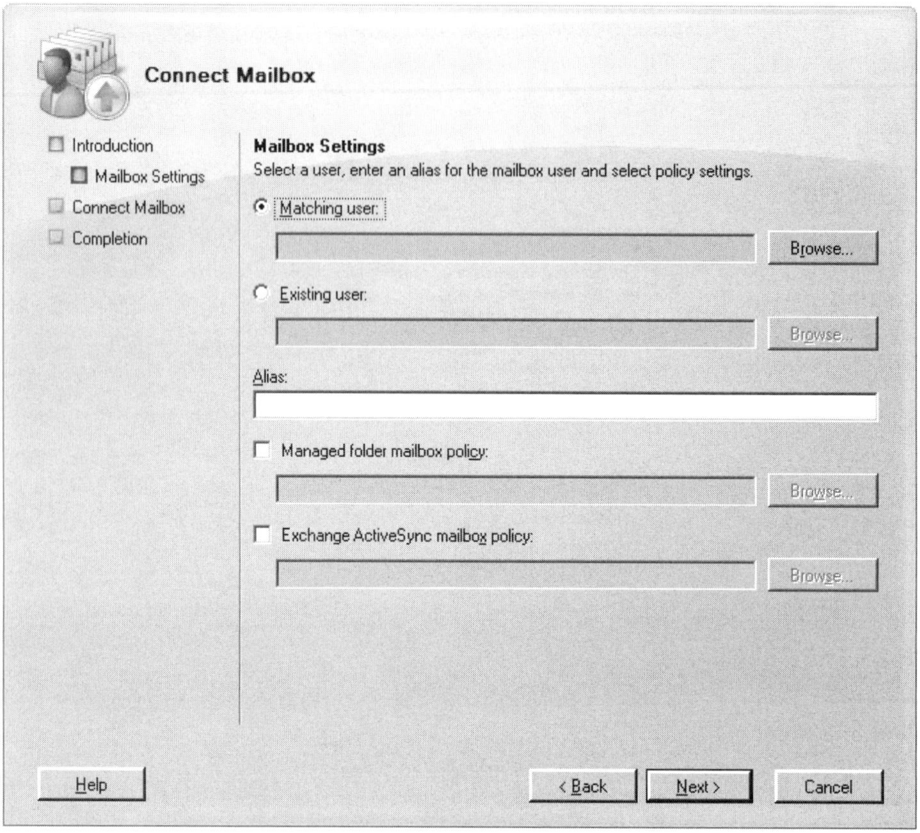

Figure 3-28. Selecting the existing user in the Connect Mailbox Wizard.

The New Mail Contact page summarizes the information you provided, and after you click the New button, the Completion page lists the outcome.

When looking at the properties of a contact (accomplished by selecting the contact in the results pane and clicking the Properties link in the action pane), most of the tabs and input boxes are self-explanatory (see Figure 3-32), so we won't go through them in great detail. However, on the General tab, you can force messages sent to this contact to be in the form of Messaging Application Programming Interface (MAPI) rich text. Select this, if appropriate.

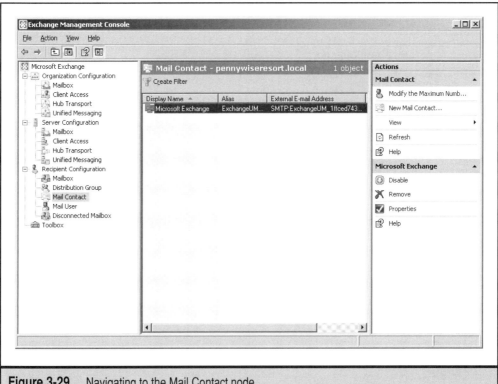

Figure 3-29.   Navigating to the Mail Contact node.

Creating and Configuring Mail Users

Mail users are actual accounts in your Active Directory, but their e-mail does not reside within your Exchange environment; they use their own messaging system, Hotmail account, etc. This may sound a lot like a contact, but the difference is that a contact is an object that represents someone who neither has a mailbox in your Exchange environment nor an Active Directory account, whereas the mail user still has an Active Directory account.

To create a mail user in the Exchange Management Console, begin by navigating to the Mail User node under Recipient Configuration in the console tree. In the action pane, click the New Mail User link (Figure 3-33) to start the New Mail User Wizard (Figure 3-34).

Since you are creating a user within Active Directory, you first need to provide user account information on the User Information page of the wizard, as shown in Figure 3-35. Then, because the user will utilize an outside messaging system, you will need to provide his or her external e-mail address, as shown in Figure 3-36.

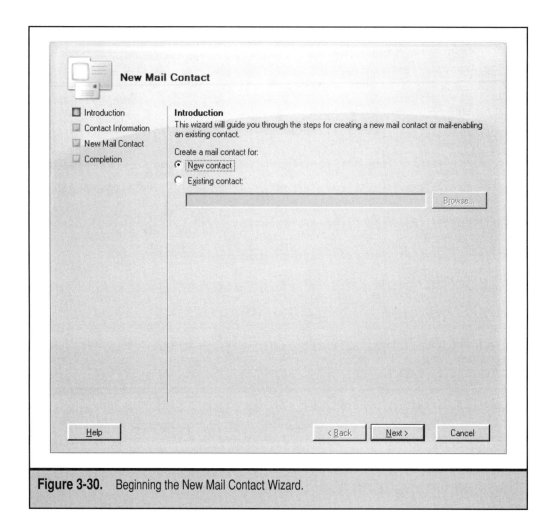

Figure 3-30. Beginning the New Mail Contact Wizard.

The properties of a mail user are extremely similar from an Exchange perspective. See the previous section for notes on what you may want to change on an existing mail user.

Creating and Configuring Distribution Groups

For the benefit of those of you who may be coming from Exchange 5.5, a distribution group is simply a mail-enabled group in Active Directory that has the same function as a distribution list did in Exchange 5.5. Sending a message to the distribution group will result in all members of the group receiving the message. Exchange 2007 supports two

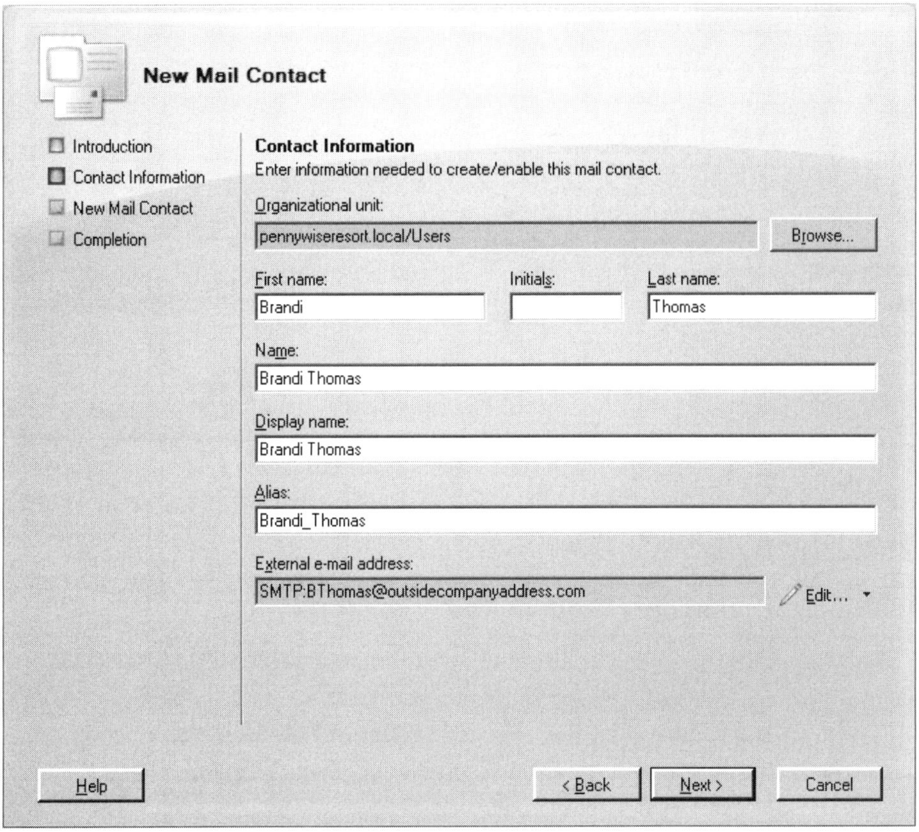

New Mail Contact

☐ Introduction
☐ Contact Information
☐ New Mail Contact
☐ Completion

Contact Information
Enter information needed to create/enable this mail contact.

Organizational unit:

pennywiseresort.local/Users   Browse...

First name: Initials: Last name:
Brandi   Thomas

Name:
Brandi Thomas

Display name:
Brandi Thomas

Alias:
Brandi_Thomas

External e-mail address:
SMTP:BThomas@outsidecompanyaddress.com   ✎ Edit... ▾

Help   < Back   Next >   Cancel

Figure 3-31. Provide contact information when creating a new contact.

kinds of distribution groups: those with a static membership (referred to simply as a *distribution group*) and those with a dynamic membership (referred to as a *dynamic distribution group*). Distribution groups act in the same manner as security groups: members are added and removed administratively. Dynamic distribution groups have their membership defined via a simple query definition.

Creating a Distribution Group

To create a distribution group in the Exchange Management Console, begin by navigating to the Distribution Group node under Recipient Configuration in the console tree.

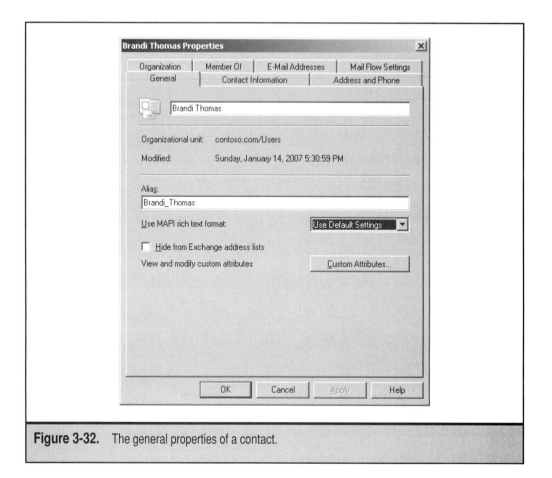

Figure 3-32. The general properties of a contact.

In the action pane, click the New Distribution Group link (Figure 3-37) to start the New Distribution Group Wizard (Figure 3-38).

On the Introduction page of the wizard, you can choose to create a new distribution group. Or, by selecting an existing group, you will mail-enable an existing security group in Active Directory. For the purposes of this chapter, I'll select New Group and click Next. On the Group Information page of the wizard (Figure 3-39), you'll need to decide whether you'll be creating a distribution or security group and provide general information about the group. The difference between the two is that a distribution group is only used for e-mail purposes, whereas the security group can be used for e-mail purposes, as well as to grant permissions to resources. Once you are done, click Next.

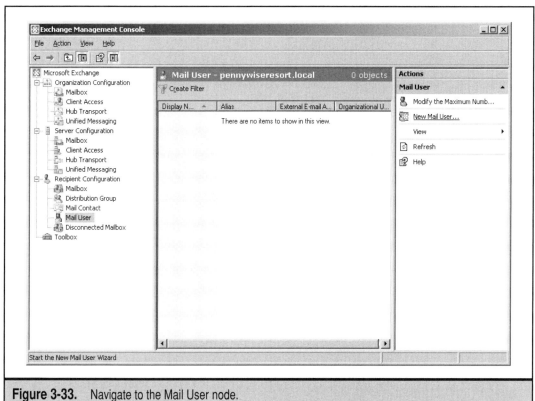

Figure 3-33.   Navigate to the Mail User node.

TIP   If you create a security group on this page, the group will be an e-mail recipient and be granted access to resources. If you create a distribution group, the group can only be an e-mail recipient.

The New Distribution Group page summarizes the information you provided. After you click the New button, the Completion page lists the outcome.

Management Shell Corner

To create a new distribution group, run the following command:

```
new-DistributionGroup -Name:'Frugle Staff Group' -
Type:'Distribution' -OrganizationalUnit:'pennywiseresort.local/
Users' -SamAccountName:'Frugle Staff Group' -DisplayName:'Frugle
Staff Group' -Alias:'Frugle_Staff_Group'
```

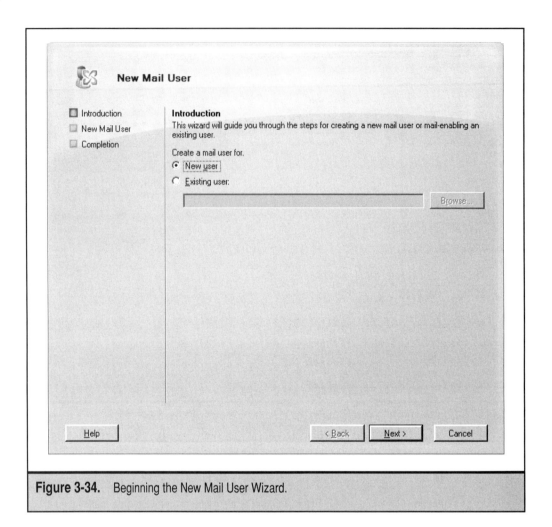

Figure 3-34.   Beginning the New Mail User Wizard.

Creating a Dynamic Distribution Group

Creating a dynamic distribution group is similar to creating a regular distribution group, with the exception of needing to establish the dynamic membership. Figure 3-40 shows the first additional wizard page where you define the recipient types that will be included in the group membership.

Once you've defined the types of recipients, the Conditions page (shown in Figure 3-41) gives you several options to choose from to further hone the dynamic membership of the group. Unfortunately, there is no way in this release of Exchange to create your own custom conditions or to use an LDAP query.

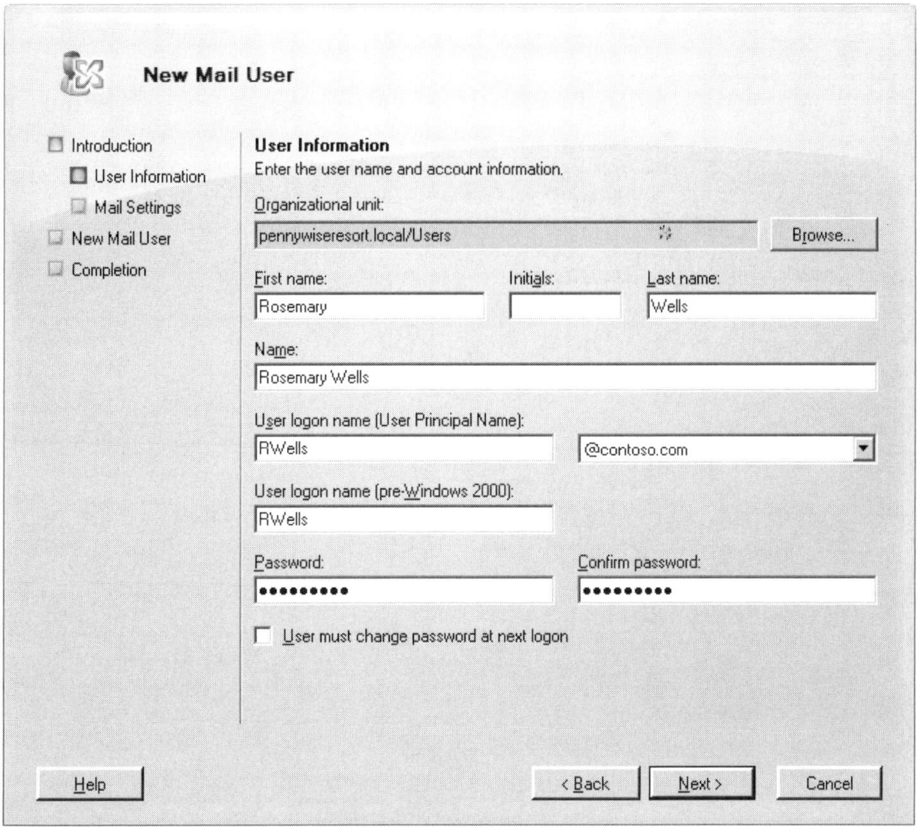

Figure 3-35.   Provide account information when creating a new mail user.

Managing Distribution Group Properties

Once a distribution group is mail-enabled, you can send messages to it, and it will act like a distribution list. The distribution group will be expanded to reveal its members, and the message will be sent to each recipient in the group. The nice thing about this is that you can minimize administrative effort by using user groups that were created for assigning permissions to resources to also act as distribution lists for those members who are mail-enabled. Of course, a mail-enabled group need not be a security group, but these two functions can be accomplished with the same Active Directory object.

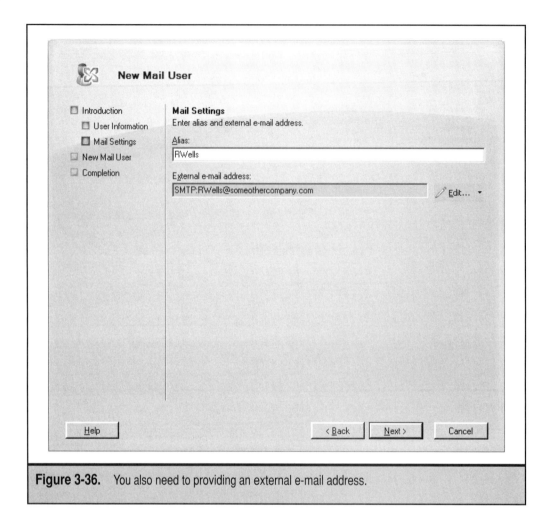

Figure 3-36. You also need to providing an external e-mail address.

Once the group is created, you can review its properties and see that there are a number of configuration options. Since many of them are self-explanatory, we'll only mention a few here.

First, on the Members tab, individual users, other groups, and mail-enabled public folders can be added. This means that a single distribution group can be used to send messages to every type of recipient available in Exchange 2007: mailboxes, groups, contacts, and public folders. On the Member Of tab, this group itself can become a member of another distribution group. When used correctly, this allows for the nesting of distribution groups to ease administrative effort.

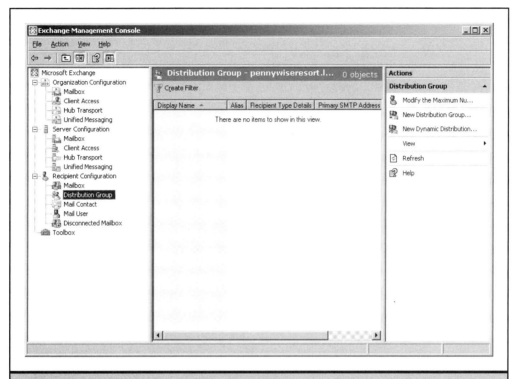

Figure 3-37.   Navigate to the Distribution Group node.

For example, let's assume you have an overall distribution group called Customers. However, inside this group, you have three other distribution groups as members, each one divided along your three product lines. Now, if you want to send an e-mail message to those in product line number one, you could send the message to the Product Line One group. However, if you had a more general message for all of your customers, such as a grand opening for a new location, then you could send the message to the Customers distribution group, and that message would, in turn, be sent to all three product line distribution groups. By nesting your distribution groups, you can efficiently select the scope of your e-mail message based on its purpose.

On the General tab, you can specify a unique alias for the distribution group. This is especially helpful if the group's name is long and you don't want to force users to type in such a long name. Also, on the Mail Flow Settings tab, message size limits can (and should) be set, as well as from whom messages will be accepted.

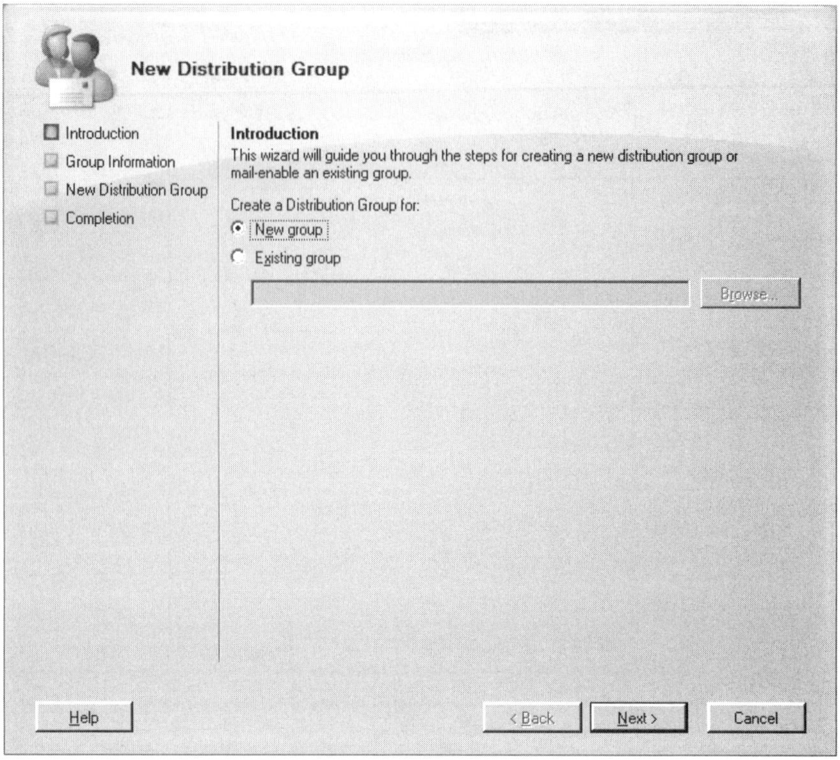

Figure 3-38.   Starting the New Distribution Group Wizard.

Now, there are a couple of things to keep in mind. First, the wider or broader the scope of the distribution group, the more tightly message originators should be controlled. For instance, you don't want to leave the default option, Accept Messages From Everyone, for the All Company Users Distribution list. Can you see it now? A disgruntled employee is on his way out the door and spams everyone in the company with pornographic images. Not a good thing, right? So increasingly tighten who can send messages to a distribution group as the group's scope widens.

Second, you'll want to limit the message size the group can receive. I once worked in a company where the owner would spam everyone in the company (80 users in three cities) with unzipped scanned images of magazine articles about the company. When dialing in over a 56.6-kilobytes per second (Kbps) connection (at the time, employees only had dial-up), it took over 20 minutes to download the e-mail, because he didn't identify it in the subject line as an e-mail with a large attachment.

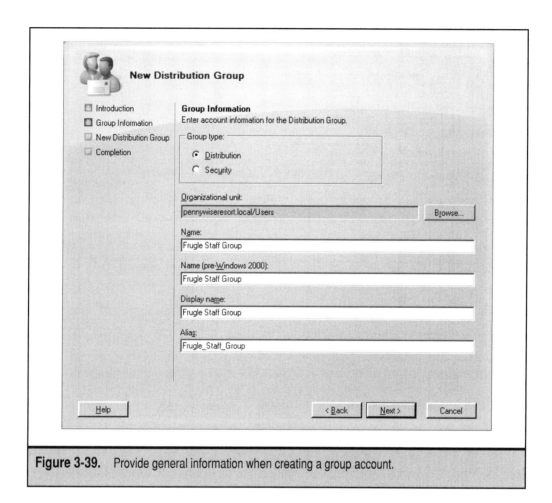

Figure 3-39. Provide general information when creating a group account.

While such situations might be politically difficult to manage, they need our attention as administrators. We should be attentive to how message size affects our remote users and, therefore, we should be diligent about enforcing message size limitations.

With the Single Instance Storage (SIS) feature of Exchange 2000 Server (see Chapter 15), we don't need to be as concerned about our databases growing out of control because of large message spamming; however, we should be concerned about the amount of bandwidth that large message spamming consumes. Be careful to perform regular capacity planning for your network, and ensure that you have set the message size limits at the largest, but optimal, setting possible.

On the Advanced tab, shown in Figure 3-42, you'll need to decide if a specific expansion server needs to be specified. This is done by using the Expansion Server drop-down list box.

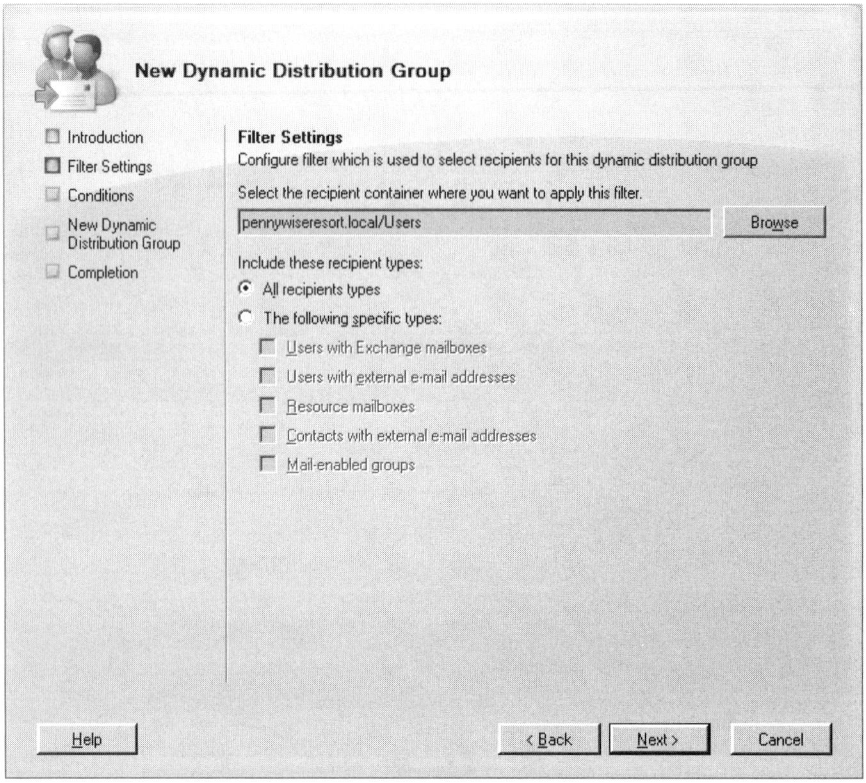

Figure 3-40.   Define the recipient types when creating a dynamic distribution group.

The purpose of the expansion server is to specify which server will expand the membership list of the distribution group, and perform its routing and selection process to send the message to each group member. This is both a RAM- and a processor-intensive activity. For groups with a small membership of fewer than 50 or 75 members, this is not a big deal and can be performed on any server in the administrative group.

But if the group contains several hundred or even several thousand members, it might be wise to dedicate a server to this function. Expanding even a simple message and then running each user through the routing and selection process, could take hours. Dedicating a server to this function, in such a scenario, just makes sense.

On the Advanced tab, you can specify how delivery reports should be handled and whether out-of-office messages from recipients should be sent to the originator of

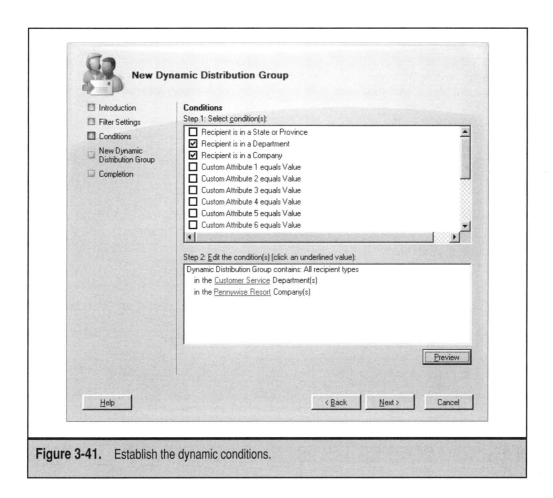

Figure 3-41.   Establish the dynamic conditions.

the message. Generally, you'll want to leave this check box unselected; but there might be certain kinds of distribution groups, such as time-sensitive messages or mission-critical groups, where having an out-of-office message sent to the originator would be a wise course of action.

TIP   Send your company-wide e-mail messages using the Bcc field instead of the To field. If the message is sent using the To field, then anyone can use the Reply To All button and send their response to everyone in the company. By using the Bcc field, the originator's name will appear as the sender of the message. Therefore, if a user uses the Reply To All button, the message will only come back to the message originator.

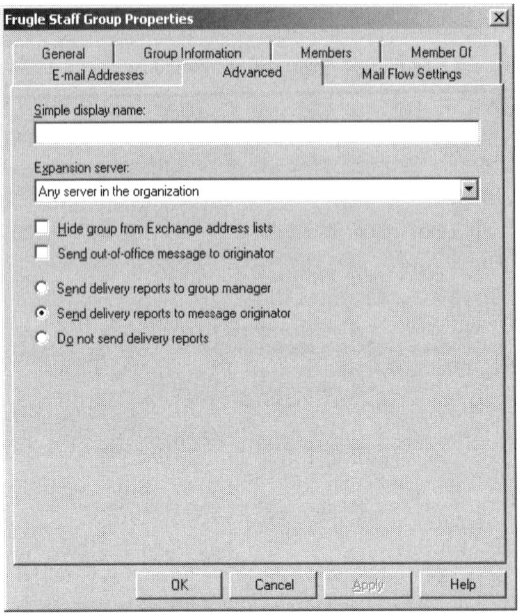

Figure 3-42. Specifying an Expansion Server

MANAGING ADDRESS LISTS

Address lists are managed in the Exchange Management Console on the Mailbox node under Organization Configuration in the console tree. They can be found by selecting the Address List tab in the results pane. Address lists are created by using filter rules—rules that search Active Directory and find objects that match a predefined set of criteria. Once all the objects are accumulated, a list is built and it becomes an address list. Figure 3-43 shows the Introduction page of the Edit Address List Wizard when editing the All Users address list. You'll notice the recipient filter in Figure 3-43 showing the LDAP filter that the list will return from Active Directory.

Default lists are provided for All Contacts, All Groups, All Rooms, All Users, and Public Folders. Additional rule sets can be created by selecting New Address List in the action pane and following the wizard. Interestingly enough, you really don't need a developer to create these rules. Exchange asks for the types of recipients and allows you to specify that the recipients belong to a certain company, department, or state/province.

An address list is another object in the directory, so it will have an Access Control List (ACL) for security purposes. This means that you can create an address list, and then specify who can access it by assigning permissions to the list using users and groups in

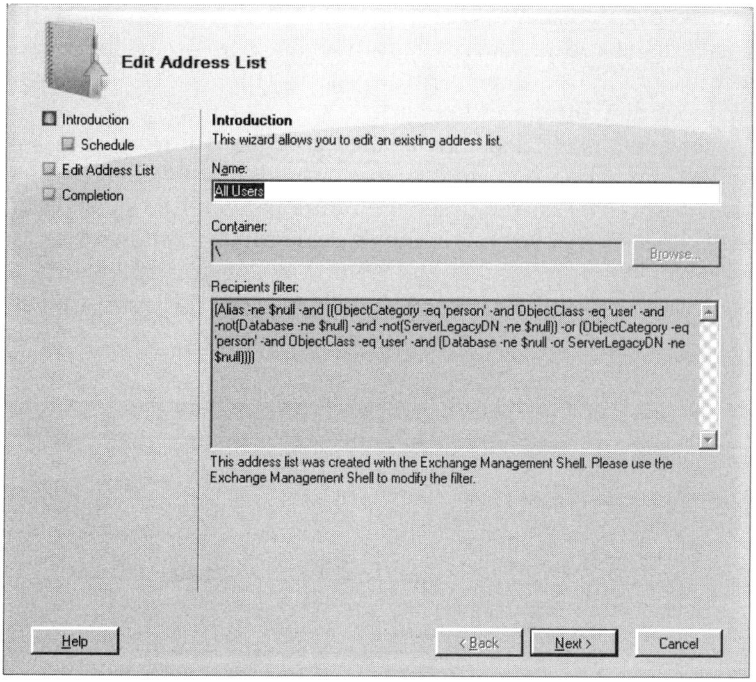

Figure 3-43.   Editing the All Users address list.

Active Directory. Some address lists, such as top corporate executives or those who hold sensitive positions, may not want their e-mail addresses available to everyone. Use the ACL to limit who can see sensitive address lists. By default, the Everyone group is not given any access and the Authenticated Users group is only given List Contents permissions.

After an address list is created, it will not update immediately. If you need it to update immediately, or if you just want to force an address list to update because new users have been added to Active Directory, you can use the Update-EmailAddressPolicy cmdlet within the Exchange Management Shell.

Offline Address Lists

An offline address list is simply an address list made up of other address lists that, when combined, are available as a single list when Outlook clients are offline. If you need certain address lists available offline, then you'll need to create them in the Offline Address Lists area of the Mailbox node under Organization Configuration. When creating an offline address list, you will need to specify the server responsible for generating the list, as well as the address lists that should be included when users are offline, as shown in Figure 3-44. You cannot copy and paste an address list from one container to another, so if you need to create an intricate set of address lists that are available both on the local area network (LAN) and remotely, you'll need to perform two steps—first create the address list and then create a corresponding offline address list.

Unlike previous versions of Exchange, where the offline address list was published in the public folders, Exchange 2007, in conjunction with Outlook 2007, supports publishing the offline address list via Web-based distribution. This allows your Outlook 2007 client to remain updated even when not in the office. Figure 3-45 shows the Distribution Points page of the New Offline Address List Wizard, where you can specify which Exchange server and corresponding Web site within that server's IIS instance will host the offline address list.

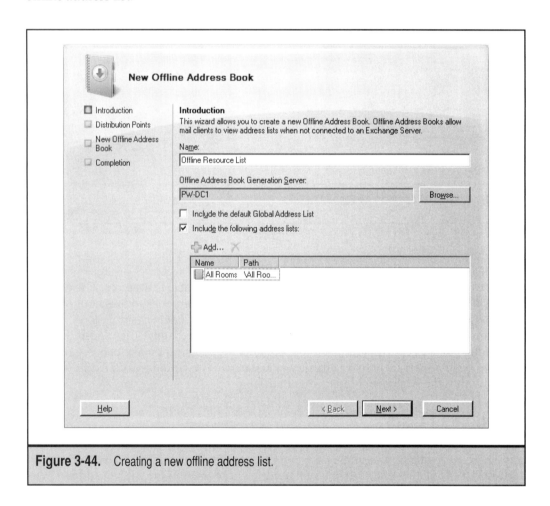

Figure 3-44. Creating a new offline address list.

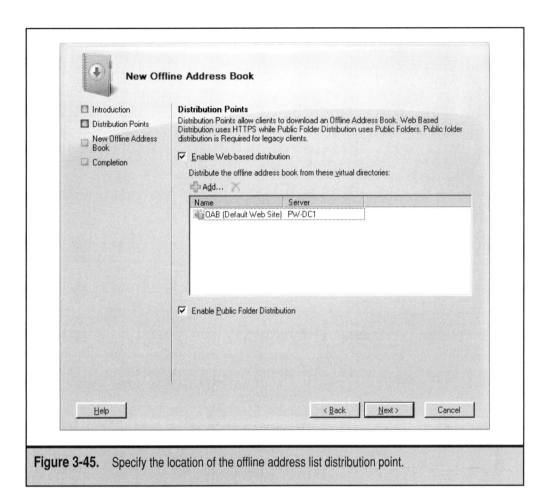

Figure 3-45. Specify the location of the offline address list distribution point.

SUMMARY

In this chapter, you learned how to create and manage mailbox, contact, and distribution group recipients. You also learned how to create and manage address lists. This was a big "how to" chapter and it should get you going on the basics of managing mailboxes in your environment.

In the next chapter, we'll take a look at how public folders are created and managed. This is a more complex topic, but just as necessary to performing good day-to-day Exchange administration. Despite solutions like SharePoint Server to make information available to multiple users, public folders are still a very large part of most Exchange installations, so don't skip over the next chapter.

CHAPTER 4

Creating and Managing Public Folders

M icrosoft Exchange information can basically be divided conceptually into two types: private and public. Private information is generally thought of as messages stored in the mailbox that is only available to an individual or delegated user. Other types of private information can include tasks, journal entries, personal contacts, and notes. Public information is generally thought to reside in public folders and is available to a wider audience than private information. Public information can take any form, including audio clips, graphics, text files, and spreadsheets.

In Exchange 2007, public folder databases are optional, as Microsoft offers more robust collaborative solutions, such as SharePoint Portal Server, to share even more types of data. While Microsoft intends on supporting public folders through 2016, you will most likely not see them in the next version of Exchange, so moving your collaborative efforts via SharePoint Portal Server would be a prudent move. However, those organizations running earlier versions of Outlook (which will need public folders to retrieve system information, such as the offline address book) or those desiring to use Exchange as a collaborative solution will need to create a public folder database. Public folders are intended to share information across organizations or across the Internet using Exchange as the point of storage and retrieval. They provide an ideal foundation for sharing data and working with collaborative applications. Whenever your organization has files and documents that must be available to multiple users, you can use public folders to distribute that information.

This chapter will introduce you to public folders and demonstrate how to create and manage them. In addition, we'll look at replication issues and strategies for managing your public folder hierarchies.

INTRODUCTION TO PUBLIC FOLDERS

Public folders provide the foundation for the Exchange Server 2007 collaborative system. Inside these folders, users can share information. More importantly, customized applications can be used as the default form, into which users can enter information, which is then transferred to a database in SQL Server via an open database connection (ODBC).

Public folders initially do not have an e-mail address associated with them. A *mail-enabled* public folder is one that not only is accessible from within Exchange, but is also addressable from outside using an assigned e-mail address. Later in this chapter, I'll discuss public folder tasks and mail-enabled public folder tasks separately.

Public folder information is held in an Exchange database that is managed by the store.exe process. This database is exactly the same as that of a mailbox store, and enjoys the benefits of transaction logging and other Extensible Storage Engine (ESE) features (these features are covered in Chapter 15).

Public Folder Hierarchy

The hierarchy for public folders is held in a public folder tree. One public folder tree is created when the first Exchange 2007 server is installed into Active Directory. This tree is automatically replicated to all the Exchange 2007 servers in the organization.

Unlike previous versions of Exchange, Exchange 2007 supports a single public folder tree, which is commonly referred to as a *hierarchy*, to give you better administrative control over workflow solutions.

Public Folder Strategies

There are advantages and disadvantages to using a single or multiple public folder strategy. When designing your Exchange 2007 organization, you'll need to design a public folder strategy. There are two basic types of strategies: standalone public folder strategy and replicated public folder strategy.

Standalone Public Folder Servers

While you might conclude that this is not the best strategy for your organization, it is the default for public folders when a public folder database is initially created in Exchange 2007. In this scenario, all public folder data is stored on the server where it was created, instead of replicating the data to other Exchange 2007 servers. The main advantage of not replicating your public folders is that no replication traffic is incurred. Furthermore, any changes to content in a given folder are immediately available to other users. Finally, a single folder strategy is both easier to manage and less expensive, since multiple servers are not necessary. It is also the only strategy available for a single-server installation, which is a high number of the Exchange deployment environments.

However, one of the largest disadvantages of this strategy is that a single point of failure exists. This isn't so much a load-balancing issue as it is one of fault tolerance. If this single server goes down for some reason, there is no other place on the network to which users can be referred for public folder information.

A single folder strategy is usually best under the following two situations:

▼   Small local area networks (LANs) with few servers

▲   No time-critical or mission-critical information is held in a public folder

Replicated Public Folder Servers

This strategy replicates public folders and their content between two or more public folder servers. These servers can be either dedicated public folder servers (that is, not containing any mailboxes, although this server would be configured with the Mailbox Server role) or dual-purpose servers, providing both public folder and mailbox servicing functions.

The main advantage of replicating public folders between servers is that fault tolerance is achieved. If you have public folder data replicated between two Exchange servers and one of the servers becomes unavailable, users can still access the public folder content on the other server. While both servers are up and running, you can load-balance public folder requests between servers. Users can work with both replicas and make changes when needed. Exchange can also send notifications when there is a conflict in changed data.

TIP   Users whose mailboxes reside on the same server where public folder data exists will attempt to access the public folder data on that server. Load-balancing comes into play for those users whose mailboxes reside on Exchange servers other than those being used for housing the public folder data. See the next section for more information.

The main disadvantage of having multiple public folder servers is the bandwidth that is consumed for data replication. This becomes a more important issue if replication must occur over a slow or unreliable wide area network (WAN) link. One other downside is that there is latency between modified content in a folder and when that modification is replicated to the other public folder servers. This means that there will be moments in time when users will be working with outdated information. Fortunately, you can set the replication schedule as needed on a per-folder basis. This is covered more fully in "Administering Public Folders" later in the chapter.

Public Folder Referrals

Exchange servers are logically organized using the Active Directory sites within which they already exist. Active Directory sites replace the concept of routing groups used previously in Exchange 2000/2003. Users first attempt to access public folders on the same server as their mailbox, and if the public folder content is not found, servers that exist within the same Active Directory site are contacted. However, if there is no copy of a public folder in the local Active Directory site, they can be (and, by default, will be) referred to Exchange 2007 servers in other Active Directory sites, which are prioritized based on proximity.

CREATING A PUBLIC FOLDER DATABASE

Unlike previous versions of Exchange, public folders can no longer be created using the Exchange Management Console, although it can be accomplished in the Exchange Management Shell. In order to create and manage public folders, you will need to have created a public folder database on at least one Exchange 2007 server configured with the Mailbox Server role. By default, no public folder database is created, so you will need to do this.

TIP   When installing Exchange 2007 into an existing Exchange 2000/2003 organization, you will be asked if you want to create a public folder (in order to support legacy Outlook clients), but in a purely Exchange 2007 environment, no public folder is created by default.

You can create a public folder database using either the Exchange Management Console or within the Exchange Management Shell. To create a public folder database in the Exchange Management Console, navigate to the Mailbox node under Server Configuration in the console tree, as shown in Figure 4-1, and select the storage group that will contain the public folder database.

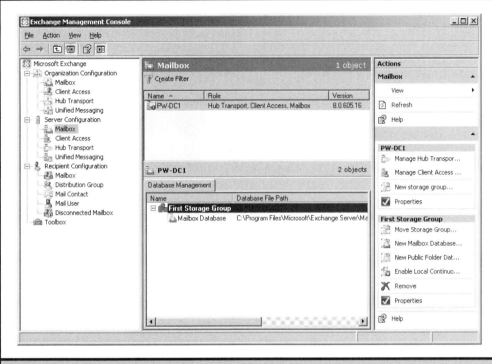

Figure 4-1.   Manage public folder databases in the Exchange Management Console.

Click the New Public Folder Database link in the action pane to start the New Public Folder Database Wizard, as shown in Figure 4-2. Give the database a name, select an alternative database location by modifying the Exchange Database File Path value (this is optional), choose to mount the database (which makes it accessible for use), and click the New button.

Management Shell Corner

To create a public folder database within the Exchange Management Shell, use the following command:

```
new-publicfolderdatabase -StorageGroup:'First Storage Group' -Name:'Public
Folder Database' -EdbFilePath:'C:\Program Files\Microsoft\Exchange Server\
Mailbox\First Storage Group\Public Folder Database.edb'
```

To mount the database, use the following command:

```
mount-database -Identity:'Public Folder Database'
```

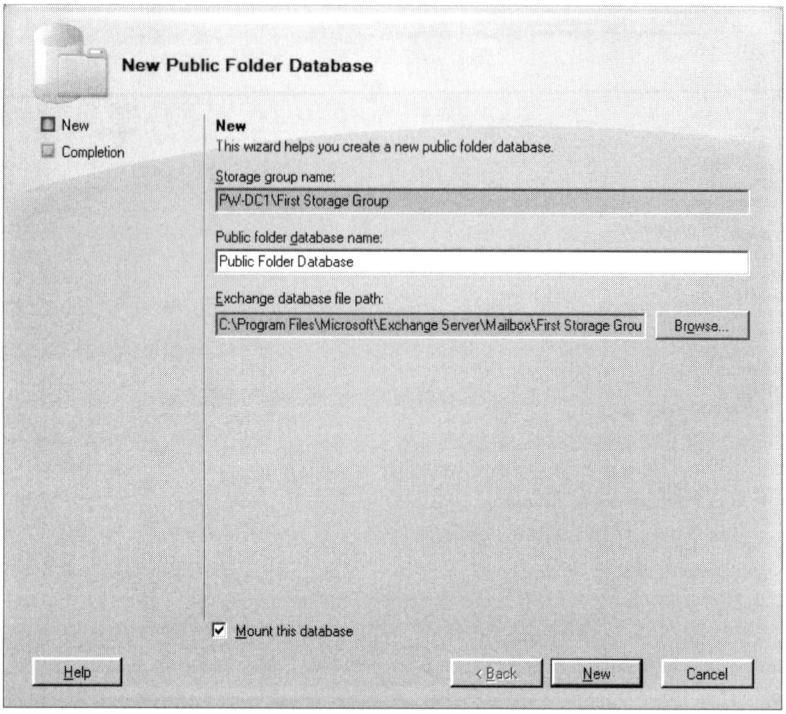

Figure 4-2.   Creating a new public folder database.

You can view the properties of the public folder database (see Figure 4-3) by selecting the database and choosing the Properties link in the action pane. Here you can the database path, backup status, and database mount status, as well as the ability to modify the maintenance schedule of the database (where the database is defragmented while online), whether the database should be mounted at startup (which you would only use in the case of maintenance or troubleshooting), and whether the database can be overwritten by a restore (more on this in Chapter 15).

DELETING A PUBLIC FOLDER DATABASE

If you need to delete a public folder database, you can easily do so from the same location within the Exchange Management Console by selecting the public folder database in question and clicking the Remove link in the action pane. If you want to remove the last public folder database in the organization, you'll need to jump through some hoops with the Exchange Management Shell. This is necessary because the implications of deleting the

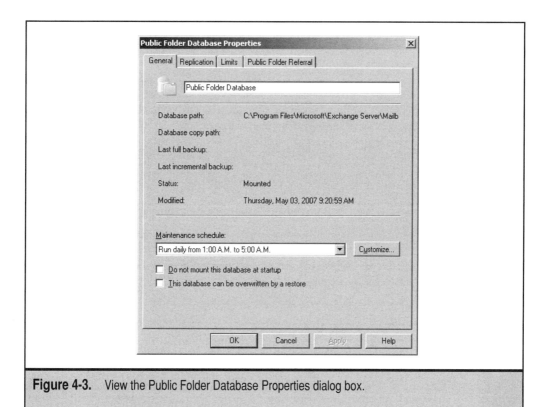

Figure 4-3.   View the Public Folder Database Properties dialog box.

last public folder database are huge in reference to Outlook 2003 clients and their ability to access system information via public folders. So, in order to remove the last public folder database, you'll need to run the following complex command in the Exchange Management Shell, shown in Figure 4-4.

```
Get-PublicFolderDatabase | Remove-PublicFolderDatabase -RemoveLastAllowed
```

As you can see in Figure 4-4, you're asked twice if you really want to perform this action and are reminded that only Outlook 2007 clients will be able to connect. Be certain here—if you need to recover the last public folder database after deleting it, you'll need to re-create the database and then restore the information from backup.

ADMINISTERING PUBLIC FOLDERS

Many Exchange features will aid your administration of public folders. In this section, we'll discuss how to configure both public folders and their replication settings. All of this can be accomplished within the Exchange Management Shell. No management of individual public folders can be accomplished within the Exchange Management

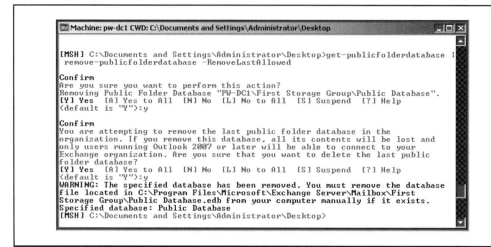

Figure 4-4. Removing the last public folder database from the Exchange Management Shell.

Console with the release to market (RTM) version of Exchange, although Service Pack 1 (SP1) incorporates a public folder management tool I'll briefly cover. In addition, some tasks can be accomplished from within an Outlook client—I'll cover each when appropriate.

Table 4-1 lists the public folder management commands I'll cover in the next few sections.

Command	Purpose
New-PublicFolder	Creates a new public folder
Get-PublicFolder	Retrieves public folder attributes
Set-PublicFolder	Sets public folder attributes
Update-PublicFolder	Starts the synchronization of a public folder
Remove-PublicFolder	Deletes a public folder
Enable-MailPublicFolder	Mail-enables a public folder
Get-MailPublicFolder	Retrieves mail-enabled public folder attributes
Set-MailPublicFolder	Sets mail-enabled public folder attributes
Disable-MailPublicFolder	Mail-disables a public folder

Table 4-1. Common Public Folder Commands

Creating and Configuring Public Folders

The creation of a public folder is a rather simple task, with the most complex part being that you must know the public folder path in which the folder will reside. The command is as follows, with an example shown in Figure 4-5:

```
New-PublicFolder -Name '<name>' -Path '<PFPath>' -Server '<ServerName>'
```

Those of you familiar with Exchange 2000/2003 are already used to the fact that creating public folders from a Microsoft management tool does not include specifying the type of content that will reside within them. The same is true here; creating a public folder from the Exchange Management Shell will result in a folder that can contain messages.

TIP If you want to create a public folder that will hold content other than messages, you will need to use Outlook and then use the Exchange Management Shell or the Public Folder Management Console (covered later in this chapter) to configure them.

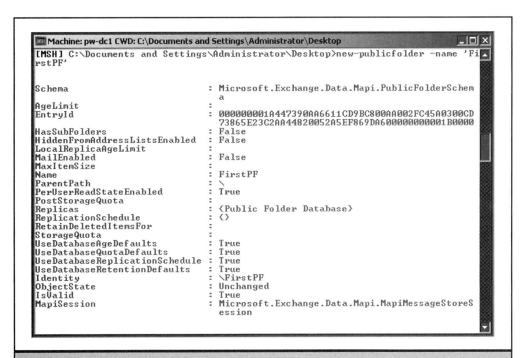

Figure 4-5. Creating a new public folder.

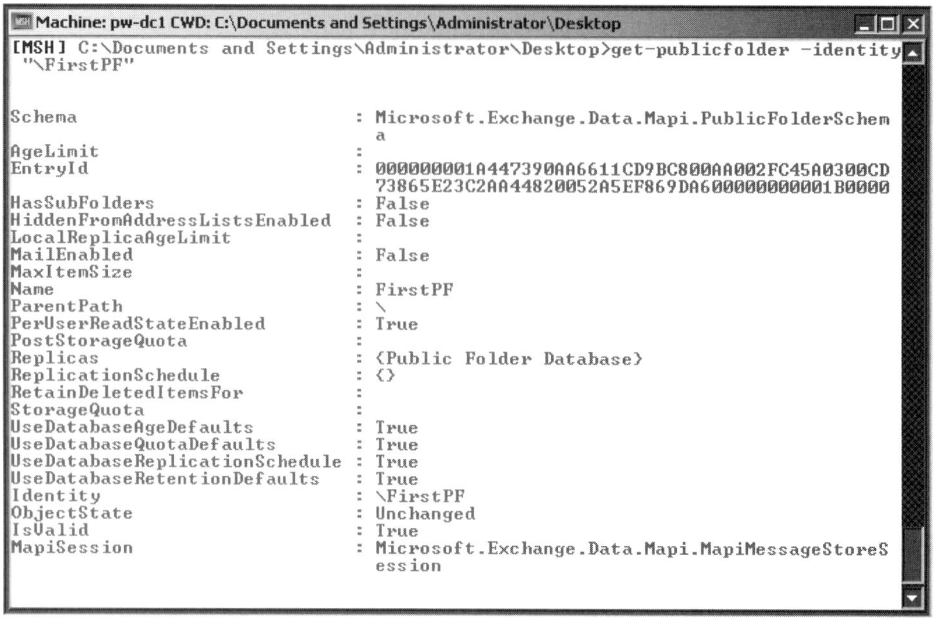

Figure 4-6. Retrieving public folder configuration information.

To retrieve the current configuration of a public folder, you will need to use the *Get-PublicFolder* command. The simplest command would be the following, with the example output shown in Figure 4-6:

```
Get-PublicFolder -Identity '<folderpath>'
```

To set attributes of a public folder, you will need to use the *Set-PublicFolder* command. The basic structure of the command is as follows. Table 4-2 lists the various fields you can configure.

```
Set-PublicFolder -Identity '<folderpath>' [attributes and values]
```

To remove an existing public folder, you should not just jump into the *Remove-PublicFolder* command; you should first remove any replicas of the public folder and then delete the contents. Once you've done this, the following command can be run:

```
Remove-PublicFolder -Identity '<folderpath>' [-Recurse] -Server
<ServerName>
```

The *recurse* parameter specifies that all child folders should also be deleted. If you exclude the parameter, the command will fail if child folders exist, as shown in Figure 4-7.

Public Folder Attribute	Purpose
Identity	Specifies the unique path and name of the public folder being managed
LocalReplicaAgeLimit	Specifies the age limit of the replica on the connected server, provided there is a replica on that server
Server	Specifies the server on which to perform the selected operations
AgeLimit	Specifies the age limit for contents housed within the public folder
HiddenFromAddressListsEnabled	Specifies whether to hide the public folder from address lists
Instance	Allows you to pass an entire object to the command to be processed; used mainly within scripts
LocalReplicaAgeLimit	Specifies an age limit for the local replica, which would override the *AgeLimit* value
MaxItemSize	Specifies the maximum item size in kilobytes (KB) that can be posted
Name	Specifies the name for the public folder
PerUserReadStateEnabled	Specifies whether read and unread status information should be maintained on a per-user basis
PostStorageQuota	Specifies the size (in KB) when a public folder will no longer allow posting
Replicas	Specifies a list of Mailbox servers to which the public folder contents should be replicated
ReplicationSchedule	Specifies the replication schedule for the folder
RetainDeletedItemsFor	Specifies the retention time for deleted items
Server	Specifies the server on which the command will be acted

Table 4-2.   Attributes for the *Set-PublicFolder* Command

Public Folder Attribute	Purpose
StorageQuota	Specifies the size (in KB) when the public folder will start issuing warnings
UseDatabaseAgeDefaults	Specifies that the public folder use the database age limit
UseDatabaseQuotaDefaults	Specifies that the public folder use the public store quota limits
UseDatabaseReplicationSchedule	Specifies that the public folder use the set replication schedule
UseDatabaseRetentionDefaults	Specifies that the public folder use the database retention defaults

Table 4-2. Attributes for the *Set-PublicFolder* Command *(Continued)*

Managing Mail-Enabled Public Folders

As I mentioned previously, by default, public folders are not mail-enabled and are not accessible from outside the Exchange organization. You may want public folders to be mail-enabled so that e-mail that needs to be read by multiple users within the organization can easily be accessed. For example, Pennywise Resorts could have a customer service e-mail address of *customerservice@pennywiseresort.com*. Rather than messages sent to this address being delivered to a single mailbox, delivering them to a mail-enabled public folder can make the message easily accessible to various individuals throughout the organization—from the customer service agents who respond to the messages to management reviewing the messages coming in.

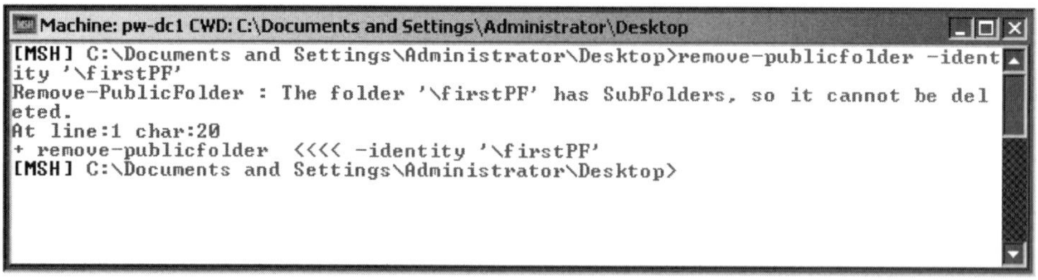

Figure 4-7. You will receive an error message when attempting to delete a public folder without deleting child folders.

Figure 4-8. Check to see if a folder is mail-enabled.

To mail-enable a public folder, you need to use the *Enable-MailPublicFolder* command:

```
Enable-MailPublicFolder -Identity '<folderpath>' [-HiddenFromAddressListsEnabled
<$true | $false>] -Server <servername>
```

TIP The *HiddenFromAddressListsEnabled* parameter should be set to *$false* only if you want internal users to be able to see the public folder in the global address list and other address lists.

You can see in Figure 4-8 that after running the *Enable-MailPublicFolder* command (which has no output on a successful run, except to leave you at a new command prompt) and looking at the *MailEnabled* attribute, the folder is now mail-enabled.

To retrieve mail-related information, you'll need to use the *Get-MailPublicFolder* command. Running a simple command like the following will yield over 60 attributes:

```
Get-MailPublicFolder -Identity '<folderpath>'
```

Figure 4-9 shows the results of running the command, but piping the output through another cmdlet, *format-list*, which only shows the listed attributes. In the case of Figure 4-9, the e-mail addresses assigned to the public folder are displayed.

Figure 4-9. Retrieve the e-mail addresses for a public folder.

To set mail-related attributes of a mail-enabled public folder, you'll need to use the *Set-MailPublicFolder* command. The basic structure of the command is as follows. Table 4-3 lists the various fields you can configure.

```
Set-MailPublicFolder -Identity '<folderpath>' [attributes and values]
```

Attribute	Purpose
Identity	Specifies the name of the public folder.
AcceptMessagesOnlyFrom	Specifies recipients the public folder can receive messages from. An empty value allows all senders.
AcceptMessagesOnlyFromDL-Members	Specifies distribution groups that can send messages to the public folder.
Alias	Specifies the mail nickname of the public folder.
Contacts	Specifies the contacts for the public folder.
CustomAttribute1-15	Specifies the values for the custom attributes.
DeliverToMailboxAndForward	Specifies whether e-mail will be sent to a forwarding address.
DisplayName	Specifies the display name of the public folder.
DomainController	Specifies the domain controller on which to perform the modifications.
EmailAddresses	Specifies e-mail addresses for the public folder.
EmailAddressPolicyEnabled	Specifies the e-mail addresses that will be affected by a recipient policy.
ForwardingAddress	Specifies the forwarding address for the folder.
GrantSendOnBehalfTo	Specifies mailboxes that can send on behalf of the public folder.
HiddenFromAddressListsEnabled	Specifies whether the mailbox is viewable from addresses lists.

Table 4-3. Attributes for the *Set-MailPublicFolder* Command

Attribute	Purpose
Instance	Allows you to pass an entire object to the command to be processed; used mainly within scripts.
MaxReceiveSize	Specifies the maximum size of e-mail messages to be received, from 1 KB to 2,097,151 KB.
MaxSendSize	Specifies the maximum size of e-mail messages that can be sent, from 1 KB to 2,097,151 KB.
Name	Specifies the name of the public folder.
PrimarySmtpAddress	Specifies the Simple Mail Transfer Protocol (SMTP) address the public folder will use.
RejectMessagesFrom	Specifies which addresses to not accept e-mail from.
RejectMessagesFromDLMembers	Specifies which distribution groups to not accept e-mail from.
RequireSenderAuthentication-Enabled	Specifies whether senders must be authenticated.
SimpleDisplayName	Specifies the friendly display name.
WindowsEmailAddress	Specifies an e-mail address for the public folder object in Active Directory.

Table 4-3. Attributes for the *Set-MailPublicFolder* Command *(Continued)*

Should you need to remove the ability to send messages to a mail-enabled public folder, you will need to run the following command:

```
Disable-MailPublicFolder -Identity '<folderpath>' -Server <servername>
```

Public Folder Permissions

Since Microsoft is attempting to encourage Exchange users to utilize SharePoint Portal Server instead of public folders, there is no management support within the Exchange Management Console. You can, however, manage permissions from within the Exchange Management Shell.

Using the Public Folder Management Console

SP1 incorporates a graphical way of managing public folders, although it is limited in functionality. The Public Folder Management Console can be accessed under the Toolbox node in the console tree. Upon launching the tool, you should see a window similar to that shown in Figure 4-10.

TIP If you do not see any public folders listed in the console pane on the left, you either need to connect to a server hosting public folders or add a public folder database to the current server.

You can create a new public folder by selecting the path within the public folder tree (which initially is empty, so anywhere in the work pane is fine) and clicking New Public Folder in the action pane. Figure 4-11 shows the simple New Public Folder Wizard, where you will only provide a public folder name. As previously mentioned, you cannot specify a message type (calendar, contact, note, etc.), so any folders created here will contain messages.

Once a folder is created, you can select the Mail Enable link (it will become a Mail Disable link when a folder is already mail-enabled). It will add the selected public folder to the global address list and allow the public folder to accept messages from outside the organization.

If you view the properties of a public folder (I'm showing you a mail-enabled folder so all of the tabs are visible), you can configure most of what you can modify with the *Set-MailPublicFolder* command shell cmdlet. Figure 4-12 shows the General tab, where you can view information on the folder, as well as specify if message-read status is maintained on a per-user basis.

Figure 4-13 shows the Replication tab, where you can specify which Exchange servers will host a replica of the public folder, the replication schedule, and the age limit of local contents.

Figure 4-14 shows the Limits tab, where you can modify the storage quotas, deleted item retention settings, and age limits on the folder.

The remaining tabs are only visible because the folder was made mail-enabled; they are nearly identical to their mailbox counterparts, which I have already covered in Chapter 3 (which you can refer to for more information).

One last option exists for you to manage your public folders from this tool. With a folder selected, you can click the Update Content link in the action pane. This forces replication of the public folder to update the selected server's replica.

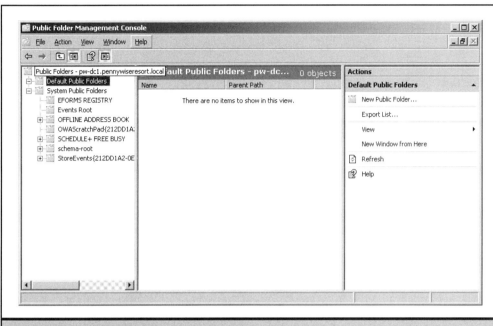

Figure 4-10.   Opening the Public Folder Management Console.

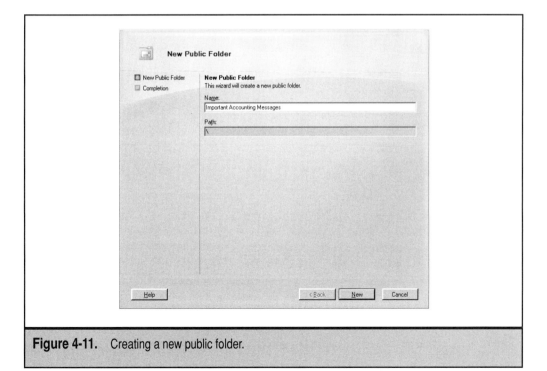

Figure 4-11.   Creating a new public folder.

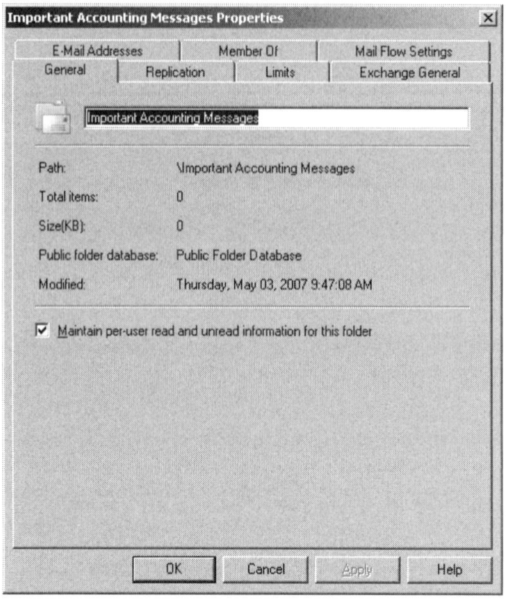

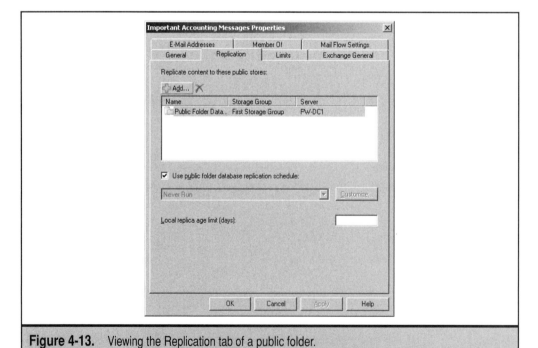

Figure 4-12. Viewing the General tab of a public folder.

Figure 4-13. Viewing the Replication tab of a public folder.

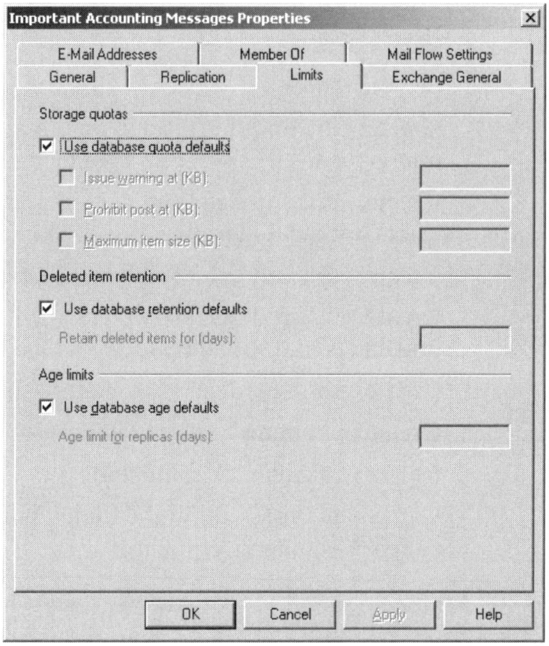

Figure 4-14.   Viewing the Limits tab of a public folder.

You can use the *Add-PublicFolderClientPermissions* and *Remove-PublicFolderClientPermissions* cmdlets to modify client permissions. Table 4-4 lists the pre-defined permission roles you can use with the *–AccessRights* parameter used to specify the permission change.

Exchange also supports giving out individual permissions that make up the permission roles. Search the Exchange Help for "configuring public folder permissions" for more information on the individual permissions.

TIP   To recursively assign permissions, use the AddUserToPFRecursive.ps1 script in the Scripts folder of your Exchange installation.

TIP   The Exchange System Manager tool used to manage Exchange 2003 environments has an extensive selection of public folder permissions-management capabilities. You can install this console onto a desktop or server not running Exchange 2007 to manage public folders. You can learn more about how to manage your public folder permissions at http://www.microsoft.com/technet/prodtechnol/exchange/2003/library/default.mspx.

Permission Role	User Is Able To:
None	See the folder
Owner	Create, edit, and delete all items; create subfolders; and is the folder owner and contact
PublishingEditor	Create, edit, and delete all items; create subfolders, but is not the folder owner or contact
Editor	Create, edit, and delete all items within the folder
PublishingAuthor	Create, edit, and delete own items within the folder and can create subfolders
Author	Create, edit, and delete own items within the folder
Non-EditingAuthor	Create own items and read items within the folder
Reviewer	Can read items within the folder
Contributor	Can create items within the folder, but has no ability to see the contents of the folder

Table 4-4. Default Folder Permission Roles

Public Folder Replication

Public folders can be replicated, either on an individual basis or as a batch by replicating an entire tree or a subset of the folders in the tree. Schedules can be set and modified as needed; if you need to make folder replication available between organizations, there are ways to accomplish this too. When managing public folder replication, you'll first need to select which folders to replicate, assign a schedule for replication, and then set the replication message priority.

Replication is conducted at the item level, meaning that if there is a change to a public folder item, the entire item is replicated. Also, you cannot schedule the replication of an individual item to another folder. The most granular level of replication can be set only at the folder level.

To set a folder to replicate, we once again need to turn to the Exchange Management Shell. Replicas of a public folder need to be established using the following command:

```
Set-PublicFolder -Identity '<folderpath>' -Replicas '<databaseID>'
```

TIP Microsoft provides a number of Exchange Management Shell scripts to handle complex tasks. One of the tasks you can accomplish is to add a replica to a public folder and all of its subfolders using the script AddReplicaToPFRecursive.ps1. You can find these scripts in the Scripts folder under the folder into which you installed Exchange.

When planning the replication of public folders, you'll need to consider how often information in the folders will change and how fast those changes need to be made available to everyone in the organization. For example, a public folder for company memos that is updated with new memos every two hours throughout the day would need a more aggressive replication schedule than a public folder that hosts the company employee manual, which might be updated once a month or so. Time-critical information will need a more frequent replication schedule than other types of information.

The schedule can be set so that replication occurs during times when WAN bandwidth usage is less. Using non-peak hours for replication of less-critical information is smart administration and should be considered if this represents a plausible solution for your environment.

Replication can be set on a per-folder or per-public folder database basis. Schedules set at the folder level override the replication schedule set on the public folder database level. To set replication for a single folder, use the *-ReplicationSchedule* parameter with the *Set-PublicFolder* command.

You may want to set replication schedules for all folders in the tree and then set special replication schedules for time-critical folders. To ensure that those folders that don't require a special replication schedule are replicated according to the public store's schedule, use the *-UseDatabaseReplicationSchedule* parameter.

To set the same replication schedule for all folders in the store, use the public folder database properties (Figure 4-15). If you click the Replication Interval drop-down list, you'll find several prebuilt replication schedules, including:

- ▼ Always Run
- ■ Never Run
- ■ Run Every Hour
- ■ Run Every 2 Hours
- ■ Run Every 4 Hours
- ▲ Use Custom Schedule

If one of the prebuilt schedules doesn't fit your needs, choose Use Custom Schedule, click the Customize button, and enter the needed schedule in the Schedule box. You'll notice that as you make different selections in the Replication Interval drop-down list, the schedule is automatically updated in the Schedule box.

You can suspend and resume public folder replication using the *Suspend-PublicFolderReplication* command in the Exchange Management Shell. This stops all replication organization-wide. The *Resume-PublicFolderReplication* command will return replication to its normal, functional state.

Interorganizational Replication

In some cases, you may need to replicate public folder information from your Exchange 2007 organization to a separate organization to coordinate meetings or appointments, or simply to make public folder data accessible from a foreign Exchange organization. Microsoft provides

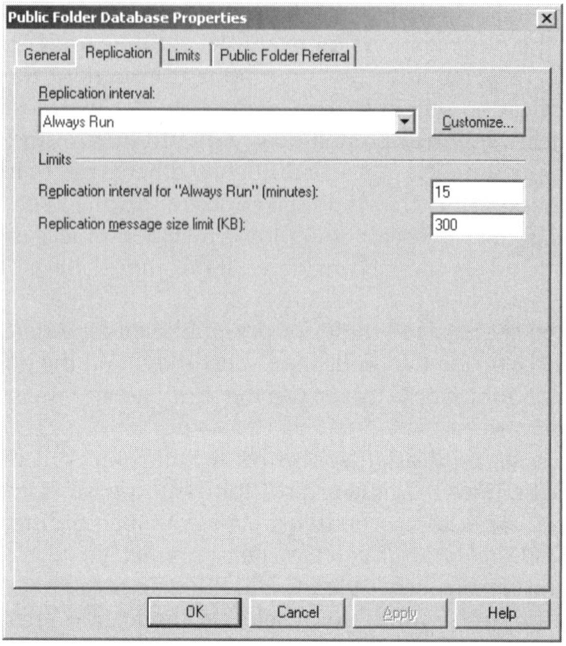

Figure 4-15. Configure replication for a public folder database.

the Inter-Organization Replication Tool to address these needs. This tool has been around since Exchange 5.5 and has had updates throughout the years. You can download the tool from the following site: http://go.microsoft.com/fwlink/?linkid=22455.

The tool replicates two kinds of information across organizations—free/busy information and public folder content—using two programs. The first is the Replication Configuration program, which sets the replication frequency, folders to be replicated, and accounts to be used. The second is the Replication service, which performs the replication. The Replication Configuration program designates one Exchange server (known as the *publisher*) and updates the configuration on a continual basis. One or more Exchange servers in the foreign organization (known as *subscribers*) receive the replicated information. Free/busy information can only be replicated in one direction, so if you want to exchange free/busy information in both directions, you'll need to set up the tool on both sides. Public folder content can be replicated in one direction with a single instance of the tool. The system requirements are as follows:

▼ Exchange 2000 SP3 running on Windows 2000 SP3.

■ A service account set up with a Messaging Application Programming Interface (MAPI) profile (so it can access the public folders)

- Owner permissions on every public folder you wish to replicate
- ▲ A public folder named *ExchangeSecurityFolder* created by you in the root of the public folder structure, with Folder Visible permissions granted to the service account

Using the Replication Configuration tool to configure a public folder session, shown in Figure 4-16, establishes the publisher and subscriber servers involved, the replication schedule, the mailbox and the Windows account to be used, and the public folders to be replicated.

The configuration of a free/busy session, shown in Figure 4-17, establishes the publisher and subscriber servers involved, the replication schedule, the mailbox and the Windows account to be used, and the Exchange sites to replicate between (this is an old Exchange 5.5 concept that is analogous to an Exchange 2000/2003 routing group).

The Replication service, shown in Figure 4-18, establishes the parameters needed for the service that will perform the actual replication. This includes the service account credentials, the configuration file created by the Replication Configuration program, the working directory used to store temporary files, and service startup options.

Once the service is started, you can sit back and let the replication begin.

Setting Public Folder Limits

Setting limits on public folders is the best way to ensure that folder content stays current and that the size of a public folder doesn't grow unchecked. There are three configuration settings you should focus on: storage limits, deletion settings, and age limits. Figure 4-19 shows these settings at the database level.

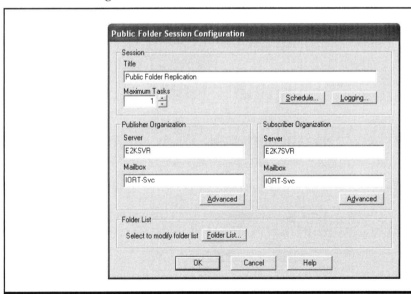

Figure 4-16. Configuring public folder replication.

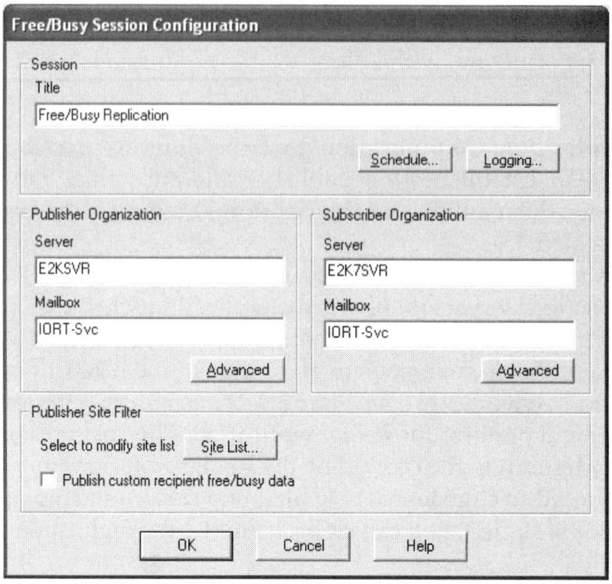

Figure 4-17. Configuring free/busy replication.

Figure 4-18. Configuring the replication service.

Storage Limits

This setting is used to control the size of the public folder and its contents. By default, storage limits are set on the public store.

The Issue Warning At (KB) setting means that when the folder reaches the specified size, a warning message is sent to the administrator. Acceptable values range from 0 to 2,097,151 KB for all three of these settings.

The Prohibit Post At (KB) setting means that when the folder reaches the specified size, users can no longer post to it. This value represents the maximum amount of KB that the public folder can hold.

The Maximum Item Size (KB) setting represents the largest allowable size for a post. Postings larger than this are returned to the user, with an error message indicating that the post exceeded the size limit on the public folder.

If you'd like different settings for a particular public folder, you can set the parameters individually using the *set-PublicFolder* command in the Exchange Management Shell using the following parameters:

▼   *-StorageQuota* specifies the issue warning value.

■   *-PostStorageReplica* specifies the prohibit post value.

▲   *-MaxItemSize* specifies the maximum item size.

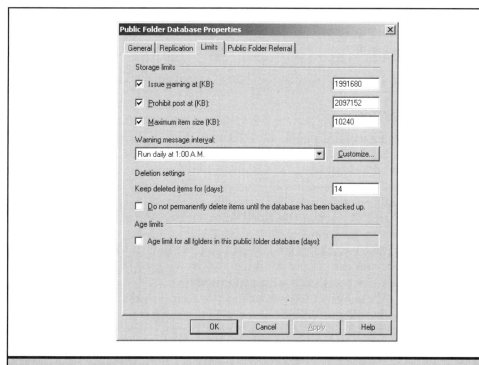

Figure 4-19.   You need to set public folder database limits.

Deletion Settings

This setting has time as its focus, whereas the storage limits setting has size as its focus. In the Deletion Settings area, you can specify the length of time deleted items are allowed to remain in the public folder before they are removed by Exchange. Again, you can allow the folder to inherit the public store settings, or they can be set individually for each folder using the *-RetainDeletedItemsFor* parameter with the *Set-PublicFolder* cmdlet in the Exchange Management Shell. Configure the Keep Deleted Items For (Days) setting as needed.

NOTE Remember that items must first be deleted in a public folder and then removed. The time period between when the item is deleted—which basically means that it is marked as hidden and stripped of its permissions—and the point at which the item is removed from the folder represents a window of time in which a deleted item can be recovered, if necessary. If you find that some items are being deleted and you wish to recover them, be sure to create a window of time long enough to allow for this.

Age Limits

This setting also has time as its focus; but unlike the deletion settings, this area is focused on active, available posts. This option specifies how long a post may be in the public folder and available for use before it is automatically deleted by Exchange. Configure the Age Limit For All Folders In This Public Folder Database (Days) setting to specify how long a replicated item may remain in the folder before being deleted. Replicated items are tracked separately from items posted directly to the public folder.

To establish an independent age limit for a public folder, use the *-AgeLimit* parameter with the *Set-PublicFolder* command in the Exchange Management Shell.

Public Folder Referrals

When a client needs to access a public folder, they initially attempt to pull the public folder data from the Mailbox server on which their mailbox resides. If the data does not reside on that server, the client needs to systematically find a server that has the data needed and is closest to the client. In previous versions of Exchange, routing concepts such as sites and routing groups were used to establish costs between separate physical locations. In Exchange 2007, Active Directory Sites are used, since they already utilize costs for Active Directory functionality.

Service Pack 1 added a new tab to the properties of a public folder database, shown in Figure 4-20, where you can choose to utilize Active Directory sites (the default) or establish a custom list of servers, each with a specified cost.

These settings will be used by users whose mailbox resides within a mailbox database that specifies the configured public folder database as its default public folder database, as shown in Figure 4-21.

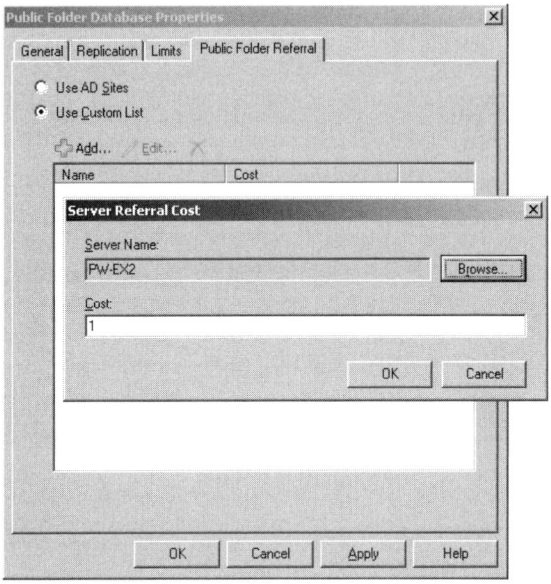

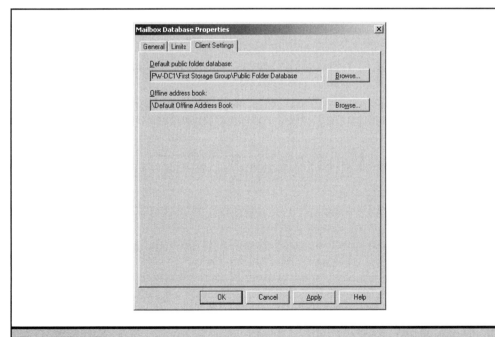

Figure 4-20.   Viewing the public folder referral properties.

Figure 4-21.   The Default Public Folder Database field specified determines referrals.

Management Shell Corner

You can manage the custom public folder referral list from the Exchange Management Shell using the `Set-PublicFolderDatabase`. To use Active Directory sites, use the following command:

```
Set-PublicFolderDatabase -Identity 'Public Folder Database'
-UseCustomServerReferralList $false
```

To use a custom list of servers, use the following command:

```
Set-PublicFolderDatabase -Identity 'Public Folder Database'
-UseCustomServerReferralList $true -PublicFolderReferralServerList
'[server & cost list]'
```

You should also note that setting the `-UseCustomServerReferralList` to a value of `$false` will overwrite a custom list of servers and costs, if a list exists.

Recovering Deleted Items from a Public Folder

Deleted items in a public folder can be recovered, provided you've set a deleted item retention time for the public folder database (or individual public folder) from which the items were deleted and the retention period for the data hasn't expired. Assuming both of these things are true, you can recover deleted items as follows.

1. In Outlook, access the public folder from which you want to recover the item.
2. Navigate to the Tools menu, and select Recover Deleted Items. The Recover Deleted Items From dialog box appears.
3. Select the item(s) you wish to recover, and click Recover Selected Items. You'll note that deleted items can only be recovered using the Outlook client.

SUMMARY

In this chapter, I briefly outlined how public folder databases and folders are created and managed. I also discussed how to replicate information between organizations using the Inter-Organization Replication Tool. As you can see, administration of public folders is a huge area and one that could easily be a full-time job in large organizations.

Another full-time job in large organizations could be the creation, management, and recovery of storage groups and databases. Since Exchange holds many organizations' mission-critical information, it is essential to understand how storage works in Exchange 2007 and how to recover in the event of a disaster.

In the next chapter, we'll look at how to create and manage Exchange storage groups and databases.

CHAPTER 5

Administering Storage

One of the most prominent features of Exchange 2000 and 2003 was their ability to use a database in the multiple-gigabyte (GB) range. It is not uncommon for some environments to be managing mailbox databases in the 40–60 GB range. While databases of this size are not terribly difficult to back up, they still represent significant challenges.

One of the main challenges of managing large databases is the time needed to restore them. Long restore times often mean that many, if not all, of a company's users are less productive because they don't have access to e-mail and public folders. In addition, most deployments don't have enough free disk space to manage a defragmentation of the database, which means that unused, but corrupted, pages could continue to cause problems for the administrator.

Microsoft addressed this problem in previous version of Exchange by implementing storage groups and *mailbox databases* in Exchange 2007 (which were previously referred to as a *mailbox store* in Exchange 2000/2003). Likewise, the public store in Exchange 2000/2003 is now called the *public folder database*.

Each database must be created inside a storage group, which is a container that can hold multiple databases, each one using the same set of transaction logs (which maintain changes to be made to the database—more about this in Chapter 15). Table 5-1 lists the storage limitations for each edition of Exchange.

There is no hard-coded size limit for each store, but the intention of giving you the ability to create multiple stores is so that no one store will become so large that it creates the same backup and restore challenges that existed in previous versions of Exchange. This is a drastic change from previous versions of Exchange, where Microsoft had promoted populating a single storage group with multiple databases. With Exchange 2007, Microsoft recommends a single database per storage group; thus, the support for multiple storage groups and an equal number of databases.

BENEFITS OF STORAGE GROUPS

Smart use of storage groups will give you the ability to accomplish three very important design goals:

▼   Host more users per server than was reasonably possible in previous versions of Exchange

Exchange Edition	Maximum Number of Storage Groups	Maximum Number of Databases
Standard	5	5
Enterprise	50	50

Table 5-1.   Storage Limits for Each Edition of Exchange

- ■ Quicken recovery time of damaged databases than was previously possible
- ▲ Minimize the number of users that are affected by a database disaster

Let's look at each of these design goals individually.

Hosting More Users

Let's do a comparison. We'll assume you have 300 users that need e-mail services, and you're not sure whether you should use Exchange Server 2003 Enterprise or Exchange Server 2007. One way to look at this is to determine how many users you'd like to have housed in a single database. In both platforms, all 300 users could be hosted by one database. If each user has 1 GB of information in his or her mailbox, this means that a total of 300 GB of information needs to be hosted. Now, in Exchange Server 2003 Standard, you have no choice but to host all this information in one database (or else move up to Enterprise Edition, which supports 20 databases); however, in Exchange 2007 Standard Edition, this information could be spread out over multiple databases. For instance, you could host five 60-GB databases on the same server. And with Enterprise Edition, you could host 30-10-GB databases.

If we continue with the same numbers, we could host 300 more users on an Enterprise Edition server just by having 20-GB databases rather than 10-GB databases (which is still a reasonable size); however, to add an additional 300 users in Exchange Server 2003 Standard, our database size would grow to 600 GB, which would represent an unmanageable-sized database for most deployments.

By spreading users across multiple databases, each server can host more users and still maintain reasonable database sizes.

Quickening Recovery Time

Continuing with the same scenario, it is now easy to understand that restoring a 10-GB database is faster than restoring a 300-GB database. And restoring a 20-GB database is much faster than restoring a 600-GB database. Again, spreading users across multiple databases means that the restoration of one database need not consume large amounts of time.

Minimizing Affected Users

Finally, when a single 10-GB database needs to be restored, the other 29 databases (going back to the previous example) can continue to operate. One of the prominent features of Exchange 2007's storage architecture is that databases can be mounted or dismounted individually. This means that if a storage group has four databases in it, three can be mounted and running while the fourth is dismounted and being restored from backup.

Hence, when any one particular database in Exchange 2007 is unavailable, only a subset of your users will lose productivity due to loss of messaging functionality. For instance, if you have four departments in your company, you could set up four databases—one for each department. If one of the databases becomes corrupted, you can restore that database from backup while the other three databases continue to operate; thus, only one department will lose messaging functionality while the other three continue to operate.

In a mission-critical environment, such as a Web-based order center, where messaging is the sales lifeline of an organization, consider spreading mission-critical mailboxes across multiple, independent databases for fault-tolerance purposes.

PLANNING FOR MULTIPLE STORAGE GROUPS

Now that you've seen how using multiple storage groups can be of benefit, the question is: How many storage groups do you need? The answer involves several factors, including:

▼ Time required to restore a database

■ Need to defragment individual stores

■ Overall amount of information that needs to be managed

▲ Ability to utilize Local Continuous Backup

Let's take a look at how this would work.

Required Restore Time

In most organizations, the loss of messaging means the loss of productivity. Such productivity loss directly impacts the bottom line of most companies. So, Exchange administrators are sometimes given maximum time periods in which to recover from a disaster so as to minimize a company's loss of productivity. These agreed-upon time periods are often known as *Service Level Agreements* (*SLAs*). SLAs can be executed within a company between the IT department and other departments; outside vendors may offer an SLA to replace hardware or to recover from a disaster within a given time frame.

The way to figure restore time is to figure out how large your databases will become based on average usage and then look at how fast your hardware will restore databases. Once you know this information, you can start to decrease the theoretical size of each database until the end result of the formula indicates that the restore time is within an acceptable range.

Let's assume that you have 1,000 users, each of whom, on average, will have 30 messages per day of an average size of 50 KB per message (assuming a portion of your messages have attachments). So, in an average day, messaging traffic will consist of 1,500,000 KB of information, or 1.5 GB ($50 \times 30 \times 1,000 = 1,500,000$). Since all of this information is also recorded in the transaction logs at some point during the day, we can safely assume that it will take 3 GB per day of disk space to handle the messaging traffic for these 1,000 users. If the transaction logs are purged on a weekly basis as a result of performing a full backup, then each week (assuming a five-day work week) will require 15 GB of disk space to hold messaging for these users in both the database and the transaction logs ($5 \times 3 = 15$).

Continuing on with this scenario, in one month (23 business days $\times$ 3 GB), 69 GB of messaging information will be generated. Add to that the disk space needed for transaction logs (5 days $\times$ 1.5 GB = 7.5 GB), and you'll need about 76.5 GB of disk space per month for messaging traffic. On an annual basis (assuming you never delete anything), you'll need 3.588 terabytes (TB) of disk space for messages and another 7.5 GB for transaction logs. Since many deployments allow users to keep messages for up to 12 months, this is a common scenario to work with.

All I've done so far is show how to figure how much messaging traffic will be incurred over the next year. The next step is to discern what the current throughput is for your backup hardware when restoring information. Let's assume your hardware will do 2 GB/min for a restore operation (as is possible with some of the newer SuperDLT drives). To restore a 3.588-TB database will require approximately 1,794 minutes, or 29.9 hours. In many deployments, a restore time this long is unacceptable.

Finally, all we need to do is to find out what an acceptable time is for your users to be without Exchange. In most environments, two to four hours is sufficient; however, in some locations, one hour would be way too long. You'll need to discuss this with your supervisor in order to find out what would be acceptable. Let's assume in our scenario that two hours is the maximum acceptable time for users to be without messaging services.

Given the numbers in our scenario, along with the two-hour SLA we just mentioned, the minimum number of databases that would be necessary is 15 (29.9/2 = 14.95), since we really can't create 14.95 databases. Because it generally takes time to diagnose a failed database and then find the backup tape from which to do the restore and catalog the tape, it is a good idea to include some troubleshooting time in the window of acceptable time to be down. In this scenario, I would recommend no less than 30 databases, with a limit of 12 GB per database, which would allow for one hour to troubleshoot and another hour to do the restore of the database. This may, of course, not work for your situation, as 1,000 users would have an average mailbox size of 358 MB, with about 33 mailboxes per database.

Defragmentation Considerations

From time to time, you might want to defragment your databases. There are different ways and reasons to defragment a database, and they are outlined in Chapter 16. For purposes of our discussion here, we need to remember that each storage group can hold up to 50 databases; however, if you ever need to restore one of those databases or conduct a defragmentation of a database, Exchange will need to create and mount a temporary database to use during the defragmentation process. So, if you place 50 active databases in one storage group and you need to restore one of the databases from tape backup, you'll need to dismount a second store in the storage group in order to perform a restore of the damaged database. You could put no more than 49 databases in a storage group so that you can conduct database administrative actions, such as defragmentation or restore, in the same storage group without having to dismount another working database.

Amount of Information to Be Managed

So far, I've looked at how many databases and storage groups we'll need to ensure we can recover within our two-hour time window, and we've allowed for room to perform database administrative functions within each storage group. However, I have not discussed how to structure these databases for future growth of our company. This part gets to be a bit more complicated, since it is often difficult to predict what the future will hold.

You can make some educated estimates and then adjust them as time goes by. In my scenario, it is likely that some databases may grow to be larger than our allowable limit of 12 GB. This being the case, there will be times when mailboxes will need to be moved to a new database within the same storage group or to another database that can accommodate the additional information.

What I have not mentioned thus far is the need to have a message-retention policy in place. The development of such a policy should involve legal counsel, since the discovery process in a legal proceeding can involve producing old messages. Having such a policy in place not only provides a level of legal protection, but it also provides a way of keeping your databases from growing out of control. The best practice is to develop a strong message-retention policy in conjunction with your legal counsel and then follow it without deviation.

CREATING AND ADMINISTERING STORAGE GROUPS

You'll recall that each mailbox server can host up to 50 storage groups. A storage group, in and of itself, is pretty useless unless it is populated with at least one store. The storage group provides the transaction logs for the stores, as well as a shell within which the databases can run. You can create a new storage group by first navigating to the Mailbox node under Server Configuration in the console tree, shown in Figure 5-1.

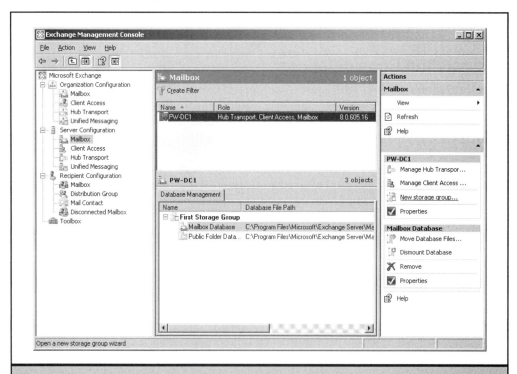

Figure 5-1.   Navigate to the Mailbox server to manage storage groups.

Choose the server in the results pane, and select New Storage Group in the action pane. You should see the New Storage Group page of the New Storage Group Wizard, shown in Figure 5-2.

In the Storage Group Name field, type the descriptive name you want for this storage group. Use the Browse button to the right of the Log Files Path and System Files Path fields to select a location for these files. The location you select must already exist. If it does not, use the Create New Folder button inside the Browse dialog box to create the folder in the desired location, and then select the newly created folder.

Remember that the transaction logs should be placed on a physically separate drive from the stores that will use them. Not only does this increase recoverability of data in the event of a disaster, but it can also improve performance if the logs are placed on a physical drive that is doing nothing other than hosting these files. A disk (or, preferably, a mirrored pair) dedicated to transaction logging will increase Exchange's performance and response time to the end user.

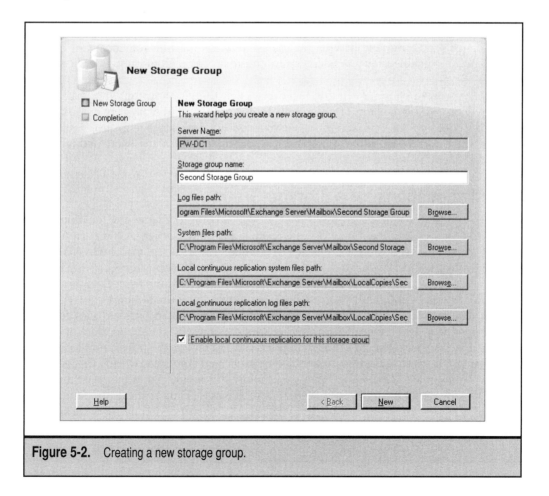

Figure 5-2.   Creating a new storage group.

Management Shell Corner

To create a storage group from the Exchange Management Shell, run the following command:

```
new-StorageGroup -Server:'PW-DC1' -Name:'Second Storage Group' -
LogFolderPath:'C:\Program Files\Microsoft\Exchange Server\Mailbox\
Second Storage Group' -SystemFolderPath:'C:\Program Files\Microsoft\
Exchange Server\Mailbox\Second Storage Group' -HasLocalCopy:$true -
CopyLogFolderPath:'C:\Program Files\Microsoft\Exchange Server\Mailbox\
LocalCopies\Second Storage Group' -CopySystemFolderPath:'C:\Program Files\
Microsoft\Exchange Server\Mailbox\LocalCopies\Second Storage Group'
```

Should you select the Enable Continuous Backup For This Storage Group check box, the fields for specifying the location for the system and log files for Local Continuous Backup become enabled for you to configure (more on Local Continuous Replication in Chapter 15).

Once you have chosen your file locations, click the New button, and the storage group will be created. It is important to note that if, at this point, you were to look inside for your folder and the transaction logs associated with the storage group, you would not find any. This is because the folder and transaction logs are actually created when the first store is created within the storage group.

Moving File Locations for a Storage Group

Sometimes, after the storage group is created, you'll want to change the location of the files. This may occur when a new drive is installed into the server, or if a current drive goes bad and you need to move the files to a reliable, working physical drive. You can change the transaction log location and system files for an existing storage group by first selecting the storage group and then selecting Move Storage Group from the action pane. The Move Storage Group Path Wizard starts, as shown in Figure 5-3.

You can browse to new locations for the transaction logs and system files for both the storage group and the Local Continuous Replication (LCR) database (more on this in Chapter 15). Because databases exist within the storage group, the transaction logs are in use. So, in order to move the logs, the databases must be dismounted during the log move and then remounted. A warning dialog box, shown in Figure 5-4, appears, stating this need. Once the log files have been moved, the databases will automatically be remounted. In addition, if you have LCR enabled, it will need to be suspended by right-clicking the storage group and selecting Suspend Local Continuous Replication in the action pane.

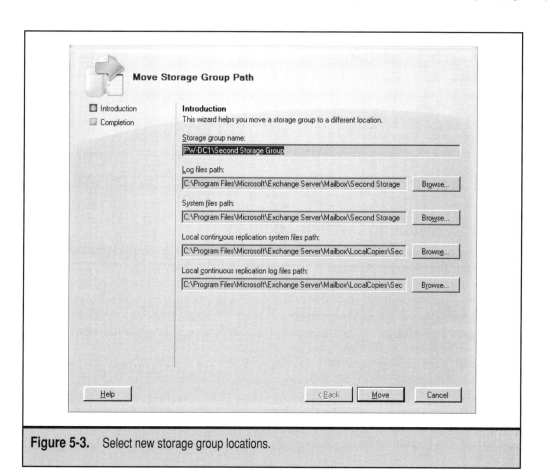

Figure 5-3. Select new storage group locations.

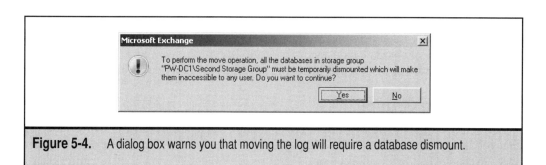

Figure 5-4. A dialog box warns you that moving the log will require a database dismount.

Management Shell Corner

To move a storage group, use the following command:

```
move-StorageGroupPath -Identity:'PW-DC1\First Storage Group' -
LogFolderPath:'C:\Program Files\Microsoft\Exchange Server\Mailbox\New First
Storage Group' -SystemFolderPath:'C:\Program Files\Microsoft\
Exchange Server\Mailbox\New First Storage Group'
```

Enabling and Disabling Circular Logging

Circular logging allows Exchange 2007 to overwrite previously created transaction log files after the data they contain has been written to the database on the disk. This feature is commonly used in environments in which the Exchange server needs to conserve disk space or in situations where recovery of data is not important, such as when Exchange is acting solely as a Simple Mail Transfer Protocol (SMTP) relay server. With circular logging enabled, you can only recover to the last full backup, and incremental and differential backups are not available.

Disabling circular logging allows for recovery of all of your Exchange data up to the point when the disaster occurred. To learn more about backup and recovery procedures, refer to Chapter 15. The best practice is to disable circular logging when creating the storage group, unless you know for certain that you won't need to recover any of the data that might be lost in a disaster since the last full backup. In most scenarios, non-recovery of data will not be acceptable.

Renaming Storage Groups

Storage groups can be renamed by editing the storage group's properties, as shown in Figure 5-5. Renaming a storage group will mean that the X.500 directory path, more commonly known as the distinguished name (DN), will change for each object inside the storage group, including mailboxes and public folders. If you are running customized software that uses the DNs of objects inside a storage group to run properly, make sure you understand the ramifications of changing the name on your third-party application.

Deleting Storage Groups

Storage groups can be deleted (referred to as "removing a storage group" within the Exchange Management Console), but all the data inside the group must first be moved or deleted. Exchange 2007 only allows storage groups to be deleted when they are empty (that is, when they contain no stores). If you attempt to remove a storage group that contains databases, you will receive an error message similar to the one shown in Figure 5-6.

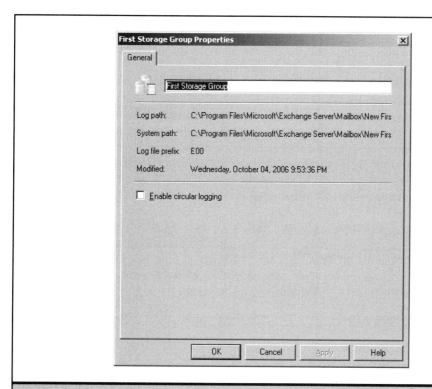

Figure 5-5.   Renaming a storage group.

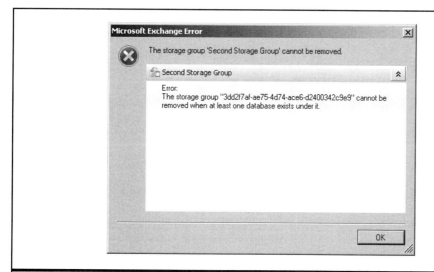

Figure 5-6.   You will receive an error message when attempting to remove a populated storage group.

CREATING AND ADMINISTERING DATABASES

New mailbox and public folder databases can be generated once the storage group is created by selecting the storage group and then selecting either New Mailbox Database or New Public Folder Database from the action pane. Once you have selected which action you wish to take, the appropriate wizard starts. In either case, you will need to provide the same details: the database name, the database path, the local continuous database path, and whether you want to mount the database after creation (see Figure 5-7). Once complete, the database will be created, along with its database files.

You'll recall that when a storage group is created, no transaction logs are created until the first store is made. Figure 5-8 illustrates the default files that are created when the first store is instantiated inside a storage group.

In Figure 5-8, you'll notice that we created a new mailbox database in Second Storage Group. The following explains each of the files:

▼ **Second Mailbox Database.edb**   Database file.

■ **E01.chk**   Checkpoint file used to track which transactions in the transaction logs have been written to disk and which have not.

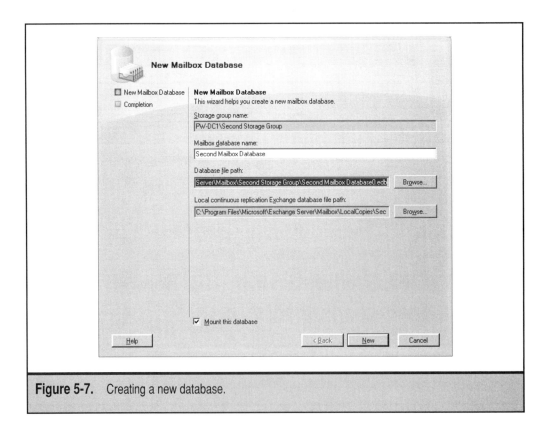

Figure 5-7.   Creating a new database.

■ **E01.log**   First generation of the transaction logs.

■ **E01xxxxxxxx.log**   Transaction logs generated by changes to the databases within the storage group.

■ **E01res00001.jrs/E01res00002.jrs**   Space holders for future transaction logs if the disk should run out of space. In this event, these two files will be converted to actual transaction logs, the transactions will be recorded, and the information store service will be shut down. These are files used only in low-disk–space situations, and the best practice is not to delete them.

■ **E01tmp.log**   Used to let Exchange know when all databases in the storage group have been dismounted. (Exchange deletes the file when all databases within the storage group are dismounted). This file is not included in a backup of Exchange.

▲ **tmp.edb**   Transaction log to record transactions while a new log is being created.

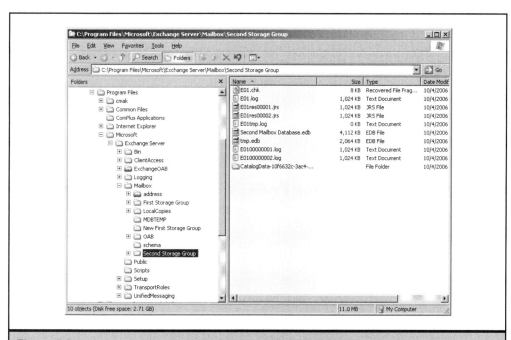

Figure 5-8.   These files are created after creating a new database.

Management Shell Corner

Two commands make up the process of creating a new database. The first creates the database, and the second mounts it. To create a new database, you'll need to run the *new-mailboxdatabase* or *new-publicfolderdatabase* cmdlet. The following example shows how the previous example in this section would be accomplished:

```
new-mailboxdatabase -StorageGroup:'Second Storage Group' -Name:'Second
Mailbox Database' -EdbFilePath:'C:\Program Files\Microsoft\Exchange Server\
Mailbox\Second Storage Group\Second Mailbox Database0.edb'
-HasLocalCopy:$true -CopyEdbFilePath:'C:\Program Files\Microsoft\Exchange
Server\Mailbox\LocalCopies\Second Storage Group\Second Mailbox Database0.edb'
```

The mounting of a database is much simpler:

```
mount-database -Identity:'Second Mailbox Database'
```

You can also dismount a database in exactly the same way, but with the *dismount-database* cmdlet.

Administering Mailbox Databases

After creating a store, the General tab (see Figure 5-9) will show you a number of different configuration options. The first section lists status information about the database, such as when the database was last backed up and whether it is currently mounted.

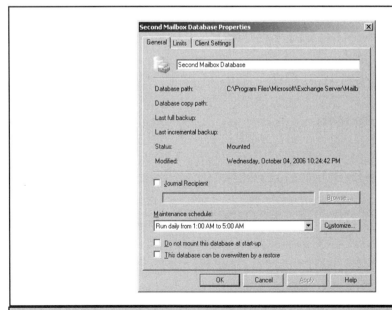

Figure 5-9. Viewing the database properties.

Selecting the Journal Recipient check box specifies a mailbox that will store a copy of all received and sent messages. Be careful with this one, as the size of the store will increase dramatically. You can schedule maintenance to run on this database at a time that makes sense. For instance, it is unwise to have the daily maintenance and backup processes running on a database at the same time. The maintenance routine performs such tasks as reindexing the database and cleaning up items that have passed the deleted-items retention time. It is best to have these routines run at different times.

Selecting the Do Not Mount This Store At Start-Up check box will keep the store from mounting when Exchange Server is booted or when the store.exe process is started. The This Database Can Be Overwritten By A Restore check box is cleared by default, but it can be selected if you want to restore an older version of the store over the current version. This can sometimes be the case when the current store has become corrupted and a clean, but older, copy of the store needs to be restored. Note that any e-mails that were sent or received since the restored version will be lost and cannot be recovered.

Use the Limits tab to configure both storage limits and deletion settings (see Figure 5-10). The storage-limit configurations can be set in several different ways:

▼ **Issue Warning At (KB)**   Sets the size limit, in kilobytes, that a mailbox can reach before a warning is issued to the user. The warning tells the user to clear out the mailbox.

■ **Prohibit Send At (KB)**   Sets the size limit, in kilobytes, that a mailbox can reach before losing its privilege to send messages. Once the mailbox is cleared, the restriction is automatically lifted. The number used is the total mailbox size.

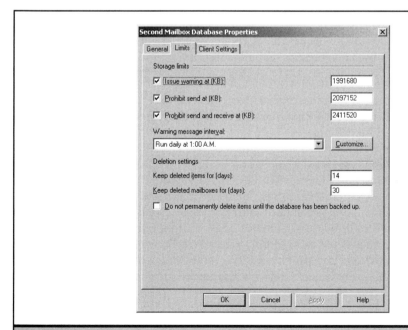

Figure 5-10.   Viewing the Limits tab of a mailbox database.

- **Prohibit Send And Receive At (KB)**   Sets the size limit, in kilobytes, that a mailbox can reach before losing its privilege to both send and receive messages. Once the mailbox is cleared, the restriction is automatically lifted. The number used is the total mailbox size.

▲ **Warning Message Interval**   Sets the interval for sending warning messages to users whose mailboxes exceed the designated limits. The default is once per day at midnight. In large environments, these messages should be generated several times per day.

In the Deletion Settings area, you can set three different configuration options:

▼ **Keep Deleted Items For (Days)**   This value sets the number of days to retain a deleted item. The default setting is 0 days, and this means that deleted messages are not retained in the database and are, therefore, not recoverable. When the value is set to something other than 0, an item that is deleted is marked as hidden and stripped of its permissions, but retained in the database with a future date and time stamp that indicates when it should be removed. If needed, the item can be recovered using the Recover Deleted Items option in the Outlook client.

- **Keep Deleted Mailboxes For (Days)**   This value sets the number of days to retain a deleted mailbox. The default setting is 30 days. The best practice is to leave this at the default setting or to increase the value. Only in rare circumstances should the value be set to 0 days. The default setting will give you 30 days to recover a deleted mailbox, if needed.

▲ **Do Not Permanently Delete Mailboxes And Items Until The Database Has Been Backed Up**   This check box ensures that deleted mailboxes and items are archived into at least one backup set before they are removed from the database.

Mailbox database limits are designed to help you control the size of your databases; therefore, it is not uncommon to enforce size restrictions on individual mailboxes. Users who exceed these limits receive warning messages and, if they are excessive enough, lose privileges in sending and receiving e-mail. Now, this loss of privilege might make some users angry, so be sure to work with your managers to obtain consensus and approval before implementing limits on users' mailboxes.

The Client Settings tab (see Figure 5-11) lists the public folder database to be associated with the mailboxes created within this database (if applicable—remember, public folder databases are not installed by default with Exchange 2007).

You also specify the offline address book (OAB) on this tab. You may use different OABs for different sets of users, based on their need. For example, you may have a group of employees whom you do not want to have access to the complete global address list when outside the office. Creating a separate OAB and specifying it here would allow you to do this.

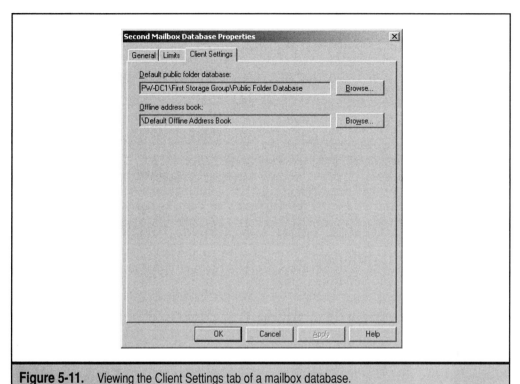

Figure 5-11. Viewing the Client Settings tab of a mailbox database.

Recovering Deleted Items

Once an item has been deleted, it can be recovered if the Keep Deleted Items For (Days) value (referred to as *deleted item retention time* within the Exchange community) has been set on the user's mailbox database. This value only refers to items that have been removed from the Deleted Items folder in Outlook. Once a user empties his or her Deleted Items folder, the value you set for deleted item retention will be enforced.

For instance, let's assume that Jenay Johnson sent John Smith an e-mail about the new ad campaign. John accidentally deleted it and then emptied his Deleted Items folder. Now, he needs to recover this e-mail. What John should do is navigate to the Tools menu in his Outlook client, click Recover Deleted Items, select the item he wishes to recover, and then click Recover Selected Items. This action will make these items appear in the Deleted Items folder in the Outlook client, at which point John can move these items to any folder he desires.

Recovering Deleted Mailboxes

Once you've set the Keep Deleted Mailboxes For (Days) value (referred to as the mailbox retention interval), you can recover a deleted mailbox as long as you're within the interval. To be honest though, the idea of deleting a mailbox is permanent; this value applies to the situation where you delete the user associated with a mailbox and the mailbox becomes "disconnected." The recovery process involves reconnecting a mailbox to an account in Active Directory. You can see the process of reconnecting a disconnected mailbox in Chapter 3.

Permanently Deleting a User's Mailbox

If you've set a deleted mailbox retention time but would like to manually purge a mailbox from a mailbox store, you can do this by performing the following steps. First, navigate to the mailbox store you wish to work with, and highlight the Mailboxes icon inside the store. Find the deleted mailbox you wish to purge (it should have an X over its icon), right-click the mailbox, and select Purge. Confirm your action, and the mailbox will be permanently removed from the mailbox store and its items will not be recoverable, unless the store is recovered from tape backup.

Reading Mailbox Summaries

Exchange 2000/2003 provided you with a summary of information about the mailboxes within a given mailbox database. In Exchange 2007, you'll need to use the Exchange Management Shell to retrieve the same information. Exchange 2000/2003 would display such information as the mailbox name, who the last user was to log on to the mailbox, the number of messages stored in each mailbox, the total size of each mailbox, the last logon time for each mailbox, and the last logoff time for each mailbox. In order to accomplish this in Exchange 2007, you'll need to utilize the *get-mailboxfolderstatistics* command.

CREATING PUBLIC FOLDER DATABASES

Public folder databases are created and managed in the same manner as mailbox databases, but with some key differences. For instance, replication configurations are available in the database's properties, but it requires more effort to administer a public folder database.

If you would like more information on how to create and manage public folder databases and public folders, refer to Chapter 4.

SUMMARY

In this chapter, you have seen how to create and manage both storage groups and individual databases. You have also seen how to move the database files for both a storage group and an individual database. Finally, you've learned how to delete and recover individual items in a mailbox database, as well as an individual database, through the use of the Exchange Management Console.

In the next chapter, we'll begin to look at the server roles in more detail, beginning with the Hub Transport role.

CHAPTER 6

Managing Hub Transport Servers

The last three chapters focused on various aspects of the Mailbox server role (recipients, public folders, mailboxes, storage, etc.). In the next four chapters, I'm going to cover the management of each of the other four server roles, beginning with the Hub Transport role. I've broken the chapters up this way to allow you to align your focus with the new server architecture of Exchange 2007. You will find through reading this chapter that some of the Hub Transport management tasks also apply to the Edge Transport role, so I'll cover transport management tasks under the premise that you would need to configure an Exchange environment *without* the optional Edge Transport role. Therefore, I'll be demonstrating management on the Hub Transport role, but I'll try to ensure that you're aware which tasks also apply to Edge Transport servers. Chapter 9 will focus on only those tasks that apply to that external, optional server role. In this chapter, I'll first cover Exchange 2007's transport architecture, followed by the management tasks you'll need to perform.

EXCHANGE 2007 TRANSPORT ARCHITECTURE

Let's begin by covering the components involved in routing messages, dive a bit deeper into each component, and then put it all together at the end to show you the flow of messages. The components that make up the transport architecture are:

- ▼ Routing topology
- ■ Transport protocol
- ■ Message flows
- ■ Connectors
- ■ Categorizer
- ■ Queues
- ■ Pickup and relay directories
- ▲ Server components

Routing Topology

In previous versions of Exchange, routing was handled by specific logical routing concepts, such as a site in Exchange 5.5 and routing groups in Exchange 2000/2003, which defined the logical groupings of Exchange servers and how each was connected. In Exchange 2007, routing has been drastically simplified by using Active Directory's site topology, eliminating the need for a separate routing topology.

Active Directory sites are connected by Internet Protocol (IP) site links, each of which has a logical cost associated with them. These costs are used by Hub Transport servers to determine the least costly route when sending messages to a Hub Transport server in another site. This does imply that if you have a Mailbox server in a given site, you must have the Hub Transport server role deployed in that same site.

Advanced Routing Considerations

Messages are sent using the principle of *direct relay*, where the source server resolves the name and IP address of the destination server and then directly sends the message to the destination server. Should the delivery be unsuccessful, the message is queued for delivery retry. To assist with more complex Active Directory site topologies, a site can be specified as a *hub site*, where messages can be routed via a transitive Hub Transport server that will simply pass the message to the intended destination server.

In addition, an Exchange-specific cost can be assigned to an IP site link should message routing not need to follow Active Directory replication paths exactly. Lastly, messages destined for multiple recipients are not expanded (where each recipient is individually identified and multiple copies of the message are sent to each) until there is a "fork" in the routing for each of the destination sites housing recipients. This decreases the bandwidth usage and speeds up delivery of messages.

Transport Protocol

I'll start with the fact that all messages are sent via the Simple Mail Transport Protocol (SMTP) and secured using transport layer security (TLS). This includes any Exchange system messages as well as user-originated e-mails. The role of a Hub Transport server is to route messages, whether they are destined for a local Mailbox server or an external messaging system across the Internet, so utilizing a single protocol makes sense to simplify the architecture.

Message Flows

When discussing the flow of messages, there are two distinct characteristics, each with two possible values that a message can take on. The first characteristic is whether the message is an *inbound* or *outbound* message. Inbound messages are sent from outside the Exchange organization, such as from across the Internet. Outbound messages originate from within the Exchange organization and are destined for external recipients.

The second characteristic applies to inbound messages, as well as those messages that originate within the Exchange organization and are also destined for a recipient within the same Exchange organization. All messages destined for an internal recipient are either *local* or *remote*. The terms are relative to the Hub Transport server processing the message. Local messages are destined for a recipient residing on a Mailbox server within the same Active Directory site. Remote messages are, therefore, destined for a recipient residing on a Mailbox server within an Active Directory site that is different from the Hub Transport server processing the message.

Connectors

Exchange 2007 uses SMTP connectors to send and receive messages between Exchange servers or with foreign messaging systems that may be either internal to your organization or across the Internet. Exchange separates SMTP connectors into SMTP send connectors and SMTP receive connectors. While you won't need to set up connectors for internal mail (they are created automatically when you install a Hub Transport server, although you will not see them, as they are implicitly based on Active Directory site topology), you can create your own connectors to define logical connections between a Hub Transport server and another SMTP host (which may be another Hub Transport server or a foreign messaging system).

The connectors are defined as objects within Active Directory—receive connectors as child objects of the server object they are logically associated with and send connectors within a special Connectors container.

Categorizer

The Categorizer's job is to process each message and perform the following tasks:

▼ Validate recipients

■ Expand the distribution list

■ Determine the appropriate routing path

■ Convert content

▲ Apply message policies

Queues

Exchange 2007 uses queues as a temporary location to store messages to be sent. Like the name implies, each message in the queue is to be processed based on the order in which it entered the queue. Messages from the Internet are queued on Edge Transport servers, and messages en route within the Exchange organization are queued on Hub Transport servers. Table 6-1 lists the types of queues used by Exchange.

Directories

Every Hub and Edge Transport server has a Pickup and a Replay directory. The Pickup directory exists for applications other than Exchange to be able to submit messages for transport, and can also be used by administrators for testing message flow. The Pickup directory is checked by Exchange every five seconds for new messages. The Replay directory is used to submit messages to Exchange recipients received from foreign non-SMTP messaging systems. In addition, administrators can export the contents of existing Exchange queues and drop those exported messages into the Reply directory for delivery.

Server Components

Two other components need to be discussed. The first component, the Mail Submission service, exists on each Mailbox server. This service notifies the Hub Transport server in the same Active Directory site of messages that need to be picked up from the sender's outbox.

Queue Type	Transport Server Role(s) Using This Queue	Receives Messages From	Messages Are Passed To
Submission	Hub Edge	SMTP receive connectors The Pickup directory The Store driver	The Categorizer
Mailbox Delivery	Hub	The Categorizer	The destination Mailbox store via Exchange Remote Procedure Call (RPC)
Remote Delivery	Hub Edge	The Categorizer	Remote servers via SMTP
Poison Message	Edge	SMTP receive connector	None
Unreachable	Hub Edge	Categorizer	None

Table 6-1.   Exchange 2007 Queue Types

The second is the Store driver, which exists on each Hub Transport server. This driver retrieves a copy of the messages in a sender's outbox and places them in the Submission queue. It also moves the message from the outbox to the sender's Sent Items folder. On the receiving side, the Store driver pulls messages from the delivery queue and hands them off to the Mailbox server.

PUTTING IT ALL TOGETHER

Let me make sense of all these moving parts by giving you a few scenarios and showing you visually how Exchange transports messages. For the purpose of this section, I'm going to show Hub Transport servers separately from Mailbox servers to clarify each server role's part in the transport process. If you have the Hub Transport role on the same server as the Mailbox role, then, of course, the communication I show between two servers will occur on the same server.

Exchange Servers in the Same Active Directory Site

The following illustration shows how a message passes from one Mailbox server to another within the same Active Directory site.

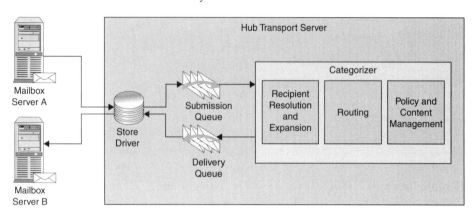

Mailbox Server A notifies the Hub Transport server of new messages, which are pulled by the Store driver and placed into the Submission queue. The message is processed by the Categorizer to validate the recipient, determine the appropriate routing for the message, and apply any message policies (such as size restrictions). When it is determined that the message is destined for a Mailbox server in the same Active Directory site (accomplished by a query to Active Directory for the mailbox server of the recipient), the message is placed in the Delivery queue destined for Mailbox Server B. The Store driver delivers the message to Mailbox Server B, where it is placed in the users Inbox.

Exchange Servers in Separate Active Directory Sites

The illustration on the next page shows how a message passes from a Mailbox server in one Active Directory site to a Mailbox server within a different Active Directory site.

Much like the previous example, Mailbox Server A notifies the Hub Transport server of new messages, which are pulled by the Store driver and placed into the Submission queue. The message is processed by the Categorizer to validate the recipient, determine the appropriate routing for the message, and apply any message policies (such as size restrictions). When it is determined that the message is destined for a Mailbox server in a different Active Directory site, the message is placed in the Remote Delivery queue destined for the Hub Transport server in the other Active Directory site. The message is handed off to the send connector and sent via SMTP, where it is received by the receive connector of the Hub Transport server in the other Active Directory site.

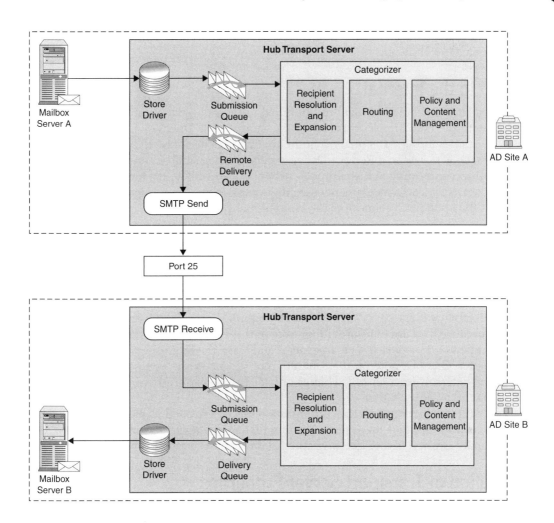

Once there, the message is processed to identify the sender and recipient, apply transport rules, and, optionally, validate content for spam or viruses. Once complete, the message is placed in the Submission queue, where it proceeds along the same path as described in the previous example.

Inbound from the Internet

Messages coming in from the Internet follow the same path as the second half of the last example, with the possible exception of the inclusion of an Edge Transport server first receiving messages from the Internet, performing a lookup in the Edge server's Active

Directory Application Mode (ADAM) directory service, and passing the message to the appropriate Hub Transport server via SMTP.

Outbound to the Internet

Messages bound for the Internet are submitted in the same way as in the previous two examples to the Hub Transport server in the same Active Directory site. It is when the message resides in the Categorizer that the routing is determined to be via the Internet. The message is placed in a Remote Delivery queue, where it is either passed to an Edge Transport server residing in the perimeter network or directly to the target domain across the Internet. Microsoft's recommended configuration includes an Edge Transport server, but Hub Transport Send connectors can be configured to send directly across the Internet.

MANAGING TRANSPORT SERVERS

Now that I've covered a bit on how the transport of messages in Exchange 2007 works, I'd like to switch gears and discuss the management of transport servers. Please note that nearly all of what I'll be covering in this section applies to both Hub and Edge Transport servers because they are both providing transport services. In this chapter, I'll cover the configuration of transport servers in general and leave the Edge-specific features for the next chapter. One last note on the separation of topics: While you can install the anti-spam and antivirus features of Exchange onto a Hub Transport server, I'm also going to cover that in the next chapter.

I'll begin this section with the configuration settings needed to properly get a transport server running and then delve into the management of the server components I conceptually covered earlier in this chapter that run on transport servers.

Configuration of Transport Server Properties

Before we get into making changes to the services a transport server will provide to meet your business needs, let's first cover a few steps you'd need to take upon the installation of a transport server by looking at the server properties.

Ensuring Transport Services

The first step after an installation is to make sure that the server is indeed hosting a Transport Server role. This is an easy task, accomplished by selecting the Hub Transport node under Server Configuration in the console tree and selecting the Properties link in the action pane, shown in Figure 6-1.

Configuring Domain Name Service (DNS) Lookups

In order for a transport server to properly communicate with other servers, it must first be able to determine the IP address of the destination server, whether it be internal or external. For example, if a Hub Transport server only pointed to a DNS server that only resolved

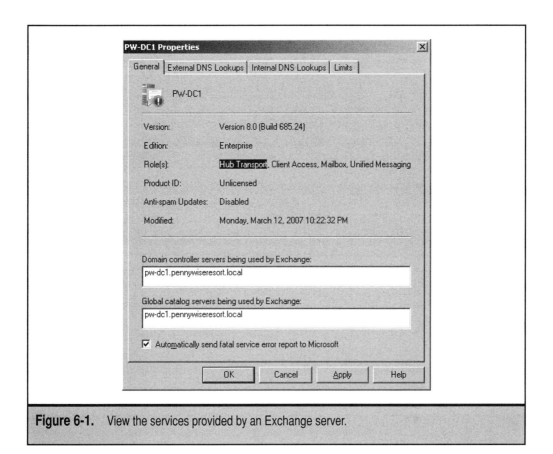

Figure 6-1. View the services provided by an Exchange server.

an internal Active Directory namespace, it would be impossible for the Hub Transport server to ever be configured to send messages to external recipients and vice versa.

By default, Exchange uses the DNS configuration of the network adapter(s) on the transport server. Should you need to override the default settings, Exchange allows you to separately configure internal and external DNS settings within the Exchange Management Console. You can view the DNS settings on the External DNS Lookups and Internal DNS Lookups tabs, as shown in Figure 6-2.

Each tab lists the settings that will be used by default (by selecting the Use Network Card DNS Settings option), and you can specify alternate DNS servers, if required. If your transport server has two network cards (presumably one for the internal network and one for the external network), you will want to identify separate DNS servers for each network.

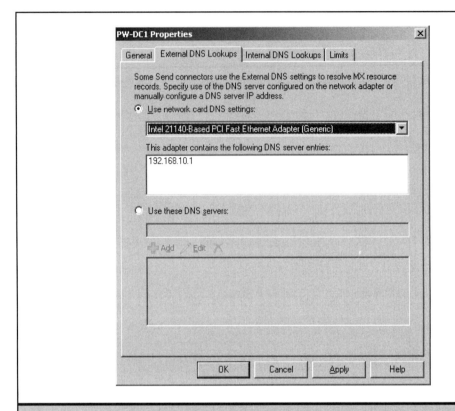

Figure 6-2. Alternate DNS servers can be configured on transport servers.

TIP If you are not logged on locally to the transport server, you will not be able to select an individual network card, but instead will be presented with an option of All Available.

Setting Transport Limits

The Limits tab, shown in Figure 6-3, establishes connection restrictions as well as message retry, expiration, and notification settings.

TIP Microsoft recommends that the default limit values be left alone, unless you are told to modify these values by Microsoft Support Services.

Table 6-2 lists each of the settings on the Limits tab, their purpose, and possible values.

Value	Description	Minimum Value	Default Value	Maximum Value
Outbound Connection Failure Retry Interval (Minutes)	Exchange will retry a failed connection after the specified number of minutes.	1	10	4320
Transient Failure Retry Interval (Seconds)	Exchange will try to reconnect to an existing session that has been disconnected after the specified interval.	15	300	43200
Transient Failure Retry Attempts	Exchange will try to reconnect to an existing session the specified number of attempts.	0	6	6
Maximum Time Since Submission (Days)	Exchange will keep a message in queue for the specified number of days before removing it.	1	2	90
Notify Sender When Message Is Delayed More Than (Hours)	Exchange will generate a delivery status notification after the specified amount of time, informing the sender of a delay in delivery.	1	4	720
Maximum Concurrent Outbound Connections	Exchange can maintain up to the specified number of connections.	1	1000	12,147,483,647
Maximum Concurrent Outbound Connections Per Domain	Exchange can maintain the specified number of connections to a single domain. (Note: This value cannot exceed the Maximum Concurrent Outbound Connections value.)	1	20	12,147,483,647

Table 6-2.   Transport Server Limits

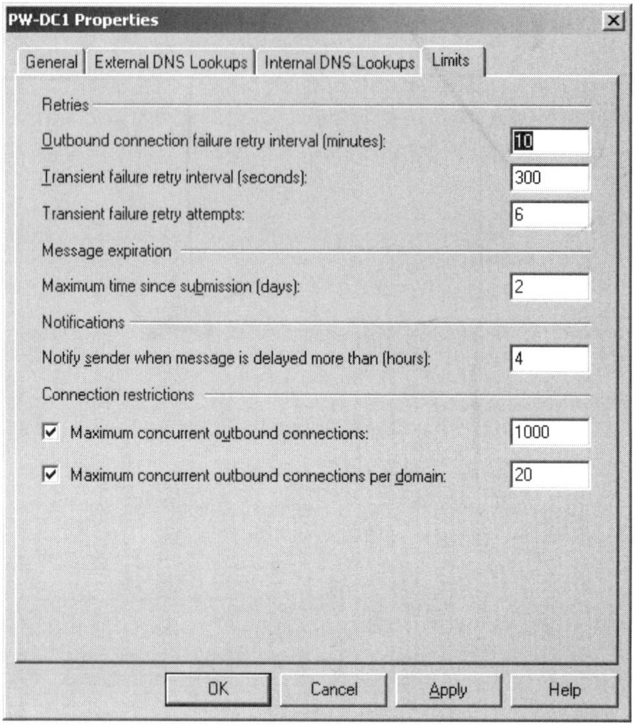

Figure 6-3. Limits for each transport server should be left alone.

The remainder of this section revolves around the various elements of transport servers that you can configure. These include:

▼ Domains

■ Connectors

▲ Queues

Managing Domains

Because SMTP is the primary namespace in Exchange 2007, SMTP domains are, therefore, the primary identifier of a messaging system. Keep in mind that a domain can represent either a foreign messaging system across the Internet or one of many SMTP namespaces equally supported by your Exchange organizations. In Exchange 2007, there are two types of domains that you need to concern yourself with: *accepted* and *remote* domains. An accepted domain is any domain namespace that in your Exchange organization is responsible for the sending and receiving of e-mail. A remote domain is a domain that Exchange will interact with, where you can specify that certain types of messages can and cannot be sent, as well as defining acceptable message formats. Let's look at the management of each, beginning with an accepted domain.

Accepted Domains

To create an accepted domain, navigate within the Exchange Management Console to the Hub Transport node under Organization Configuration in the console tree. Select the Accepted Domains tab in the results pane, and select New Accepted Domain from the action pane, shown in Figure 6-4.

TIP Configuring an accepted domain should typically be done on the Hub Transport server role. Edge Transport servers should be configured via EdgeSync subscriptions instead of directly (more on this in Chapter 9).

Accepted domains only need a name (for the created object), the SMTP domain, and the domain type, as shown in Figure 6-5.

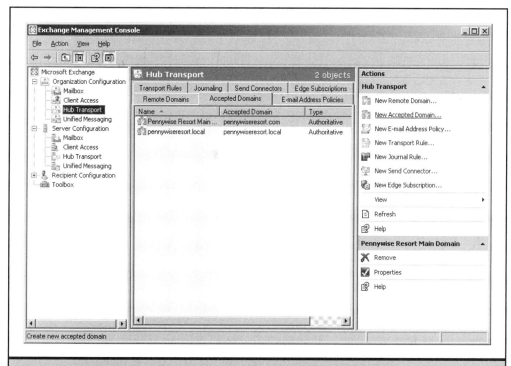

Figure 6-4. Navigate to the Hub Transport node to manage accepted domains.

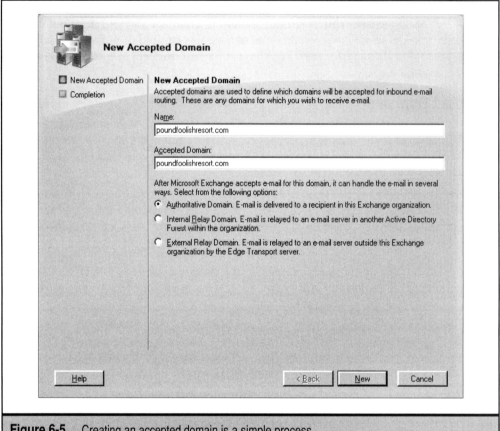

Figure 6-5.   Creating an accepted domain is a simple process.

Three domain types exist:

▼ **Authoritative**   If Exchange is configured to be the authority of a specified domain, it means that (from Exchange's point of view) your Exchange organization is *the* messaging system hosting that domain name. No other Exchange organization or messaging system will host that domain.

■ **Internal relay**   Exchange will accept mail destined for the specified domain, but assumes that the authoritative system is not the Exchange system that received the mail, and will immediately work to route the mail to another internal messaging system (Exchange or otherwise), as defined by your internal DNS. A good example of this would be a larger organization with multiple business units, where the corporate office wants all mail to be routed through

---

Management Shell Corner

You can create an accepted domain using the `New-AcceptedDomain` command:

```
new-AcceptedDomain -Name 'Pound Foolish Resort' -DomainName 'pound-
foolishresort.com'
```

You can also modify a remote domain using the `Set-AcceptedDomain` command.

Edge Transport servers that provide appropriate protection against spam and viruses before being routed to individual Exchange systems that exist within the corporate office, but are in separate Active Directory forests.

▲ **External relay** Exchange will accept mail for this domain at the Edge Transport server (essentially outside your organization), makes the same assumption that the mail is destined for a system other than Exchange, and will work to route the mail to the appropriate external messaging system without allowing the mail to be routed within Exchange.

You'll notice if you view the properties of the object that you can only modify the type of domain.

Remote Domains

Creating a remote domain is a similar process to that for creating accepted domains. While still on the Hub Transport node in the console tree, select the Remote Domains tab, and click the New Remote Domain link in the action pane (you can, of course, always click this link when any tab is selected under the Hub Transport node). This causes the New Remote Domain Wizard to start, shown in Figure 6-6. The wizard is simple, requiring only three fields: the object name, the remote domain name, and whether to include sub-domain names.

When creating the remote domain, you may not see the value until you view its properties, beginning with the General tab, shown in Figure 6-7. It is important to remember that the very presence of a remote domain in Exchange permits it to handle messages destined for that domain as a relay. Without the remote domain, any messages received by Exchange destined for that domain will not be delivered.

Here, you can configure whether out-of-office messages will be sent to the remote domain at all, by Exchange 2007 clients and Exchange 2003 or lower clients. On the Message Format tab, shown in Figure 6-8, you can do a whole lot more than configure message formats (which are set at the bottom of the dialog box). This tab basically continues the thought process started on the General tab: Configure the types of system messages that will be supported (it is assumed that you want to allow normal messages to be sent to this domain). These are self-explanatory, so I won't go into detail.

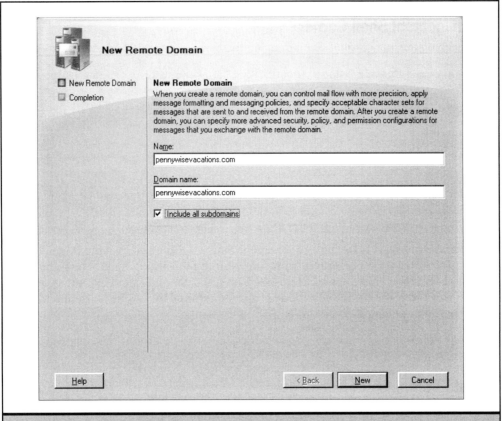

Figure 6-6.   Creating a remote domain is also simple.

Management Shell Corner

You can create a remote domain using the New-RemoteDomain command:

```
new-RemoteDomain -Name 'pennywisevacations.com' -DomainName 'penny-
wisevacations.com'
```

You can also modify a remote domain using the Set-RemoteDomain command.

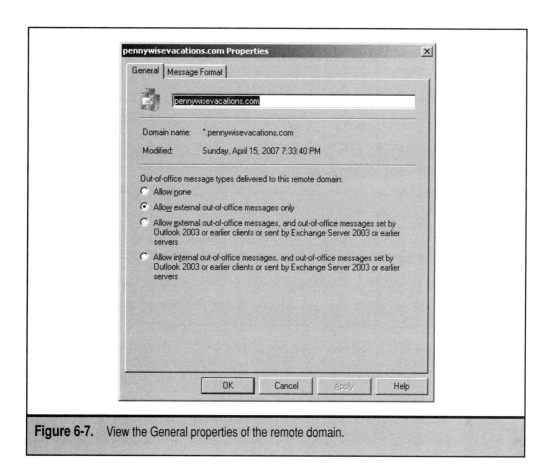

Figure 6-7.   View the General properties of the remote domain.

Now that we've looked at configuring the domains that will be supported with Exchange, let's look at how Exchange will establish communication with connectors.

Managing Connectors

Exchange connectors are logical representations of message connectivity between two servers. Exchange does create implicit connectors based on the logical network topology using Active Directory site link costs. You'll never see these in the Management Console or in the Management Shell, however. These are the connectors between Hub Transport servers, so you won't need to worry about creating connectors just to make your Exchange environment work. The only time you'll really need to create a connector is

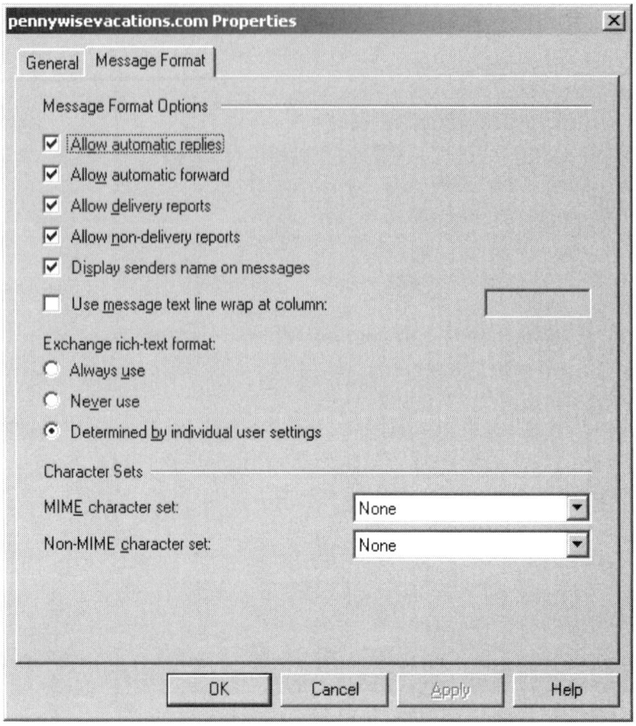

Figure 6-8. View the message formats of the remote domain.

if you want some kind of unique configuration to a specific external domain. Exchange supports three types of connectors: send, receive, and foreign. I've already covered the first two at the beginning of this chapter: send connectors for sending mail and receive connectors for, yep—you guessed it—receiving messages over SMTP. Foreign connectors utilize the Drop directory on a Hub Transport server to move messages to a foreign messaging system. A foreign connector could use SMTP as its protocol, but other protocols, such as X.400, can be used to communicate.

Send SMTP Connectors

In the Exchange Management Console, send connectors are managed within the Hub Transport node under Organization Configuration. Send connectors are managed at the organization level, because the Hub Transport server specified is a subset of the connector and not the other way around. By navigating to the Hub Transport node under Organization

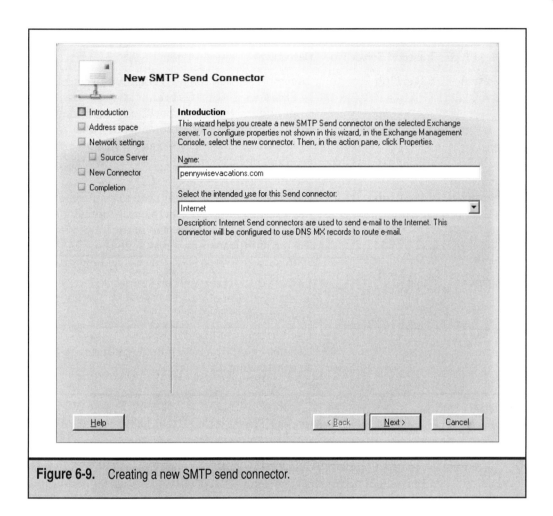

Figure 6-9.   Creating a new SMTP send connector.

Configuration and selecting the New Send Connector link in the action pane, you start the New SMTP Send Connector wizard, shown in Figure 6-9.

Each connector needs a name (if I'm connecting to an outside domain, as in the example here, I usually put the domain name as the name of the connector) and the intended use of the connector. Table 6-3 describes the types of connector uses.

Upon selecting the type and clicking Next, you'll be presented with the Address Space page of the wizard. Here, you will define one or more SMTP domain names that will be transported via this connector. Clicking Next again displays the Network Settings page of the wizard, shown in Figure 6-10. Here you specify whether Exchange will determine the target server address using DNS or via a smart host (which is an SMTP relay that presumably knows how to properly route messages to the target domain).

Usage Type	Transport Server Type	Description
Internal	Edge, Hub	Transport servers can be configured to connect to Exchange 2000/2003 bridgehead servers, from Edge to Hub Transport servers (although this is usually created automatically), and from Hub to Hub (again, usually an automatic creation, but cross-forest transport may use this type of send connector).
Internet	Edge, Hub	Either server can be configured to connect to the Internet, although Microsoft recommends using an Edge Transport server or, at the very least, a Hub Transport server with the anti-spam and antivirus features installed manually.
Partner	Edge	Edge Transport servers can connect to an external domain via SMTP using TLS authentication.
Custom	Edge, Hub	Used to connect to a third-party message-transfer agent or an Exchange environment in a separate forest.

Table 6-3. SMTP Send Connector Types

The Source Server page, shown in Figure 6-11, is where you choose which Exchange server(s) will send messages across this connector. This is where you see the individual Hub Transport server as a subset property of the overall connector. You can add multiple Hub Transport servers if you want to establish connector redundancy.

Clicking New and then clicking Finish completes the wizard.

Management Shell Corner

An SMTP send connector can be created using the following command :

```
new-SendConnector -Name 'pennywisevacations.com' -Usage 'Internet'
-AddressSpaces 'smtp:pennywisevacations.com;1' -DNSRoutingEnabled
$true -UseExternalDNSServersEnabled $false -SourceTransportServers
'PW-DC1'.
```

Additional settings can be used to further configure the connector as it is being created.

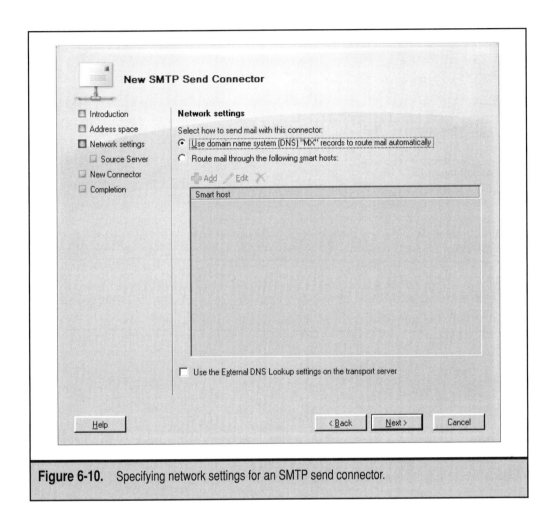

Figure 6-10.   Specifying network settings for an SMTP send connector.

When creating send connectors of other usage types, the process is much the same, but in some cases, such as when creating a connector where authentication will be required, such as when you create an internal connector or a partner connector, you will be prompted to provide authentication settings, as shown in Figure 6-12.

You can see a few of the parameters that are not asked for when using the New SMTP Send Connector Wizard in Figure 6-13. This includes a logging level should you need to troubleshoot this connector and the fully qualified domain name (FQDN) the connector will use when establishing an SMTP session with another server.

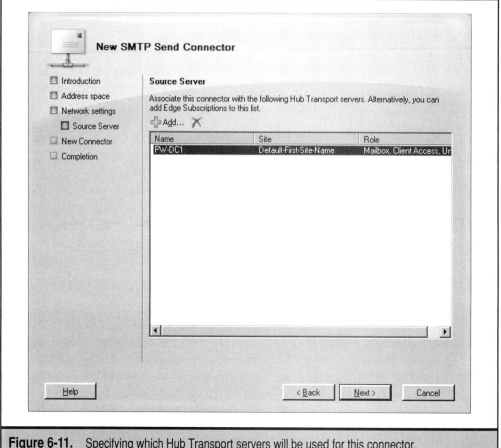

Figure 6-11. Specifying which Hub Transport servers will be used for this connector.

You may need to disable a connector for troubleshooting purposes to force traffic via a particular route or to view messages in a queue. You can do this by choosing the connector in question and selecting the Disable link in the action pane.

Management Shell Corner

You can view a connector's properties from the management shell using the `Get-SendConnector` command, shown in Figure 6-14. Equally, the `Set-SendConnector` can be used to modify a connector's properties using the `-Identity` switch to name the connector and the appropriate `-<PropertyName>` specifier and value.

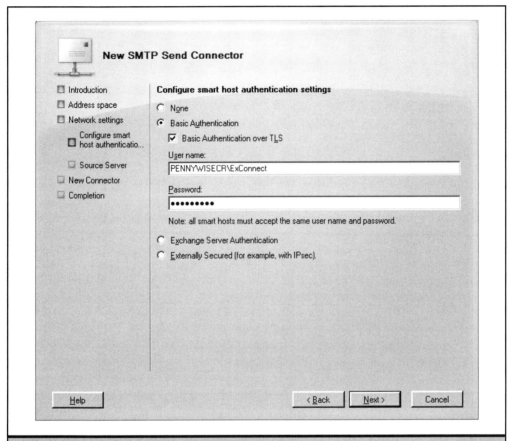

Figure 6-12.   Provide credentials for authenticating over an SMTP connector.

Receive SMTP Connectors

Receive connectors are managed on a per-server basis, so you'll first need to navigate to the Hub Transport node under Server Configuration in the console tree and select the server you wish to manage in the work pane to see the receive connectors in the results pane, as shown in Figure 6-15. You'll notice there are two connectors by default: the default and the client connectors. The client connector is automatically created to receive messages being submitted from Post Office Protocol Version 3 (POP3) or Internet Message Access Protocol Version 4 (IMAP4) clients. The default connector is automatically created to accept messages from Exchange 2007 and legacy Exchange servers, as well as still supporting Exchange clients.

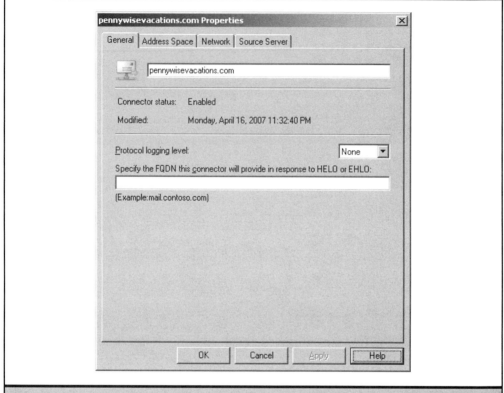

Figure 6-13. Viewing the connector's properties shows additional settings.

By choosing a connector and selecting the Properties link in the action pane, you can see the General tab of the receive connector, as shown in Figure 6-16. Here, like the send SMTP connectors, you can specify the FQDN of the server and the logging level for troubleshooting.

On the Network tab, shown in Figure 6-17, you can restrict which local IP addresses on the transport server will be used for this connector, as well which IP addresses can send messages to it. You may want to restrict each of these settings in order to force communications along a specific path instead of the default paths calculated based on your Active Directory site topology.

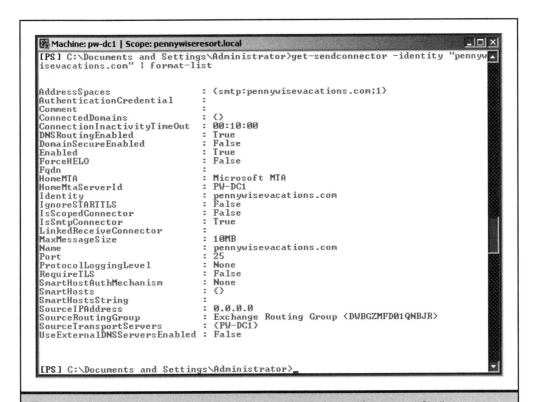

```
Machine: pw-dc1 | Scope: pennywiseresort.local                              _ □ ×
[PS] C:\Documents and Settings\Administrator>get-sendconnector -identity "pennyw
isevacations.com" | format-list


AddressSpaces                : {smtp:pennywisevacations.com;1}
AuthenticationCredential     :
Comment                      :
ConnectedDomains             : {}
ConnectionInactivityTimeOut  : 00:10:00
DNSRoutingEnabled            : True
DomainSecureEnabled          : False
Enabled                      : True
ForceHELO                    : False
Fqdn                         :
HomeMTA                      : Microsoft MTA
HomeMtaServerId              : PW-DC1
Identity                     : pennywisevacations.com
IgnoreSTARTTLS               : False
IsScopedConnector            : False
IsSmtpConnector              : True
LinkedReceiveConnector       :
MaxMessageSize               : 10MB
Name                         : pennywisevacations.com
Port                         : 25
ProtocolLoggingLevel         : None
RequireTLS                   : False
SmartHostAuthMechanism       : None
SmartHosts                   : {}
SmartHostsString             :
SourceIPAddress              : 0.0.0.0
SourceRoutingGroup           : Exchange Routing Group {DWBGZMFD01QNBJR}
SourceTransportServers       : {PW-DC1}
UseExternalDNSServersEnabled : False



[PS] C:\Documents and Settings\Administrator>
```

Figure 6-14. Viewing the connector properties from the Exchange Management Shell.

The Authentication tab, shown in Figure 6-18, specifies which methods will be accepted to identify the sending server:

▼ **Transport Layer Security**   Since SMTP itself has no secure version, TLS is used as an application-independent encryption protocol on which SMTP resides. If selected by itself, the SMTP session will be encrypted, but messages would be passed anonymously.

■ **Basic Authentication**   Use this to pass a user name and password insecurely across the network. This is not recommended, but it is supported. Note the option to only offer basic authentication after a TLS session is established to protect the security of the password.

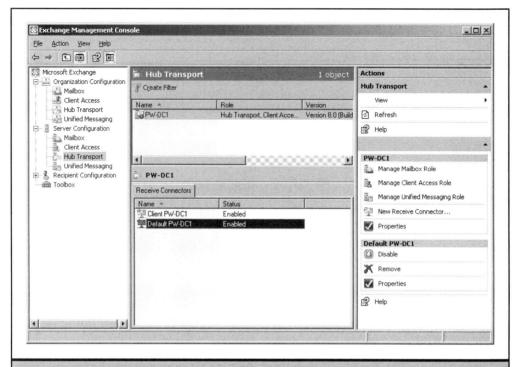

Figure 6-15. Navigating to the receive connectors on an Exchange 2007 server.

■ **Exchange Server Authentication** This option supports both 2007 and legacy versions of Exchange by utilizing a client/server authentication called the Generic Security Services Application Programming Interface (GSSAPI) and an Exchange-specific SMTP "protocol sink" extension called EXPS.

■ **Integrated Windows Authentication** This method uses the credentials of the currently logged-on user or process that connects to the server hosting the receive connector.

▲ **Externally Secured** This option leaves the security to a third party and causes Exchange to assume that the line is secure, so no Exchange-specific authentication is needed.

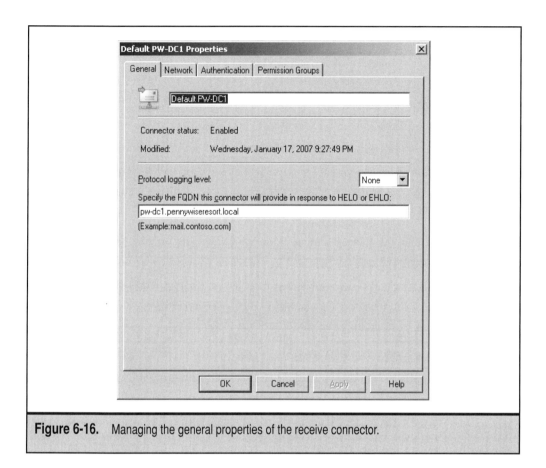

Figure 6-16. Managing the general properties of the receive connector.

The Permission Groups tab, shown in Figure 6-19, lists which clients and/or servers are allowed to connect to this connector. Table 6-4 describes the permissions that can be granted.

TIP If you're not going to use an Edge Transport server to receive e-mail from the Internet and instead will be directing Internet traffic to a Hub Transport server, you will need to enable anonymous users on the default receive connector.

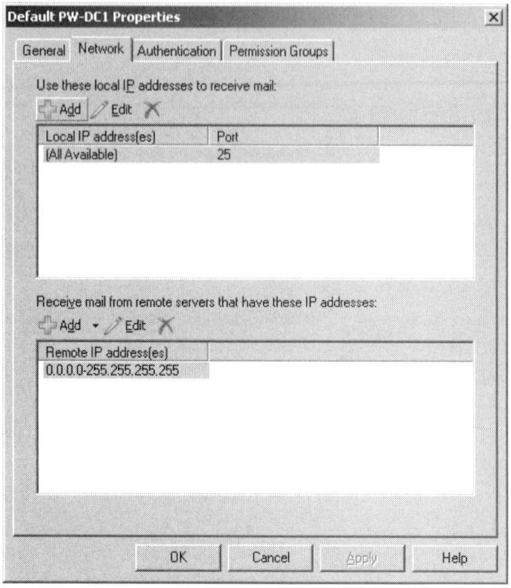

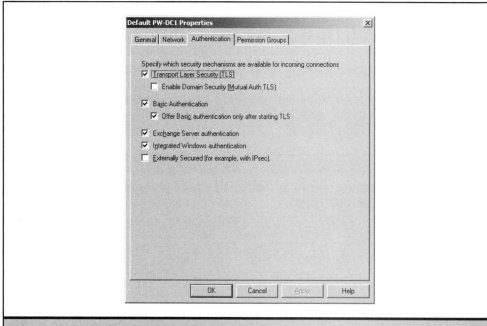

Figure 6-17. Restrict access to the connector on the Network tab.

Figure 6-18. Select the authentication methods to be supported.

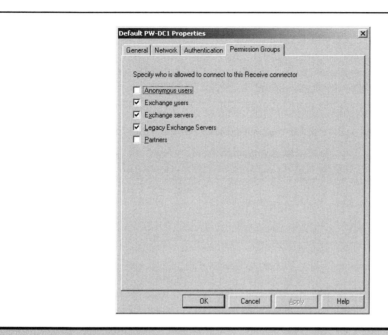

Figure 6-19. Specify who is permitted to connect to this connector.

Permission Group	Description
Anonymous	Use this option if you wish Exchange to accept SMTP connections from any other server without authentication.
Exchange Users	Use this option to allow authenticated users to utilize the connector.
Exchange Servers	Use this option to allow Hub and Edge Transport server and any other externally secure server to utilize the connector.
Legacy Exchange Servers	Use this option to allow Exchange 2000/2003 servers to communicate via this connector. The servers must be members of the Exchange Legacy Interop security group.
Partners	Use this option if you have externally granted partner servers permissions to access this connector.

Table 6-4. Receive Connector Permission Groups

Foreign Connectors

If you have the need to connect Exchange directly to another messaging system, you will need to create a foreign connector. This is really nothing more than a logical definition of an address namespace (such as an X.400 address) and a directory in which to drop the messages destined for that foreign system. To create a foreign connector, you will need to follow three steps in the Exchange Management Shell, shown in Figure 6-20:

1. Create the foreign connector using the `New-ForeignConnector` command.

2. Set the drop directory for the transport server on which you created the foreign connector using the `Set-TransportServer` command.

3. Specify that the foreign connector use the drop directory using the `Set-ForeignConnector` command.

Managing Queues

Queue management became big in Exchange 2000, where Exchange shifted from essentially a single queue, where all messages stacked up when something went wrong, to multiple queues that were dynamically created for each destination. Exchange 2007 continues

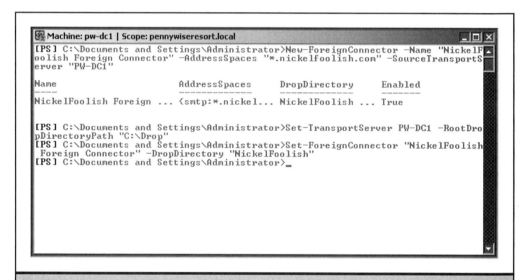

Figure 6-20. Create a foreign connector and the associated drop directory.

the improvement of queue management by providing easy management of the queue databases and settings, as well as a queue management console that has more filtering and searching capabilities to make identifying queue-related problems easier. The management of queues will fall into two distinct tasks in this section: managing the queue databases and settings, and queue management.

The Queue Database and Settings

All of the Exchange queues (I previously listed them in the "Queues" section in this chapter) are stored in an extensible storage engine (ESE) database located, by default, in the *C:\Program Files\Microsoft\Exchange Server\TransportRoles\data\Queue* folder. The contents of the folder are listed in Table 6-5.

The Microsoft Exchange Transport service, which is responsible for processing messages in the queues, is configured via the EdgeTransport.exe.config file (an XML file), found in the *C:\Program Files\Microsoft\Exchange Server\Bin* folder. The values you can modify will be found within the `<appSettings>` section of the file. Each value you modify (and they are case-sensitive) will be entered using the `<add key="Option" value="Value" />` format within this section. Some of the more common parameters you may need to modify are listed in Table 6-6.

Database File	Description
mail.que	The queue database file
tmp.edb	A temporary database used to validate the schema of the queue database at startup
trn.*.log	The transaction log file user to track changes to the database
trn.chk	The checkpoint file for tracking the progress of each database change
trnres00001.jrs, trnres00002.jrs	Reserved transaction log files used if the volume storing the transaction logs runs out of disk space

Table 6-5. Files That Make Up the Queue Database

Parameter	Default Value	Description/Notes
QueueDatabasePath	C:\Program Files\Microsoft\ Exchange Server\ TransportRoles\ data\Queue	Ensure the target folder exists before you change this value, and give Full Control permissions to Network Service, System, and Administrators.
QueueDatabase-LoggingPath	C:\Program Files\Microsoft\ Exchange Server\ TransportRoles\ data\Queue.	Ensure the target folder exists before you change this value, and give Full Control permissions to Network Service, System, and Administrators.
QueueGlitchRetry-Count	4	Defines how many times transmission should be retried. Only change this if queues are continually put into a state of retry and you consider your network to be unreliable.
QueueGlitchRetry-Interval	1 minute	Defines how often to retry transmission. Only change this if queues are continually put into a state of retry and you consider your network to be unreliable.
MailboxDeliveryQueue-RetryInterval	5 minutes	Defines how often a Hub Transport server should retry to send messages destined for a Mailbox server.

Table 6-6. Commonly Used Queue Configuration Parameters

Queue Management

Those of you familiar with Exchange 2000/2003's queue management will find the management in Exchange 2007 relatively similar, with some new features to hone in on messages you are trying to find. You will find queue management within the Exchange Management Console by navigating to the Toolbox node in the console tree and double-clicking the Queue Viewer icon in the results pane, as shown in Figure 6-21.

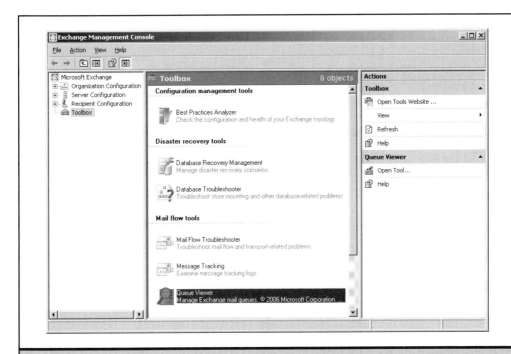

Figure 6-21. Navigating to the Queue Viewer in the management console.

Queues are dynamically created based on destination, so in my basic example in Figure 6-22, you can see there are only two queues. You should note that with a queue selected, you are presented with options in the action pane such as:

▼ **View Messages**   Opens a new tab and displays the messages contained within the queue.

■ **Suspend**   Pauses the queue and replaces "Suspend" with "Resume" as an action in the action pane.

■ **Remove Messages (With NDR)**   Deletes the message and sends the originator of the message a non-delivery report (NDR), stating that the message was not delivered.

▲ **Remove Messages (Without Sending NDRs)**   Deletes the message, but does not send an NDR to the message originator.

If you select to view the messages, a new tab appears for the related queue, as shown in Figure 6-23, and you are presented with a list of messages in that queue (if appropriate). Note first a similar set of actions in the action pane that will apply only to the message(s) you choose before selecting the appropriate actions link.

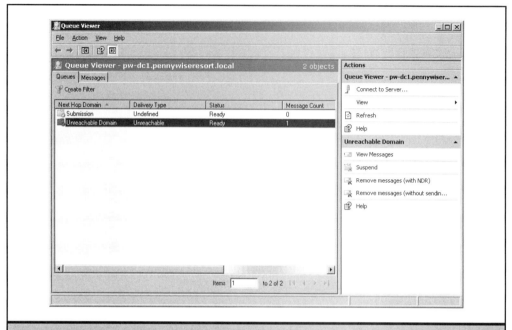

Figure 6-22. Managing queues in the Queue Viewer

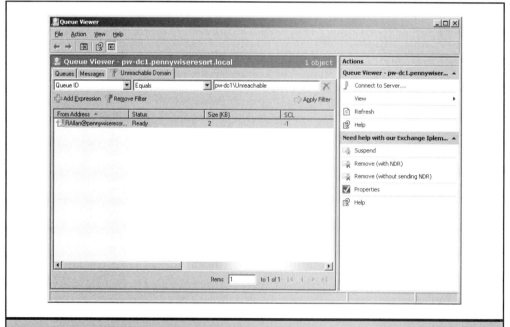

Figure 6-23. Managing messages in a single queue.

Selecting the Properties link in the action pane will show you detailed information on the selected message, including message ID, source IP address, the error causing the message to remain stuck in the queue, e-mail addresses of both the sender and recipient, and more, as shown in Figure 6-24.

The last thing you should notice about queue management is the improved filtering interface, shown in Figure 6-25, which allows you to quickly and easily narrow the focus from hundreds or potentially thousands of messages in a queue to the few or one message of interest. This can be based on 12 different criteria that map to nearly every piece of information presented in the message properties.

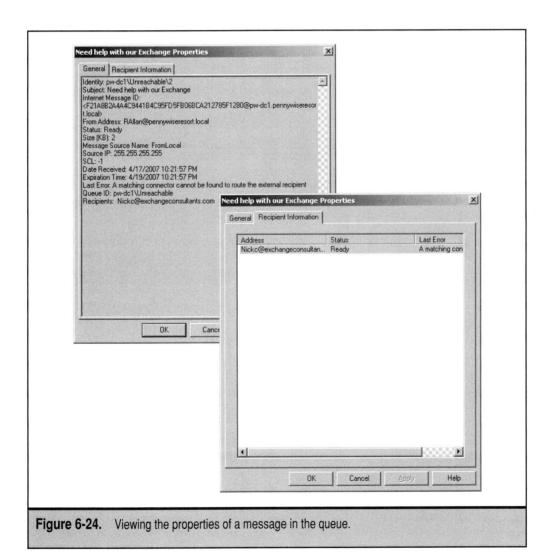

Figure 6-24.   Viewing the properties of a message in the queue.

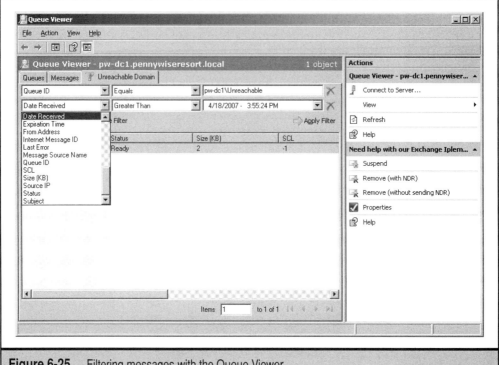

Figure 6-25.   Filtering messages with the Queue Viewer.

SUMMARY

In this chapter, I covered the routing basics of Exchange, discussed the various routing elements, how they all work together, and how to manage them. At this point, you should have a working understanding of how routing works in Exchange, although there is much more detail that you can dive into. You can find more on Microsoft's Web site should you desire to explore this.

In the next chapter, I'll switch gears and cover the newest addition to Exchange: Unified Messaging and then cover Edge Transport-specific features and management in Chapter 9.

CHAPTER 7

Managing Unified Messaging

One of the most prominent feature changes in Exchange 2007 is the inclusion of Unified Messaging services. If you aren't familiar with this concept, take your voice mail system and fax solution and marry it with Exchange. Well, OK, that's oversimplifying it a bit. Let me elaborate. Unified Messaging (UM) in Exchange combines voice mail, faxing, and traditional e-mail messages and provides access to them via your Exchange mailbox. Access to any of these message types is available from Office Outlook, Outlook Web Access (OWA), and mobile devices. Voice and e-mail messages can also be accessed by a new service, Outlook Voice Access (OVA), where voice messages can be played and e-mail messages and calendar items can be read, created, and managed. Using a single storage medium for three different message formats provides you with the ability to reduce the number of servers (no separate fax or voice mail server for storage needed), as well as your backup strategy (you only need to back up your mailbox databases). In this chapter, I'll look at the configuration and utilization of the UM server role.

UM ARCHITECTURE

Before I cover how to install and configure UM, let me first briefly cover how this new functionality fits into the messaging architecture of Exchange by showing the transport and availability of voice and mail messages through a UM server, and then by covering each of the components and concepts surrounding a UM installation. The following illustration shows a basic UM deployment that I will refer to throughout the discussion of the components and concepts behind UM. There are three realms that the UM server needs to play in, which I will use as a way to present the architecture: the worlds of telephony, Active Directory and Exchange.

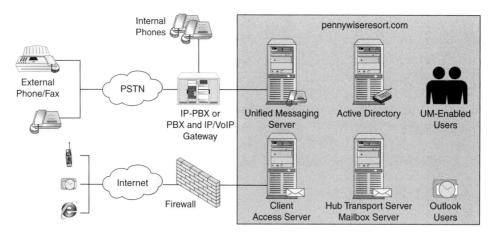

UM and Telephony

The UM server cannot simply live in the world of Exchange, or there is no way for it to receive voice and fax messages, so it will always have one arm grasping your phone system.

Unified Messaging Licensing

Remember that to take advantage of UM services, you will need to purchase a Microsoft Exchange Enterprise Client Access License (CAL) in addition to the Exchange Standard CAL.

In this section, I'll cover the following concepts by discussing how a voice message comes in from outside your office and into Exchange:

▼ Circuit-switched and packet-switched networks

■ Public Branch Exchange (PBX)

■ Voice over the Internet Protocol (VoIP)

■ VoIP gateway

▲ IP-PBX

Circuit-Switched and Packet-Switched Networks

Before a voice message or fax message ever exists within Exchange, it must come from outside Exchange over a traditional phone network. The most common is the public-switched telephone network, or PSTN, which is a circuit-switched network. In a circuit-switched network, a dedicated circuit exists for communication, allowing two nodes (one at each end) to communicate. Another kind of network is a packet-switched network (such as the Internet), which does not establish an end-to-end circuit, but instead breaks the communication into smaller data sets called packets, and each packet is sent to the same destination, but over the best available route. Exchange can communicate with both network types, but requires different hardware to interface with each, as I will explain in the next few sections.

VoIP

VoIP facilitates voice communications to occur across the Internet. It can be software only or combined with a hardware solution. VoIP solutions can communicate directly with Exchange.

PBX

A PBX participates in a circuit-switched network by connecting a limited number of phone lines outside an organization to many individuals within the organization. This allows organizations with potentially dozens or hundreds of internal users to share a few phone lines for both incoming and outgoing calls.

IP/VoIP Gateways

A PBX itself cannot communicate directly with Exchange, as it only connects external phone lines to internal ones. And while a VoIP system can communicate with Exchange, it has no ability to accept inbound calls from regular telephone lines. So the two are brought together by a gateway that allows a legacy PBX to communicate over IP to Exchange (or just a VoIP solution if Exchange wasn't in the picture).

IP-PBX

Not all PBXs are using legacy technology. Today's modern IP-PBXs already join PBX's ability to connect to analog phone lines and a VoIP solution, where internal phones are IP-based.

UM and Active Directory

To process messages appropriately, Exchange doesn't simply connect to a phone system and save a message; it provides an architecture where policies can be established to define the customer experience and ensure that messages are properly routed. Exchange stores a number of new object types in Active Directory to configure exactly how voice and fax messages should be handled. Table 7-1 lists the UM-related Active Directory objects and their purpose.

UM and Exchange

Once Exchange has the ability to receive voice and fax messages via one of the previously mentioned phone solutions, it needs to do something with the message to eventually get it to your inbox and make it available. I'd like to break this section down into two basic areas,

Object	Description
Dial Plan	A logical representation of one or more PBXs (or IP/PBXs) and the extensions hosted on them.
Hunt Group	A logical representation of one or more shared extensions within a PBX or IP/PBX. UM Hunt Groups are used to identify the PBX an incoming call came from.
IP Gateway	A logical container object that represents either an IP/VoIP gateway or an IP/PBX.
Auto Attendant	Represents a recorded set of voice prompts to help callers navigate to the correct extension within the organization.
Messaging User	A UM-enabled mailbox.
Mailbox Policy	A security policy for UM-enabled users that defines settings such as greeting duration, logon failures, and PIN settings.

Table 7-1.   UM-Related Active Directory Objects

first discussing what happens to a message once it enters the Exchange environment to get it to your inbox and then briefly talking about any services required to make that same voice or fax message available to you from a variety of clients. Remember, at this point in the chapter, I'll be covering this from a high level and will dive into detail later in the chapter.

Incoming Messages

To make this simple, think of when you call a colleague at his or her office, and assume with me that your colleague has Exchange's UM as part of their telephone system. When you call them and they are, of course, away from their desk working on some important project, you are forwarded to Exchange so that a message can be recorded. With a PBX, the call would be routed or forwarded to an IP/VoIP gateway and on to the UM server. With an IP-PBX, the call is routed or forwarded directly to the UM server. The Exchange server running the UM server role will route messages to the Hub Transport server, which then routes the message to the appropriate Mailbox server.

TIP   You can read more about how messages are routed within Exchange in Chapter 6.

Accessing Messages from Within Exchange

You can access voice and fax messages from Office Outlook directly from the Mailbox server. Outlook Web Access, Windows Mobile clients, and Office Outlook clients connecting via Outlook Anywhere (formerly known as RPC over HTTP) access voice and fax messages via Client Access servers. Voice messages, along with e-mail, contacts, and calendar items, can be retrieved from OVA by interacting with Exchange via a PBX/IP-PBX.

INSTALLING AND ENABLING UNIFIED MESSAGING

A typical installation of Exchange does not include the Unified Messaging server role, so you'll need to run the Exchange setup on the server that you wish to install the role, and on the Server Role Selection page of the setup wizard, select Unified Messaging Role, as shown in Figure 7-1.

Once installed, you will still need to enable the server role on a per-server basis. This is accomplished within the Exchange Management Console by navigating to the Unified Messaging node under Server Configuration, selecting the server that has the Unified Messaging role installed, and selecting Enable UM Server from the action pane, as shown in Figure 7-2.

TIP   The Unified Messaging service is not started by default. You should restart the server for the service to start correctly.

You can, of course, view the properties of a UM server, but I'll leave this for later in the chapter so that some of the management behind the properties you'll see will make more sense. The remainder of the chapter will be split into three areas of management: UM objects, UM servers, and UM users.

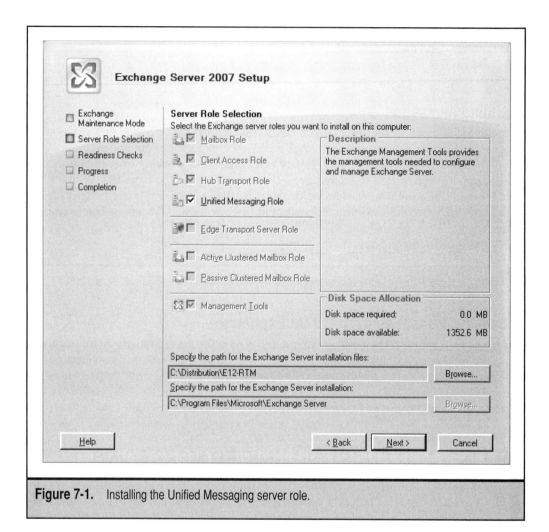

Figure 7-1. Installing the Unified Messaging server role.

Connecting UM to Your Phone System

There are two parts to this process. The first is configuring Exchange to use the IP/VoIP gateway you currently use, and the second is configuring your IP/VoIP gateway to communicate with Exchange. I will show you later in this chapter how to create and configure UM IP gateway objects that represent your IP/VoIP gateway. Configuring your IP/VoIP gateway is not a part of this book, as there are many brands and models of gateways possible. So the best way I can handle this aspect of the process is to refer you to Microsoft's Telephony Advisor Web page found at www.microsoft.com/technet/prodtechnol/exchange/telephony-advisor.mspx.

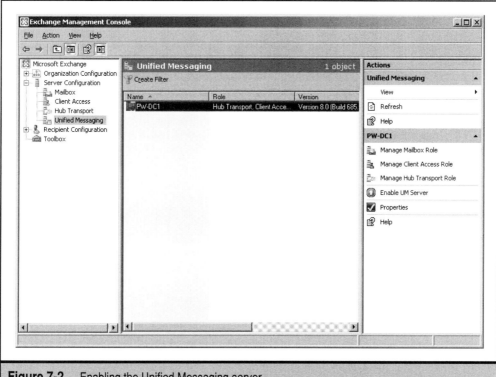

Figure 7-2. Enabling the Unified Messaging server.

MANAGING UM OBJECTS

In order for a UM server to function properly within Exchange, as I described before in the chapter, you will need to define how it will interact with the phone system. Exchange does this through your configuration of the Active Directory objects previously defined in this chapter. The following objects will need to be created and configured:

- ▼ UM Dial Plans
- ■ UM IP Gateways
- ■ UM Hunt Groups
- ■ UM Mailbox Policies
- ▲ UM Auto Attendants

Each of these objects is managed by first navigating in the Exchange Management Console to the Unified Messaging node under Organization Configuration, as shown in Figure 7-3.

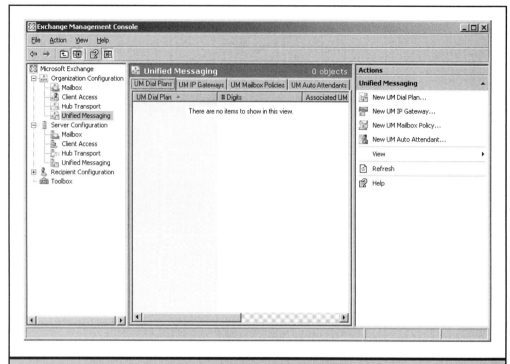

Figure 7-3. UM Active Directory objects are managed together.

Creating and Managing a UM Dial Plan

Creating a UM dial plan is simple: Select the New UM Dial Plan link in the action pane, and complete the four-step wizard, shown in Figure 7-4. After you've provided the name of the object and the number of extension digits used within your PBX, you'll need to address two advanced options: the uniform resource identifier (URI) and the VoIP security model.

The URI field supports three methods of identifying a user: telephone extension ('TelExtn'), E164 phone number addressing ('E164'), and Session Initiation Protocol ('SIP') information, with the last two being new with Exchange 2007 Service Pack 1. The VoIP Security field supports the extensions being unsecured, secured (via some outside method), and SIPSecured, where the SIP-based communication is secured over a transport layer security-encrypted channel.

TIP You can read more about the E164 phone number addressing at www.e164.org.

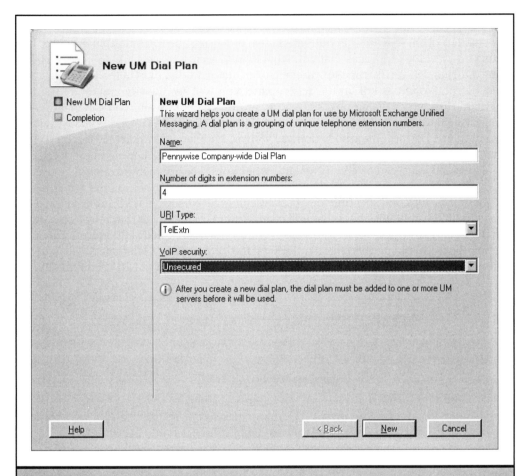

Figure 7-4.   Creating a UM dial plan.

Management Shell Corner

Creating a UM dial plan is accomplished using the new-UMDialPlan cmdlet, like
the following:

```
new-UMDialPlan -Name 'Pennywise Company-wide Dial Plan'
-NumberOfDigitsInExtension '4' -URIType 'TelExtn' -VoIPSecurity
'Unsecured'
```

Existing UM dial plans can be managed from the Exchange Management Shell
using the Set-UMDialPlan cmdlet.

Configuring a UM Dial Plan

The creation of the dial plan is not where any of its real configuration takes place. It is when you view the properties that you will begin to see far more detail than the creation of the dial plan lets on. By choosing the newly created UM dial plan in the work pane and selecting the Properties link in the action pane, you will see the General tab of the UM dial plan's Properties dialog box, shown in Figure 7-5. On this tab, you can view which UM servers and IP gateways are associated with the dial plan (which, initially, will be none until you perform the association), as well as whether a non-delivery receipt (NDR) should be sent to the administrator if message delivery fails, whether members of the dial plan (specified later) can receive faxes, and what VoIP security method should be used.

On the Subscriber Access tab, shown in Figure 7-6, you can configure the .wav file that will play as the welcome greeting for a user reaching the UM system, the informational announcement (an announcement that will change more frequently than the welcome greeting), whether the informational announcement can be interrupted with voice commands or phone keys (this is specified upon modifying the Informational Announcement field), as well as the subscriber access number that will be used to access the UM server via OVA.

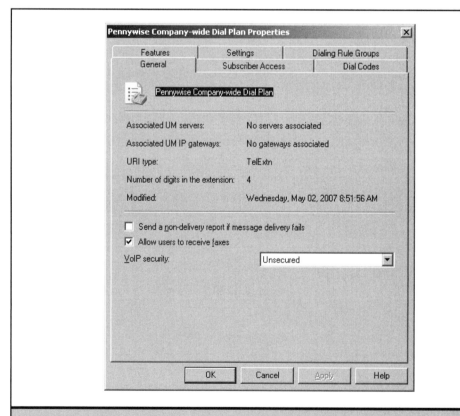

Figure 7-5.   Managing the General Properties tab of a UM dial plan.

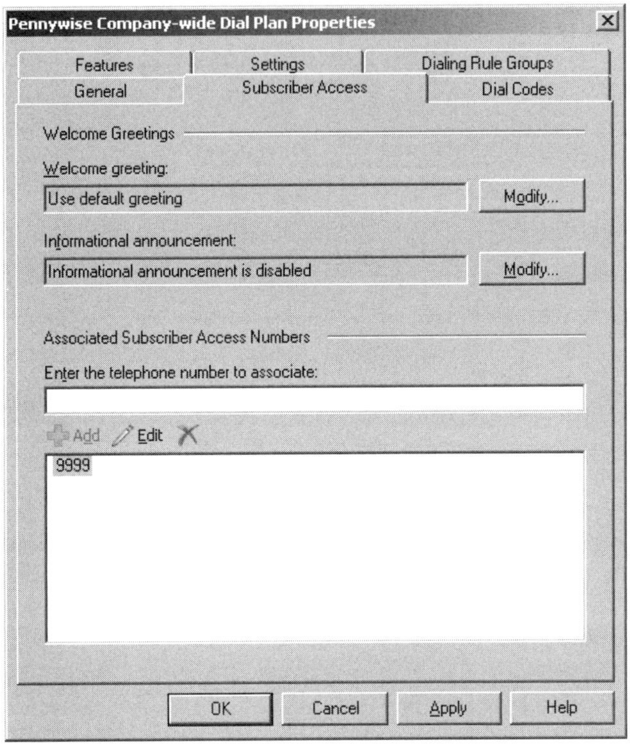

Figure 7-6.   Configuring the Subscriber Access tab of a UM dial plan.

On the Dial Codes tab, you can specify the various incoming and outgoing prefixes and number formats. The Features tab, shown in Figure 7-7, is where you can specify whether users associated with this dial plan when calling in via OVA can transfer calls as well as messages to other users within the dial plan. If one or both of the first two options are selected, the Callers Can Contact options will be available to specify who can

Understanding the Greetings

If you're a little confused about the use of the welcome greeting and the informational announcement, think of them this way: you call Exchange via OVA, and the first thing you hear is, "Welcome to the Pennywise Voice Messaging System," followed by, "The system will be unavailable from Friday at 7 P.M. until Monday at 7 A.M." The welcome greeting would be the first recording, and the informational announcement would be the availability message.

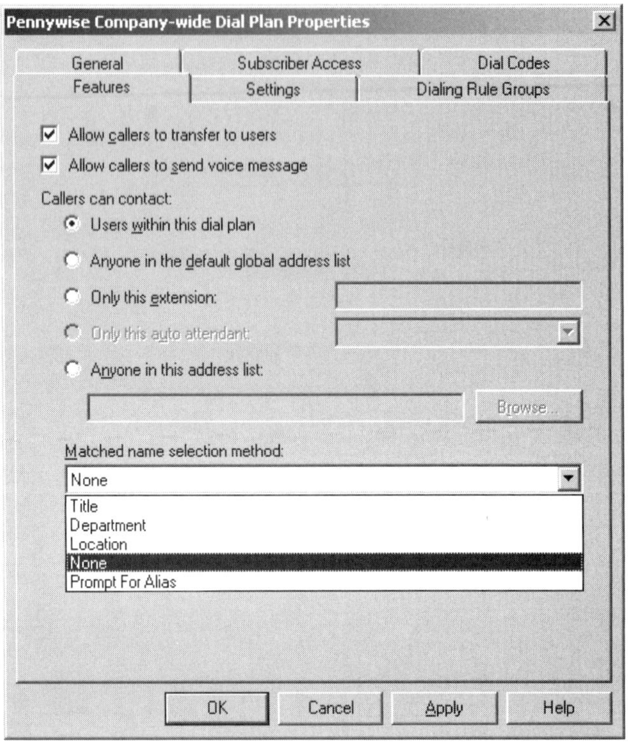

Figure 7-7. Configuring the Features tab of a UM dial plan.

be transferred messages and/or calls. When a caller wants to specify the person to whom they will transfer a call or message, the value specified in the Matched Name field will be listed, should there be more than one John Smith, for example, in an effort to uniquely identify the desired John Smith.

The Settings tab, shown in Figure 7-8, contains quite a number of settings related to finding users within the UM system, call timeouts, and language settings. Table 7-2 lists the various settings you can specify on this tab.

The Dialing Rule Groups tab, shown in Figure 7-9, is for establishing dialing rules when a phone number needs to be modified before it is sent out to the PBX for outbound dialing. For example, if a seven-digit phone number is to be used to reach a user found via a directory search, the local number may require an area code to meet the local 10-digit dialing requirements. So a dialing rule would establish that the seven digits listed (each represented as an "x" wildcard value within the dialing rule) instead be pre-pended with a 9 for outside dialing and the area code. Exchange supports different rules for in-country and international numbers.

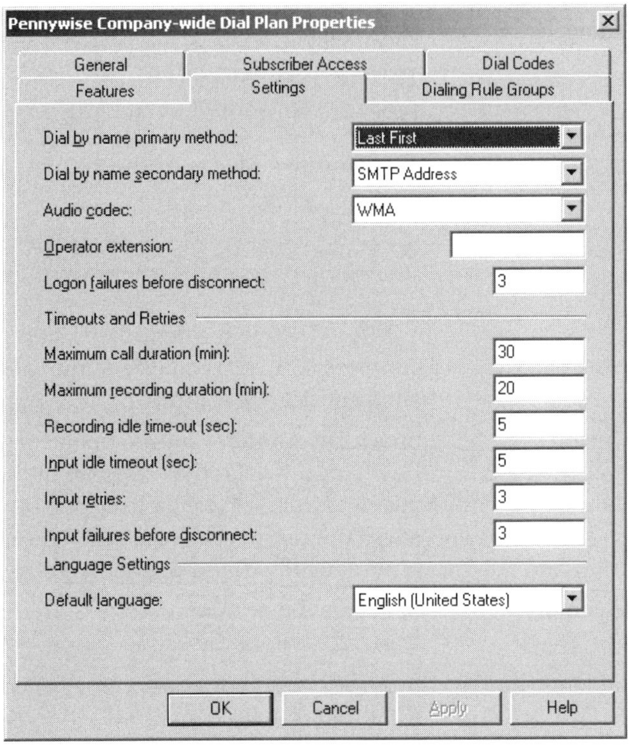

Figure 7-8.   Configuring the Settings tab of a UM dial plan.

UM Dial Plan Setting	Description
Dial By Name Primary Method Dial By Name Secondary Method	These two fields are used to determine what a caller will specify when attempting to locate a specific user. The choices are Last Name, First Name, and SMTP Address.

Table 7-2.   UM Dial Plan Settings

UM Dial Plan Setting	Description
Audio Codec	This field specifies the format of messages. Three types are supported by default: ▼ Windows Media Audio (WMA) ■ Pulse Code Modulation (PCM) ▲ Global System for Mobile Communication (GSM) WMA (which is the default selection) has high compression, high-quality audio, and has the smallest storage footprint.
Operator Extension	Specifies a number for the operator. This can be internal within the dial plan or an external phone number. When a user presses the # key or says "operator" or "reception," the system will automatically dial the specified extension.
Logon Failures Before Disconnect	Specifies the number of logon attempts (between 1 and 20) before the call is ended.
Maximum Call Duration	Specifies how long (between 10 and 120 minutes) a call can remain connected without being transferred to an extension.
Maximum Recording Duration	Specifies how long (between 5 and 100 minutes) a message can be.
Recording Idle Timeout	Specifies the number of seconds of silence (between 2 and 16) that a message can have before the call is ended.
Input Idle Timeout	Specifies the number of seconds (between 3 and 32) the system waits for user input before any voice commands are presented.
Input Retries	Specifies the number of retries (between 1 and 16) the system will allow before a caller is transferred to the operator extension.
Input Failures Before Disconnect	Specifies the number of invalid input attempts before a call is ended.
Default Language	Specifies the language used by callers. Language packs are available from Microsoft.

Table 7-2.   UM Dial Plan Settings *(Continued)*

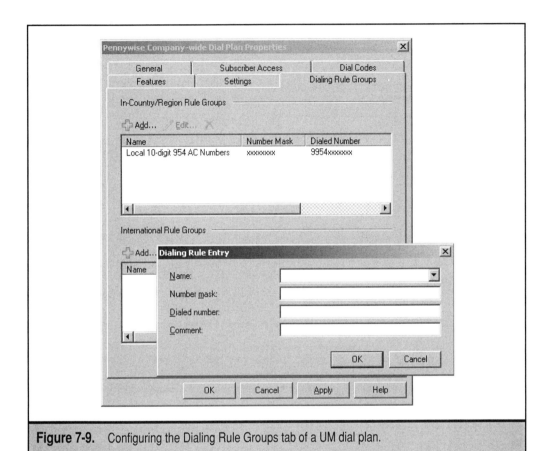

Figure 7-9. Configuring the Dialing Rule Groups tab of a UM dial plan.

Specifying a UM Dial Plan for a UM Server

One of the first things I pointed out when looking at the UM dial plan Properties dialog box was the lack of an associated UM server. Associating a server requires that you navigate to the UM server in question under Server Configuration node, view the properties of the Server object in the work pane, and select the UM Settings tab, shown in Figure 7-10. Here you can choose the UM dial plan, as well as specify the supported prompt language(s) and call concurrency.

Creating and Managing UM IP Gateways

Like the UM dial plan, creating a UM IP gateway is a simple process; with the Unified Messaging node under Organization Configuration selected, choose the New IP Gateway link in the action pane to start the New UM IP Gateway Wizard, shown in Figure 7-11. This wizard creates the logical representation of an actual IP/PBX or an IP gateway. By filling in the name and either IP address of fully qualified domain name (FQDN), such as *ipgtwy.pennywiseresort.com*, and selecting a dial plan to associate the IP gateway with, you can finish the wizard.

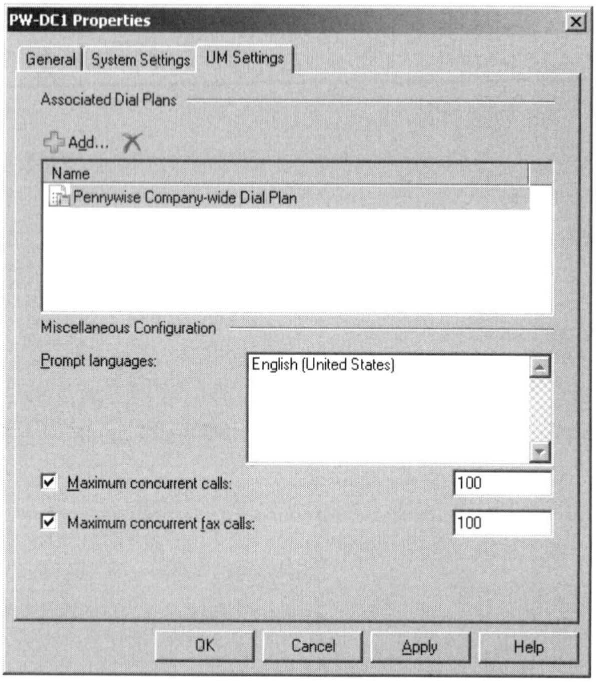

Figure 7-10. Associating a UM dial plan to a UM server.

Once the UM IP gateway is created, you will notice that a default UM hunt group is associated with the UM IP gateway. I'll cover hunt groups in the next section. Before I do, I want to backtrack just a bit to show you the completion of the dial plan's Properties dialog box, where both the UM Server and UM IP Gateway fields are now populated, shown in Figure 7-12.

Management Shell Corner

To create a UM IP gateway, you will use the `new-UMIPGateway` cmdlet like the following:

```
new-UMIPGateway -Name 0Pennywise IP Gateway' -Address '10.1.1.250'
-UMDialPlan 'Pennywise Company-wide Dial Plan'
```

Existing UM IP gateways can be managed from the Exchange Management Shell using the `Set-UMIPGateway` cmdlet.

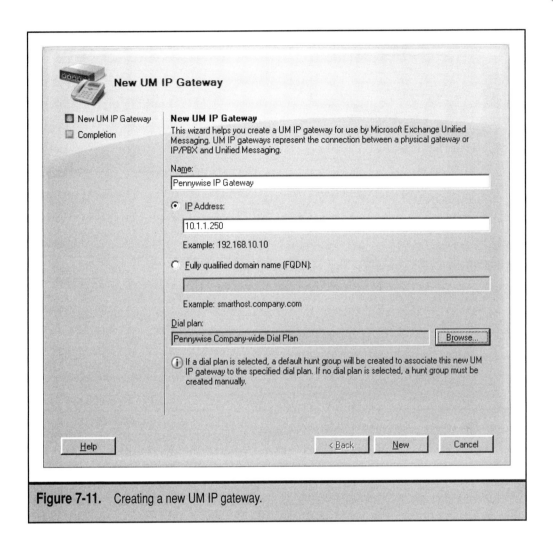

Figure 7-11.   Creating a new UM IP gateway.

Creating and Managing UM Hunt Groups

Remember that a hunt group represents the extensions supported by a given PBX. So when you create a UM IP gateway and a dial plan is selected, a default UM hunt group is created. To properly show you the settings in a UM hunt group, look at the New UM Hunt Group Wizard, shown in Figure 7-13, which is started by selecting the UM IP Gateway link and then New UM Hunt Group in the action pane.

In the wizard, you must specify an object name and associate a UM dial plan and a pilot identifier. A pilot identifier is the phone number (or numbers) associated with the hunt group. Multiple values can be separated by commas. You'll need to get this from those managing your phone system.

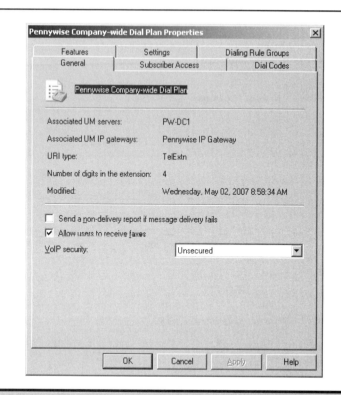

Figure 7-12. A fully associated UM dial plan.

TIP Since there is no way to manage a UM Hunt Group object from either the Exchange Management Console or the Exchange Management Shell, should you need to modify a value, you will need to instead remove and re-create the UM hunt group.

Creating and Managing UM Mailbox Policies

A UM Mailbox policy is created with a single-step wizard that asks you for the name of the object and a dial plan to associate with it. Similar to a default UM hunt group being created

Management Shell Corner

You can create a UM hunt group using the `new-UMHuntGroup` cmdlet, as follows:

```
New-UMHuntGroup -Name 'Pennywise PBX Hunt Group' -PilotIdentifier
9545550127  -UMDialplan 'Pennywise Company-wide Dial Plan' -UMIP-
Gateway 'Pennywise IP Gateway'
```

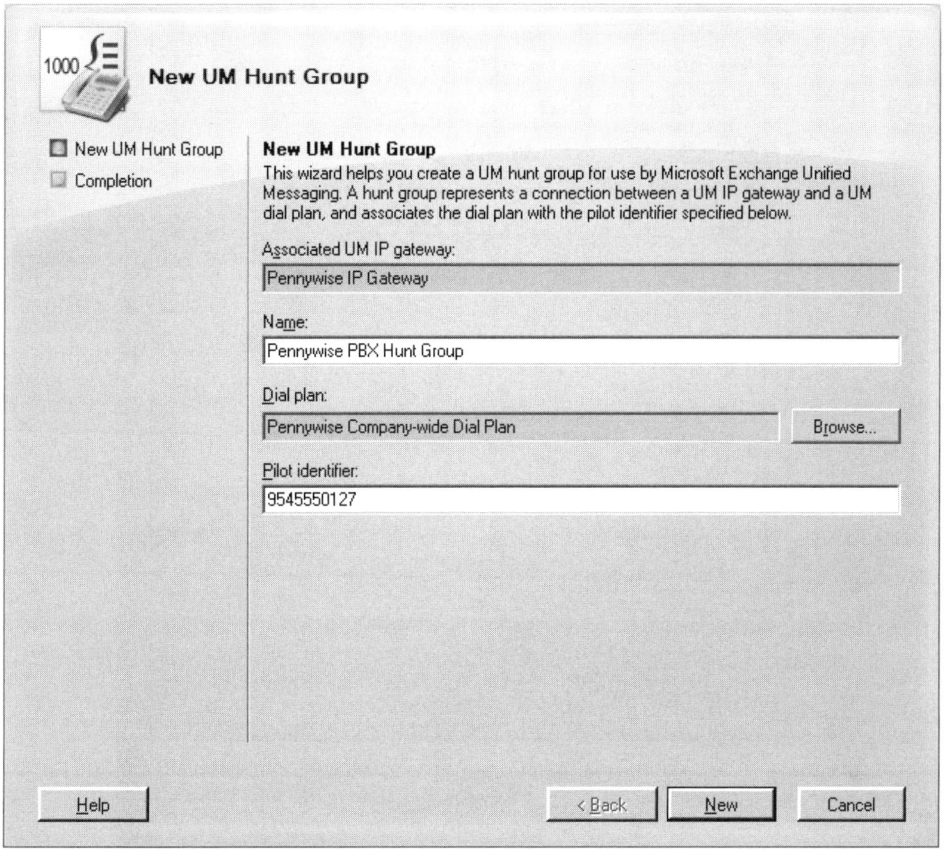

Figure 7-13. Creating a new UM hunt group.

when you create a UM IP gateway, when you create the first UM dial plan, Exchange creates a default UM Mailbox policy, found on the UM Mailbox Policies tab in the results pane of the Exchange Management Console. By viewing the Properties dialog box of the policy object, as shown in Figure 7-14, you can see the settings that are available for configuration.

The General tab lists the associated dial plan and allows you to set the maximum amount of time a user's greeting can last, with the maximum being 10 minutes, and whether Exchange should send the user a notification e-mail that a call was received. On the Message Text tab, you can specify the text that should be included in several different notification e-mails. While no text exists in the fields, Exchange does have default message content for all listed messages. If you provide text here, it will replace the default message settings.

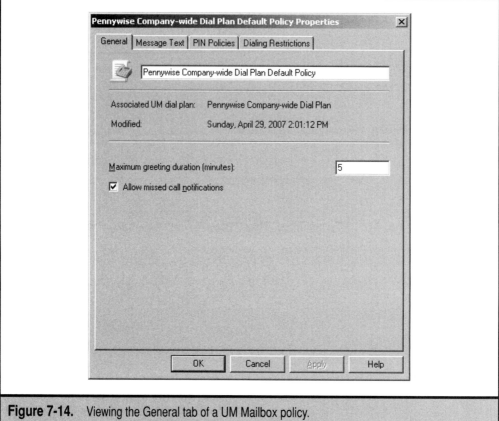

Figure 7-14. Viewing the General tab of a UM Mailbox policy.

On the PIN Policies tab, shown in Figure 7-15, you can modify the PIN settings for users associated with this Mailbox policy. While most of these settings are self-explanatory, let me address the last three. The Allow Common Patterns In PIN option, when selected, disallows the following PIN patterns:

▼ Sequential numbers (e.g.: '1234' or even '12')

■ Repeated Numbers (e.g.: '1111' or even '11')

▲ Use of the extension as a PIN suffix (e.g. using '13544' when your extension is '3544')

The two fields within the Failed Logons section are easy enough to understand, but I would like to address some specifics on values and the impact of the settings. Both address what happens when you continually use an incorrect password. With the first setting, where the PIN is reset, you can specify a value of zero to disable the resetting of PINs and the locking out of UM mailboxes. You can establish a value of up to 999 attempts (although this is not recommended, as it gives way to malicious attempts to access your UM mailbox). The second setting, where the UM mailbox is disabled, must be a value

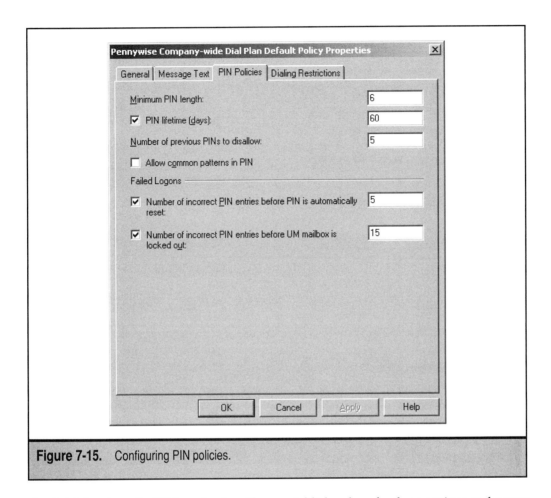

Figure 7-15.   Configuring PIN policies.

that is higher than the PIN reset value. If you establish values for these settings and a user reaches one or both of the maximum numbers of incorrect attempts, you will need to reset the PIN and/or unlock the UM mailbox manually within the Exchange Management Console (available under Recipient Configuration for a UM-enabled recipient—more on this later in the chapter).

On the Dialing Restrictions tab, shown in Figure 7-16, you can configure which numbers UM users are able to dial, whether they should be internal (as in the case of users within the same dial plan or internal extensions, regardless of dial plan), or external (as in the case of regional/national numbers or international numbers). The last two fields are selected from the associated UM dial plan. This allows you to use a single UM dial plan for multiple UM Mailbox policies, but have each UM Mailbox policy have its own set of acceptable numbers to be called.

Creating and Managing UM Auto Attendants

Like the other UM objects, the process to create a UM auto attendant is simple. A single-step wizard, shown in Figure 7-17, requires the object name and associated dial plan to

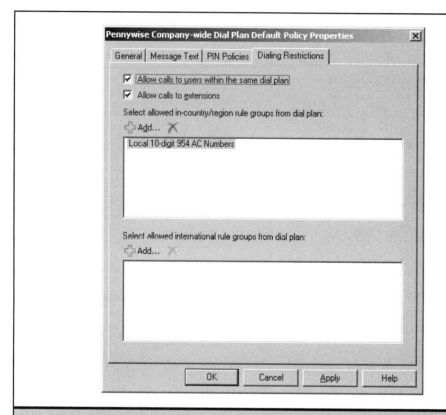

Figure 7-16. Configuring dialing restrictions based on dial plan values.

be created. You can optionally add an extension to reach this attendant (although none is needed, as in the case of the initial attendant users will hear), as well as choose to immediately enable the attendant and/or make it speech-enabled.

Management Shell Corner

You can create a UM Mailbox policy using the `New-UMMailboxPolicy` cmdlet, as follows:

```
New-UMMailboxPolicy -Name 'Pennywise Default Mailbox Policy'
-UMDialPlan 'Pennywise Company-wide Dial Plan'
```

You can modify an existing UM Mailbox policy using the `Set-UMMailboxPolicy` cmdlet.

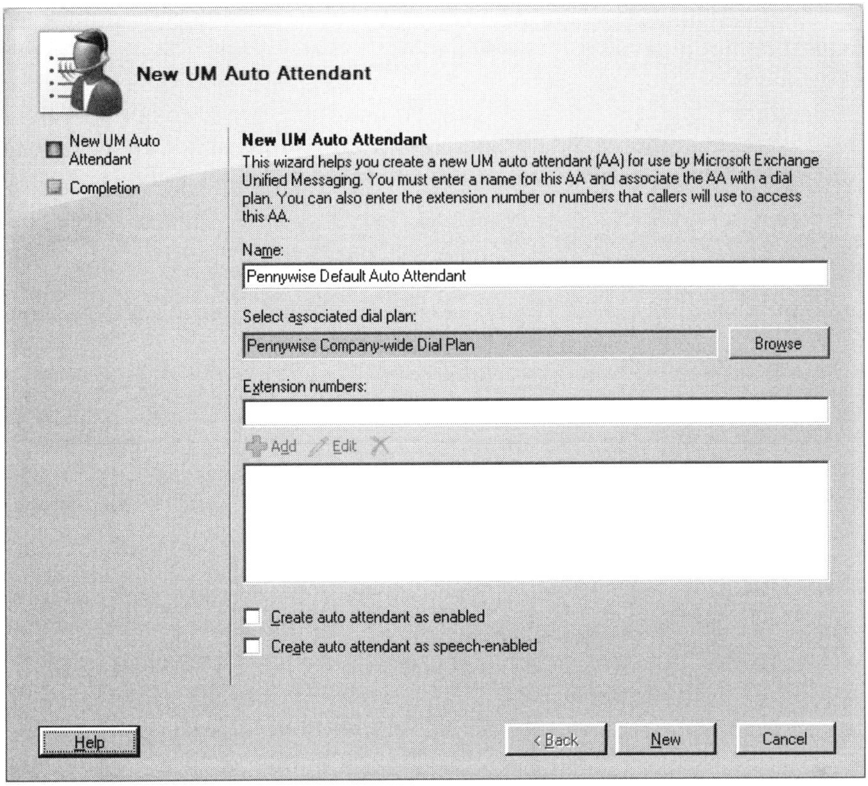

New UM Auto Attendant

- New UM Auto Attendant
- Completion

New UM Auto Attendant

This wizard helps you create a new UM auto attendant (AA) for use by Microsoft Exchange Unified Messaging. You must enter a name for this AA and associate the AA with a dial plan. You can also enter the extension number or numbers that callers will use to access this AA.

Name:

Pennywise Default Auto Attendant

Select associated dial plan:

Pennywise Company-wide Dial Plan   [Browse]

Extension numbers:

[   ]

[Add] [Edit] [X]

[ ] Create auto attendant as enabled
[ ] Create auto attendant as speech-enabled

[Help]   [< Back] [New] [Cancel]

Figure 7-17.   Creating a new UM auto attendant.

TIP   To make an auto attendant speech-enabled, you must also install the appropriate UM language pack that contains Automatic Speech Recognition (ASR) support, as well as configure the properties of the auto attendant to use this language (which I'll cover next). You can add a language pack by running Exchange setup from a command prompt using the /AddUmLanguagePack switch.

Management Shell Corner

To create a new UM auto attendant, use the new-UMAutoAttendant cmdlet, as follows:

```
new-UMAutoAttendant -Name 'Pennywise Default Auto Attendant'
-UMDialPlan 'Pennywise Company-wide Dial Plan' -PilotIdentifierList
-Status 'Disabled' -SpeechEnabled $false
```

with the configuration of the UM auto attendant being done using the set-UMAutoAttendant cmdlet.

Once created, you can view the properties (where most of the configuration actually takes place) by selecting the Auto Attendant object and choosing Properties from the action pane. On the General tab, shown in Figure 7-18, you can reconfigure the settings allowed during the creation of the auto attendant, as well as specify a fallback auto attendant (one that is not speech-enabled) to be used in the event your speech-enabled auto attendant cannot understand the speech commands of a user. With the fallback auto attendant in place, the user can at least navigate using phone key presses.

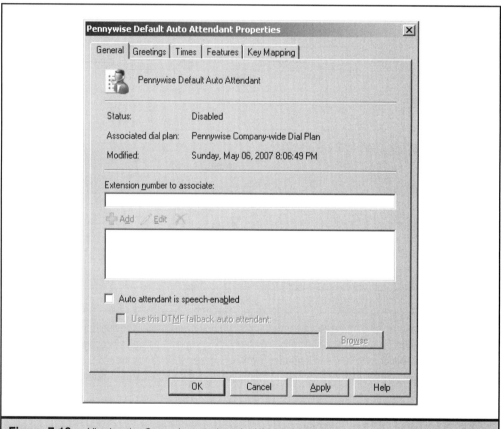

Figure 7-18.   Viewing the General properties of a UM auto attendant.

The Greetings tab, shown in Figure 7-19, is where you will configure the .wav files that should be played for the user to both greet them and provide menu choices. The default greetings are rather bland (for example, the default greeting the dialog box refers to simply says, "Welcome to the Exchange auto attendant"), so you will want to create your own customized greeting that includes your company name, etc.

To define when the specified greetings and menu prompts should be played, the Times tab (shown in Figure 7-20) defines when "business hours" are, as well as when holidays require a separate greeting to inform of special hours of operation, etc.

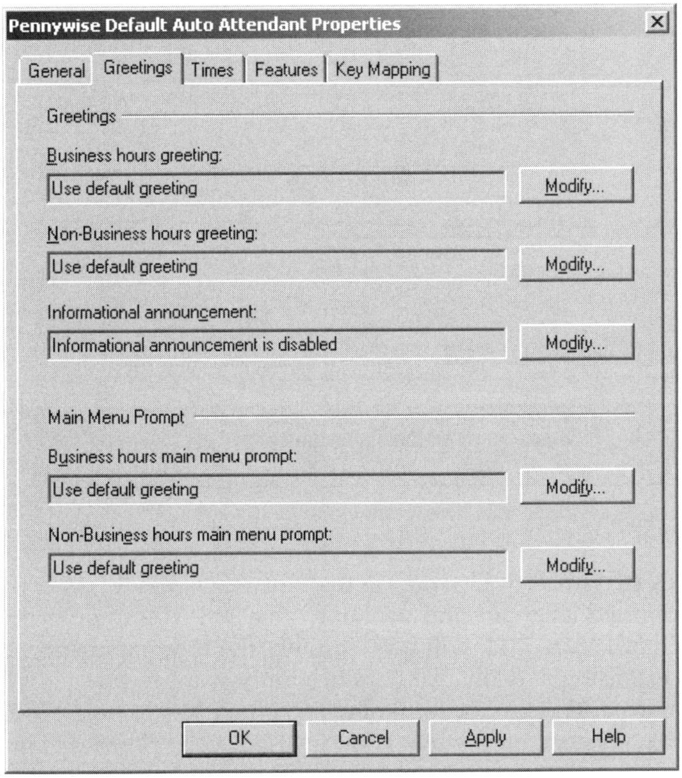

Figure 7-19.   Auto attendant greetings can be customized.

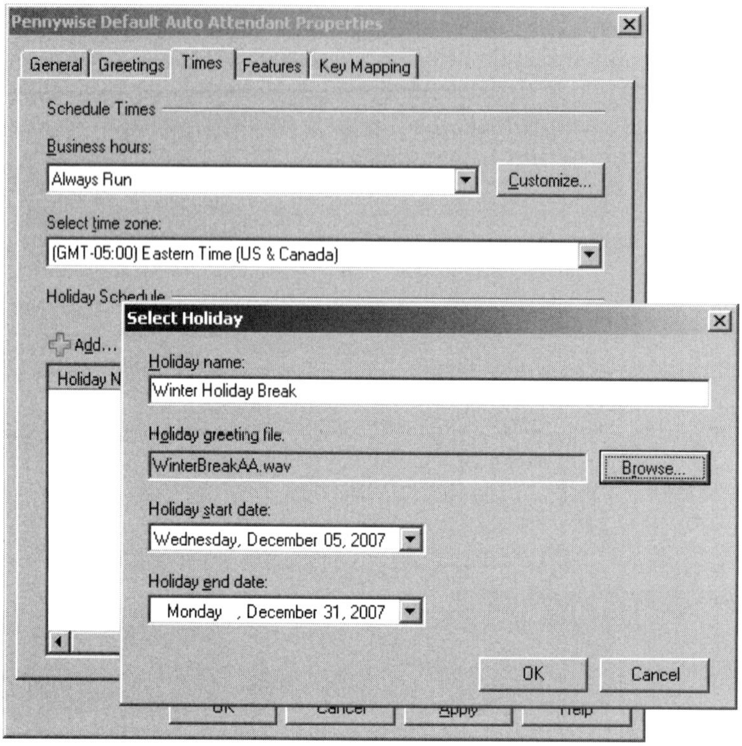

Figure 7-20. Define business hours on the Times tab.

The Features tab is nearly identical to the Features tab in a UM dial plan, with the addition of supported language and operator extension. The settings on the Key Mapping tab, shown in Figure 7-21, will help simplify the user experience. For example, if the operator's extension is really 5000, users simply want to press '0.' This tab allows the desired user experience (in the form of which phone key to press) to line up with the needs of the phone system. Notice that you can also specify phrases to invoke an action, as well as appropriate responses, such as .wav files to play, extension transfers, or running subsequent auto attendants.

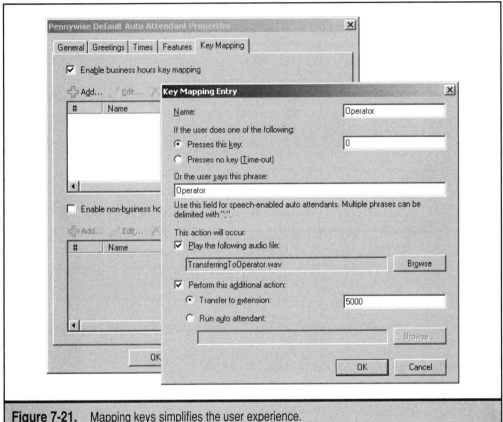

Figure 7-21.   Mapping keys simplifies the user experience.

MANAGING UM USERS

Once your Exchange environment is configured to support UM, you still need to establish which users are to be utilizing it and how they should be configured.

Enabling and Configuring a Mailbox

By default, no users are configured to use UM services, so you'll need to first enable the mailbox in question by navigating to the Mailbox node under Recipient Configuration in the console tree within the Exchange Management Console. This starts the Enable Unified Messaging Wizard, shown in Figure 7-22.

On the Introduction page of the wizard, you'll first need to select a Mailbox policy to establish which PIN policies and dialing restrictions apply to the selected user, and for the PIN generation for the mailbox.

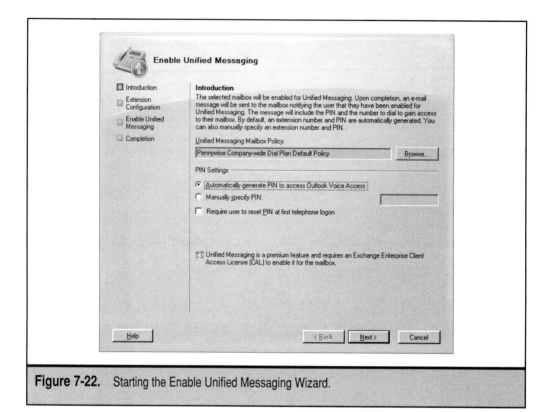

Figure 7-22. Starting the Enable Unified Messaging Wizard.

TIP While you appear to be selecting a Mailbox policy, because there is a one-to-one relationship between UM dial plans and UM Mailbox policies, Exchange has you actually select a UM dial plan—this is key for the next step in the wizard.

Clicking Next reveals the Extension Configuration page of the wizard, shown in Figure 7-23, where you specify the mailbox extension and, if appropriate, the SIP resource identifier, which is available with Exchange 2007 SP1 (this defaults to the mailbox's SMTP e-mail address). Clicking the Next and Finish buttons will complete the wizard.

Management Shell Corner

You can UM-enable a mailbox using the `Enable-UMMailbox cmdlet`, as follows:

```
Enable-UMMailbox –Identity 'pennywiseresort.local/Users/Ryan Allan'
-PinExpired $false -UMMailboxPolicy 'Pennywise Company-wide Dial
Plan Default Policy' -Extensions '5235' -IgnoreDefaultScope $false
```

You'll modify the UM-enabled mailbox using the `Set-UMMailbox cmdlet`.

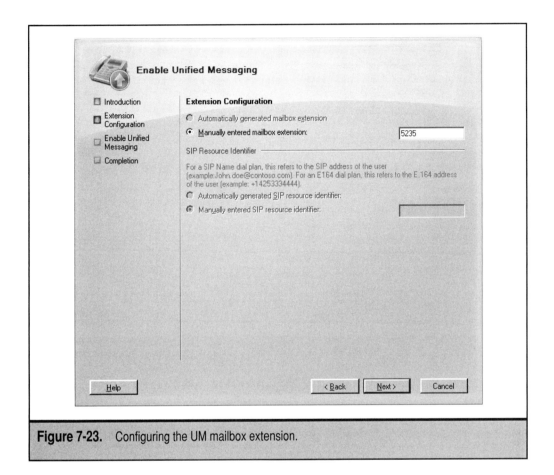

Figure 7-23. Configuring the UM mailbox extension.

TIP You'll only be able to configure the SIP Resource Identifier section if the associated UM dial plan (see my last tip) has the URI Type value set to SipName.

When you view the properties of the newly UM-enabled mailbox, it will not appear at first that anything has changed; the same number of tabs exist, and it is difficult to see what's different. It's not until you select the Mailbox Features tab and view the Properties dialog box of the enabled UM feature, shown in Figure 7-24, that you can now see where you can modify the UM settings for the mailbox.

A few of the settings are self-explanatory, but some of them need explaining. The Lockout Status is determined by the PIN policy and whether a user attempts to access the UM services via OVA and uses the incorrect PIN. If the Enable For Automatic Speech Recognition checkbox is cleared, the mailbox user will need to use the phone keypad to enter their PIN, choices, etc. If you want to enforce that all messages left for users are done so by a caller with Caller ID enabled, you will want to clear the Allow Diverted Calls Without A Caller ID To Leave A Message check box. Lastly, the Personal Operator

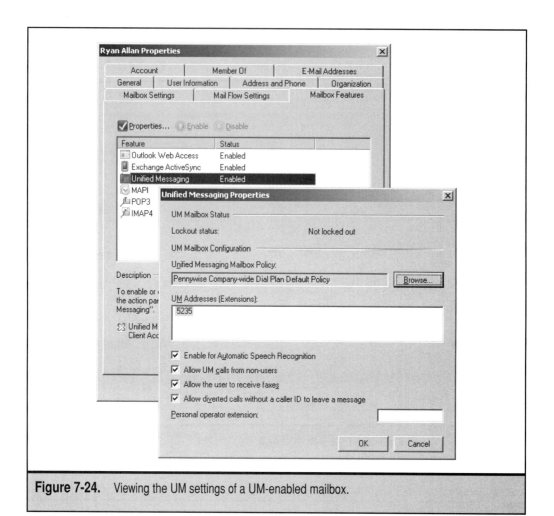

Figure 7-24. Viewing the UM settings of a UM-enabled mailbox.

Extension isn't what you think—it has nothing to do with the company operator; this setting defines the internal extension that all calls to the UM user will be forwarded to. A good use-case for this setting is someone on maternity leave; there is no point in taking weeks of messages (the mailbox size restrictions probably wouldn't allow it anyway), so instead all calls are forwarded to a secondary extension.

SUMMARY

In this chapter, I've discussed the basic architecture behind Exchange's new UM services, as well as the processes to install and configure them. In the next chapter, I'll continue the management of the server roles by covering Client Access servers.

CHAPTER 8

Managing Client Access Servers

Microsoft has always wanted Exchange to be the "anytime, anywhere, any client" messaging platform, and with each release they have taken great strides to make it so. In Exchange 2007, messaging information is available through such a variety of devices with improved accessibility and functionality, that with the current version, I believe it is safe to say that Exchange is at an all-time peak in accessibility.

In this chapter, I will focus on the Client Access server role, which is responsible for providing access to Exchange data for every client possible. I will cover the server-side aspects of four key elements of the Client Access role: Outlook Web Access, ActiveSync, POP3/IMAP4, and Outlook Anywhere. Afterwards, I will cover two new services in Exchange 2007: the Autodiscover service and the Availability service. The client-side configurations that correspond to each of the topics discussed in this chapter are covered in Chapters 10 and 11.

NOTE   Not all of the Client Access administration you will need to do will be accomplished within the Exchange Management Console; you may need to find yourself within the Exchange Management Shell, the Internet Information Services (IIS) Manager, or even the registry. When appropriate, I'll cover the Exchange-specific tasks you will need to accomplish with each of these solutions.

CONFIGURING OUTLOOK WEB ACCESS

When using Outlook Web Access (OWA), it seems rather simple: open a Web browser, put in the Uniform Resource Locator (URL), log on, and get your mail. But on the server side, while Exchange does a great job in setting up an initial environment that works well, there are so many aspects of OWA that you can modify. On the server side, you can do the following:

▼ Manage OWA-related virtual directories

▲ Manage authentication

To improve the client experience, you can do the following:

▼ Manage attachment handling

■ Disable Web beacons

▲ Configure OWA features

Each of these directories can be managed from within the Exchange Management Shell, the Exchange Management Console, or IIS Manager, with varying capabilities.

Managing Virtual Directories

When the Client Access role is installed on a server, Exchange automatically creates several virtual directories in the default WEB site within IIS to facilitate access to OWA. Table 8-1 lists the directories and describes the purpose of each.

Virtual Directory	Description
/owa	Used to access mailboxes on an Exchange 2007 server
/exchange	Used to access mailboxes on an Exchange 2000/2003 server when in a mixed environment
/public	Used to access public folders that exist on an Exchange 2000/2003 server only
/exchweb	Stores additional graphics and files used by OWA
/exadmin	Used to manage public folders

Table 8-1.   Default Virtual Directories

To manage virtual directories within the Exchange Management Console, you will navigate to the Client Access node under Server Configuration in the console tree, as shown in Figure 8-1. Here, you will modify settings that will affect the user experience. I'll cover these specific settings later in this chapter.

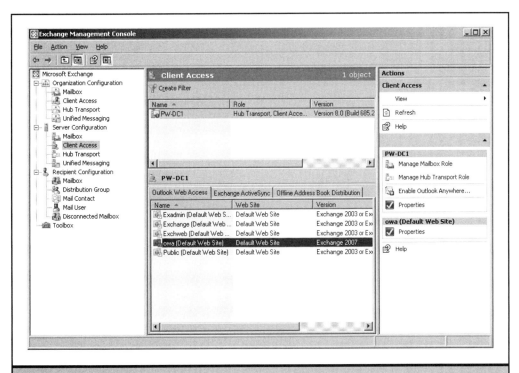

Figure 8-1.   Manage virtual directories within the Exchange Management Console.

Creating a New Virtual Directory

At first glance, you may not see the need to create an additional virtual directory; after all, all the virtual directories that you need are already created, right? Well, not exactly. You may want to create separate OWA experiences for different sets of users within your organization. (This is possible by limiting access to a virtual directory with IIS permissions and restricting certain OWA features through a feature you'll see later in this chapter called *segmentation*.) So if you need to create a new virtual directory, you will do so in the Exchange Management Shell by running the *New-OwaVirtualDirectory* command.

To manage virtual directories within the IIS Manager, you will navigate to Default Web Sites under Web Sites, as shown in Figure 8-2. Here, you will modify the settings that pertain to how IIS will handle access to OWA. This includes security settings, such as Secure Socket Layer (SSL) connection settings, and Internet Protocol (IP) address restrictions.

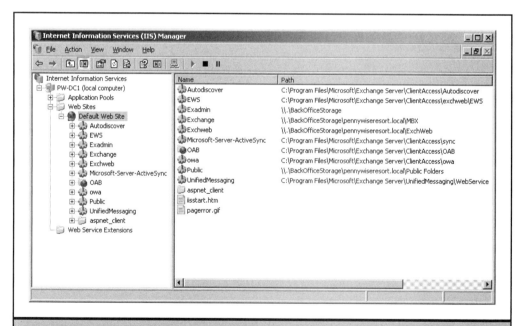

Figure 8-2. Manage virtual directories within the IIS Manager.

Let's dig a bit deeper and look at some of the settings you can manage within a virtual directory to customize the user experience within OWA.

Managing Authentication

The first experience the user has with OWA is the need to log on. By default, your user name and password are sent across the network (or Internet) unencrypted, as shown on the Properties dialog box for the virtual directory within the Exchange Management Console (see Figure 8-3). You can support additional authentication methods (or change to an alternate method). Integrated Windows Authentication will take the user's current user name and password and automatically pass it through to Exchange. This presumes that you are currently logged on as a domain user, which probably won't be the case when using OWA across the Internet. Digest authentication adds an extra layer of security by passing your password across as a hash value. Figure 8-4 shows the rather drab user experience.

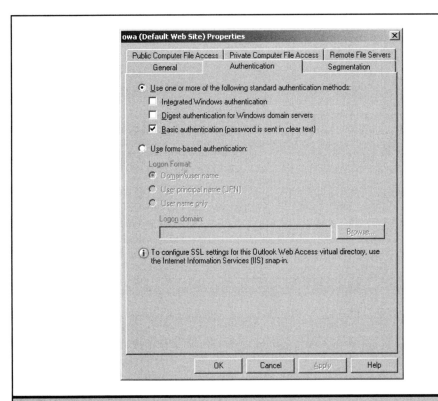

Figure 8-3.   Authentication settings for a virtual directory.

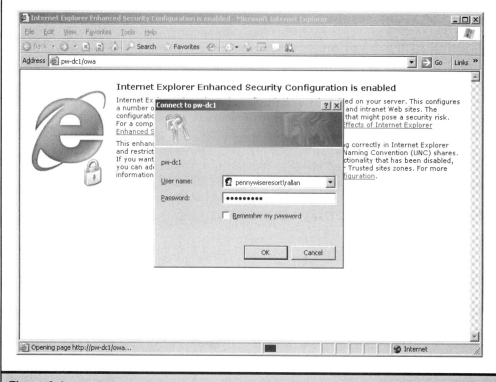

Figure 8-4. Logging on to OWA using standard authentication methods.

Forms-based authentication provides a much more inviting experience, where the OWA user can log on using an authentication Web page and provide as little as their user name (no domain name needs to be specified) and password to log on. Figure 8-5 shows the forms-based authentication settings, and Figure 8-6 shows the resulting OWA experience.

Using SSL

The assumption with all authentication settings from within the Exchange Management Console is that you will set up an SSL connection to secure the data over in the IIS Manager. If you do not implement an SSL connection for OWA traffic, anyone that can intercept the Web traffic (which is not so easy to do) and has a protocol analyzer can literally read the user name and password in clear text. If you configure OWA to use forms-based authentication, Exchange will automatically self-sign a secure sockets layer (SSL) certificate. You can find out how to establish SSL in the section titled 'Installing an SSL certificate' later in this chapter.

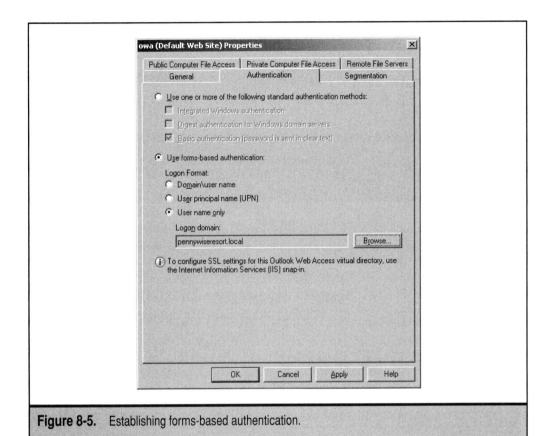

Figure 8-5. Establishing forms-based authentication.

Managing Attachment Handling

One of the new advancements in OWA with Exchange 2007 is comprehensive management of attachments and user access to them. Exchange 2007 separates the configuration of how users access attachments by whether the client computer is specified as a *public* or *private* computer (accomplished with forms-based authentication on the initial logon page). Figure 8-7 shows the configuration of the public computer settings (the interface is identical for private). Here, you can manage the attachment types users can access and view.

The Direct File Access section determines which attachments can be accessed (opened, saved, etc). Clicking the Customize button displays the Direct File Access Settings dialog box (shown in Figure 8-8), where you can determine which attachments can be accessed, which are always blocked, which can only be saved to the local computer, and what to do with unknown file types.

The Allow, Block, and Force Save buttons each display the dialog box shown in Figure 8-9, although each dialog box maintains its own settings. Here, you can specify based on extension or Multipurpose Internet Mail Extensions (MIME) types. Remember, you'll separately edit these settings for the attachments you wish to allow access to, block access to, and force the saving of.

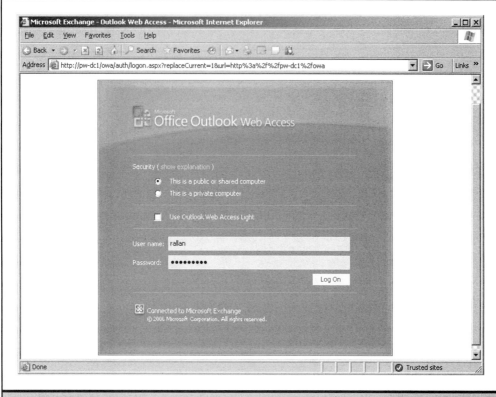

Figure 8-6.   Logging on to OWA using forms-based authentication.

In addition, since there are obviously so many extension possibilities that you may not identify one and how it should be handled, you can specify what OWA should do when encountering such an attachment using the drop-down list in the Unknown Files section of the Manage Direct File Access Settings dialog box, shown previously in Figure 8-8.

Management Shell Corner

To modify direct file access settings for the OWA virtual directory I've been showing you in this chapter, you would use the following commands:

```
Set-OwaVirtualDirectory -Identity 'Owa (Default Web Site)' -AllowedFileTypes
<extension list> -AllowedMimeTypes <mime type list>
Set-OwaVirtualDirectory -Identity 'Owa (Default Web Site)' -BlockedFileTypes
<extension list> -BlockedMimeTypes <mime type list>
Set-OwaVirtualDirectory -Identity 'Owa (Default Web Site)' -ForceSaveFileTypes
<extension list> -ForceSaveMimeTypes <mime type list>
```

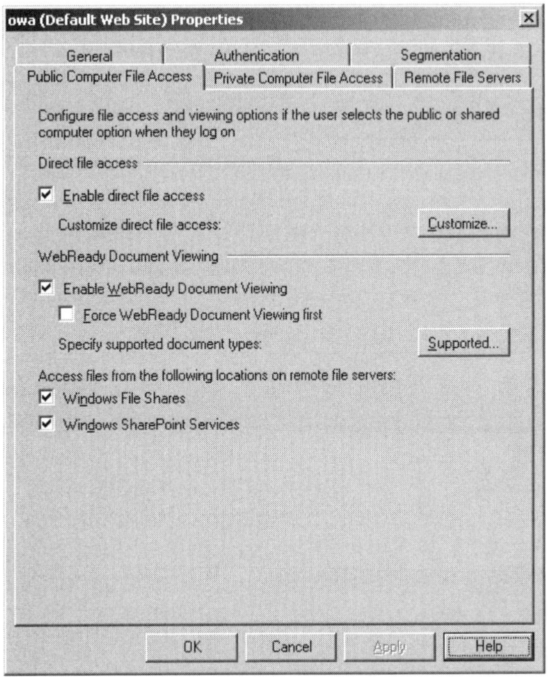

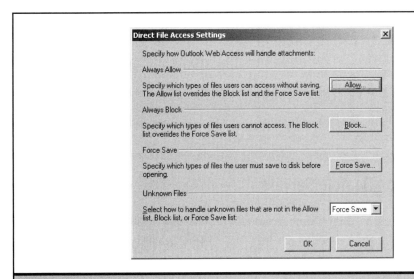

Figure 8-7. Public computer file access settings.

Figure 8-8. Managing direct file access settings.

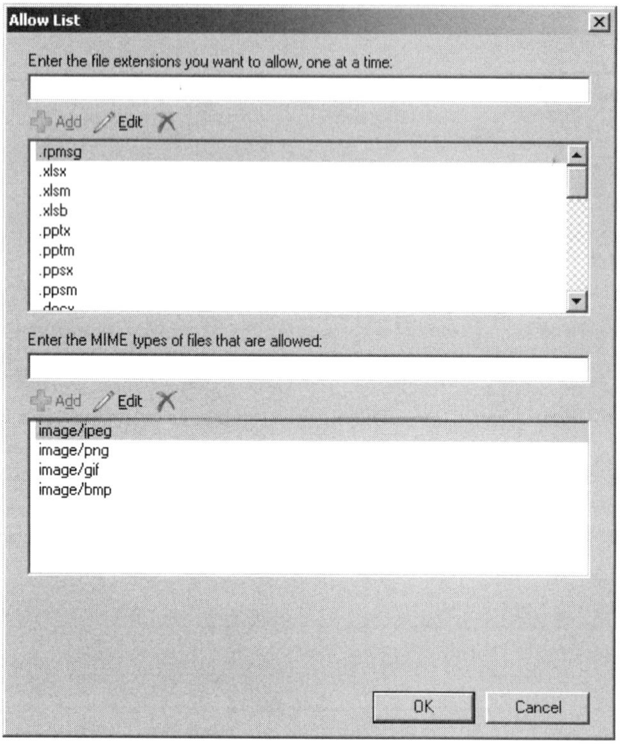

Figure 8-9.   Specify attachment extensions and MIME types to allow access to.

In addition to establishing settings for which files can be access directly, OWA provides the ability to open certain file types without the need to install the normally appropriate client application. This feature is known as *WebReadyDocument Viewing* (or *transcoding* in geek speak). By default, the list of documents is short (Word, Excel, PowerPoint, and Adobe PDF). This list, shown in Figure 8-10, can be edited by clicking the Supported button on the virtual directory Properties dialog box (shown previously in Figure 8-7).

Accessing Files on Remote Servers

Lastly, Exchange now supports access from within OWA directly to data stored on either Windows file shares or on a SharePoint server (also called link access). You can configure OWA to allow data access from either of these sources, shown previously in Figure 8-7.

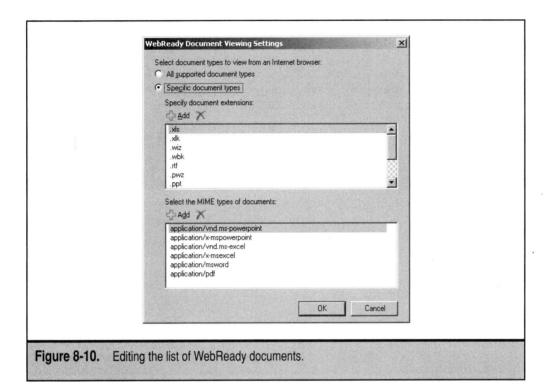

Figure 8-10.   Editing the list of WebReady documents.

On the Remote File Servers tab of the virtual directory's Properties dialog box (see Figure 8-11), you can specify the names of servers that you can allow and/or block access to.

TIP   Accessing internal servers from within OWA poses a security risk. To maintain a secure environment, the Unknown Servers section should be configured to block access so that only servers listed in the Allow List are accessible externally via OWA.

Configuring OWA Features

You may want to restrict the user experience within OWA so that certain features are disabled. For example, for security reasons, you may not want to allow users to change their password from OWA for fear that the computer they are on may have a keystroke logger application running. On the Segmentation tab, shown in Figure 8-12, you can enable or disable nearly all the features of OWA.

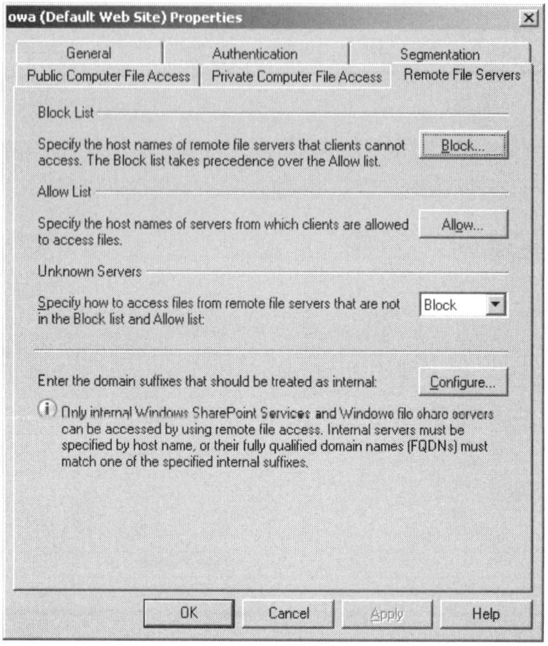

Figure 8-11.   Configure remote servers to be accessed from OWA.

Disabling Web Beacons

Outlook has long provided the security feature of blocking the automatic download of graphics and other Web content from external servers. Exchange 2007 supports configuring this for OWA clients. Individual clients can configure this from within their OWA session (more on this in Chapter 11), or Web beacons can be configured universally from with the Exchange Management Shell. To enable or disable Web beacons, use the following command:

```
Set-OwaVirtualDirectory -identity "Owa (Default Web Site)" -
FilterWebBeaconsAndHtmlForms <setting>
```

The settings you can use when configuring Web beacons are:

▼ **ForceFilter**   This setting causes OWA to block all Web beacons.

■ **DisableFilter**   This setting causes OWA to allow all Web beacons.

▲ **UserFilterChoice**   This setting causes OWA to prompt the user to allow or block Web beacons.

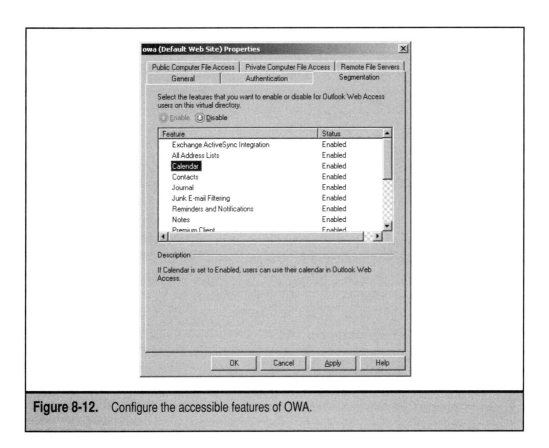

Figure 8-12. Configure the accessible features of OWA.

Disabling User Access to OWA

By default, all users have OWA enabled. You can verify and/or modify this by looking at the Mailbox Features tab within the properties of a user mailbox, as shown in Figure 8-13.

CONFIGURING ACTIVESYNC

ActiveSync has been around since the now-defunct Mobile Information Server (MIS), when the functionality was moved into Exchange 2003. The basic idea of ActiveSync is to provide access to Exchange information via a secure Web connection to Exchange using a push technology that automatically updates client messages, schedules, contacts, and tasks. Synchronization of data entered on the mobile device also works back to the Exchange server in some cases. The Client Access server utilizes the same Web services as OWA to allow Windows mobile devices (or other devices supporting the Exchange Active-Sync protocol) to access Exchange mailboxes, calendar information, address books, and more. In Exchange 2003, ActiveSync was moved from MIS into Exchange and given some slight enhancements. However, in Exchange 2007, significant strides have been taken to

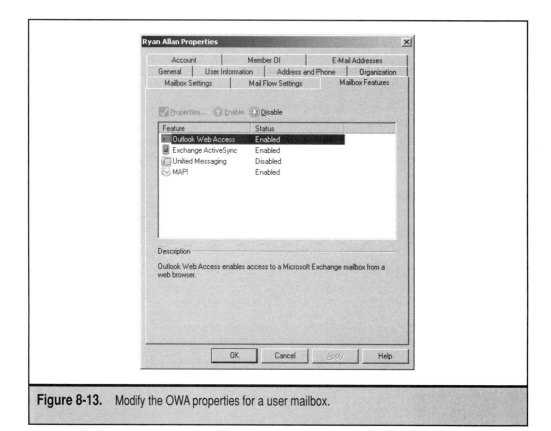

Figure 8-13. Modify the OWA properties for a user mailbox.

make mobile devices a truly viable option as a primary Exchange client for mobile users. Table 8-2 lists some of the enhancements found in Exchange 2007's ActiveSync.

Most of these features will require a device running Windows Mobile version 5.0 (code-named "Crossbow").

On the server side, Exchange 2007 has limited amount of ActiveSync configuration capabilities available, and is generally properly configured to facilitate connections from mobile devices. Figure 8-14 displays the ActiveSync virtual directory within the IIS Manager where you can manage the normal settings usually associated with a virtual directory within IIS. The Exchange-specific settings are all managed within the Exchange Management Console. You can edit the ActiveSync settings by navigating to the Client Access node under Server Configuration in the console tree, as shown in Figure 8-15, choosing the ActiveSync tab in the results pane, selecting the Microsoft-Server-ActiveSync entry, and clicking the Properties link in the action pane.

Only a small number of settings are related to ActiveSync. The first is shown in Figure 8-16 on the General tab. Here, you can establish an external URL; by default, the external URL is the server name followed by /Microsoft-Server-ActiveSync. If you want to use a different URL, you can provide the alternate value in the External URL field.

ActiveSync Feature	Description
Autodiscover	Once configured with the URL of the Autodiscover service, mobile devices can be automatically configured for synchronization.
Over-the-air provisioning	Working hand-in-hand with the Autodiscover service, mobile devices do not need to initially be connected to a computer running Windows to start the configuration/synchronization process.
Faster message retrieval	ActiveSync only downloads a portion of larger messages. Mobile devices can now pull the remainder of a message on demand, rather than waiting for the next sync interval.
Support for HTML messages	Hypertext Markup Language (HTML) messages are no longer converted to plain text, but are instead sent in their original format.
Follow-up flags	Like in Outlook, you can now flag a message for follow-up, and the flag will be synchronized back to Exchange.
Attendee status on calendar items	Information on the status of attendees and their global address book information can be accessed.
Enhanced search capabilities	To compensate for a default of only three days' worth of messages on a mobile device, it is now possible to search for messages on the Exchange server that are no longer stored on a device.
Access to SharePoint and file share-based data	Devices can now access files that are stored on servers other than the Exchange server.
Password access	Exchange can require a password be entered on the mobile device after a specified period of inactivity to ensure security of Exchange data.

Table 8-2. New Features in Exchange 2007 ActiveSync

The Authentication tab, shown in Figure 8-17, provides some basic settings, including whether to support basic authentication (where your user name and password are sent across the Internet in clear text), as well as whether to support client certificates that would be stored on a smart card or on the mobile device itself.

Figure 8-14. You can view the ActiveSync virtual directory in IIS Manager.

TIP Basic authentication should only be used when you have an SSL session established or when you publish ActiveSync via ISA Server 2006. With the session secured, passing clear text is not an issue. You can find out more on how to establish an SSL session and basic use of ISA Server 2006 in Chapter 12.

The last tab available is Remote File Servers, where you can specify which servers are accessible from a Windows mobile device. Like OWA, with Exchange 2007, mobile clients can access data on servers other than the Exchange server hosting e-mail and public folder data. These settings are identical to that of OWA in the previous section.

ActiveSync Mailbox Policies

Exchange 2007 allows you to establish a policy defining the connection settings users will need to utilize in order for their devices to connect to Exchange. You create these policies within the Exchange Management Console by first navigating to the Client Access node under Organization Configuration in the console tree, as shown in Figure 8-18, and then selecting the New Exchange ActiveSync Mailbox Policy link in the action pane.

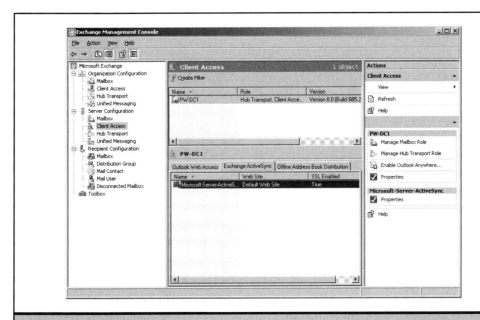

Figure 8-15. Manage ActiveSync settings within the Exchange Management Console.

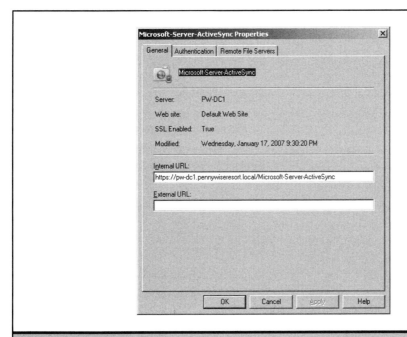

Figure 8-16. Setting an alternate URL for ActiveSync.

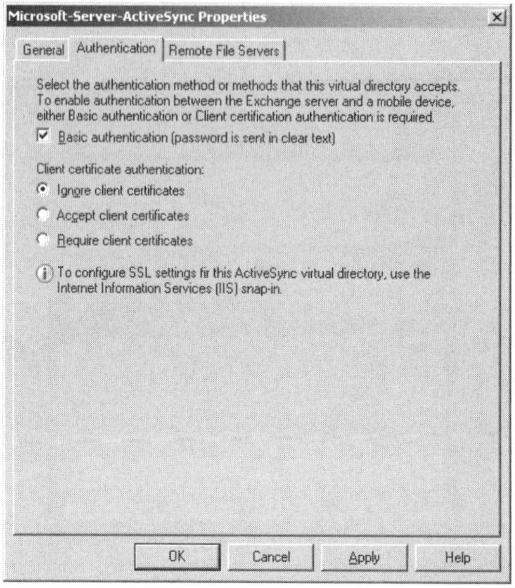

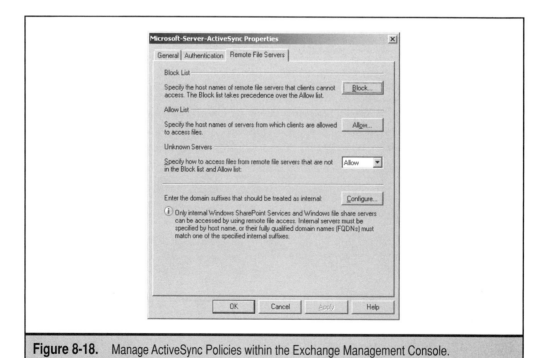

Figure 8-17. Configure authentication settings for ActiveSync.

Figure 8-18. Manage ActiveSync Policies within the Exchange Management Console.

ActiveSync Mailbox Policy Setting	Description
Allow Non-Provisionable Devices	Allows devices that do not support the Autodiscover service to connect
Require Password	Requires a password be entered on the mobile device after a period of inactivity
Enable Password Recovery	Allows the device password to be recovered from the Exchange server within OWA

Table 8-3.   An Explanation of Certain ActiveSync Mailbox Policy Settings

Once you click the link, the New Exchange ActiveSync Mailbox Policy Wizard starts, as shown in Figure 8-19. Table 8-3 lists the settings requiring explanation that you can configure as part of the policy.

Once configured, click the New button, and the policy will be created.

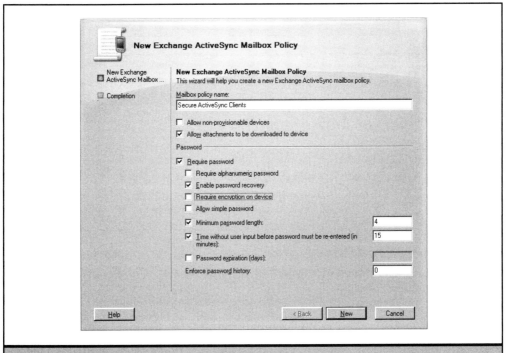

Figure 8-19.   Creating a new ActiveSync mailbox policy.

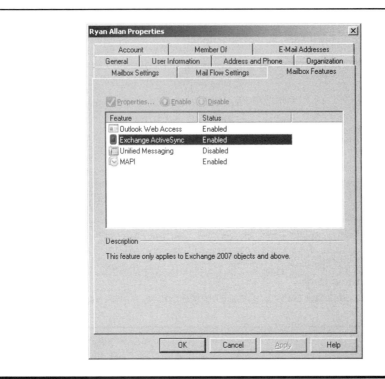

Figure 8-20. You can modify the ActiveSync properties for a user mailbox.

Configuring a User for ActiveSync

By default, all users have ActiveSync enabled. You can verify and/or modify this by looking at the Mailbox Features tab within the properties of a user mailbox, as shown in Figure 8-20. By selecting the Exchange ActiveSync entry and clicking the Properties button, you can specify an ActiveSync mailbox policy that should be applied to this user.

Management Shell Corner

To create the policy shown in Figure 8-18, use the following command:

```
New-ActiveSyncMaiboxPolicy -Name PolicyName -DevicePasswordEnabled:$false
-AlphanumericDevicePasswordRequired:$false -MaxInactivityTimeDeviceLock:'
unlimited' -MinDevicePasswordLength:$null -PasswordReciveryEnabled:$false
-DeviceEncryptionEnabled:$false -AttachmentsEnabled:$true
```

You can also modify an existing policy by using the set-ActiveSyncMail-boxPolicy command.

> ## Management Shell Corner
>
> If you wish to configure a number of mailboxes to use the same policy, run the following command for each mailbox you wish to configure:
>
> ```
> Set-CASMailbox <Mailbox> -ActiveSyncMailboxPolicy(Get-ActiveSyncMailboxPol-
> icy "<Policy-Name>").Identity
> ```
>
> Or, you can first create a query against the user mailboxes by assigning a variable to query results (in the following example, I am assigning a variable, $a, to be the resultant set of mailboxes that reside on the server "pw-dc1"):
>
> ```
> $a = get-Mailbox | where {$_.server -eq 'pw-dc1'}
> ```
>
> and then putting the variable into the command:
>
> ```
> Set-CASMailbox $a -ActiveSyncMailboxPolicy(Get-ActiveSyncMailboxPolicy
> "<Policy-Name>").Identity
> ```

CONFIGURING POP3/IMAP4

Post Office Protocol version 3 (POP3) and Internet Message Access Protocol version 4 (IMAP4) clients, while in the Exchange world are probably considered legacy clients, are still a viable access media from clients other than Outlook or OWA. Outside of the necessity for POP3 and IMAP4 clients to access e-mail, Exchange itself does not require the use of those protocols. However, let's assume that you need both protocols and take a look at the process of getting both up and running. If you have no intent of using either protocol, you can safely skip this section and move on to the "Configuring Outlook Anywhere" section later in this chapter.

Since the configuration of both protocols is so similar, I am going to cover them jointly, discussing each individually only when necessary. As you will see, POP3 and IMAP4 are configured entirely within the Exchange Management Shell with the RTM version of Exchange. Each of these procedures and commands, unless indicated otherwise, will be run on the specific Exchange server providing either POP3 or IMAP4 service. Service Pack 1 (SP1) also incorporates some of the management I'll cover within the Exchange Management Console.

Enabling and Managing POP3 and IMAP4

So, the first question is whether you want (or need) to enable POP3 or IMAP4 access to Exchange. By default, both protocols are disabled and set to a startup type of Manual for a number of reasons. First, Exchange provides so many other more robust methods of access (Outlook, OWA, and ActiveSync), and when enabled, both protocols provide insecure access to e-mail. The first thing you'll need to do is enable the protocol(s) you

Management Shell Corner

While I doubt you'd actually enable and configure the services from the Exchange Management Shell, you can both start the service and set its startup type to Automatic with the following commands:

```
Set-service <service-name> -startuptype automatic
```

and

```
Start-service <service-name>
```

where *<service-name>*, in this case, is either *msExchangePOP3* or *msExchangeI-MAP4*.

require within the Services MMC snap-in by starting the following services and setting their startup value to Automatic:

- ▼ Microsoft Exchange IMAP4
- ▲ Microsoft Exchange POP3

Protocol Configuration

Both POP3 and IMAP4 are basic enough protocols that there are just a few configuration options you have to choose from for each protocol within Exchange. Each option is configured via the Exchange Management Shell and not in the Exchange Management Console.

To manage the configuration for each protocol, you will use either the `Set-PopSettings` or `Set-ImapSettings` command within the Exchange Management Shell. Table 8-4 lists the parameters you can use to configure both POP3 and IMAP4, as well as the command parameters you will use.

There are more values than those specified in Table 8-4, but I have focused on some of the more common values you may need to modify.

Configuring User Access to POP3 and IMAP4

Once configured, you should consider limiting user access to Exchange via either protocol by only allowing those users that require access. Remember, by default, all users can use both protocols and also, by default, both protocols are insecure. To limit which users can use these protocols, you need to disable the protocol(s) on a per-user basis. You can do this only via the Exchange Management Shell by using the following commands to enable or disable the protocols:

```
Set-CASMailbox <mailbox> -PopEnabled $true | $false
Set-CASMailbox <mailbox> -Imap4Enabled $true | $false
```

Remember, you can utilize a variable, like in the example in the ActiveSync section of this chapter, to run these commands on multiple mailboxes in one motion.

Setting	Command Parameter	Default Value	Value Range
Maximum number of connections	-MaxConnections	2,000	1 – 25,000
Maximum number of connections from a single IP address	-MaxConnectionsFrom-SingleIP	20	1 – 1,000
Maximum number of connections from a single user	-MaxConnectionsPerUser	10	1 – 1,000
Connection timeout before authenticating	-PreAuthenticatedConnect-ionTimeout	00:01:00	00:00:10 – 00:60:00
Connection timeout for idle sessions	-AuthenticatedConnection-Timeout	00:30:00	00:00:30 – 24:00:00
Banner to be displayed upon connection	-Banner	"Microsoft Exchange Server 2007 <service> service ready"	As desired
Domain controller to use for authentication	-DomainController	Automatically established	As desired
Logon Method	-LoginType	PlainTextLogin	PlainTextLogin PlainTextAuthentication SecureAuthentication
Calendar retrieval options	-CalenderItemRetrieval-Option	0	0 – uses iCalendar standard 1 – Specify internal URL 2 – Specify external URL 3 – Specify OWA URL

Table 8-4.   POP3 and IMAP4 Command Parameters

Managing POP and IMAP from the Exchange Management Console

SP1 introduces managing much of this section's tasks within the Exchange Management Console. Figure 8-21 shows the updated Results pane of the Client Access Node under Server Configuration in the console tree: a new *POP and IMAP* tab.

As I mentioned before, the configuration of both protocols is nearly identical, so I'll focus on showing the management of POP3. The graphical management of these two protocols does not include enabling each protocol, or starting the related services, only the equivalent of the `Set-PopSettings` and `Set-ImapSettings` commands within the Management Shell. By viewing the properties, shown in Figure 8-22, you can see the Banner string presented upon establishing a session with a client.

Figure 8-23 shows the IP addresses and port settings for secure POP or IMAP sessions, Figure 8-24 shows the supported authentication method, Figure 8-25 shows the settings described in the previous "Protocol Configuration" section in this chapter, and Figure 8-26 shows the message sort order and attachment format, as well as calendar item retrieval method.

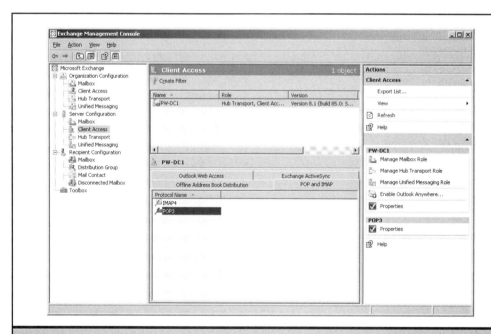

Figure 8-21. Viewing the New POP and IMAP Tab

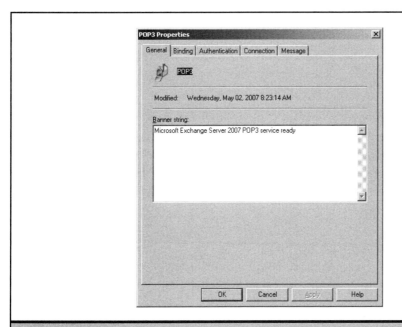

Figure 8-22. Viewing the General Properties

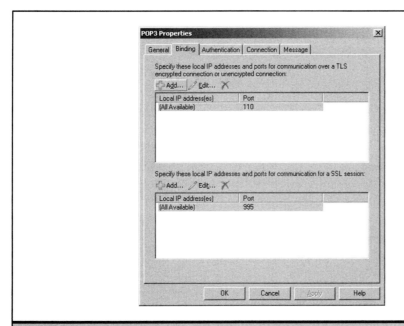

Figure 8-23. Viewing the Binding Settings

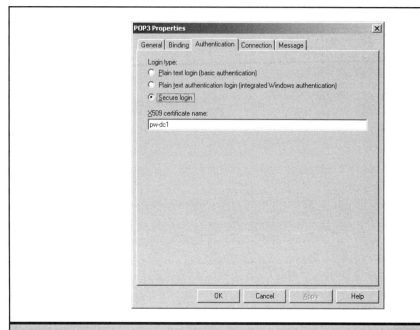

Figure 8-24. Viewing the Authentication Settings

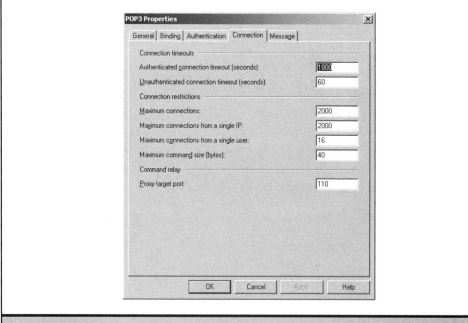

Figure 8-25. Viewing the Connection Settings

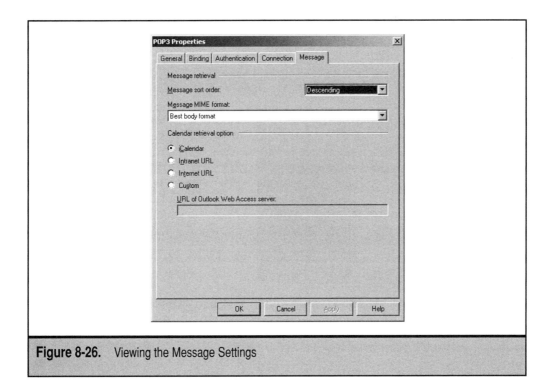

Figure 8-26. Viewing the Message Settings

CONFIGURING OUTLOOK ANYWHERE

Outlook Anywhere is the new version of what was referred to as *RPC over HTTP* in Exchange 2003. It allows you to run Outlook 2003/2007 natively within a virtual private network (VPN) and access Exchange data by first establishing a secure Hypertext Transfer Protocol (HTTP) connection and then passing the normal remote procedure call (RPC) traffic between the Exchange server and the Outlook client.

There are three steps to getting Outlook Anywhere up and running.

1. Install an SSL certificate from a trusted certification authority (CA).

2. Install the RPC over HTTP Proxy component.

3. Enable and configure Outlook Anywhere on an Exchange server running the Client Access role.

Installing an SSL Certificate

SSL certificates are not specific to Outlook Anywhere, but to IIS. Outlook Anywhere is accessed by Outlook as a secure HTTP session. Therefore, to install an SSL certificate, you'll need to do so within the IIS Manager. Navigate to the default web site's properties, select the Directory Security tab, and click the Server Certificate button. The Web Server Certificate Wizard (see Figure 8-27) is used to generate the certificate request to be presented to a CA, such as VeriSign, as well as to install the certificate created by the CA. You can

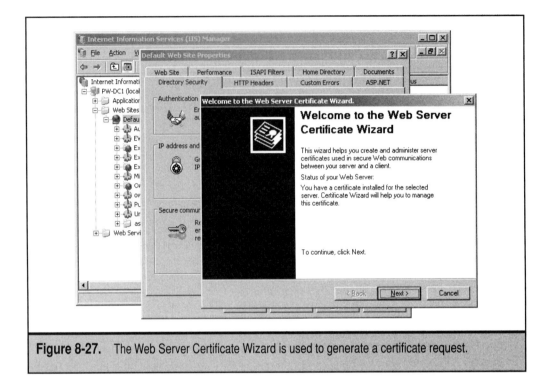

Figure 8-27. The Web Server Certificate Wizard is used to generate a certificate request.

find out more on how to do this process at http://support.microsoft.com/kb/228821. Remember—you'll need to perform this process for the default web site.

TIP During the Exchange setup, a default SSL certificate is created and installed automatically. However, this certificate is not trusted by the client, so you should consider obtaining a certificate from a trusted authority.

Installing the RPC over HTTP Proxy

This is a pretty easy step. Open up Add/Remove Programs in Control Panel. Then click the Add/Remove Windows Components button on the left. Select Networking Components and click the Details button. Select RPC Over HTTP Proxy (shown in Figure 8-28), and click OK twice. You may need to insert a Windows Server 2003 CD to complete this step.

Enabling and Configuring Outlook Anywhere

As you will see, the configuration of Outlook Anywhere is far easier than RPC over HTTP in Exchange 2003, despite the improvements Microsoft made in the service packs for Exchange 2003. Once you have installed the RPC over HTTP Proxy, you need to enable Outlook Anywhere. This is accomplished within the Exchange Management Console by navigating to the Client Access node under Server Configuration in the console tree and then clicking the Enable Outlook Anywhere link in the action pane, as shown in Figure 8-29.

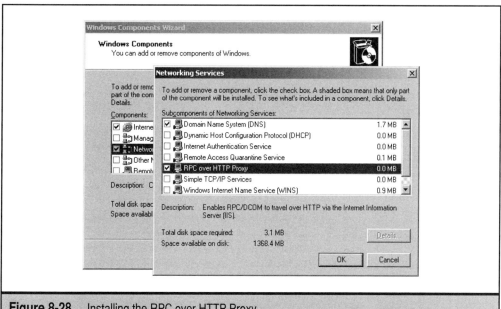

Figure 8-28.   Installing the RPC over HTTP Proxy.

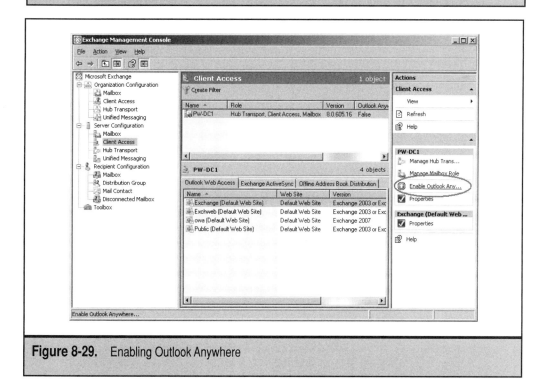

Figure 8-29.   Enabling Outlook Anywhere

Management Shell Corner

To enable Outlook Anywhere, use the following command:

```
enable-OutlookAnywhere -Server:'PW-DC1' -
ExternalHostname:'oa.pennywiseresorts.com' -ExternalAuthenticationMethod:'B
asic' -SSLOffloading:$false
```

You can also use the `disable-OutlookAnywhere` command to disable Outlook Anywhere. There are a few options not shown in the wizard that you can use from within Exchange Management Shell. For example, the –ExternalAuthenticationMethod parameter also supports digest, forms-based, and Windows integrated authentication using the `Digest`, `Fba`, and `WindowsIntegrated` parameter values, respectively.

The Enable Outlook Anywhere Wizard starts and requires that a few elements be configured to complete it. As shown in Figure 8-30, you will need to provide an external host name (a URL) that will be used to configure Outlook 2003/2007 clients with access to Exchange; an authentication method (remember, if you choose basic authentication, SSL should be used); and whether you will be using a server in front of the Exchange server running the Client Access role to handle the SSL session, such as an ISA server. If you choose the last option, the Exchange server will assume that the SSL session will terminate at a front-end firewall server (again, such as an ISA server) and will be utilizing non-SSL sessions.

If you need to make changes to the settings you used when enabling Outlook Anywhere, right-click the server object in the results pane, and click the Outlook Anywhere tab, shown in Figure 8-31.

TIP If you will be running a 2003/2007 mixed environment with 2003 back-end servers (those hosting mailboxes), you should ensure that all back-end 2003 servers are running at least Service Pack 1 to facilitate automatic configuration of the Outlook Anywhere environment.

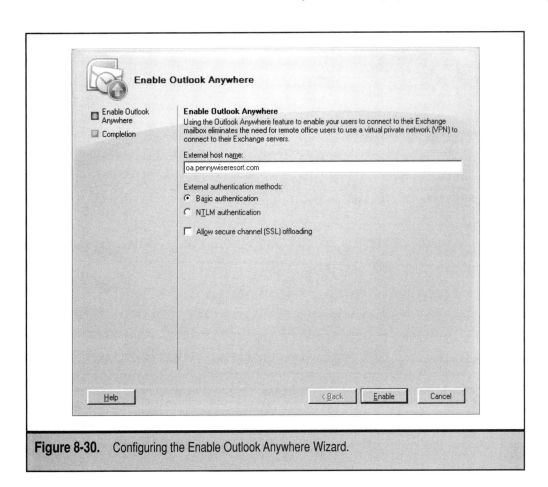

Figure 8-30.   Configuring the Enable Outlook Anywhere Wizard.

THE AUTODISCOVER SERVICE

The Autodiscover service is a new feature with Exchange 2007 that works with Outlook 2007 and Windows mobile devices to automatically configure their profile for the right Mailbox server, Outlook Anywhere settings, display-name URLs to data sets like the offline address book or free/busy information, and more.

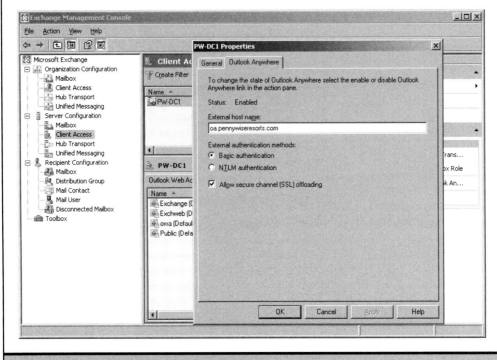

Figure 8-31. Modifying Outlook Anywhere settings.

When an Exchange server is configured with the Client Access role, an IIS virtual directory with the name *Autodiscover* is created, as shown in Figure 8-32. This virtual directory is used by clients to retrieve URLs of available services stored in an autodiscover .xml file.

How Outlook Finds the Autodiscover URL

The answer lies in Active Directory. When the Client Access role is installed, an object in Active Directory is created called the service connection point (SCP) that contains the URL to the Autodiscover service. When Outlook 2007 is connected to the network and Active Directory is accessible, the SCP object is queried and the URL is returned by Active Directory.

Even though a virtual directory is automatically created in the same Web site as the other Exchange virtual directories, Microsoft recommends that you run the Autodiscover service in a separate virtual site. This requires a few steps to be taken in order to configure a new site.

1. You will need to create a new virtual site using the following Exchange Management Shell command: `New-AutodiscoverVirtualDirectory -Websitename <sitename>`.

2. You will need to configure the site to use an SSL certificate. Review the information in the URL listed in the "Configuring Outlook Anywhere" section earlier in this chapter.

3. You should remove the default Autodiscover virtual directory (although this is optional). You can do this using the `Remove-AutodiscoverVirtual-Directory` Exchange Management Shell cmdlet.

THE AVAILABILITY SERVICE

The Availability service is another new service in Exchange 2007 that provides the most recent free and busy information available to Outlook 2007 clients. The Availability service and Autodiscover service are related, in that Outlook 2007 obtains the URL for the

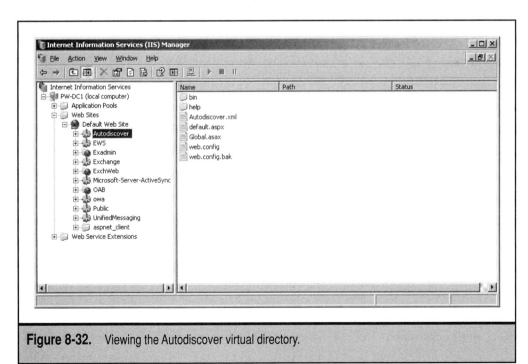

Figure 8-32. Viewing the Autodiscover virtual directory.

Availability service via the Autodiscover service. This only applies if the mailbox accessed by Outlook 2007 is on an Exchange 2007 server; if the mailbox is located on an Exchange 2003 server, free and busy information is obtained from public folders. If you happen to still be running Outlook 2003, free and busy information will still be obtained via public folders, regardless of whether the mailbox exists on an Exchange 2003 or 2007 server.

SUMMARY

In this chapter, I've taken a look at the various ways the Client Access server role supports Exchange clients and how to configure them. Remember, the client-side configuration that corresponds to the services listed in this chapter will be covered in Chapters 10 and 11. In the next chapter, I'll take a look at how to manage the Edge Transport server role.

CHAPTER 9

Managing Edge Transport Servers

In Exchange 2000/2003, Microsoft began enhancing Exchange's ability to ensure the security of e-mail messages by including a SmartScreen-based technology developed by Microsoft Research known as the Intelligent Message Filter (IMF), which identified and appropriately dealt with spam messages and other unwanted e-mail. In Exchange 2007, Microsoft has taken a giant leap forward to secure messages by introducing the Edge Transport server role. This server role resides on your perimeter network and scans messages using an antispam agent. In addition, the Edge Transport server provides management of messages using transport rules, as well as some presentation services, through a new feature called Address Rewriting. In this chapter, I'm going to cover the architecture, installation, and configuration of Edge Transport services. Be aware that this chapter focuses strictly on the configuration aspects of the Edge Transport server that are not shared with the Hub Transport server (which you can read about in Chapter 6).

EDGE TRANSPORT CONCEPTS

The Edge Transport server is made up of a few different components, which I will address individually first and then bring together by showing the path a message takes through an Edge Transport server, including:

▼ Antispam and antivirus functionality

■ Address Rewriting

■ Active Directory Application Mode (ADAM)

▲ Edge subscriptions

Antispam and Antivirus Functionality

The Edge Transport server has a number of technologies at its disposal to determine if a message is spam. Rather than attempt to keep up with the latest virus signatures, Exchange focuses its energies on detecting spam, as most email-borne viruses are not from the sender they purport to be.

TIP   Remember, you can activate the antispam features on a Hub Transport server without an Edge Transport server by using the Install-AntispamAgents.psi script in the Scripts folder, which is located in C: \Program Files\Microsoft\Exchange Server.

Filters

Exchange touts several filters, each with a specific tactic to remove spam and, therefore, viruses. The basic principle is to have a message pass through so many different filters looking for a different aspect of a spam e-mail that if a message is indeed spam, it will be caught by one of the filters. Table 9-1 lists each filter and its purpose.

Filter	Description
Attachment	Removes attachments based on name, extension or Multipurpose Internet Mail Extension (MIME) type. Attachments can be stripped from a message, or the entire message can be blocked and deleted.
Connection	Uses Internet Protocol (IP) address Block and Allow lists to identify potentially unsafe messages.
Content	This is the revised version of the Intelligent Message Filter, where messages are identified as spam using Microsoft's SmartScreen technology.
Recipient	Uses a replicated copy of recipients from Active Directory, as well as a Block list to determine the proper course of action for a message.
Sender	Blocks messages based on the sender.
Sender ID	Utilizes the new Sender ID technology that queries the sender domain's Domain Name System (DNS) to verify the sending IP address as being from the claimed domain.

Table 9-1.   Exchange Filters Used to Reduce Spam and Viruses

Sender Reputation

In addition, Exchange utilizes a number of other technologies to detect spam. The first is Sender Reputation, which works by establishing a sender reputation level (SRL) using four tests:

▼ **HELO/EHLO Analysis**   Exchange looks at the HELO or EHLO command (whichever is used to establish the Simple Mail Transfer Protocol [SMTP] connection) and attempts to match the claimed domain name with the IP address of the sender.

■ **Reverse DNS Lookup**   Sort of a reverse of the previous test, where the IP address is checked to see if it matches the domain claimed. This test and the HELO/EHLO Analysis together ensure that a message is truly from where it claims.

■ **Sender Open Proxy**   Exchange tests to see if the sender is an open-proxy server (an open-proxy server is often used by spammers to hide the true origination of a spam message).

▲ **Spam Confidence Level (SCL) Rating**   The SCL rating of the sender is checked to see if messages from this sender are consistently in question.

Exchange takes the outcome of these tests and assigns an SRL to the sender from 0 to 9. A level of 0 means that the sender is not a spammer; 9 means it is very likely a spammer. The sender filter is triggered to block this sender based on a configurable SRL block threshold, where any senders whose SRL is over the block threshold will be subject to the blocking configuration of the sender filter.

Safelist Aggregation

You are probably familiar with the Safe Senders lists used in Outlook 2003 and 2007. Exchange 2007 introduces the ability for the individual Safe Senders lists, Safe Recipients lists, and Safe Domain lists to be aggregated from each user's mailbox (where these lists are stored) to Active Directory. This aggregated data is replicated to the Edge Transport server to be used centrally.

Address Rewriting

Edge Transport servers also provide the ability to take the domain value in inbound and outbound messages and rewrite them for the purpose of maintaining a consistent namespace for an Exchange organization. For example, let's say Pennywise Resort expands to four locations, each with its own subdomain under pennywiseresort.com:

▼ cancun.pennywiseresort.com

■ dubai.pennywiseresort.com

■ miami.pennywiseresort.com

▲ bahamas.pennywiseresort.com

Without Address Rewriting, messages sent from each of the locations would look like <user>@cancun.pennywiseresort.com (with the appropriate subdomain, of course). With Address Rewriting, as the messages are sent via the Edge Transport server, they can be rewritten as "@pennywiseresort.com" addresses to maintain a single company namespace outside the organization. Likewise, as an e-mail comes in to an "@pennywiseresort.com" address, the Edge Transport server would rewrite the address to be the appropriate subdomain to ensure proper routing.

Table 9-2 lists the addresses that can be rewritten by an Edge Transport server.

TIP For outbound rewriting to work properly, you must ensure that each rewritten address is unique across your Exchange organization and that the rewritten address is included in the proxy addresses for the intended recipient.

Edge Subscriptions

In order to be an effective first point of contact for inbound messages and last point of contact for outbound messages, the Edge Transport server will exist in the perimeter network. Being on the perimeter network usually means that you need to open a number of holes in the firewall to make the Edge Transport server communicate with Active Directory.

Address	Inbound Messages	Outbound Messages
Envelope From (specified in the `MAIL FROM` SMTP command)	Not Rewritten	Rewritten
Envelope To (specified in the `RCPT TO` SMTP command)	Rewritten	Not Rewritten
Body To Body CC	Not Rewritten	Rewritten
Body From Body Sender	Not Rewritten	Rewritten
Body Reply-To Body Return-Receipt-To	Not Rewritten	Rewritten
Body Disposition-Notification-To	Not Rewritten	Rewritten
Body Resent-From Body Resent-To	Not Rewritten	Rewritten

Table 9-2.   Message Addresses Rewritten by Edge Transport Servers

Instead, Microsoft has taken a more secure approach and designed the Edge Transport server to *not* be a member of the internal domain and instead get its directory information by means of a one-way synchronization process between Active Directory and the Edge Transport server. This is done using an Edge Subscription. Edge Subscriptions define the elements of Active Directory that will be replicated to the Edge Transport server to be stored in the ADAM directory service. Some implementations will have the Edge Transport server installed as a member of a perimeter domain (which is not part of the internal forest) for ease of patching and monitoring.

> **TIP**   You only need Edge Subscriptions if you plan on using the antispam, recipient lookup, safelist aggregations, or secure communications via mutual Transport Layer Security (TLS) features of an Edge Transport server. These all require information from Active Directory to function.

By creating an Edge Subscription, you'll enable an Edge Transport server to first synchronize needed information from Active Directory and utilize this information to provide the services listed previously in this chapter. The Microsoft Exchange EdgeSync service, which runs on Hub Transport servers, is responsible for the synchronization of data from Active Directory to ADAM.

Active Directory Application Mode (ADAM)

ADAM is an LDAP-based directory service that provides a read-only copy of Active Directory information to applications that need to access it, but do so from a potentially insecure location. ADAM synchronizes itself with Active Directory via a subscription process where data is replicated from Active Directory to ADAM (and not the other way) using Hub Transport servers, giving ADAM a viable copy of Active Directory to work with while not exposing it to modification. The Edge server only needs the following specific subsets of Active Directory to be functional:

▼   Schema extensions

■   Exchange Configuration data

Accessing Active Directory Through a Firewall

Because the Edge Transport server exists in the perimeter network, you'll need to ensure that the server only has the needed access to complete its job, but at the same time keep the number of holes in the firewall to an absolute minimum. The following ports are required on the *internal* firewall to allow the Edge Transport server to synchronize data via the Edge Subscription:

▼   **TCP 25**   for e-mail communications

■   **TCP 50389**   for access to Active Directory using the Lightweight Directory Access Protocol (LDAP)

■   **TCP 50636**   for secure access to Active Directory using LDAP

▲   **TCP 3389**   for remote administration over the Remote Desktop Protocol (RDP)

Assuming there is an *external* firewall as well, you'll need to open the port TCP 25 for e-mail communications.

These opened ports will facilitate a smooth Edge Subscription, as shown in the following illustration.

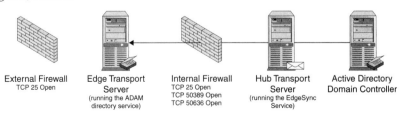

External Firewall	Edge Transport	Internal Firewall	Hub Transport	Active Directory
TCP 25 Open	Server	TCP 25 Open	Server	Domain Controller
	(running the ADAM directory service)	TCP 50389 Open TCP 50636 Open	(running the EdgeSync Service)	

- ■ Recipient information
- ▲ Topology information

Schema Extensions Edge servers need specific attributes of the ms-Exch-ExchangeServer object to support the authentication and management of the synchronization process.

Configuration Information The Edge Transport server is still a transport server, so there are numerous settings in Active Directory that it needs to properly process messages. Table 9-3 lists the Active Directory configuration data that is synchronized with an Edge Transport server and a description of that data.

Recipient Information Edge Transport servers also need a listing of internal recipients (excluding distribution groups) so it can properly find the right recipient, apply address rewriting, etc. Only a subset of recipient information is replicated. Table 9-4 lists the recipient configuration data that is synchronized with an Edge Transport server and a description of that data.

Configuration Information	Description
Hub Transport server objects	Used to identify the internal Hub servers that the Edge server will communicate with.
Accepted domains	Lists all authoritative, internal relay, and external relay domains so the Edge server knows which domains are supported by your Exchange organization. More on this in Chapter 6.
Message classifications	If synchronized, the Edge server can apply message classifications that may include the immediate deletion of messages before they enter the organization. More on this in Chapter 17.
Remote domains	Define the message format used and out-of-office replies to specific external domains. More in Chapter 6.
Send connectors	These define the end-to-end communications from your organization to the Internet.
Internal SMTP servers	Those servers listed will be ignored by Sender ID and connection filtering.
Domain secure lists	Lists the external domains the Edge server can establish a secure SMTP session with.

Table 9-3. Active Directory Configuration Information Synchronized to Edge Servers

Recipient Information	Description
Recipients	Only valid recipients are replicated to ADAM (deleted mailboxes, those disallowed from receiving e-mail from outside, etc. won't be in this list).
Proxy addresses	All proxy addresses for valid recipients are replicated for use by the Edge server. The proxy information is secured with a hash to ensure that it is never exposed should the server be hacked.
Safe Senders and Safe Recipients lists	This falls under the aggregation mentioned earlier in the chapter so that Edge Transport servers can validate senders appropriately.
Per-recipient antispam settings	It is possible to override the organization-wide spam settings on a per-mailbox basis. This is replicated so individual configuration can be used prior to messages entering the organization.

Table 9-4. Recipient Configuration Information Synchronized to Edge Servers

INSTALLING AN EDGE TRANSPORT SERVER

For the most secure installation of an Edge Transport server, there are two basic criteria:

▼ The server should be placed in your perimeter network.

▲ The server should not be a member of the internal domain.

I'm going to assume you've got that covered and move on. Before you can install the Edge Transport server, you'll need to install ADAM (remember, ADAM is not proprietary to Exchange, but to any application that will utilize Active Directory information to function). If you are running the R2 release of Windows 2003 Server, ADAM is already built into the operating system and is available through the Optional Component Manager. ADAM is available for download at www.microsoft.com/adam.

Like any other Exchange server installation, you'll need to install the prerequisites (.NET Framework 2.0, the Microsoft Management Console 3.0, and PowerShell 1.0) before you can get into the meat of the Exchange installation.

When you start the Exchange installation (you can refer back to Chapter 2 if you need a refresher on the Exchange installation process), you'll need to accept the license agreement, address whether you want to participate in error reporting, and finally choose to perform a Custom Exchange Server Installation, as shown in Figure 9-1.

After clicking Next, you will select only the Edge Transport Server Role check box, shown in Figure 9-2. You'll notice that all the other roles become unavailable, as you cannot install the Edge Transport role on the same server as any other role. Also note that the Management Tools checkbox is automatically selected.

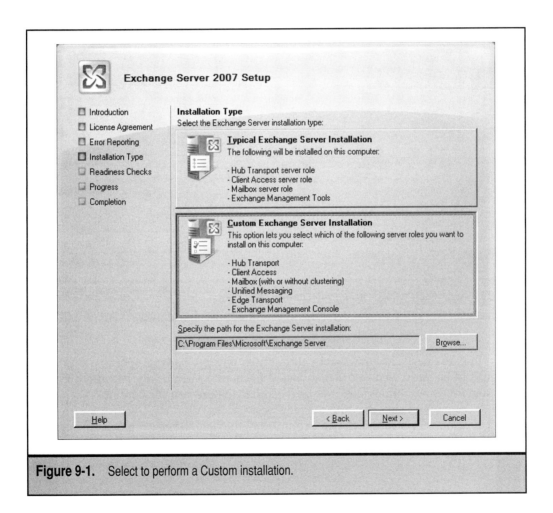

Figure 9-1.   Select to perform a Custom installation.

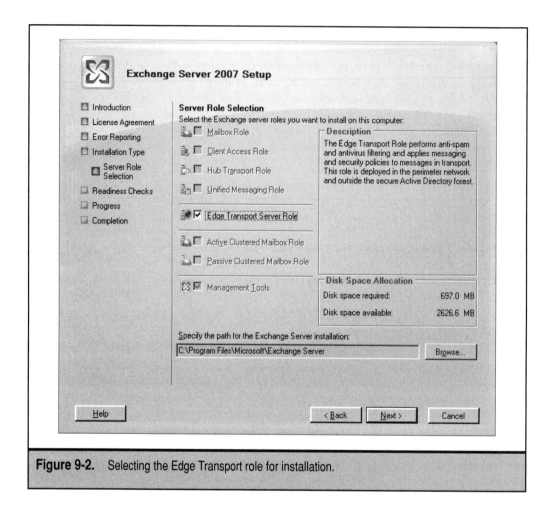

Figure 9-2. Selecting the Edge Transport role for installation.

On the next page, Exchange goes through its normal readiness checks. Any issues that need to be addressed in order to install Exchange, such as any required updates, DNS domain name settings, etc., will be listed here before you can continue.

With the prerequisites met and the readiness checks complete, the installation of the Edge Transport server can start. Once completed, the default selection has the Exchange Management Console starting automatically, shown in Figure 9-3. You'll notice it is very much an Edge Transport–focused view of Exchange management.

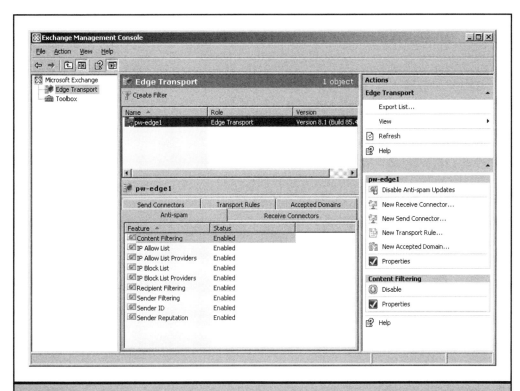

Figure 9-3. The Exchange Management Console on an Edge Transport server.

Setting the DNS Suffix

You might forget to do this, but because the server is not part of an Active Directory domain, the DNS suffix needs to be set (it is automatically set when you join a domain, and I'd guess that you, like most, set up very few servers that are not part of a domain). To set the DNS suffix, right-click the My Computer icon in the Start menu, and choose Properties, shown in the following illustration. Click the Computer Name tab, click the Change button, and on the Computer Name Changes dialog box, click the More button.

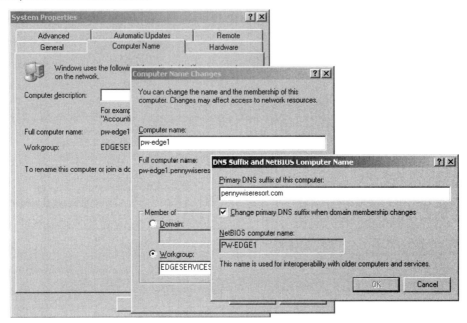

On the DNS Suffix And NetBIOS Computer Name dialog box, enter the appropriate DNS suffix for the server, and click OK three times to complete the process. This change will require a reboot to take effect (no, a disable/enable of the network card doesn't do it—I tried it too!).

CONFIGURING AN EDGE TRANSPORT SERVER

The configuration of an Edge Transport server entails most of the concepts previously discussed in this chapter. In this section, I'll cover the following aspects of Edge Transport management:

▼ Set up of an Edge Subscription

▲ Configuration of antispam features

Creating Edge Subscriptions

Creating an Edge Subscription is a two-step process, involving both the Edge Transport server and at least one Hub Transport server. The prerequisites are relatively simple:

▼ The two servers involved in the synchronization must be able to resolve each other's name in DNS.

■ The appropriate ports need to be opened in the firewall.

▲ You need local administrator permissions on the Edge Transport server to start the process and Exchange Organization Administrator rights in the Exchange organization to complete the process.

The process includes the creation of an Edge Subscription file on the Edge Transport server and the installation of that file on the Hub Transport server in the Exchange organization.

TIP   Remember that before you create the Edge Subscription, you should configure the settings for the objects in Active Directory that will be replicated to the Edge Transport server, including internal SMTP servers, accepted domains, and remote domains.

To begin, you'll need to open the Exchange Management Shell and run the `New-EdgeSubscription` cmdlet, shown in Figure 9-4.

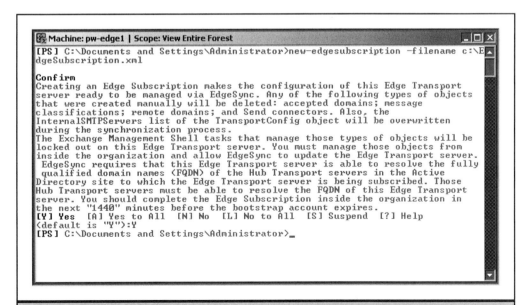

Machine: pw-edge1 | Scope: View Entire Forest

```
[PS] C:\Documents and Settings\Administrator>new-edgesubscription -filename c:\E
dgeSubscription.xml

Confirm
Creating an Edge Subscription makes the configuration of this Edge Transport
server ready to be managed via EdgeSync. Any of the following types of objects
that were created manually will be deleted: accepted domains; message
classifications; remote domains; and Send connectors. Also, the
InternalSMTPServers list of the TransportConfig object will be overwritten
during the synchronization process.
The Exchange Management Shell tasks that manage those types of objects will be
locked out on this Edge Transport server. You must manage those objects from
inside the organization and allow EdgeSync to update the Edge Transport server.
 EdgeSync requires that this Edge Transport server is able to resolve the fully
 qualified domain names (FQDN) of the Hub Transport servers in the Active
Directory site to which the Edge Transport server is being subscribed. Those
Hub Transport servers must be able to resolve the FQDN of this Edge Transport
server. You should complete the Edge Subscription inside the organization in
the next "1440" minutes before the bootstrap account expires.
[Y] Yes  [A] Yes to All  [N] No  [L] No to All  [S] Suspend  [?] Help
(default is "Y"):Y
[PS] C:\Documents and Settings\Administrator>_
```

Figure 9-4.   Creating the Edge Subscription file.

This newly created file will then need to be copied to the Hub Transport server that will be utilized in the subscription process. The eXtensible Markup Language (XML) file contains information such as the Edge server name, the public key of the Edge server's certificate, the user name and initial password to be used, date, validity duration of the credentials, and licensing.

TIP   The user name and password are stored in clear text within the XML file, so you should immediately delete the file once you have completed the subscription process.

To import the Edge Subscription file, on the Hub Transport server, navigate within the Exchange Management Console to the Hub Transport node under Organization Configuration in the console tree, shown in Figure 9-5.

Once there, select the Edge Subscriptions tab, and click the new Edge Subscription link in the action pane. This starts the New Edge Subscription Wizard, shown in Figure 9-6.

The Active Directory site selected determines the Hub Transport server(s) that will participate in the synchronization process. The Edge Subscription file should be selected; clicking New will complete the subscription process.

TIP   The credentials for the replication account are only valid for 24 hours, so you will need to start and finish the subscription setup within that timeframe.

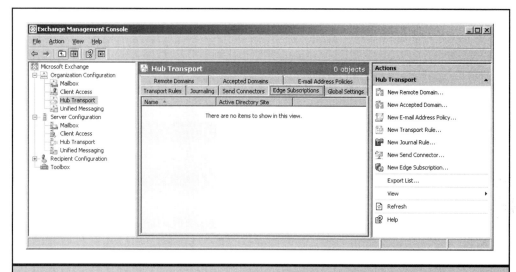

Figure 9-5.   Navigating to the Edge Subscriptions in the Exchange Management Console.

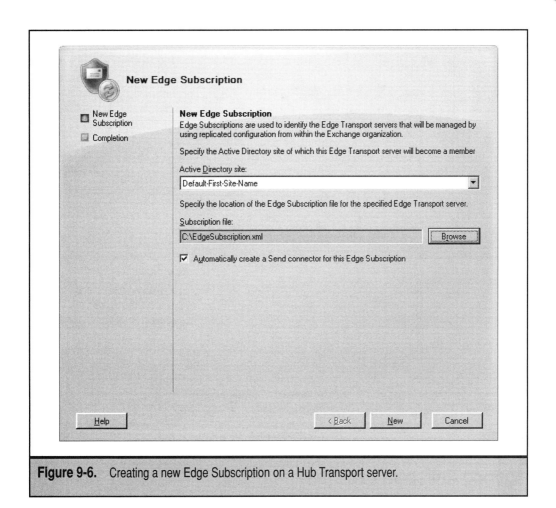

Figure 9-6.   Creating a new Edge Subscription on a Hub Transport server.

Once the subscription is complete, on the Hub Transport server, you should see a new object in the Edge Subscriptions tab. In addition, on the Edge Transport server, you will see the replicated data begin to populate in the Send Connectors, Receive Connectors, and Accepted Domains tabs in the results pane, as shown in Figure 9-7.

The only maintenance you will need to do with an Edge Subscription is forcing the synchronization using the `Start-EdgeSynchronization` cmdlet, removing an Edge Subscription, and resubscribing a subscription.

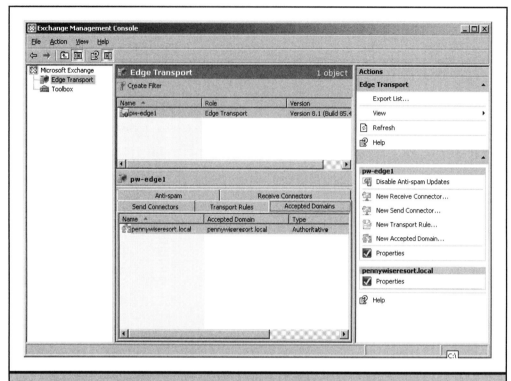

Figure 9-7. Viewing replicated Active Directory data on the Edge Transport server.

Configuring Antispam Features

Let's take a look at the antispam features that are available on an Edge Transport server. There are nine separate features I'll cover. You can see which agents/features are enabled using the Get-TransportAgent cmdlet, as shown in Figure 9-8.

I'm going to cover in this section *in the order they are processed*. This will help you see which feature supersedes another. All of them are managed within the Exchange Management Console on the Edge Transport server by navigating to the Edge Transport node in the console tree and selecting the Anti-Spam tab in the results pane, as shown in Figure 9-9.

General Configuration Issues

You can enable or disable (as appropriate) each of the features by selecting the feature and clicking the appropriate link in the action pane. Antispam updates from Microsoft

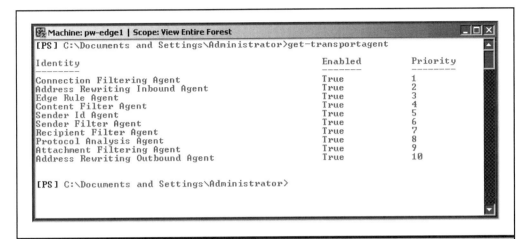

Figure 9-8. Viewing the transport agents.

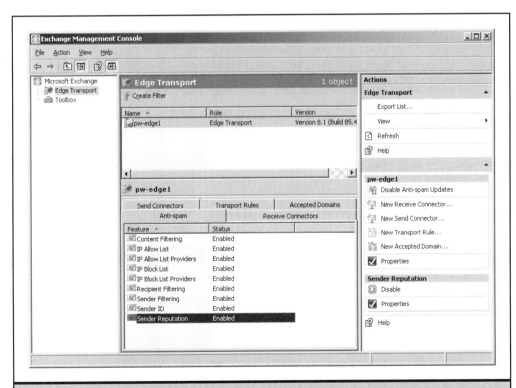

Figure 9-9. Managing the antispam features in the Exchange Management Console.

(which occur several times a day) can also be disabled using the Disable Anti-Spam Up-dates link in the action pane.

The server itself has a few options you can configure, which are identical to that of Hub Transport servers. These include internal and external DNS lookup settings, as well as connection retry and restriction values. For more information, see Chapter 6.

Connection Filtering

Four features are associated with Exchange's first line of defense: connection filtering. The basic premise here is if a message is coming from somewhere you have specified that you want blocked, the contents of a message from this sender are irrelevant.

IP Allow and Block Lists   Exchange uses IP Allow and Block lists built by you to identify specific IP addresses and address ranges as allowed or blocked, as shown in Figure 9-10. The Allow and Block dialog boxes are identical.

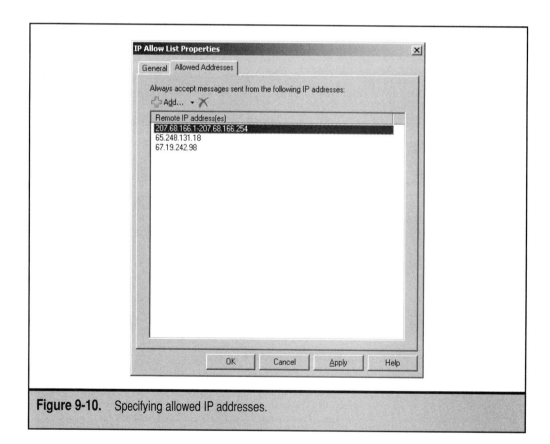

Figure 9-10.   Specifying allowed IP addresses.

IP Allow and Block Providers Next, Exchange uses Allow/Block lists from external providers, such as Spamhaus (www.spamhaus.org), that constantly update their database of known IP addresses of spammers. Configuring the options for either the IP Allow list or the IP Block list can get a bit hairy, as Exchange provides a rather generic, but effective, interface, as shown in Figure 9-11.

The basic fields are the name and domain to point to in order to query the Block list. However, you may need to configure the Return Status Codes section based on the format of the responses so that Exchange knows when the Block or Allow list is returning an affirmative value. The IP Block List properties also allows for a set of exception e-mail addresses, where the Block list value should be overridden when an e-mail is received from a specific address.

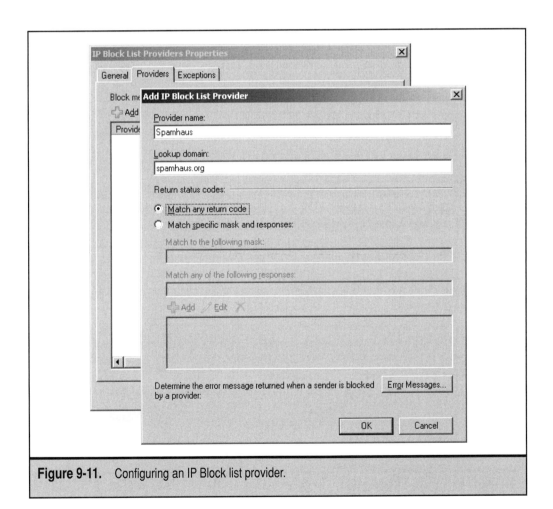

Figure 9-11. Configuring an IP Block list provider.

Address Rewriting

Exchange supports two rewriting agents, one for inbound (which runs just after the connection filter) and one for outbound (which runs last). Since they are managed the same, I'm going to cover them both here. Exchange supports rewriting using three scenarios:

▼ Rewriting a single recipient address

■ Rewriting a single domain

▲ Rewriting multiple subdomains

All three scenarios will be accomplished within the Exchange Management Shell using the `New-AddressRewriteEntry` cmdlet. Figure 9-12 shows an example of each scenario.

Transport Rules

The transport rules you establish within the Exchange organization are replicated via the Edge Subscription process. See Chapter 17 for a brief primer on transport rules.

Content Filtering

By selecting the Content Filter feature and selecting Properties, a brief description of the purpose of the feature and its current status is displayed on the General tab. With this

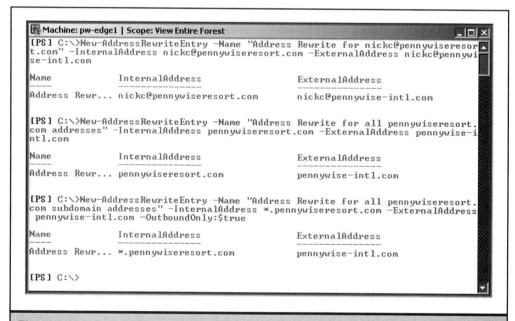

Figure 9-12. Adding address-rewrite entries.

feature enabled, Exchange uses Microsoft's SmartScreen technology to identify spam messages. You can add to Microsoft's efforts by using the Custom Words tab, where you can specify the words that will trigger the filter to block a message. The Exceptions tab lists the recipients that will receive messages, regardless of the content. The Content Filtering agent also utilizes the safelist aggregation feature, where the safelists from Outlook and Outlook Web Access clients are combined to be used centrally by the Edge Transport server.

TIP You manually aggregate the safelist information using the `Update-Safelist` cmdlet. You will need to schedule this command to run using the AT command.

Using the SCL The Actions tab, shown in Figure 9-13, defines the actions to be taken based on the SCL (which is determined using the various features configured on the Anti-Spam tab of the results pane of the Exchange Management Console). The options on the Actions tab are relatively easy to understand.

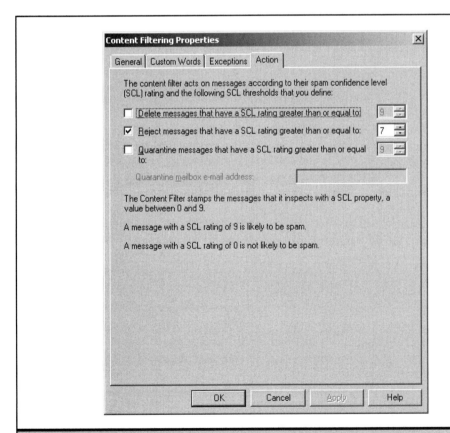

Figure 9-13. Configuring the actions to be taken based on the SCL.

Determining the Right SCL

The challenge is to determine what SCL you should use for each value: An SCL set too low on any of the three choices will result in valid messages being deleted or rejected; an SCL set too high will allow too many messages to reach users' mailboxes. Unfortunately, there is no universal set of SCL values, as each organization has a different experience with the amount and nature of spam messages.

The way to determine the appropriate SCL for your organization is relatively simple:

1. Enable filtering on the Edge Transport server.

2. Leave all three of the check boxes in the Action tab (shown previously in Figure 9-13) cleared.

3. Set up a counter log using the Performance Logs and Alerts MMC snap-in that monitors the 10 "Messages with SCL X" counters (where X represents values 0 through 9), shown in the following illustration.

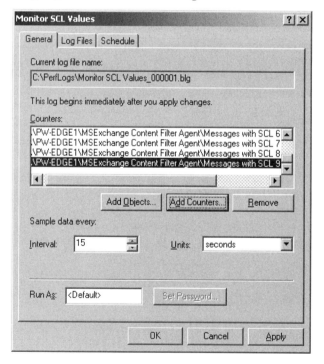

4. Allow messages to enter the organization without any action being taken by the Edge Transport server for at least 24 hours.

5. Review the data recorded in the counter log to see what SCL values are most prevalent.

6. Find the SCL value where the number of messages having that value takes a spike from the lower values, and begin your configuration of the three Action check boxes based on what action(s) you want taken. For example, if the number of messages with an SCL of 0 to 7 is relatively even and then the number messages with an SCL of 8 is much higher than 0 to 7, start there.

7. Watch the effects of the configuration; you may need to raise or lower the SCL choices if too many valid messages are being deleted/rejected/ quarantined (in which case you should raise the SCL values used) or if too many spam messages are getting through (in which case you should lower the SCL values used).

8. Remember this is still a "best-effort" method of implementing SCL in your organization.

Sender ID

We've all received spam messages where the sender purported to be from a reputable domain ("Bill Gates will give you a million dollars if you forward this message to 10 friends!"). With Sender ID, Exchange takes the IP address of the sender, along with the claimed source domain, and queries the sender's domain to see if the IP address is authorized to send messages from that domain. To use this feature, the source domain administrator would need to publish sender policy framework (SPF) records in their DNS.

You can choose among three options when configuring how the Sender ID filter will act, as shown in Figure 9-14. Because not every domain has SPF records set up, the default setting is to stamp the Sender ID result, which has an effect on the SCL rating for the message (which I'll address just a bit later in this chapter), and allow the message to pass through.

Sender Filtering

Once a message has passed the IP address scrutiny of the connection filter, Exchange focuses on who the sender claims to be, based on e-mail address. The Blocked Senders

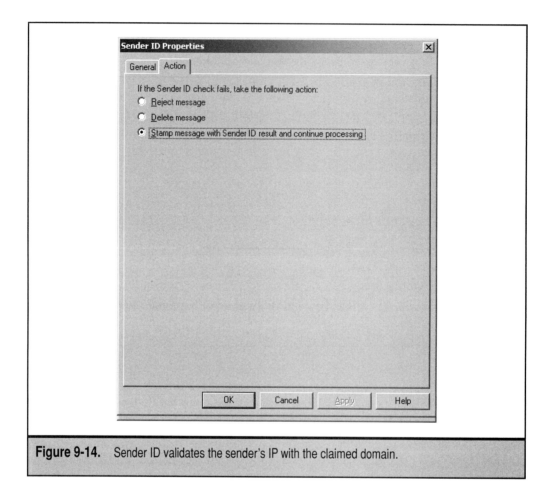

Figure 9-14.   Sender ID validates the sender's IP with the claimed domain.

tab on the Sender Filtering properties, shown in Figure 9-15, allows you to enter both individual e-mail addresses as well as entire domains that should be blocked (you can include subdomains with a single entry). You can use this feature if there is a domain you feel you are receiving spam from (even though the sender believes their own messages to be legitimate); the sender may not meet the criteria of an IP Block list provider and their IP addresses may change periodically (a symbol of the sender being a spammer), so blocking based on sender address makes sense.

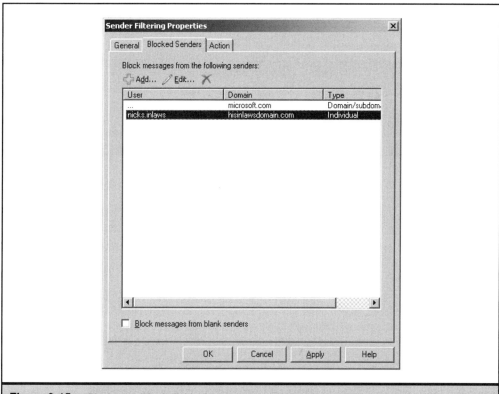

Figure 9-15.   Block e-mail by individual addresses and domains.

Recipient Filtering

This feature is useful when you don't want specific internal addresses to receive external messages. As shown in Figure 9-16, you can block messages sent to addresses hidden from the global address list, as well as identify those recipients that should not receive external messages.

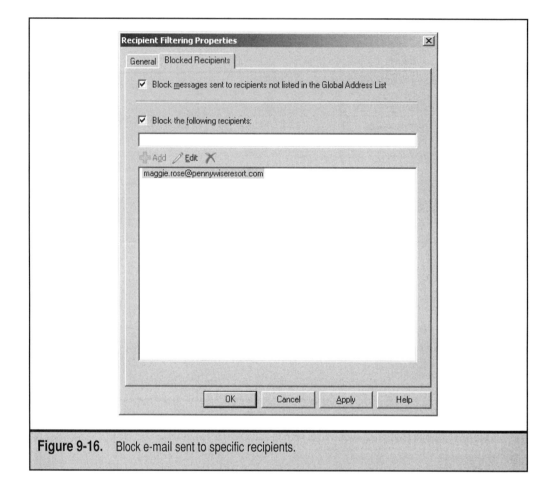

Figure 9-16. Block e-mail sent to specific recipients.

Sender Reputation (Protocol Analysis)

As previously mentioned in this chapter, Exchange calculates an SRL based on a few tests:

▼ HELO/EHLO analysis

■ Reverse DNS lookup

■ Analysis of SCL ratings on messages from the same domain

▲ Sender open-proxy tests

The first three tests happen without any configuration on your part. The sender open-proxy test can be separately enabled or disabled on the Server Confidence tab of the Sender Reputation Properties dialog box.

Like the SCL, the SRL for a given sender is value from 0 to 9. You can establish the threshold level of a non-reputable sender and choose what Exchange should do on the Actions tab of the Sender Reputation Properties dialog box, shown in Figure 9-17.

The only action Exchange takes based on SRL is to move the sender to the IP Block list (which, oddly enough, can contain more than just IP addresses) for the period you specify. The range is from 0 to 48 hours. The premise behind not making the block permanent is that this is an issue of reputation (which can change over a period of time). Don't worry—if a sender continually is sending spam that triggers a high SRL, the sender will continually remain on the IP Block list.

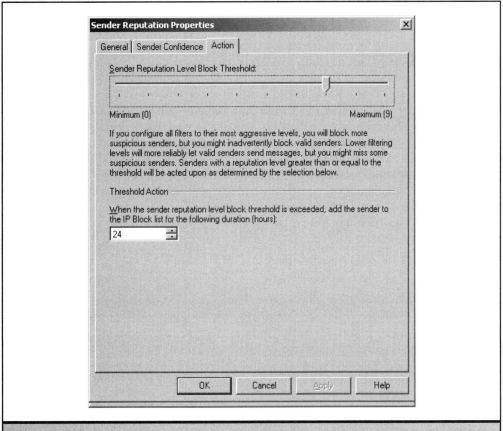

Figure 9-17.   Determining the action to take based on SRL.

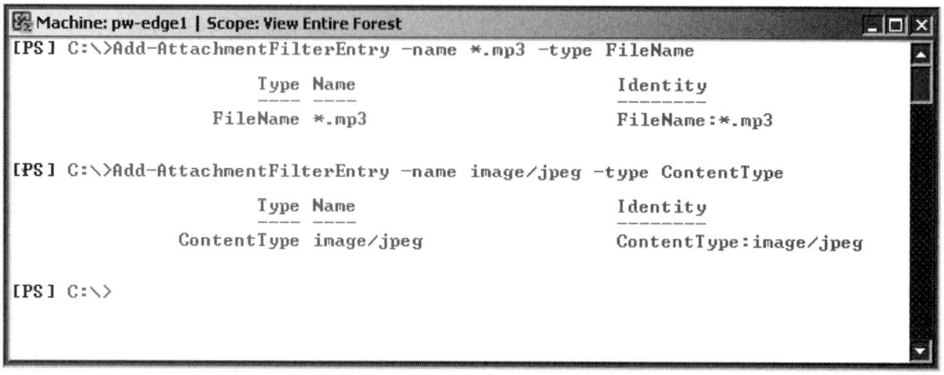

Figure 9-18. Adding an attachment filter.

Attachment Filtering

This feature is last because the outcome of this filter is the removal of the attachment and not the message. Therefore, all of the message-specific filters will determine if a given message can enter the organization, and then the attachment filter determines if the attachments are allowed. Exchange allows you to block attachments based on either file name or MIME type. File names can be either exact matches (such as "maliciousfile.exe") or simply an extension (such as "*.mp3"). You can find a list of MIME file types at www .iana.org/assignments/media-types.

To add an attachment filter, you will need to open the Exchange Management Shell and use the `Add-AttachmentFilterEntry` cmdlet. An example of both commands can be found in Figure 9-18.

SUMMARY

Microsoft has gone to great lengths to keep Exchange a productive messaging solution by introducing the Edge Transport server role. By moving many of the functions previously accomplished internally on an Exchange server to a dedicated external server, internal messaging will function more efficiently and more securely.

This is the last server role–focused chapter in the book. In the next chapter, I'll switch gears and focus the next two chapters on administering Exchange clients.

PART

Administering Clients

CHAPTER 10

Administering Exchange 2007 Clients

Until now, I have focused on the server side of Exchange 2007 Server because this book is about administering Exchange. However, it would do us well to go over the various clients that exist for Exchange 2007 Server and that you might find in your environment:

▼ Microsoft Outlook 2007

■ Previous versions of Microsoft Outlook

▲ Microsoft Outlook Express and other Post Office Protocol version 3 (POP3)/ Internet Messaging Access Protocol 4 (IMAP4) clients

While each of these clients can be used in an Exchange 2007 environment, I suspect that eventually most of you will be using Microsoft Outlook 2007. Now there is not enough room in this book to cover each of these clients in depth, so I will first cover the various types of supported clients and then spend most of this chapter focusing on Outlook 2007 and some of its new Exchange-specific features. You'll also notice that Outlook Web Access and Outlook Anywhere (formerly RPC over HTTP) are not present in the list of clients covered in this chapter; these clients will be covered in Chapter 11.

OUTLOOK 2007

The release of Outlook 2007, like the overall release of Office 2007, represents a completely new mode of working by completely changing the interface, keeping user productivity in mind, and more tightly integrating functionality with other Microsoft technologies, like SharePoint Server 2007 and InfoPath. In this section, I'll take a look at what's new with Outlook, give you a basic primer on what you should expect as you begin using it, and the Exchange-related features that are new to Outlook 2007.

Outlook Editions

Microsoft now offers Outlook 2007 in eight ways: as a standalone and in any one of seven flavors of Office. However, Outlook 2007 itself comes in two editions: Standard and Professional. While they are nearly identical, Table 10-1 lists the major functional differences in the products, which I will address in detail.

IRM Support

Within the context of Outlook, Information Rights Management (IRM) allows you to control what recipients of an e-mail (and corresponding documents for other Microsoft solutions) can do to the e-mail as well as to the attachment. For example, in order to protect the confidential information within an e-mail you are sending to your company's legal counsel, you could decide that the e-mail and any attachments can be read by the recipient, but not copied, printed, forwarded, etc. Outlook 2007 Standard can only be the recipient of messages and attachments protected with IRM, while the Professional

Outlook Feature	Outlook 2007 Standard	Outlook 2007 Professional
Information Rights Management (IRM)	Can only utilize existing IRM-protected content	Can create and utilize IRM-protected content
InfoPath form integration	Supported	Supported
Workflow support	Can receive workflow notifications	Can initiate and complete workflow tasks
Support for managed folders	Supported	Supported

Table 10-1. Differences in Outlook Editions

edition can generate messages and attachments protected with IRM. Plan your edition purchases and deployments accordingly if you plan on implementing IRM.

You can find out more about Rights Management technologies on Microsoft's Web site at www.microsoft.com/rm.

InfoPath E-mail Forms

Unlike previous versions of Outlook, where electronic forms were created and managed from within Outlook, Outlook 2007 now integrates with InfoPath 2007 to facilitate the creation and management of electronic forms. Outlook 2007 has a new type of folder, the *InfoPath Forms folder*, to store forms and related data. In order to take advantage of this new technology, you will need to have Microsoft Office InfoPath 2007 installed and Outlook configured to use InfoPath forms. More information on using InfoPath forms can be found on Microsoft's Web site at www.microsoft.com/infopath.

Is IRM Foolproof?

IRM's goal is to keep protected information safe. Microsoft has done a great job of ensuring that all their solutions that provide access to information (Office, Internet Explorer, etc.) all work in concert to maintain security. However, I did see an example of a "manual printscreen" that can bypass IRM in the form of a picture of someone who had put a computer monitor on their photocopier! While a silly example, it does bring the more practical method, taking a picture with your cell phone camera, to mind. So within the context of your PC, IRM is fairly secure, but people can still be the weakest link.

Workflow Support

Outlook 2007 integrates Microsoft Office SharePoint Server 2007 to facilitate workflow tasks. In previous versions, Outlook supports the most basic workflow, such as getting someone's approval using a custom form, but the use of SharePoint 2007 empowers the Professional edition of Outlook 2007 to initiate and complete tasks. The Standard edition can only receive notifications within a workflow and not participate in the process.

Managed Folder Support

One of the new features of Exchange 2007 is the concept of managed folders. Outlook 2007 fully supports the creation of managed folders, the retention of content within those folders, and the automatic journaling (copying) of folder content to other locations. More on managed folders can be found in Chapter 17.

New Exchange Features

Because there are far too many changes and new features put into Outlook 2007 to cover in this book, this section will strictly focus on the changes in Outlook 2007 that relate to its interaction with Exchange 2007. One of the first things you will notice is that everything looks different. Don't be fooled—the placement of options and features has been moved around to make you more productive when using Outlook, but under the covers, nearly all detailed dialog boxes remain the same.

Account Settings

One of the first things you'll notice with Outlook 2007 (mostly because you'll need to do this before you can access Exchange) is the change in how Outlook configures the e-mail profile. When you first start Outlook, you are asked to create a new e-mail account. The difference you will see is that Outlook 2007 utilizes the new automatic account setup. The basic idea is that with workstations that are members of Active Directory that is hosting Exchange, you will only need to provide some basic information, and Outlook will configure everything else via the Autodiscover service discussed in Chapter 8. In the example I'll show you, I've logged on as a domain user, so some of the information is already available to Outlook (such as user account).

Outlook Licensing

Unlike previous versions of Exchange, the purchase of an Exchange client access license (CAL) does not include an Outlook 2007 license. Only those customers purchasing an Exchange 2007 Server CAL, Core CAL Suite, or Enterprise CAL Suite that also have Software Assurance as of November 30, 2006, will be granted a license of Outlook 2007 for each Exchange CAL purchased. Those same customers will retain the ability to upgrade to the next version of Outlook as long as their Software Assurance is intact. Should none of this apply to you, you can simply purchase Outlook 2007 as a standalone product or as part of an Office suite.

Figure 10-1 shows what you will see when you initially set up an Outlook profile. Outlook 2007 automatically populates information it can ascertain (such as the full name of the user) and prompts you to provide the e-mail address of the account. You should note that Outlook does allow you to manually configure all aspects of the profile instead of going with the automated steps you will see in this section.

Once an e-mail address has been provided, Outlook 2007 utilizes the Autodiscover service to connect to Exchange, find a Global Catalog server, look up the e-mail address within Active Directory, and find the corresponding users' Exchange server, as shown in Figure 10-2.

Once configured, Outlook 2007 has a new account settings look and feel that allows you a far easier view of all aspects of an e-mail account. Figures 10-3 and 10-4 show the E-mail and Data File settings tabs of the Account Settings dialog box. While this dialog box has a new look, should you modify any of the settings, you will see the familiar detailed dialog boxes you are used to from Outlook 2003.

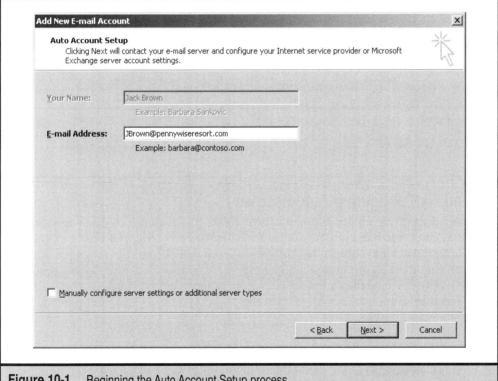

Figure 10-1.   Beginning the Auto Account Setup process.

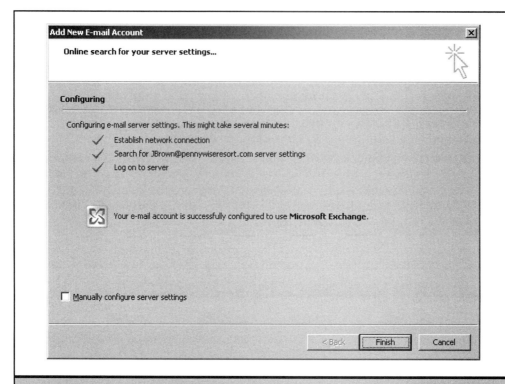

Figure 10-2. Automatically determining Exchange settings.

Manually Configuring Autodiscover

While Microsoft recommends that you utilize the server-based Autodiscover service, in some cases, you may want to localize the Autodiscover configuration; for example, you may not want to publish the Autodiscover eXtensible Markup Language (XML) file on the Internet, or perhaps you simply want to test the Autodiscover process when connectivity to the Autodiscover server is unavailable. To manually configure the location of the Autodiscover XML file, you'll need to create an entry in the following registry key:

```
HKEY_CURRENT_USER\Software\Microsoft\Office\12.0\Outlook\AutoDiscover
```

You'll create a REG_SZ value that will have the name of your e-mail domain, such as "pennywiseresort.com," and a value of the path to the Autodiscover XML file. Microsoft has a downloadable document on its Web site that details the format of the XML file, should you desire to create your own. Search for a document entitled "Outlook Automatic Account Configuration."

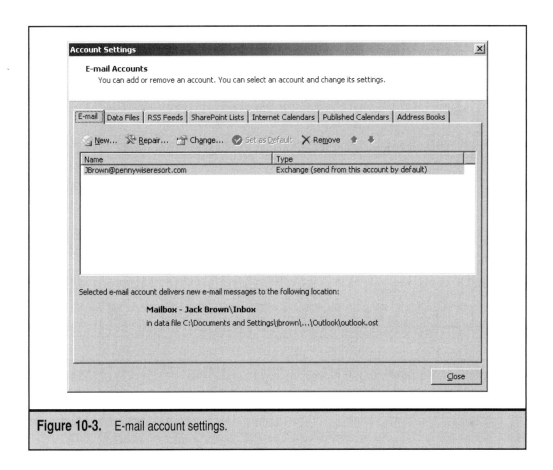

Figure 10-3.   E-mail account settings.

Scheduling Assistant

In previous versions of Outlook, if you wanted to invite a number of people to a meeting, you did have the opportunity to have Outlook show you the next timeslot that all attendees were free to meet. But sometimes, finding out that the only time all the attendees are free is tonight after work simply will not do. So Outlook 2007 has a new Scheduling Assistant that not only tells you when all attendees are free, but also when just a portion of the attendees are free, as shown in the lower-right area of Figure 10-5.

Protection from Spam and Phishing

In an effort to improve protection against malicious e-mail, Outlook 2007 has a few new smaller options I'd like to cover. Hopefully, none of you have been a victim of phishing, where an e-mail claims to be from a legitimate company (such as a bank) and invites you to provide personal information (such as a social security number) by making you think there is a problem with your account at the legitimate business. Outlook 2007's Junk E-Mail Options dialog box has a new feature that disables phishing functionality in suspect messages, shown in Figure 10-6.

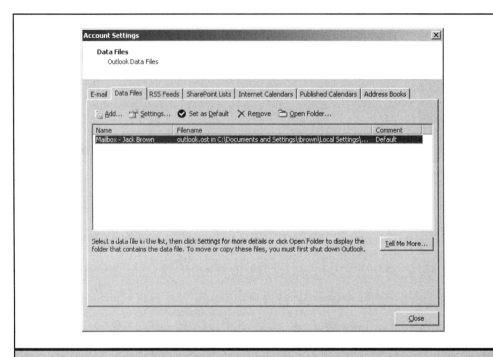

Figure 10-4. Data file account settings.

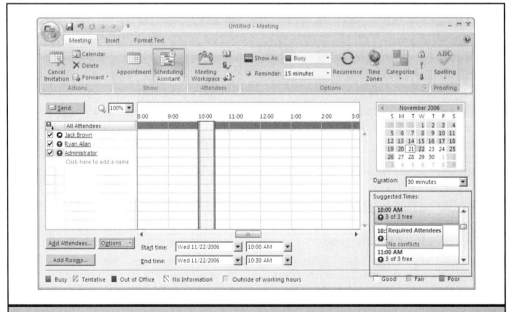

Figure 10-5. Finding the right meeting time with the Scheduling Assistant.

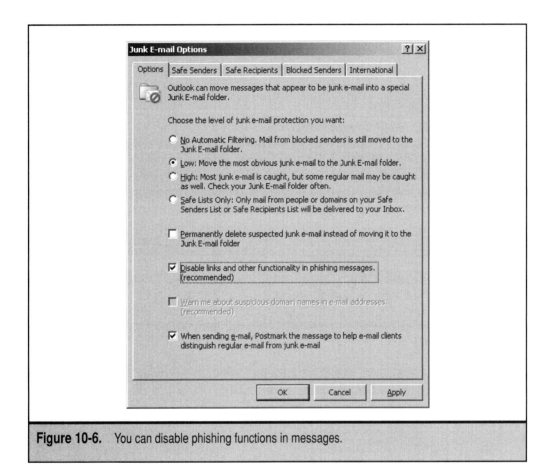

Figure 10-6.   You can disable phishing functions in messages.

You can also take a more aggressive step to block spam and phishing messages by blocking country-specific top-level domains. I can remember receiving a ton of e-mail from specific countries in the Middle East a few years back, so I can see the value of this new feature, shown in Figure 10-7.

One of the other junk e-mail–related capabilities Outlook has is the aggregation of Outlook Safe Senders lists to an Edge Transport server to minimize the number of false positives that may occur at the Edge server. There is no configuration within Outlook; instead, a *safelist collection* is stored within the user's mailbox (although I do cover how to enable safelist aggregation for a given mailbox in Chapter 9). The safelist collection includes the following lists from each user:

▼   Safe Senders

■   Safe Recipients

- ■ Blocked Senders
- ▲ External Contacts

The safelist collection can have up to 1,024 entries in total.

Out of Office Assistant

When providing details about why you're not in the office, where you are, how you can be contacted, etc., it makes sense that you may want to provide different sets of information to those inside and outside of your organization. Outlook 2007 now provides different out-of-office settings for internal and external recipients. Figures 10-8 and 10-9 show how you can establish different messages to be used when messages are sent to you while you are out.

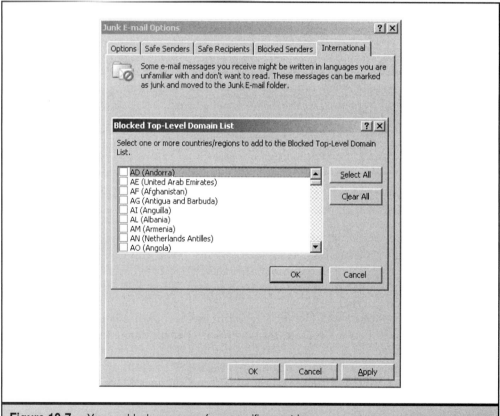

Figure 10-7. You can block messages from specific countries.

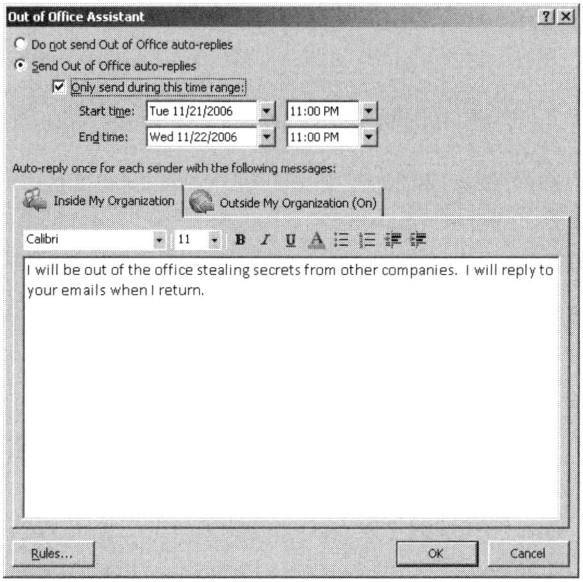

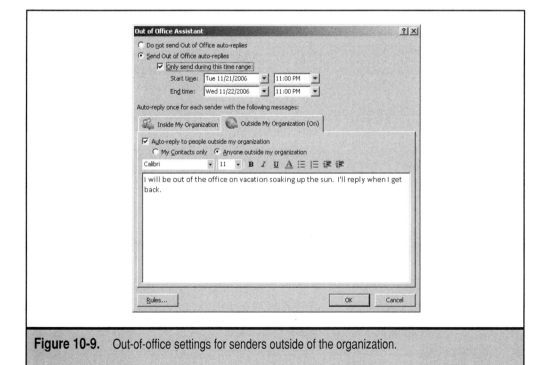

Figure 10-8.   Out-of-office settings for senders within the organization.

Figure 10-9.   Out-of-office settings for senders outside of the organization.

PREVIOUS VERSIONS OF OUTLOOK

From experience, I suspect that when you migrate to Exchange 2007, you'll selectively deploy Outlook 2007, which leaves the majority of your Outlook clients on versions before 2007. From the client-experience perspective, earlier Outlook clients will provide the same functionality as with Exchange 2000/2003.

Table 10-2 lists the various Outlook clients that exist, as well as the compatibility and functionality with Exchange 2007.

TIP Remember, if you plan on using a version of Outlook prior to 2007, you will need to implement public folders (which are not installed by default) in order to take advantage of the offline address book, free/busy information, and Outlook security settings, all of which reside within public folders.

Outlook Version	Compatibility with Exchange 2007	Notes
Outlook 2007	Yes	Preferred client, with complete usage of Exchange 2007 functionality.
Outlook 2003	Yes, but limited in functionality	Newer features are not supported in this version of Outlook, such as improvements in the Out of Office Assistant, scheduling, Autodiscover, and Unified Messaging.
Outlook 2002/XP	Yes, but limited in functionality	Newer features are not supported in this version of Outlook, such as improvements in the Out of Office Assistant, scheduling, Autodiscover, and Unified Messaging.
Outlook 2000	Partially	Outlook 2000, while functional with Exchange 2007 at a basic level, was not tested with Exchange 2007 and, therefore, is not supported by Microsoft as an Exchange 2007 client.
Outlook 97/98	Partially	Outlook 97 and 98, while functional with Exchange 2007 at a basic level, were not tested with Exchange 2007 and, therefore, are not supported by Microsoft as an Exchange 2007 client.

Table 10-2. Outlook Version Compatibility with Exchange 2007

MICROSOFT OUTLOOK EXPRESS

Outlook Express ships and installs with Internet Explorer. Its main advantage over Outlook 2000 is that it has a Network News Transfer Protocol (NNTP) client that works well with Internet newsgroups. It also has the ability to send and retrieve e-mail, and possesses both the POP3 and IMAP4 clients. Outlook Express can also query X.500-based directories over Lightweight Directory Access Protocol (LDAP). In an Exchange environment, Outlook Express does not query a directory via Exchange. Instead, it will query Active Directory directly over TCP port 389 via a specified domain controller.

Where Outlook Express falls short is in its inability to connect to public folders and its lack of calendaring abilities. In my consulting experience, I have generally recommended Outlook Express primarily as a newsgroup reader and Outlook for all other functions.

OTHER CLIENTS

Because Exchange 2007 and Windows Server 2003 are standards-based platforms, nearly any POP3 or IMAP4 client will be compatible with Exchange 2007, but limited to the scope of functionality provided by each standard. If you are running other Internet mail clients, you can use Exchange 2007 Server as your messaging server, although some functionality may be sacrificed in this situation.

In our discussions in this book, I have readily assumed a complete Windows operating system environment. However, there are many UNIX and Macintosh deployments as well, and we need to consider how non-Windows–based clients can connect to Exchange 2007 Server.

UNIX Clients

There is no Outlook or Exchange client for the UNIX operating system, so UNIX users have one of two choices to make.

The first option is that a standards-based POP3 or IMAP4 client may be used to access messages from the Exchange 2007 Server. If access to public folders is necessary, then an IMAP4 client should be utilized, because a POP3 client cannot access public folders.

The second option is to install a browser on the UNIX computer and use Outlook Web Access (OWA) to access e-mail. This might be a preferred method in some environments, since the same utility can be used for more than one purpose.

> ### Using POP3/IMAP4
> By default, Exchange has both of these services disabled. See how to enable and configure these protocols in Chapter 8.

Macintosh Clients

There are several choices that can be made for a Macintosh client. First, there is a Macintosh version of Outlook (Entourage 2004 for Mac) that will work with all versions of Exchange. The Entourage client is being updated on a regular basis. Usually, this client lacks some of the functionality of the Windows-based versions (especially Outlook 2007), and my consulting experience suggests that it tends to require more administrative effort to install and maintain. Like UNIX clients, a second choice would be for Mac users to install and use a generic POP3 or IMAP4 client. Finally, a third choice for Macintosh users would be to use OWA for e-mail from a Macintosh-based browser.

SUMMARY

In this chapter, you have learned about the various clients that are available as messaging clients for Exchange Server 2007. Moreover, you've learned how Outlook 2007 can configure more on its own and seen some of the new Exchange-specific features. I really just scratched the surface of this client. There are entire books out there that can be referenced for every detail of this powerful client.

In the next chapter, I'll continue the client discussion and focus on how mobile clients can utilize Outlook Web Access, ActiveSync, and Outlook Anywhere.

CHAPTER 11

Administering Mobile Clients

In the previous chapter, I focused on the traditional clients available for Exchange. But as I've mentioned several times in this book, Microsoft's ever-present goal for Exchange is to provide "anytime, anywhere, any device" access to your messages. In order to meet this goal, several mobile clients are available for your use to remotely access Exchange. Now, to be clear, when I say "mobile," I don't necessarily mean a Pocket PC type of client; I really mean any client that is mobile—this could be a laptop, a roaming user logging on from a friend's home computer, or a mobile phone browser, as well as the Pocket PC (now called Windows Mobile) type clients. In this chapter, I'll cover the latest versions of several mobile clients you may take advantage of in your environment:

▼ Outlook Web Access (OWA) Premium for Web-based access

■ OWA Light for dial-up Web-based access

■ Outlook Anywhere (formerly RPC over HTTP) for external access to Exchange within Outlook

■ Windows Mobile devices

▲ Outlook Voice Access for retrieving voice and e-mail messages via phone

Remember, in this chapter, in all cases I'll be focusing on the *client-side* features and configuration. The server-side configurations can be found in Chapter 7, where I covered the Unified Messaging server role and Chapter 8, where I covered the Client Access server role.

OUTLOOK WEB ACCESS PREMIUM

Many OWA users have desired to utilize it as a primary client. While the OWA in Exchange 2003 was close to this, the latest version of OWA is even closer (if not there). The primary focus of OWA is to provide access to messages, schedules, contacts, tasks, and read-only access to external data, such as Windows file and SharePoint servers, all from a lightweight browser-based client. The Premium edition is a fully functional client; the Light edition is used for those clients with slower connectivity or with a legacy browser.

NOTE   To use OWA Premium, you'll need to be running at least Windows 98 and Internet Explorer version 6 or later.

The first thing you'll notice when logging on to OWA is the number of options available to you before you even provide your credentials (see Figure 11-1). First, you must specify whether the computer you are using is public or private—this is basically asking you whether you want an extended session time before OWA logs you off. If you're on your private laptop, the session can leave you logged on longer because there is less of a security risk. The public computer setting uses a shorter timeframe to promote a more secure use of OWA. The selection of Outlook Web Access Light will use a limited version

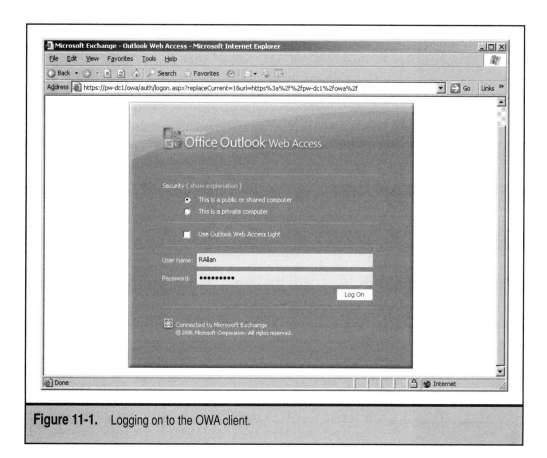

Figure 11-1.   Logging on to the OWA client.

of OWA, which I will cover later in this chapter. On your first logon to OWA, you will be asked if you wish to use the blind and low vision experience, as well as what your primary language and time zone are.

Logon Credentials

Depending on the way you configure OWA, you can log on using the following types:

- ▼ DOMAIN\User name
- ■ Principal name (for example, MRose@pennywiseresort.com)
- ▲ User name

For more information on how to configure OWA to support these credential types, refer to Chapter 9.

Once logged on, you'll notice the interface has been updated to have a similar look and feel to that of Outlook 2007, as shown in Figure 11-2. For those of you new to OWA entirely, this client can be used as an effective means of managing message, calendar, contact, and task items within your mailbox, which make up most of your mailbox contents. It does not provide the means to manage the Outlook journal or the Really Simple Syndication (RSS) feed features of Outlook 2007. Don't get me wrong; OWA is a rich client with plenty of additional functionality, which I will spell out in this section, but it still doesn't hold a candle to Outlook 2007, Exchange's primary client.

In this section, I'm going to assume that even if you're new to Exchange, you have used a Web-based e-mail client of some kind, so I won't be going through things like how to create and send an e-mail, etc. Instead, I want to focus on the features that make OWA a uniquely effective Web-based messaging client.

Familiar Interface

One of the most important features that Microsoft has achieved with OWA is its similarity to that of Outlook 2007. The reason I bring this up as a "feature" is that having a common

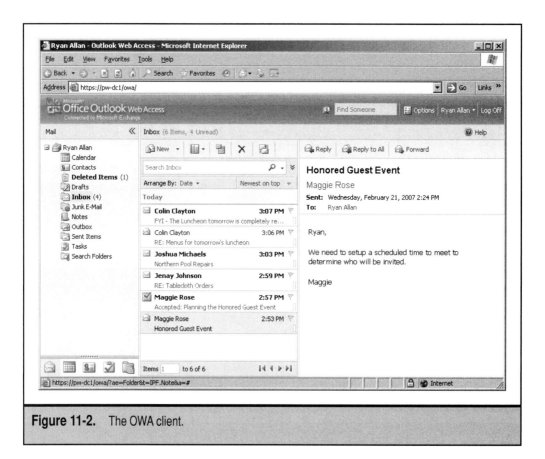

Figure 11-2.   The OWA client.

interface for Outlook users who need to switch (either temporarily or permanently) to OWA carries a minimal (if nonexistent) learning curve. You can see in Figure 11-3 the similarity between OWA and Outlook 2007. These similarities include (starting in the lower-left area of the OWA window and moving clockwise within the same window for reference):

▼ The Navigation pane that can be used to quickly access specific commonly used folders

■ The Folder list showing the various folders within a mailbox and appropriate icons to denote content types

■ Access to the indexed search and arrangements when viewing messages

■ A context-sensitive toolbar

▲ The ability to search both the global address list and local contacts

Keep in mind that I've only focused on the similarities when a folder containing messages is selected. The same look and feel exists when managing your calendar, contacts, and tasks.

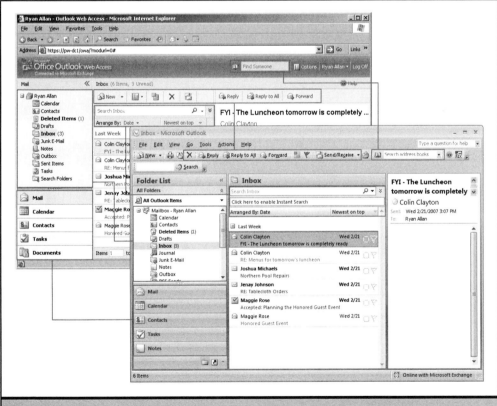

Figure 11-3.   Similarities between OWA and Outlook.

Access to External Data

Earlier versions of OWA restricted users to only working with the data within their own mailbox and accessible public folders. But users today need access to many sources of collaborative data, and securely providing access to a user who is potentially outside the confines of the corporate network would be an extremely productive feature set. The new version of OWA allows easy access to a number of data sets beyond that of its predecessors, giving users the ability to touch not just their individual e-mail, but also the collaborative data they require to be effective.

Access to Additional Mailboxes

OWA can now easily open other user's mailboxes using an interface similar to that of Outlook. Shown in Figure 11-4, OWA uses an Outlook-like interface to open the mailbox of another user and even provides the AutoFill function to simplify the process. Keep in mind that you will, of course, need appropriate permissions to open another user's mailbox. There is no method for keeping another mailbox open all the time—you'll need to switch between the various mailboxes you are interested in by using the same Open Other Mailbox feature.

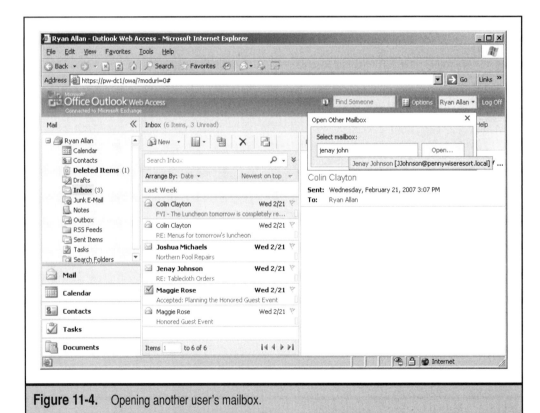

Figure 11-4.   Opening another user's mailbox.

NOTE   Mailbox permissions are viewed and managed in the Exchange Management Shell. See Chapter 13 for more information.

Access to Public Folders

While not available for Exchange 2007–based public folders, I thought I'd mention that the public folders are accessible from OWA in a mixed Exchange 2000/2003 and 2007 environment when the public folders reside on a legacy Exchange 2000/2003 server. They are accessible using the default Uniform Resource Location (URL) of *<servername>/public*.

Access to Shares and SharePoint

One of the best new features of OWA is its ability to directly access both folder shares and SharePoint sites without the need for a virtual private network (VPN), providing read-only retrieval of data. The server hosting the Client Access server role proxies the requests to retrieve the documents so that no internal servers are ever exposed to the Internet. Access is accomplished by first selecting the Documents link in the Navigation pane, resulting in the view shown in Figure 11-5. The location path specified must be first allowed on the specific server hosting OWA (which you can find out more about in Chapter 8).

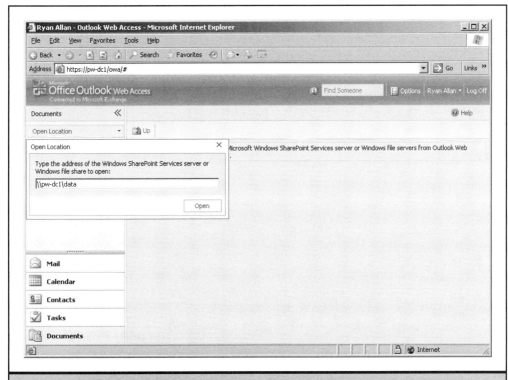

Figure 11-5.   Specifying a file server in OWA.

The path can be either a universal naming convention (UNC) path to a folder share or the Web address to a SharePoint site. In the case of a folder share, you can see in Figure 11-6 that OWA lists the folders and files contained within the path you specified. (In the example of Figure 11-6, I've opened the initial set of folders and drilled down one level deep, as indicated by the UNC path "\\pw-dc1\data\Event Planning" in the upper-middle section of the OWA window, to show a listing of various files that are accessible to an OWA user, regardless if he or she is internal or external to the corporate network.

WebReady Document Viewing

Another of the new technologies I discussed in Chapter 8 is viewing WebReady documents. This gives your OWA users the ability to view documents for programs they may not have installed (such as any products from the Microsoft Office suite) and also maintain the security of the document being viewed by not having to download it in its original format (the read document is converted to HTML) to be exploited by other users or processes on the computer.

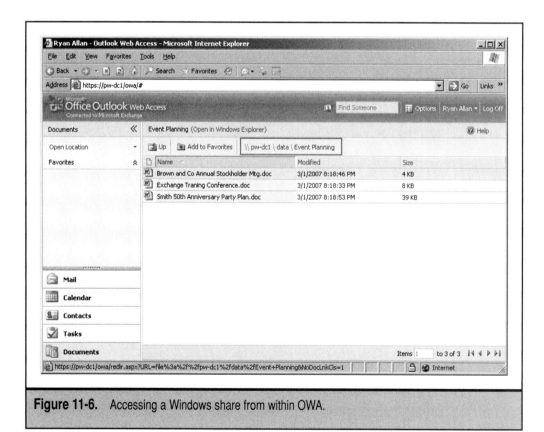

Figure 11-6.   Accessing a Windows share from within OWA.

The default applications supported are:

▼   Microsoft Word

■   Microsoft Excel

■   Microsoft PowerPoint

▲   Adobe Acrobat

This list may be lengthened in a service pack, as Microsoft has made the architecture extensible to include additional file types. If the attachment you wish to open is supported as a WebReady document, the attachment will have a special link, shown in Figure 11-7, to open the attachment as Hypertext Markup Language (HTML).

When you select the Open As A Web Page link, the attachment will be *transcoded* (that is the technical term for this process) into HTML and presented in a new window, as shown in Figure 11-8.

Configurable Client Experience

One of the issues with many Web clients is a lack of customization functionality beyond that of messaging (that is, e-mails, address book, Inbox/Sent Items folders, etc.). If you think in terms of the Outlook client, many settings can be configured to customize the user experience to specifically meet their needs. While OWA in Exchange 2007 is nowhere near Outlook, it has plenty of options to create an individual experience for the user. Figure 11-9 shows the Options pane (which is accessed by clicking the Options link in the upper-right area of any of the non-Option views of OWA). Table 11-1 lists the various sections and the types of settings you can configure.

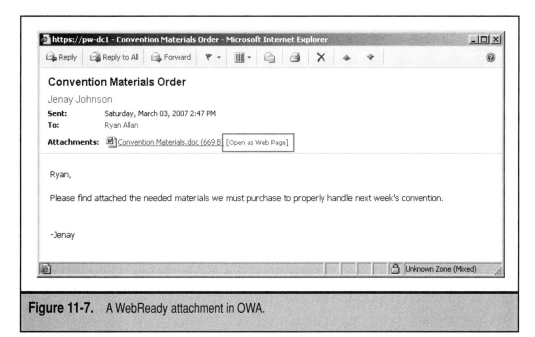

Figure 11-7. A WebReady attachment in OWA.

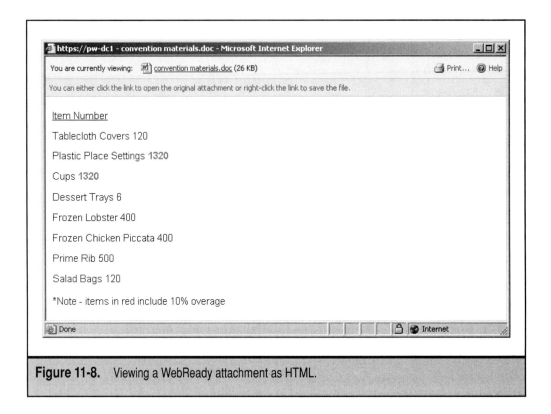

Figure 11-8. Viewing a WebReady attachment as HTML.

There are many other enhancements to OWA that are specific to each data type (message, calendar, task, note) that mirror OWA to Outlook 2007, each one improving the productivity of users as well as the viability of OWA as a full-fledged client. It's worth spending a little time to review these on your own. For now, let's move on to the next mobile client: OWA Light.

OUTLOOK WEB ACCESS LIGHT

While I believe you will agree that Outlook Web Access Premium is a feature-rich Web-based client, OWA Light is not too far behind. OWA Light is a restricted (and yet still feature-rich) version of OWA that should be used when connectivity is an issue, when using a third-party browser, or when using higher security settings that may not allow OWA Premium to function properly. Table 11-2 lists the browser and operating system requirements to run OWA Light.

NOTE   If you have Macintosh or UNIX/Linux clients, you can look at the Safari, Firefox, and Netscape Navigator browsers to meet your needs.

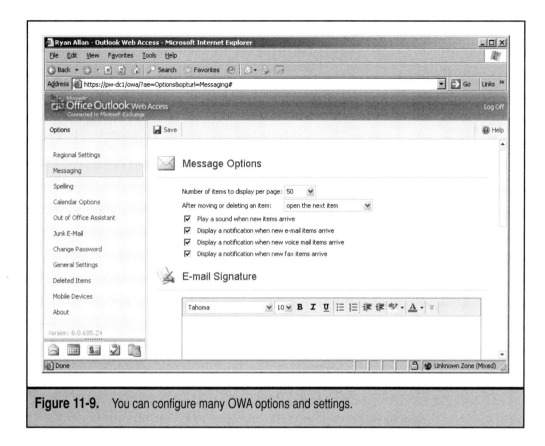

Figure 11-9.   You can configure many OWA options and settings.

Figure 11-10 shows what the OWA Light experience is like. While at first glance it is a reasonably good interface that seems to have most of the user experience covered, the following is a non-exhaustive list of features *not* found in OWA Light:

▼   Reading pane

■   Spelling check

■   Flags and categories

■   Notifications and reminders

■   Access to Windows shares and SharePoint

■   Drag-and-drop capability

■   Right-click menus

▲   Printing (although you can print the entire Web page)

OWA Option	Description
Regional Settings	Establish language, date, and time preferences
Messaging	Establish notification, signature, message format, and message-tracking preferences
Spelling	Select spell-checking options and the language of the dictionary used
Calendar Options	Set calendar presentation, reminder, and scheduling options
Out Of Office Assistant	Configure the out-of-office messages for both internal and external recipients
Junk E-MAIL	Enable junk filtering as well as manage safe senders, blocked senders, and safe recipients lists
Change Password	Modify the password for your Active Directory user account
General Settings	Establish name resolution priority, OWA themes, and accessibility settings
Deleted Items	Choose whether to empty the Deleted Items folder upon exit
Mobile Devices	Remotely wipe your mobile device, and display the mobile device's recovery password

Table 11-1.   Configurable Options in OWA

Operating System	Supported Internet Explorer Versions	Supported Third-Party Browsers
Windows 95	Not supported	Not supported
Windows 98	Internet Explorer 5.01 or later	None
Windows ME	Internet Explorer 5.5 or later	None
Windows 2000	Internet Explorer 5.01 or later	None
Windows XP/2003 Server	Internet Explorer 6 or later	Firefox 1.8 or later Opera 7.54 or later

Table 11-2.   Browser and Operating System Requirements for OWA Light

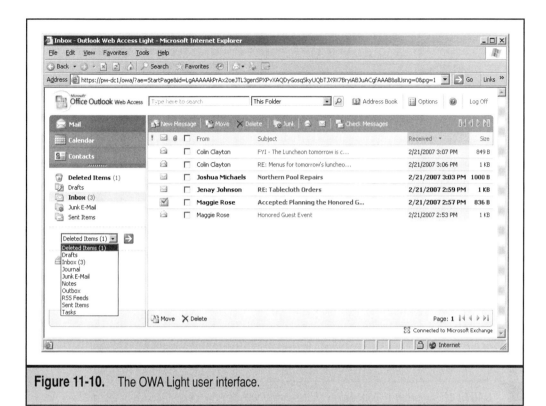

Figure 11-10.   The OWA Light user interface.

OUTLOOK ANYWHERE

In the previous chapter, I covered what was new with Outlook 2007. The one thing I purposely did not cover is Outlook Anywhere. It was previously referred to as RPC over HTTP (that is, Remote Procedure Calls over Hypertext Transfer Protocol) in Outlook 2003. I left it for this chapter because it is what allows Outlook 2007 to run from anywhere in the world outside of the reaches of the corporate network, making Outlook a mobile client.

What Outlook Anywhere does is take the RPC traffic that normally travels within your corporate network between the Outlook client and the Exchange server to make and serve messaging requests and instead sends them over a secure HTTP connection, presumably across the Internet, as shown in the following illustration. So without Outlook Anywhere, if you wanted to make Outlook function externally, you'd need to set up VPN access to the internal network, have the client first connect the VPN client, and then load Outlook. With Outlook Anywhere, the client simply launches Outlook, and the RPC traffic is automatically sent over HTTP (which can either be allowed directly to the Client Access server or via an ISA server for added security) to connect the Outlook client to Exchange.

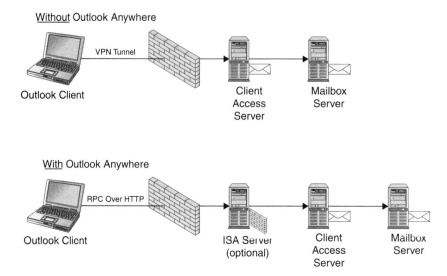

So the only differences to the end user between running on your network and using Outlook Anywhere are the transport protocol (which they will, of course, be oblivious to), the speed at which the user connects (as I would think it safe to assume that the connection speed is slower than your corporate network), and the location you are running Outlook from.

CAUTION   In order to connect to Outlook via Outlook Anywhere, there must be a Client Access server with Outlook Anywhere enabled (this is covered in Chapter 8), ready to accept connections from Outlook 2007 and 2003 clients.

Configuring Outlook Anywhere

Each Outlook client needs to be configured to support connectivity to Exchange over HTTP. Let me first show you how to do this manually within Outlook 2007 and then address how Exchange assists with the configuration automatically.

Manual Configuration

You need to edit the Outlook profile to configure Outlook Anywhere. You can access the profile settings by either running the Mail applet in Control Panel or from within Outlook by selecting Account Settings from the Tools menu. (Note: While I'll be covering the specifics for Outlook 2007, Outlook 2003 is nearly identical.) On the Account Settings dialog box, shown in Figure 11-11, select the Exchange settings and click the Change button.

For best performance, Outlook Anywhere requires the profile be in Cached Mode (if you're not familiar with Cached Mode, it is an offline version of your Exchange mailbox available whether you are connected to the Exchange server or not). This enhances performance of the client, as there is less need to pull data constantly from the Exchange server. On the Change E-mail Account dialog box, shown in Figure 11-12, select the Use

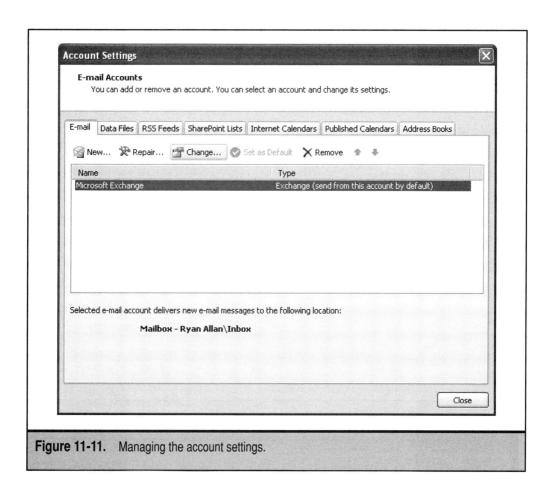

Figure 11-11. Managing the account settings.

Cached Exchange Mode check box—this will automatically create an offline folder file (.ost) and configure Outlook to use it. The next time you open Outlook, the OST file will be used and Outlook will synchronize it with your mailbox. To continue the Outlook Anywhere configuration, click the More Settings button.

If you want to configure the offline folder file further, select the Advanced tab and click the Offline Folder File Settings button, as shown in Figure 11-13. Here you can select the file location, compress the OST (to preserve disk space), and disable offline use (which you can also do by clearing the Use Cached Exchange Mode check box shown earlier).

The Outlook Anywhere settings are found on the Connections tab. You first need to select the Connect To Microsoft Exchange Using HTTP check box and then click the Exchange Proxy Settings button to display the Microsoft Exchange Proxy Settings dialog box, shown in Figure 11-14. You will need to provide a URL to connect to (and this URL must be accessible from the Internet, either directly or via an ISA server), choose to use a secure sockets layer (SSL) connection (which is recommended to the point that it should

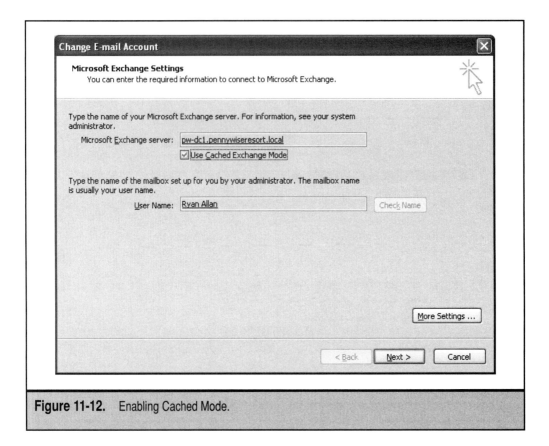

Figure 11-12.　Enabling Cached Mode.

be an absolute must). You can also determine whether Outlook should attempt the default RPC over TCP/IP before trying over HTTP using the last two check boxes in the Connection Settings section. You would nearly always have Outlook configured to use HTTP first on slow networks. You may also have a need for HTTP first on fast networks if you know that a particular user will almost always be outside of the corporate network but will still be on a high-speed network (as in the case of a contractor). You may also configure HTTP first on a fast network when you want to test connectivity to the Outlook Anywhere URL while you are still on your corporate network.

Enhancing Security

Additional security is accomplished by selecting the Only Connect To Proxy Servers That Have This Principal Name In Their Certificate check box and putting in the URL of the Client Access server's external URL using the format *MSSTD:<url>*.

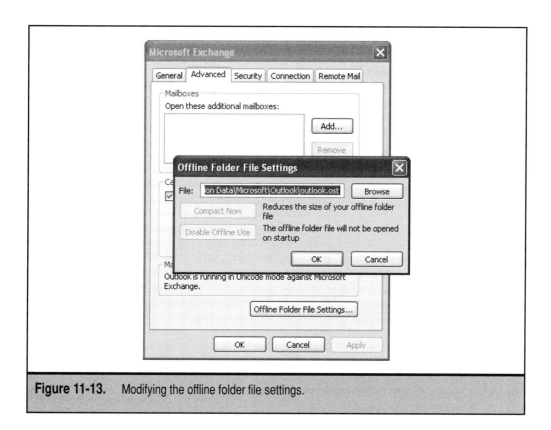

Figure 11-13. Modifying the offline folder file settings.

Lastly, you can select basic or NT LAN Manager (NTLM) authentication. The default is NTLM authentication, which will use your current logon credentials and pass them on to Exchange. Selecting basic authentication will cause Outlook to prompt you for credentials each time you start it. You would only use this if you need to log on to Windows with one set of credentials and Exchange with another.

To complete the process, the usual several clicks of OKs, a Next, and a Finish will preserve these settings.

Automatic Configuration

In Chapter 8, I briefly covered the Autodiscover service that provides, among other data sets, information related to your Outlook Anywhere configuration when using Outlook 2007. To recap, several other settings Outlook 2007 requires to function externally are automatically configured using the Autodiscover service. These include URLs defining where to access the offline address book, the availability service (which provides free/busy information), and unified messaging services. Even with these automatically configured, you will need to perform the steps covered in the previous section.

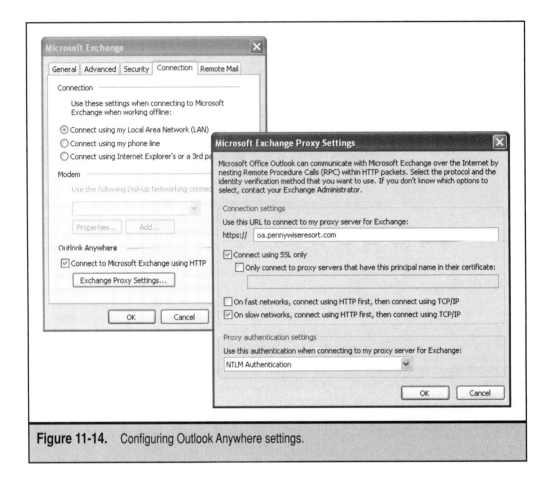

Figure 11-14.   Configuring Outlook Anywhere settings.

You can use a few different tools to automate the Outlook Anywhere configuration steps from the previous section. Microsoft has the Office Customization tool for use when you initially deploy Outlook. Should you need to make changes once Office has been deployed, you can use third-party solutions, such as ScriptLogic's Desktop Authority to keep Outlook Anywhere settings up to date.

WINDOWS MOBILE

Windows Mobile clients exist in a couple of varieties: Pocket PCs have been around for quite a number of years, but the Windows Mobile integrated cellular phones have truly made Windows Mobile a viable mobile client for Exchange.

For those of you new to what Windows Mobile clients can do with regards to your interaction with Exchange, the history goes something like this: Microsoft first introduced Mobile Information Server (MIS) as a platform to deliver information to mobile clients. The first execution of MIS was for Windows CE/Pocket PC clients (the former names for what is now Windows Mobile) to retrieve messages, contacts, and calendar information wirelessly. MIS eventually became integrated into Exchange 2003, where ActiveSync services played the role of an MIS server, and Windows Mobile 2003 replaced Pocket PC 2002 and began to include more and more cellular-based clients accessing their Exchange data from across the Internet wirelessly.

Today, Windows Mobile clients enjoy much of the same basic functionality as the previous versions: synchronizing your Inbox, calendar items, contacts, and tasks. The difference is that today Windows Mobile includes Direct Push technology that allows Exchange to notify clients of new updates for the client to pull down. Instead of getting your new messages when your Windows Mobile client hits the next interval, Direct Push technology works much like the RPC traffic in Outlook; Exchange notifies the client that there are updates, and the client requests the new information from Exchange. This way, you get your new messages and other data items as soon as they come in (and the client is notified, of course).

Initial Device Configuration

Assuming that your Windows Mobile device has wireless access (in the case of being within your company's wireless network) or cellular access (for external access) to Exchange, the configuration of the mobile device would be as follows: Select ActiveSync from the Start menu to launch the ActiveSync application, shown in Figure 11-15 and 11-16. Selecting the Set Up Your Device To Sync With It link starts the Edit Server Settings Wizard, which configures the mobile device's connection to Exchange.

On the first page of the Edit Server Settings Wizard, you will need to provide the address of either the Exchange server hosting the Client Access role with ActiveSync configured or an ISA server that proxies the requests to the Exchange server. This address needs to match the external address specified within Exchange (see Chapter 8 for more information on this setting), as well as the common name on the SSL certificate. Select whether you will be using an encrypted connection, and click Next to continue the wizard.

On the next page of the wizard, shown in Figure 11-17, provide the user credentials to log on and access the Exchange mailbox. Advanced settings allow you to determine how the mobile device should handle conflicts when synchronizing data, as well as whether to log events for troubleshooting purposes. Click Next to continue the wizard.

On the next page, you can select which data sets should be synchronized, as shown in Figure 11-18. You can configure how far in the past you want calendar and e-mail items to be synchronized, as well as e-mail and attachment size limits, security options, and the primary e-mail address for the account.

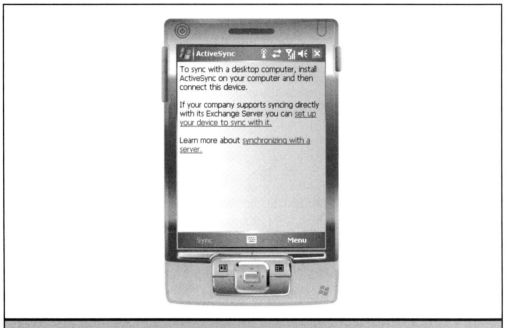

Figure 11-15. Launching ActiveSync on your mobile device.

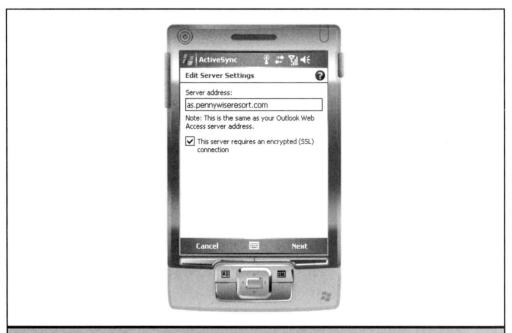

Figure 11-16. Specify the URL of your ActiveSync Exchange server.

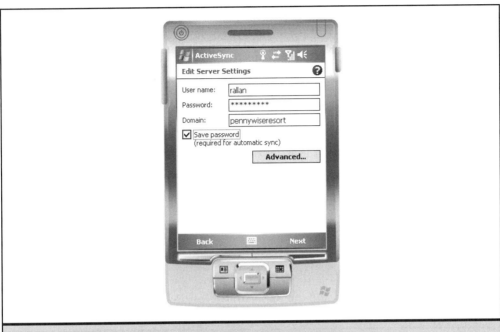

Figure 11-17. Configuring user credentials.

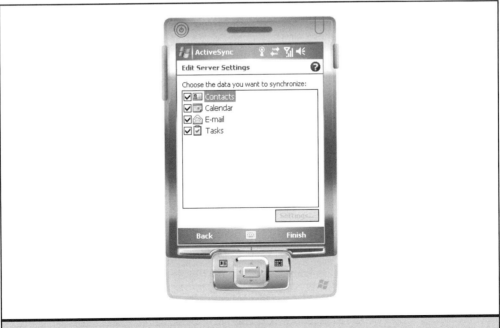

Figure 11-18. Configuring which data to synchronize.

Upon completion, ActiveSync will attempt to synchronize immediately with Exchange. You can modify the schedule the mobile client uses to synchronize by clicking the Menu button in the lower-right area of the ActiveSync application screen and choosing Schedule from the menu. On the Schedule screen, shown in Figure 11-19, you can specify when to synchronize based on "peak" and "off-peak" times. ("Peak" time defaults to Monday through Friday, 8:00 a.m. through 6:00 p.m.).

Windows Mobile 6.0

The screenshots I've shown you (which, by the way, were done using the standalone Windows Mobile Emulator) are using version 5.0 of Windows Mobile. The next version of Windows Mobile (code-named "Crossbow"), was just announced while I was writing this chapter and was unavailable to demo. However, it will have several new Exchange-related features:

▼ Improved rendering of e-mail messages and embedded elements, such as pictures and tables

■ Improved e-mail experience, including setting out-of-office replies, message storage management, and the Reply To All feature

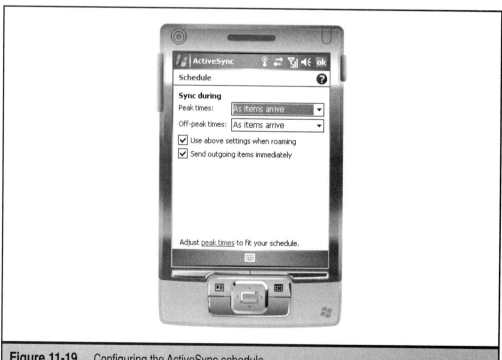

Figure 11-19.   Configuring the ActiveSync schedule.

- Search for messages stored on the Exchange mailbox
- Direct access to SharePoint and internal folder shares linked to from within messages
- ▲ Use of follow-up flags

The process of setup and configuration of the Windows Mobile 6.0 client will be basically the same as the Outlook 2007 Autodiscover feature.

OUTLOOK VOICE ACCESS

The last mobile client is the one that has no graphical user interface (GUI). With Microsoft's introduction of unified messaging, they have also introduced a mobile ability to access all of your messages, be they e-mail, voice, or fax. Outlook Voice Access (OVA) allows you to access all three of the message types from any phone in the world. E-mail messages can be read to you, you can (of course) listen to your voice messages, and faxes can be sent to a fax number you specify (no, not read to you—who really wants to hear about low mortgage rates and health insurance anyway?).

OVA will prompt users in the following supported languages:

- ▼ English (U.S.)
- English (U.K.)
- English (Australia)
- German
- Spanish (Spain)
- Spanish (Mexico)
- French (France)
- French (Canada)
- Italian
- Japanese
- Korean
- Dutch (Netherlands)
- Portuguese (Brazil)
- Chinese (China)
- Chinese (Taiwan)
- ▲ Swedish

While prompts can be heard in these languages, OVA will only accept spoken commands in English; users of other languages will need to use their telephone keypad to enter responses.

Since this is a client-configuration chapter, I would normally discuss how to configure this mobile client. The truth is that OVA is a simple phone-based interface that has no real configuration, only usage instructions. So I want to take the opportunity to point out the most useful configuration document I could find on the subject: Microsoft's Outlook Voice Access Quick Reference Guide. It does a fantastic job of covering how users interact with OVA to retrieve and manage all message data.

Download the OVA Quick Reference Guide at http://go.microsoft.com/fwlink/?LinkId=64645.

SUMMARY

In this chapter, I covered the various mobile clients available that can access Exchange 2007. With each of these clients, Exchange becomes more and more accessible from anywhere, anytime, and just about anyhow. In the next chapter, I will switch gears, from focusing on client management to advanced management tasks, beginning with securing Exchange.

PART IV

Advanced Administration

CHAPTER 12

Securing Exchange 2007

Throughout the book, I've touched on the security measures available for nearly every part of Exchange. Even so, no specific focus has been on security. Exchange obviously cannot run in a vacuum; it needs to be accessible to and from the Internet, which means your Exchange servers need to be hardened to protect your environment from malicious attacks. So I want to take a chapter and specifically address securing Exchange.

Microsoft has included plenty of security measures (and not just the patches we hear about on Patch Tuesday), both in Windows and Exchange:

▼ The hardening of Windows using the Security Configuration Wizard

■ Secure communication methods

■ The use of certificates and authentication prior to communication

▲ Exchange support in Microsoft's Internet Security and Acceleration (ISA) Server

In this chapter, I will touch on securing Exchange in general, as well as for each specific server role. I'll start by covering a few common security concepts, follow up with the hardening of Windows using the Security Configuration Wizard, and then focus on each of the server roles and the security measures you can implement. If I've already covered some of the steps to securing a particular role, I'll reference you back to the content in the corresponding chapter.

COMMON SECURITY CONCEPTS

Before I delve into the specifics of securing your Exchange server, I first want to discuss a few concepts that will be used throughout all of Exchange. This way, when I write something as simple as "implement a Secure Sockets Layer," you already have an understanding of how complex that may actually be.

Encryption

Encryption is the process of taking readable information and scrambling it using a predefined algorithm or, as it is commonly referred to, a *key*. The result is a data set that is unreadable. Once unreadable, it would be safe to send the information across an unsecured medium, such as the Internet, to the intended recipient without fear that someone else will read its contents. The only way to make the data readable again is for the recipient to have the appropriate key that will decrypt the message. Once decrypted, the message is returned to its original state and is read by the intended recipient.

To demonstrate encryption, take the following example of a simple phrase, such as "I Love Exchange," and let's encrypt it using a simple key: replacing each letter with the one just after it in the alphabet. The result of the encryption is "J Mpwf Fvdibohf"—a completely unreadable piece of text. If you know the encryption key, you can easily reverse the process. This is similar to what happens when a message is encrypted.

The preceding example was accomplished using *symmetric keys,* one of two types of encryption keys. Symmetric keys are identical. That means you use the same key to both encrypt and decrypt the message. The preceding example used the same key to both encrypt and decrypt the text message. This type of key is not very secure; once someone knows your key from interacting with you initially, they can access information not intended for them. The other key type is an *asymmetric key.* Asymmetric keys are far more secure because they use two keys, a public encryption key and a private encryption key, to handle the encryption. Only the owner of the key pair knows the private key, while the public key is available to anyone. These two keys are the only two keys that will work with each other. The use of this key pair makes up the Public Key Infrastructure (PKI), used to either encrypt or digitally sign. Let's look at how these two keys are used in implementing message encryption, and we'll discuss just how both the sender and recipient retrieve these keys in the "Digital Signatures" section in this chapter.

The Encryption Process

When encrypting information, as shown in the following illustration, the sender needs to know the recipient's public key. (Don't be the least bit worried that senders need to know your public key; all they can do with it is encrypt messages. On top of that, they would only be readable by you!) The sender uses the recipient's public key so that the recipient can use his or her own private key to decrypt the message. Since only the recipient knows his or her own private key, only the intended recipient can decrypt the message. Think about it: If the keys were used in reverse, where the sender uses his or her own private key to encrypt and the recipient used the sender's public key to decrypt, because the public key is available to everyone, *anyone* could decrypt the sender's message! Also, if the sender used his or her own public key (and not the recipient's), how would the recipient decrypt the message? Only the sender can know his or her own private key, and that private key is the only other half of the key pair that can decrypt a message.

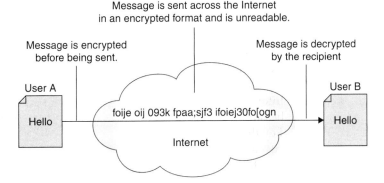

Digital Signatures

Because it is possible for someone to send data claiming to be someone else, a digital signature is used to allow the recipient to verify that the data actually came from the sender. The signature is only considered valid because it is validated by a trusted source: a *certificate authority* (CA). You can't just create your own digital signatures; they have to be created by a certificate authority and then assigned to the service requiring encryption. It is this third party, trusted by both parties, which ensures you that senders are really who they say they are. For instance, if a close friend introduced you to someone you had never met before and said the stranger's name was Bob Johnson, would you believe your friend? Of course you would, because the source of that information is trusted. In a similar way, a digital signature is valid because the recipient trusts its source. Within an organization, the authority can be a Windows 2003 server running certificate services, but communications between two separate organizations will require either a trusted third party or the importing of each other's certificates to establish that each party trusts the other as an authority.

Secure Sockets Layer

Secure Sockets Layer (SSL) and its successor Transport Layer Security (TLS) encrypt communications to prevent the reading, tampering, or forgery of the secured data. The encryption (and decryption) is usually accomplished at the endpoints of the communication, but can sometimes be handled by a proxy server, such as ISA Server. SSL is commonly used to provide secure Web browsing (as in the case of Outlook Web Access, Outlook Anywhere, and Exchange ActiveSync and its related functionalities), Post Office Protocol version 3 (POP3), and Internet Message Access Protocol version 4 (IMAP4) sessions. Exchange auto-generates an SSL certificate for all Web-based traffic, so out of the box, you have SSL capabilities. But it is recommended that you utilize a certificate from a trusted authority for permanent security.

Transport Layer Security

While Transport Layer Security (TLS) is a newer implementation of SSL, the terms are not necessarily interchangeable; there are many protocols, such as Simple Mail Transfer Protocol (SMTP), that do not support SSL but do support TLS. Some of the differences between TLS and SSL are:

▼ TLS has more secure encryption using a more up-to-date hashing method

▲ TLS does not require certificates to trace back to the root CA (which is the actual trusted party); TLS can use intermediary certificates

Authentication

Windows uses authentication as a simple means of identifying each party as part of the communication process. Authentication is used in addition to securing a channel;

even though a certificate used to help secure communications has a digital signature, that signature usually does not identify the specific user initiating the communications. Four methods of authentication can be used with Exchange: plain-text, NT LAN Manager (NTLM), Kerberos, and forms-based authentication.

Plain-Text Authentication

This is the least secure (well, actually, completely insecure) method of authentication. Using plain-text means that you are literally sending the user name and password across the communications channel in plain text. For example, anyone with a packet sniffer watching a POP3 client not using security can see the user name and password in the traffic (I've done it myself for clients). And in the case of a POP3 client connecting to Exchange, that means you'd be using the same user name and password as you would to log on to Windows—VERY scary.

TIP Anytime you must use plain-text authentication, ensure that you have a secure channel, such as SSL, implemented to secure the user name and password, as well as the data that follows.

NTLM Authentication

NTLM is a challenge-response authentication protocol that is supported in Windows 2003 for legacy clients that do not support Kerberos (covered in the next section), when the client involved is authenticating against an Active Directory forest that is different from the client's or when ports used by Kerberos are blocked by a firewall. With NTLM, both the client and the server send "challenge" data to ensure the identity of the other, as well as user name and password information.

Kerberos Authentication

Windows 2000 and 2003 Active Directory environments use Kerberos as the default authentication method. One of the main benefits of Kerberos over NTLM is its ability to allow both the client *and* server to verify the credentials of the other party without the client and server exchanging credentials. This is accomplished using a Key Distribution Center (KDC) as a mutually trusted authority between the client and server, where the client and server exchange tickets (distributed from the KDC) rather than credentials.

Forms-Based Authentication

Outlook Web Access has the ability to authenticate the user using a set of Web-based forms that utilize cookies as part of the authentication process. The benefit is primarily in the user experience; the user is not presented with a plain IIS-based authentication dialog box, but instead is presented with a well-designed logon page. When using forms-based authentication, be sure to use SSL to encrypt the session.

THE SECURITY CONFIGURATION WIZARD

Microsoft released the Security Configuration Wizard (SCW) with Windows 2003 Service Pack 1 as a tool to harden Windows servers using server role-specific templates. The hardening of the server is based on a few simple actions:

▼ Blocking ports not used by the server

■ Placing restrictions on ports in use by the server

■ Disabling services not used by the server

■ Securing communications

■ Setting up auditing of event log entries

▲ Locking down Internet Information Services (IIS)

Installing the SCW

By default, the SCW needs to be installed using the Add Windows Components Wizard within Add/Remove Programs. It's in the main list, as shown in Figure 12-1, so you won't need to use the Details button to see a subset of components.

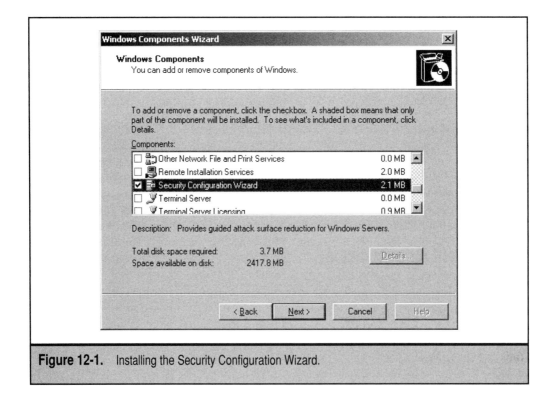

Figure 12-1. Installing the Security Configuration Wizard.

NOTE   You'll need to be a local administrator on the server you install the SCW, as well as having at least Exchange Server administrator privileges.

Once installed, you can find the SCW in the Administrative Tools folder on the Start menu. While I'm covering the running of the SCW and the registering of extensions in reverse order to show you a before and after comparison, in practice, you'll want to install the Exchange 2007 extensions before you run the SCW on an Exchange server.

Running the SCW

The SCW is a pretty simple application; a security policy can be created, applied, and even removed using the wizard. The wizard runs through five sections, each with its own purpose. Table 12-1 lists the five sections of the SCW and the purpose of each.

 NOTE   The SCW only addresses individual Exchange server roles in the first two sections, Role-Based Service Configuration and Network Security, where it determines the appropriate services that are allowed to run and the ports and applications that can communicate over the network.

SCW Section	Purpose
Role-Based Service Configuration	Informs the SCW of the server roles (such as a domain controller, Exchange Mailbox server, file server, etc.) that will be run on the selected server so that only the appropriate services will be running.
Network Security	Establishes which ports should be opened or closed, which applications are approved for communications, Internet Protocol Security (IPSec) settings, the restriction of specific network connections, IP addresses or subnets, and authentication requirements.
Registry Settings	Sets registry values that modify the communication signature settings, as well as accepted authentication levels, for both inbound and outbound communications.
Audit Policy	Defines the level of auditing the server will maintain in the security log.
Internet Information Services (IIS)	Secures IIS content and virtual directories.

Table 12-1.   SCW sections and their purposes

Microsoft Exchange Server 2007: A Beginner's Guide

When you start the SCW, the page just after the Welcome page inquires as to which action you'd like to perform. Since this is the first time running the SCW, I've chosen to create a new policy, as shown in Figure 12-2.

Upon clicking Next, you'll need to select the server you want to use as a baseline. This is an important step, as the extensions to be used (an extension is a list of services, ports, etc. that should be secured) will default to those actually installed on the server selected. The SCW then processes the extensions to see which are applicable to the server selected and allows you to view the configuration database before you begin the remainder of the SCW, as shown in Figure 12-3.

Viewing the Registered Extensions

By default, the SCW only has two Exchange 2003 extensions registered, and since you're running Exchange 2007 and not 2003, the Exchange 2007 services won't even show up in the list of installed roles, as shown in Figure 12-4. You can view the installed roles (meaning those roles detected as being installed on the server, such as Exchange, File and Print, DNS, etc.), all roles the SCW knows about (based on registered extensions), uninstalled roles (meaning those that are not currently detected as being installed), and only the selected roles (to eliminate viewing those you don't care about).

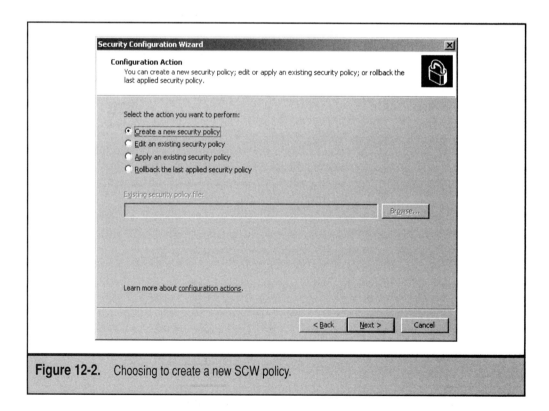

Figure 12-2. Choosing to create a new SCW policy.

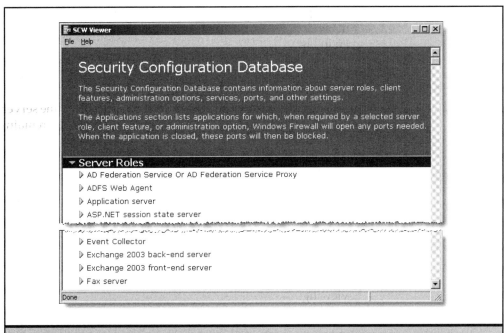

Figure 12-3. Reviewing the configuration database

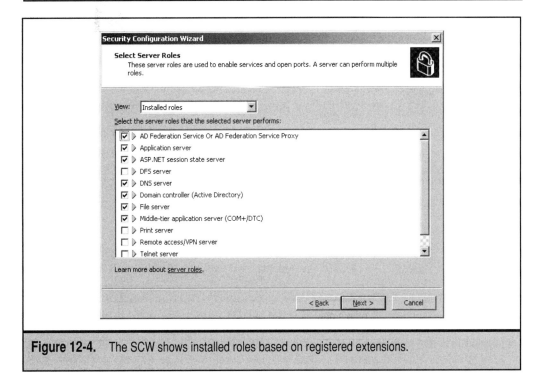

Figure 12-4. The SCW shows installed roles based on registered extensions.

Registering the Exchange 2007 Extensions

In order for the SCW to know about the Exchange roles, their services, dependencies, etc., the SCW schema needs to be extended to include Exchange 2007–specific information. This is accomplished using two eXtensible Markup Language (XML) files found in the Scripts folder under the installation path for your Exchange install. The following table lists the files and their corresponding server role.

File Name	Supported Exchange Server Roles
Exchange2007.xml	Mailbox, Hub Transport, Unified Messaging, Client Access
Exchange2007Edge.xml	Edge Transport

To register an extension file with SCW, run the following command at a command prompt:

```
scwcmd register /kbname:Ex2007KB /kbfile: <path_to_xml_file>
```

Note that when registering the extension, do so from the default folder at the command prompt (C:\Documents and Settings\Administrator in my case). I always like to run commands from the root of C: (so that I can see more of the command on a single line), and when I ran this from the root of C:, I got an "access is denied" error message and found other people on the Internet with similar problems.

The next screen, shown in Figure 12-5, shows the SCW running *after* the Exchange 2007 extensions have been registered, causing the Exchange 2007 server roles to be installed. You'll notice that the Exchange 2007 server roles now show up because the extensions for Exchange 2007 were registered. By expanding a role, the required services can be seen.

The next few screens specify the client features (such as the Microsoft networking client and the server being a domain member), the administrative options (such as backup software or error reporting), any additional services that should be allowed, and whether you want to leave the resultant set of unnecessary services alone or disable them. What is going on with all of these screens (from the server roles through the last four screens) is you are providing the SCW with enough information to determine which services should be disabled. Figure 12-6 shows the summary of service changes to be accomplished on your Exchange server.

The next section of the SCW, Network Security, focuses on the ports that need to be opened, with the goal being only opening those ports that absolutely need to be. It does so by first using well-known ports, such as Transmission Control Protocol (TCP) port 389 for Lightweight Directory Access Protocol (LDAP) access, as well as by specifying allowed applications for when specific ports are not known so that all ports used by a specified application will be allowed. The result, shown in Figure 12-7, is a summary of all ports that will be opened or closed (as appropriate).

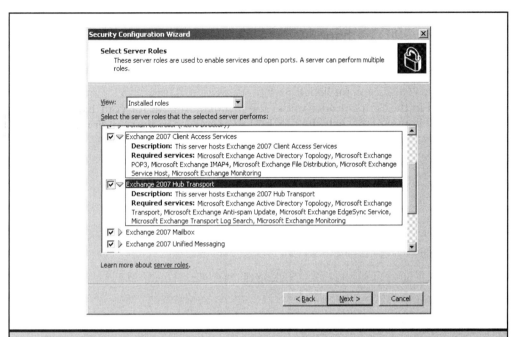

Figure 12-5.   Reviewing the installed server roles.

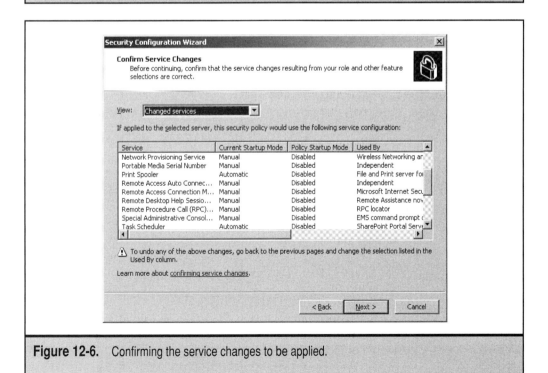

Figure 12-6.   Confirming the service changes to be applied.

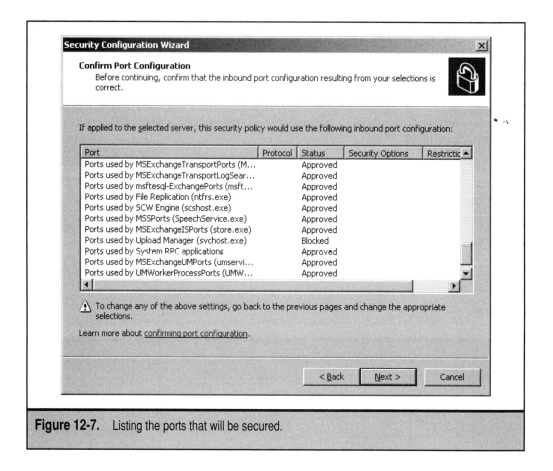

Figure 12-7. Listing the ports that will be secured.

The next section, Registry Settings, doesn't secure the registry; it makes changes to several registry values that secure the following:

▼ Server Message Block (SMB) security signatures

■ LDAP signing

▲ NTLM authentication levels for inbound and outbound communication

The next section, Audit Policy, determines which system events should be audited. These can include the success and/or failure for:

▼ Logons

■ Account management

■ Directory service access

■ Object access

- Policy changes
- Process tracking
▲ System events

NOTE   Should you audit object access, you'll need to configure which files, folders, registry keys, printers, and certificates will be audited and for whom. You can get started with Microsoft Knowledge Base article 310399.

The SCW allows you to choose to audit either the success only or the success and failure of events. However, in some cases, even if you choose just success auditing, the SCW will still audit failure events for logon and system events.

The final section, Internet Information Services, performs three functions: removing unnecessary or undesirable Web service extensions (shown in Figure 12-8), determining

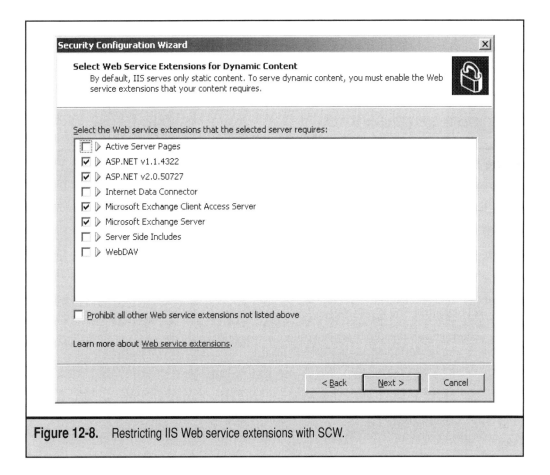

Figure 12-8.   Restricting IIS Web service extensions with SCW.

the virtual directories that should be retained (be careful here—this can have adverse effects if you remove needed virtual directories!), and whether the IIS server will support anonymous access.

At the end of the wizard, you will save the policy and have the option to apply the policy then or later by re-running the wizard (remember, one of the initial options is to apply an existing policy). You will want to consider creating separate policies for each server role (should you have multiple servers), test the functionality of your Exchange servers once the policy has been put in place, and lastly be aware that you can remove the policy settings within the SCW as easily as you applied it.

SECURING EXCHANGE SERVER ROLES

Each of the server roles has its own security needs, from physical placement, availability to/from the Internet, use of SSL/TLS, use of authentication, etc. This section will address each of the roles separately, providing information on the possible security measures you can implement.

Securing the Client Access Role

This role has many exposure points you need to concern yourself with. Just listing the various clients that can utilize this role should get your wheels turning:

▼ Outlook Web Access (OWA)

■ File server resource access via OWA

■ SharePoint resource access via OWA

■ Outlook Anywhere

■ ActiveSync

■ Autodiscover service

■ Availability service

■ Offline Address Book (OAB) distribution

■ POP3

■ IMAP4

▲ Interaction with other server roles

Starting to see how this is critical? Because there are so many ways to connect to the Client Access role, this role has more potential exposure to security threats than any of the other four roles. The good news is that because all of these services provided by the Client Access role are Web-based, they can be secured using either SSL or TLS. While in previous versions of Exchange, Web-based services were placed in the perimeter network, the Client Access role should be placed on the internal network and accessed via either ISA Server or protected behind a firewall.

Web-Based Client Access Services

The following services provided by the Client Access role are all Web-based and are, therefore, capable of securing using SSL within the IIS Manager:

▼ OWA

■ Outlook Anywhere

■ ActiveSync

■ OAB distribution

▲ Autodiscover

All of these services will require credentials, so implementing SSL is imperative for the security of the sessions. You can utilize an ISA server to securely publish any of these services and not require SSL to be implemented on the Exchange server itself, but instead on the ISA server. Should you wish to implement SSL on the Exchange server, or if you do not have an ISA server, you can read more about implementing SSL in Chapter 8 in the section titled "Installing an SSL Certificate."

POP3/IMAP4

Both of these protocols have no security of their own and are, therefore, a security risk. As I mentioned earlier in the chapter, packet-sniffing a POP3 session will quickly yield a user name and password for the user being monitored (the same applies to an IMAP4 session). I'm treating these two as one, as the configuration of each is identical.

Securing the Session Exchange 2007 supports securing POP3/IMAP via SSL/TLS. Using Exchange's self-signed SSL certificate that ships with the product, the only configuration you need to do is modify (if desired) the ports used for SSL using the Exchange Management Console, if you have Exchange 2007 Service Pack 1 (SP1) installed (shown in Figure 12-9). If you're not running SP1, use the `Set-PopSettings` and `Set-ImapSettings` cmdlets within the Exchange Management Shell.

Securing the Authentication Again, if you have SP1 installed, you can modify the authentication settings from the Exchange Management Console, shown in Figure 12-10 (if you're not running SP1, you'll need to use the `Set-PopSettings` and `Set-ImapSettings` cmdlets).

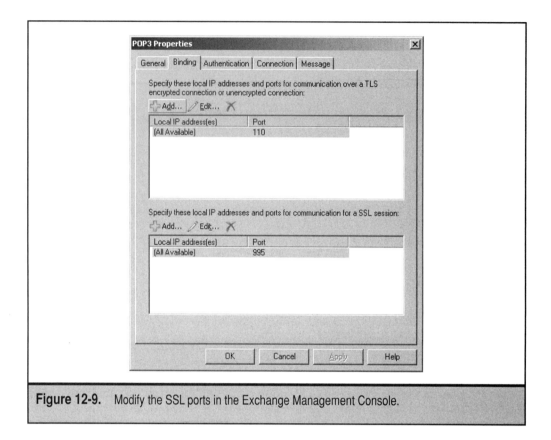

Figure 12-9. Modify the SSL ports in the Exchange Management Console.

Table 12-2 lists the values and their implications on the use of SSL/TLS with POP3 and IMAP4.

Other Server Roles

While there is no need to configure how the Client Access role interacts with other roles, I think it is important for you to be aware of the various ports and authentication methods used. Table 12-3 lists the roles, ports, supported authentication, and encryption methods when the Client Access role communicates with other servers.

Securing the Hub Transport and Edge Transport Server Roles

There are a few different aspects of security that apply to the Transport roles. The first issue that should come to mind when considering the security of the Transport roles is the fact that one of your transport servers (whether Hub or Edge) may be (depending on your configuration) directly exposed to the Internet. In addition, there is communication between a Hub Transport server and other server roles that needs to be secured.

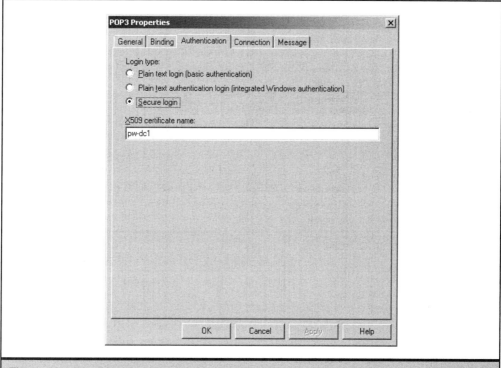

Figure 12-10. Modifying the authentication settings from the Exchange Management Console.

Internet Exposure

If you're not using an ISA server, at least one of your Transport servers will be receiving e-mail from the Internet. This can mean the server is exposed, but there are several simple and secure workarounds:

- ▼ Use an SMTP proxy, keeping the Transport server protected from external exposure.

- ■ Publish SMTP services via an ISA server (this is your most secure option, as the ISA server adds its own layer of security).

- ▲ If you only have the Hub Transport role to receive e-mail from the Internet, configure your firewall to only allow access to the needed ports (more on this later).

Securing Connectors

The send and receive connectors used by the Transport servers are secured using TLS and authentication, as shown in Figure 12-11. Depending on the connector, the TLS may or may not be enabled (see Table 12-3 at the end of this section for specifics on when TLS is enabled). Microsoft automatically takes care of the security for default send and receive connectors, but should you need to create your own (more on this in Chapter 6), ensure that TLS is used to maintain security of your messages as they traverse your network.

Authentication Value	Description
Plain Text Login	TLS is not required. Credentials will be sent unencrypted unless TLS or SSL is implemented. It will be up to the client to specify secured POP3 or IMAP4 ports (995 for POP3 with SSL and 993 for IMAP4 with SSL).
Plain Text Authentication Login	TLS is not required on standard POP3 and IMAP4 ports (110 for POP3 and 143 for IMAP4). However, basic authentication is only allowed on a port secured by TLS or SSL.
Secure Login	Standard POP3 and IMAP 4 ports must be secured with TLS before authentication is allowed.

Table 12-2. POP3/IMAP4 Authentication Settings

Server Role	Ports	Authentication	Encryption
Mailbox (2007)	RPC (uses many ports)	Kerberos (default) NTLM	RPC Encryption (enabled by default)
Mailbox (earlier versions)	TCP 80, TCP 443 (SSL)	Kerberos (default) NTLM (default fallback) Basic (optional)	None by default, but can use IPSec
Unified Messaging	TCP 5060, TCP 5061, TCP 5062, dynamic ports	IP address only	TLS (used by default)
Other Client Access (ActiveSync or OWA)	TCP 80, TCP 443 (SSL)	Kerberos (default)	SSL (enabled by default using self-signed certificate)

Table 12-3. Secure Client Access Communication with Other Server Roles

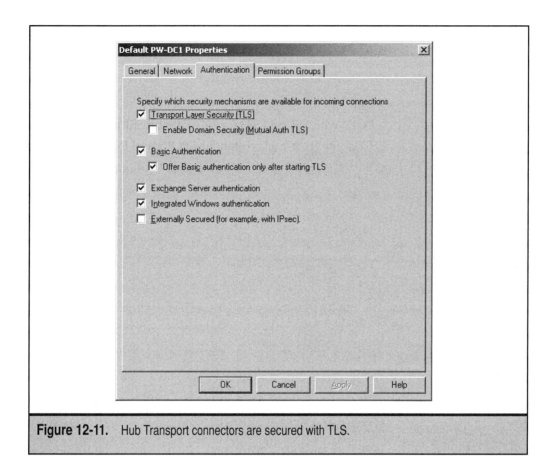

Figure 12-11. Hub Transport connectors are secured with TLS.

Other Server Roles

Table 12-4 lists the security methods used when a Hub Transport server interacts with other Exchange servers. Again, while you won't need to modify any of this, it is helpful to see Microsoft's position on the need to implement security for nearly all Exchange communication.

Server Role	Ports	Authentication	Encryption
Hub to Hub	TCP 25 (TLS), TCP 587 (SSL)	Kerberos (default)	TLS (enabled by default)
Hub to Edge/Edge to Hub	TCP 25 (TLS)	Direct trust (default)	TLS (enabled by default)
Edge to Edge	TCP 25 (TLS), TCP/UDP 389	Anonymous/ certificate (default)	TLS (not enabled by default)
Hub to Mailbox via MAPI	TCP 135	NTLM (default) Kerberos	Remote Procedure Call (RPC) encryption (enabled by default)
Hub to Active Directory Access	TCP/UDP 389 (DC), TCP 3268 (GC), TCP/UDP 88 (Kerberos), TCP/UDP 53 (DNS), TCP 135 (RPC)	Kerberos (default)	Kerberos (when appropriate)
EdgeSync Service (to Active Directory)	TCP 50636 (SSL), TCP 50389	Basic (default)	SSL
Active Directory Application Mode	TCP 50389	NTLM/Kerberos (default)	none

Table 12-4. Secure Hub Transport Communication with Other Server Roles

Securing the Unified Messaging Server Role

The interaction between fax or voice and the Unified Messaging (UM) server is secured via the IP address of the IP-PBX (public branch exchange) or IP/VoIP (voice over IP) gateway specified in the UM IP Gateway object, shown in Figure 12-12.

The remainder of the security is accomplished by default settings and do not require your interaction, with the exception of the UM Web service, where you can implement your own certificates in place of the self-signed certificates installed by default. Table 12-5 lists the security measures that are in place for a UM server's interaction with other servers.

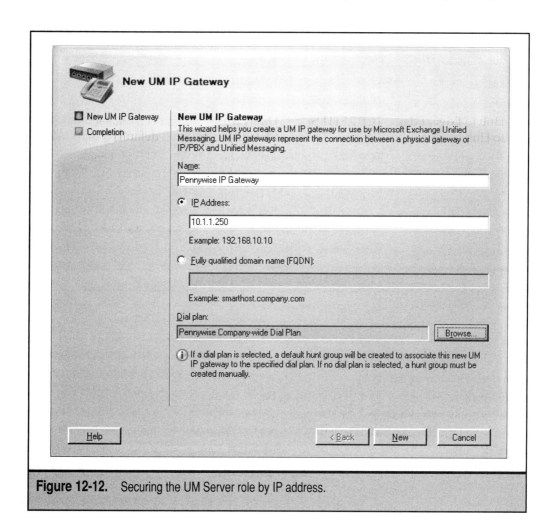

Figure 12-12.   Securing the UM Server role by IP address.

Securing the Mailbox Server Role

Since Mailbox servers primarily are accessed by users for mailbox content retrieval, it is really only the Mailbox server's interaction with Active Directory that requires security. This is accomplished automatically, so no intervention on your part is necessary. Table 12-6 lists the security in place for a Mailbox server's interaction with other servers.

Service	Ports	Authentication	Encryption
UM Fax	TCP 5060, 5061, 5062, dynamic port	IP address (default)	Media not encrypted
UM Phone	TCP 5060, 5061, 5062, dynamic port	IP address (default)	Media not encrypted
UM Web services	TCP 80, TCP 443 (SSL)	Basic, digest, Windows Integrated (default)	SSL (enabled by default)
Hub Transport	TCP 25 (TLS)	Kerberos (default)	TLS (enabled by default)
Mailbox	TCP 135 (RPC)	NTLM/Kerberos (default)	RPC encryption (enabled by default)

Table 12-5.   Secure Unified Messaging Communication with Other Services

Service	Ports	Authentication	Encryption
Messaging Application Programming Interface access	TCP 153 (RPC)	NTLM/Kerberos (default)	RPC encryption (enabled by default)
Active Directory access	TCP/UDP 389 (DC), TCP 3268 (GC), TCP/UDP 88 (Kerberos), TCP/UDP 53 (DNS), TCP 135 (RPC)	Kerberos (default)	Kerberos (when appropriate)
Active Directory topology service	TCP 135 (RPC)	NTLM/Kerberos (default)	RPC encryption (enabled by default)
OAB accessing Active Directory	TCP 135 (RPC)	Kerberos (default)	Kerberos (enabled by default)
Outlook clients accessing OAB	TCP 80, TCP 443 (SSL)	NTLM/Kerberos (default)	SSL (not enabled by default)

Table 12-6.   Secure Mailbox Server Communication with Other Servers

SUMMARY

In this chapter, I've covered some of the basic security concepts used in Exchange to protect user information, data, and all communications. I've discussed how you can use the Security Configuration Wizard to harden an Exchange server, as well as addressed some basic security considerations for each server role.

In the next chapter, I'll be discussing scripting in Exchange 2007 using Windows PowerShell.

CHAPTER 13

Scripting in Exchange 2007

A s intimidating as scripting can be, it is one of the most rewarding skills to develop as an information technology professional. Even a beginning scripter can produce impressive results with just a little bit of effort. The goal of this chapter is to help you overcome the initial fears of scripting that you might have. Let's be realistic: There is not one chapter in any book that is going to turn you into a scripting "guru." But if this chapter can take the mystery out of scripting, get you excited about the possibilities, and provide you with some scripts that can give you some instant gratification, then that will be significant.

In this chapter, I'll cover some scripting basics, not specific to Exchange or an individual scripting language. Next, I'll provide a general introduction to Windows PowerShell, followed by what you're really looking for: scripting with Exchange.

START WITH WHAT YOU DO

When you arrive at work on Monday morning and you begin your daily Exchange administrator routine, what is it that you do? Is any of what you perform the same every day, week, or month? The idea of scripting for administration is to reduce the time you have to spend on routine or repetitive tasks. The first step in becoming a successful scripter is to be able to clearly detail the process you go through to complete an administrative task. If you can do this for each task, you can begin to look for and customize scripts that automate them. Notice I didn't say *write* scripts. As a general rule of thumb, writing scripts from scratch is not a good place for a beginning scripter to start. That can—and will—come in time if you stick with it, but it is lacking that instant gratification that we need initially to keep you going.

Define a Process

Grab a blank sheet of paper or open up Visio and draw out a process. You can use step-by-step lists or a flow chart. Use whatever method works best for you to detail the process. For practice, don't even use an administrative task. Use something far more familiar, something that you have been doing for a long time. Detail something like brushing your teeth. Try to define the process as if you were teaching a child to do it for the first time.

Example Process: Brushing Your Teeth

1. Squeeze some toothpaste onto a soft-bristled toothbrush.

2. Gently brush the outer tooth surfaces and gumline of two to three teeth at a 45-degree angle, using short, back-and-forth brushing motions.

3. Move brush to the next group of two to three teeth and repeat.

4. Gently brush the inside surfaces with up-and-down motions to clean the inert tooth surfaces and gumline.

5. Tilt brush vertically behind the front teeth. Make several up and down strokes using the front half of the brush.

6. Brush your back molars.

7. Spit out the toothpaste, and rinse your mouth with water or mouthwash.

8. Repeat every morning.

9. Repeat after eating lunch.

10. Repeat before going to bed.

Did you find yourself critiquing the steps as you read through them? Thinking how you brush your teeth and how you could do a better job? If so, that is fantastic. That means you are a detail-oriented person and you have the potential to become a great scripter. It also probably means you have really clean teeth. When scripting, the better you can define each step of the process, the more likely it is that you will be able to successfully automate it with a script. Just like the better instructions you give someone, the greater the likelihood that they will be able to successfully complete the task. Remember the computing adage: "Garbage In Garbage Out."

Define a Problem

Many times, scripts are used to solve problems. As an administrator, you are often presented with only symptoms of problems to go by. You have learned processes that help you diagnose symptoms and deliver the actual source of the problem. Methods for troubleshooting and problem solving can help reduce the amount of time it takes to restore systems to good health. Sound methodologies can also prevent you from creating new problems along the way.

They say necessity is the mother of all inventions. So you could say that problems are the mothers of all scripts. If you can define a problem and you already have knowledge of methodologies to diagnose and solve it, you can use that knowledge to help you build scripts to solve problems. Here are some problems that scripts could potentially solve (in no particular order):

▼ Information Store Service keeps shutting down.

■ Fifty new users were just hired and they need user accounts, mailboxes, and computers by yesterday.

■ You have been too busy to check the event logs in two weeks on the Exchange servers.

▲ Outlook clients in Sao Paulo office are timing out when connecting to Exchange.

Can you think of the problems that you have faced at work in the past? How about the ones you are facing right now? Here is the fun part—can you think of the problems you are likely to face in the future? Here is a hint: Just look to your past. Now think of a process that could solve the problem or maybe even prevent a problem from happening in the first place. If the process involves many steps, then a script might just be the answer.

THANK GOODNESS FOR PROGRESS

Some years back, circa 1994, I regularly taught classes on how to write batch files in MS DOS. People have been writing batches for DOS much longer than that. It is amazing, but I still use that knowledge today to automate administrative tasks from the Windows command line (cmd.exe and command.exe). The basic construct for working at the command line has not changed in over a decade. What has changed is the arsenal of commands and tools that you can use from the command line. One dictum has held true: If you can run it from a command line, you can automate it. Of course, there are limitations to writing batch files. While there is often a need to get beyond the limitation of a basic batch, there is rarely, if ever, a need for administrators to program a full-fledged application. Usually, a sign that you need a better way to automate a task is when it starts to feel like you are framing a house with your stapler.

Higher-Level Languages

Higher-level scripting languages have been developed, and have evolved, to fill the need for advanced methods of automation and error checking. The term *higher level* implies that more computer instruction can be accomplished by a single statement. But even as powerful as they are, they should not be confused with actual programming languages that have much more stringent requirements. Programming languages also require many more lines of code to accomplish identical tasks, so they are impractical for writing scripts. In Figure 13-1, you can see that scripting languages are much higher-level languages than programming languages. But scripting-level languages are not practical for writing applications because they are less efficient than programming languages with system resources.

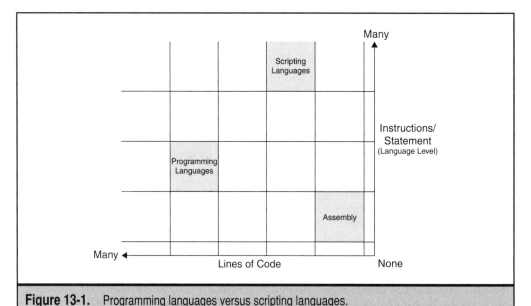

Figure 13-1. Programming languages versus scripting languages.

It might help to think of scripting languages as sports cars and programming languages as hybrid gas/electric vehicles. Both get you there; they just vary on how. But be careful not to take that analogy too far. After all, we wouldn't want to start comparing administrators to hot rods and programmers to environmentally sound cars, too, would we?

The Spice of Scripting Life

It has been said that diversity is the spice of life. If that holds true for scripting languages, then scripting is "muy picante" (very spicy). There are so many scripting languages, in fact, that I'm not even going to name them all. Suffice it to say that there are at least seven different types of scripting languages/interpreters and close to 100 individual scripting languages/interpreters. Fortunately for you, this is a book on Exchange Server 2007 administration. This immediately limits our discussion to a Windows environment and, furthermore, to Exchange. Also good for you is the fact that everything we're going to talk about is going to be condensed to the length of this chapter, which, like a script, will be short and to the point (relatively).

Microsoft Scripting

All high-level scripting languages utilize interpreters to execute the scripts. Programming languages compile their code. It is important to have some idea of what is available to use for scripting. Some of the Microsoft scripting language interpreters are also interactive shells known as command-line interpreters (CLIs). Table 13-1 gives a brief description of Microsoft scripting languages and interpreters.

Technically, it is possible to load third-party interpreters onto Windows to process other scripting languages. Most of the time, it is much easier to just load up another interpreter than it is try to re-create a script in another language. In other words, if you find a script that solves your problem, load up the interpreter so that you can use it before you spend a long time porting it over to another language.

And Then There Was One

A problem that Microsoft has had difficulty with in the Windows environment is making it possible to automate, or even just perform, all of the administrative tasks that can be done via the graphical user interface (GUI) from the command line. Windows Scripting Host was created to bridge the gap between GUI tools like Active Directory Users and Computers and the CLI of cmd.exe. While it was certainly an improvement, WSH has its shortcomings. It was quickly exploited after its release, which made Windows systems susceptible to malicious code. It was not widely adopted by administrators because of the programming skill level required to take advantage of it. In addition, documentation was not readily available or comprehensive.

Acknowledging the automation and command-line limitations inherent in their Windows platforms, Microsoft began a project in 2004 to correct this problem. The result of the project was Monad, which is now called PowerShell. If you are just learning how to script today, this is great news. It means that you can start by learning PowerShell. You may find that it might just be possible to handle all of your administrative tasks with it.

Interpreter	Description
command.exe	Default shell/interpreter for DOS (Disk Operating System); supports two operating modes (interactive and batch).
cmd.exe	A native shell/interpreter for Windows that supports the same functions as command.exe and also supports non-DOS programs.
Windows Scripting Host (WSH)/ CScript.exe	Language-independent interpreter available on Windows 98 and higher. WSH files can contain multiple scripting languages, such as VBScript, JScript, PearlScript, etc. Uses cscritp.exe as a CLI.
VBScript	COM objects–friendly, high-level language that can be used to script Web pages for Internet Explorer and administrative tasks. It derives many of its conventions from Visual Basic. Note: VBScript's pending demise does not affect administrative task automation (see the scripting FAQ at www.microsoft.com/technet/scriptcenter/scrptfaq.mspx).
Jscript	Microsoft's implementation of the ECMA-262 specification. It can be interpreted by Microsoft Windows Scripting Host and Web browsers like Internet Explorer that support the standard. The latest revision of this is JScript.net. The other major implementation of this standard is JavaScript by Netscape.
Active Server Pages (ASP)	A server-side scripting engine that primarily executes VBScript for the rendering of active content on Web pages. It can run any script that references the ASP built in COM objects such as JScript and PearlScript. The latest implementation is ASP.NET.
Windows PowerShell	Extensible CLI based on Microsoft .NET Framework. Available in Windows XP and higher, including Windows Server 2008. Available in both 32- and 64-bit versions. It is the basis for all of the Exchange Server 2007 administrative tools (EMS and EMC).
Exchange Management Shell	Extended version of Windows PowerShell created by the Exchange product group at Microsoft. Includes Exchange-specific commands not available in Windows PowerShell by itself.

Table 13-1. Microsoft Scripting Languages and Interpreters

With that thought in mind, the remainder of this chapter will focus on Windows Power-Shell and the Exchange Management Shell.

Before you continue reading the remainder of this chapter, you might find it helpful to install Windows PowerShell. If you have Exchange Server 2007 installed on the computer you are working on, you already have Windows PowerShell installed.

To install Windows PowerShell:

1. Verify that .NET Framework 2.0 or higher is installed. If you are running .NET Framework 2.0, make sure that Hotfix KB926776 is installed, as it is required for the Exchange Management Shell.

2. Download the version of Windows PowerShell that is appropriate for your operating system. If you need help determining the correct file to download, you can refer to the TechNet article called: "How to Get Windows PowerShell 1.0" at www.microsoft.com/technet/scriptcenter/topics/msh/download.mspx.

3. Run the executable that you downloaded. For example, the Windows Server 2003 SP1 32-bit version is WindowsServer2003-KB926139-x86-ENU.exe.

4. Click Next when the Windows PowerShell 1.0 install wizard appears.

5. Select I Agree and then click Next.

6. Click Next.

7. Click Install.

8. Click Finish when the installation completes.

WINDOWS POWERSHELL

Microsoft emphasizes that Windows PowerShell is designed specifically for administrators and the automation of administrative tasks. Where Windows PowerShell excels and other administrative automation tools have lacked is apparent in the following characteristics of Windows PowerShell:

▼   **Discoverability**   Ease in which you can learn how to use Windows PowerShell

■   **Consistency**   Transferability of knowledge from one command to another

■   **Interactive and scripting environments**   Improved alternative to cmd.exe and WSH that provides administrators access to object-based commands called cmdlets, COM objects, and the .NET Framework, all in one interface.

■   **Object orientation**   Commands and scripts are .NET object–based rather than text-based; in short, this means you can do more from the command line then ever before

▲   **Easy transition to scripting**   Ease with which you can switch from issuing a command to executing a script

Cmdlets

There are 129 cmdlets (pronounced "command-lets") in PowerShell 1.0. Each one references a .NET object. As a Windows PowerShell beginner, you do not need to know or understand the .NET Framework or the methods that are employed by cmdlets. What you do need to learn to start taking advantage of them, however, is their syntax. A big part of the discoverability and consistency of Windows PowerShell is the syntax for the command-line interface. In the following illustration, you can see the basic anatomy of the cmdlet in Windows PowerShell.

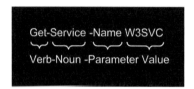

Each cmdlet is comprised of a verb-noun combination. Parameters and their associated values are used to define with greater detail the action you want to perform with the cmdlet. It is possible to specify multiple parameters.

If you can learn the verbs, then you are well on your way to being able to perform all of your administrative tasks right from the command line. The really great news is that there are only 40 verbs. Table 13-2 provides a complete list of the verbs in Windows PowerShell.

Basic Windows PowerShell Skills

There are some basic skills that you must acquire in order to truly be comfortable working from the Windows PowerShell command line. If you start with the following skills, your initial experience with the Windows PowerShell will be much more pleasant and rewarding.

Add	Clear	Compare	ConvertFrom	Convert
ConvertTo	Copy	Export	ForEach	Format
Get	Group	Import	Invoke	Join
Measure	Move	New	Out	Pop
Push	Read	Remove	Rename	Resolve
Restart	Resume	Select	Set	Sort
Split	Start	Stop	Suspend	Tee
Test	Trace	Update	Where	Write

Table 13-2. PowerShell Cmdlet Verbs

Skill #1: Get-Help

Some of the verbs are more commonly used than others. But it is easy to discover what each verb does. The first verb you will want to learn is Get. The first cmdlet you should become familiar with is Get-Help. You can use Get-Help to discover the meaning of each verb, as well as each and every cmdlet.

To use Get-Help to discover cmdlets:

1. Start the Windows PowerShell.

2. Type **Get-Help** and press ENTER. Review the results.

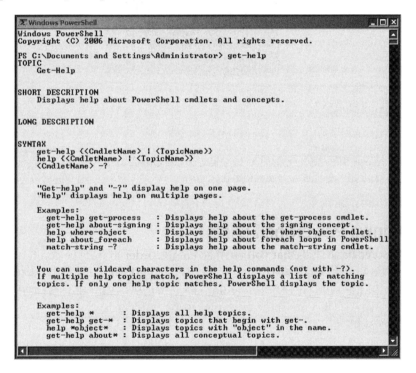

3. Type **Get-Help Get-Service** and press ENTER. Review the detailed description.

4. Type **Get-Help Get-Service -Detailed** and press ENTER. Review the parameters.

5. Type **Get-Help Get-Service -Full** and press ENTER. Review the parameters again.

You should have been able to use the -detailed and -full parameters to learn even more about the Get-Service cmdlet. You can consistently repeat this process for each of the cmdlets that you are interested in learning about. You probably also picked up on some other syntactical information just by reviewing the examples that are given by Get-Help. We are going to review additional syntax options. But first, there is a hidden feature for you to learn that is going to come in handy before you move forward. That is the use of Tab Expansion.

Skill #2: Tabbing

You may be thinking that you are already familiar with using the TAB key to auto-complete a path in cmd.exe. It is true that Tab Expansion is not a unique Windows PowerShell feature. But Windows PowerShell expounds upon it even further—in fact, much further. I would venture to say that it is the single most important skill to utilize if you are a Windows administrator discovering how to perform administrative tasks from the command line for the first time. Here are some examples of how Tab Expansion can save you time and frustration with working from the command line:

Path Example:

```
[PS] C:\>CD /w
```

Now press the TAB key until you get to the Windows directory, and then press ENTER.

```
[PS] C:\>CD /Windows
[PS] C:\Windows
```

Cmdlet Example:

```
[PS] C:\>Get-d
```

Now press the TAB key, and you should see Get-Date. Press the ENTER key, and you will see a display of the current date and time.

```
[PS] C:\>Get-Date
[PS] C:\>Sunday, May 20 2007 1:11:56 PM
```

Skill # 3 Wildcards and Positional Values

Wildcards are fully supported in Windows PowerShell. Combining the Tab Expansion feature with the Wildcard feature will make quick work out of most Windows Power-Shell commands. Here are some examples using wildcards:

Wildcard Example 1:

```
[PS] C:\>Get-Command -Verb g*
```

Did you use your TAB key while typing the cmdlet and the parameter? The "*" was used as the wildcard and will return all of the cmdlets with verbs that start with the letter G, shown in the following illustration.

Wildcard Example 2:

```
[PS] C:\>Get-Command *
```

Using a wildcard immediately following a command is not necessarily the same thing as not specifying a wildcard. For example, if you were to type **Get-Command** and press ENTER, you would see all of the Windows PowerShell cmdlets. On the other hand, if you were to type **Get-Command** * it will enumerate every executable file and application-related files, such as .dll files. The lesson here is to be careful what you ask for—you just might get it.

Positional values are implied values. When you are working interactively with the PowerShell, it is assumed that you are working with the local computer. Therefore, it is not necessary to specify the computer you want to run the command on. The same is true of values associated with parameters that you put in. Simply specifying the value of a parameter is usually good enough to execute the command.

Positional Parameter Example 1:

```
[PS] C:\>Get-Command -Name Group-Object
```

This is the formal syntax for getting a specific command. But with positional values, you can do this instead to save time:

```
[PS] C:\>Get-Command Group-Object
```

Windows PowerShell will determine the parameter you are implying based on the value you put in. This will not work in every case, but it will in most.

Skill #4 Piping

Many times, it is beneficial to take the results of one command and use them in another command. In other scripting languages, this is accomplished with text files and text parsers. Since Windows PowerShell is an object-oriented language, the results of a command are stored as objects. We depend on the Windows PowerShell to interpret the data into text that we see on the screen. But it is possible to take the object's data and *pipe* it into another command. This is called *linking commands*. The pipe command | is used in the command-line syntax to link commands together.

Piping Example 1:

```
[PS] C:\>Get-Command | Measure-Object
```

In this example, the results are piped to a command that measures the total number of commands, the result of which is 129.

```
Count       :129
Average     :
Sum         :
Maximum     :
Property    :
```

Piping Example 2:

```
[PS] C:\>Get-ChildItem -Filter *.exe | Get-Acl
```

In this example, the folders and files on the root of the C: drive are enumerated. A filter displays only the .exe files. The data is linked to a command that displays the owner of the file.

```
Directory:
Microsoft.PowerShell.Core\FileSystem::C:\


Path                        Owner
----                        -----
Bginfo.exe                  BUILTIN\Administrators
winscp382.exe               BUILTIN\Administrators
```

Skill #5 Sorting

If the resulting data from a command is not displayed by default in the order that you were hoping for, you can use the Sort-Object command to rearrange the data.

Sort Example 1:

```
[PS] C:\>Get-Service | Sort-Object -Property Status
```

When you run the Get-Service command, it will sort all services by name. However, administrators usually want to see services sorted by their status. In this example, the Sort-Object command is invoked with the -Property parameter.

Sort Example 2:

```
[PS] C:\>Get-Service | Sort-Object -Property Status -Descending
```

In Example 1 for sorting, the services are returned with the stopped services listed first. By adding the -Descending parameter, you can see the running services first.

Skill #6 Variables

A discussion on variables can certainly lead to advanced topics outside the scope of this book. But do not let variables intimidate you. They can be used by even a beginning scripter to make the process of scripting a whole lot easier. In the Windows PowerShell, you declare a variable with a "$" sign.

Variable Example 1:

```
[PS] C:\>$a = Get-Service | Sort-Object -Property Status -Descending
```

By typing **$a =** at the beginning of the cmdlet, the entire results of the linked command will be stored as a variable. Now type **$a** by itself, press ENTER, and you should be able to see the stored results.

```
[PS] C:\>$a
```

Variable Example 2:

```
[PS] C:\>$a | Group-Object -Property Status
```

Of course, the real power of a variable is to be able to pass the information in it on to another command. The results of the second example, shown in the following illustration, will tell you exactly how many services are running and how many are stopped. Another cool thing about variables is that they are "point-in-time" collections. So if you want to compare the status of the services in the variable to the status of the same services an hour later, you can.

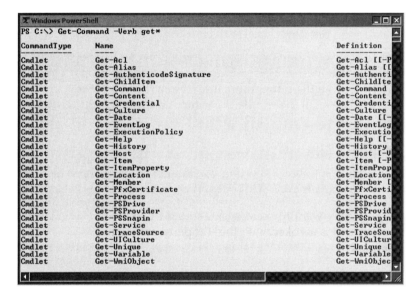

I hope by now you are feeling comfortable with what we have covered in terms of basic skills. In order for you to show the world your new skills, we need to cover some basics in terms of output.

Additional Output Skills

The reason why we are able to see the results of our commands on the screen is that PowerShell is appending the Out-Host Cmdlet to them. Output to the host computer is only good for interactive sessions. In order for you to go to the next step in scripting, you need to acquire additional output skills.

Skill # 7 Formatting

Windows PowerShell does not return every parameter for objects in a result set. However, that doesn't mean the data doesn't exist. In order to see some of the values of an object, you will need to use the Format-Table cmdlet.

Formatting Example 1:

```
[PS] C:\>Get-Service | Format-Table -Property *
```

If you don't know the name of the property you want to display, a good technique to employ is just to display them all by calling a wildcard. Then, once you know the property name you are looking for, you can re-run the command and specify one or more properties.

```
[PS] C:\>Get-Service | Format-Table -Property ServiceName
```

Formatting Example 2:

```
[PS] C:\>Get-Service | Format-Table -Property ServiceName, Status
-AutoSize
```

When you specify only one property, you will only get back one column of data. If you want additional values, you can add them by specifying property names separated by commas. You can run the same command without the -AutoSize parameter, but you may not be able to see all of the results. To ensure that you do see all results, it is a good idea to use -AutoSize.

Skill #8 Output to File

Windows PowerShell supports exporting command results to three file types. You can export to TXT files, CSV files, and XML files. There are specific cmdlets for each file type.
Output Example 1:
Export to TXT:

```
[PS] C:\>Get-Service | Format-Table -Property * | Out-File C:\services.txt
```

Export to CSV:

```
[PS] C:\>Get-Service | Format-Table | Export-CSV C:\services.csv
```

Export to XML:

```
[PS] C:\>Get-Service | Format-Table | Export-Clixml C:\services.xml
```

Output Example 2:
If you want to be able to see the files that you have created, you can use the Invoke-Item cmdlet.

```
[PS] C:\>Invoke-Item C:\services.txt
```

Skill #9 Convert to HTML

If you want to easily share the data that you are generating with your cmdlet, a Hypertext Markup Language (HTML) file may prove handy. The ConvertTo-Html cmdlet makes quick work of creating HTML files.

```
[PS] C:\>Get-Service | sort-object Status -descending | ConvertTo-HTML
-Property Name,Status > C:\service-report.html
```

After you have created an HTML file, you can publish it to a Web server directory for multi-user viewing.

Skill #10 Output in Color

For visual impact, it is possible to change the color of the text output. Write-Host supports changing both the foreground and background colors. It is not as easy as it might sound; however, if you use the Get-Help Write-Host -Full, you will discover that Write-Host cmdlet doesn't support pipeline input. So it will take an advanced skill to report results in color. What you can use is the ForeEach-Object cmdlet.

Output Color Example 1:

```
[PS] C:\>$a = Get-Command -Verb S*
[PS] C:\>Write-Host $a -f yellow
```

In this example, a variable is used to collect the data. Write-Host then enumerates the variable to generate the custom color text. This is not a dynamic way to accomplish this, however.

```
[PS] C:\>Get-Service | ForEach-Object {Write-Host -F Magenta -B DarkBlue $_.Name
$_.Status}
```

The problem with Example 1 is that it isn't looking for a specific condition to take action on. In this second example, the ForEach-Object was used to loop through the object's data and perform a specific action based on the singular condition that the service exists and can be enumerated. But then again, changing the color of all the text does not necessarily add any significant meaning to it.

If Statements

In some cases, the ForEach-Object Cmdlet is not sufficient enough to accomplish the task at hand. ForEach by itself can only check on one condition. However, "If" statements can be written to check on multiple conditions. In layman's terms, an If statement would be like saying: If (if) the nail is small, use a small hammer, but if (elseif) the nail is medium, use a medium hammer; for any other (else) size nail, use a big hammer. If you need additional granularity to define multiple conditions, you can incorporate If statements. The complete syntax for an If statement is as follows:

```
if (condition) {command(s) to execute}
elseif (condition2) {command(s) to execute}
else{command(s) to execute}
```

It is not common, or even required, to use the Elseif condition. However, the Else condition can be helpful as a catch-all for any condition outside of the If condition. The condition after the If statement can be used to do comparisons using a variety of operators. In the following example, you can see how the If statement is used to do a comparison on the results of the all *<td>* cells in an HTML table using a "-like" condition.

```
[PS] C:\> get-service | ConvertTo-Html -Property Name,Status | foreach { if ($_
-like "*<td>Running</td>*") {$_ -replace "<tr>", "<tr bgcolor=green>"} else {$_
-replace "<tr>", "<tr bgcolor=red>"}} > C:\service-alert.html
```

If the status of the service is running, then the entire table row <tr> is changed to green. If the status is anything "else" other then running, the table row color is changed to red.

Windows PowerShell Comparison Operators

Windows PowerShell administrators can use a number of different operators. When writing If statements, the comparison operators that are most common to use are listed in Table 13-3.

Operator	Description
-eq	Equal to
-ne	Not equal to
-gt	Greater than
-ge	Greater than or equal to
-lt	Less than
-le	Less than or equal to
-like	Uses wildcards for pattern matching
-notlike	Uses wildcards for pattern matching
-match	Uses regular expressions for pattern matching
-notmatch	Uses regular expressions for pattern matching
-replace	Replace
-contains	Determine elements in a group (returns $True or $False)
-notcontains	Determine excluded elements in a group (returns $True or $False)
>	Redirect
>>	Append

Table 13-3. PowerShell Comparison Operators

For more details about using comparison operators and other, operator types:

```
[PS] C:\>get-help about_operator
```

EXCHANGE MANAGEMENT SHELL

Now for what you have been waiting for! If you worked your way through the examples earlier in this chapter, then you have built the basic set of Windows PowerShell skills necessary to begin to take advantage of the Exchange Management Shell. From this point forward, we take the basic skills outlined earlier and apply them to the Exchange Management Shell.

The Exchange Management Shell (EMS) is an extended version of Windows PowerShell created by the Exchange Product group. You can use the extensions to perform every single Exchange administrative task. This is evident in the fact that the graphical tool, the Exchange Management Console (EMC), works by passing commands through EMS. But even with what the EMC can do, there are still many tasks that are only possible to perform in the EMS. This includes being able to automate tasks.

Before you continue with the rest of this section, you will want to open the Exchange Management Shell. I suggest that you practice these examples in a lab environment until you are comfortable with them.

TIP You can refer to Chapter 2 for information on performing a custom installation that only includes the Exchange Management tools.

To start the Exchange Management Shell:

1. Verify that you are on a computer on which the Exchange Management tools have been installed. Note: They are installed as part of a "Typical Installation."
2. Click Start, click All Programs, click Microsoft Exchange Server 2007, and select Exchange Management Shell.

Exchange Extensions to Windows PowerShell

There are exactly 381 new cmdlets that only exist in the Exchange Management Shell. Most of these are based on existing verbs, like "get-," but there are seven new verbs. The verbs that are specific to Exchange Server 2007 are:

▼ Disable
■ Dismount
■ Enable
■ Install

- ■ Mount
- ■ Retry
- ▲ Uninstall

Other than increasing the vocabulary of the Windows PowerShell, the Exchange Management Shell does not change the way in which the Windows PowerShell works, because it is, in fact, the Windows PowerShell with Exchange extensions.

There are some niceties that the Exchange team included in the EMS to help us get started. In Figure 13-2, you can see that a Welcome screen was added. There is no such screen by default in the Windows PowerShell. Cosmetically, you will also notice a change in the default background color.

One of the nicest things is the completion of a quick reference guide. Just by typing **quickref**, you can have helpful information about using the Exchange Management Shell. This would be an excellent guide to print out and keep close by while you are using the EMS.

Basic Exchange Tasks

There are two broad categories in which we can place each Exchange administrative task. One category is recipient management and the other is system management. While we have already covered many of the basic Exchange tasks throughout this book, I want

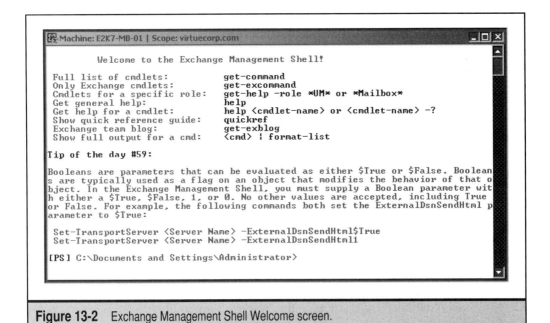

Figure 13-2   Exchange Management Shell Welcome screen.

to review a few of the core tasks that the average administrator will perform in each of these two categories. These represent the most repetitive tasks that can be performed from the Exchange Management Shell.

Recipient Management

Recipient management makes up the majority of administration that takes place on a day-to-day basis. There are some new recipient types in Exchange Server 2007 that are derivatives of the mailbox-enabled User object. For brevity's sake, we are only going to review some of the PowerShell commands for contacts, mailboxes, and distribution groups.

Mail Contacts   The Windows PowerShell can be used to create new contacts with external e-mail addresses or to assign external e-mail addresses to existing contacts:

```
[PS] C:\>New-MailContact "Sales Contact" -alias salescontact -external-
EmailAddress salescontact@pennywiseresort.com
 [PS] C:\>Enable-MailContact "Sales Contact" -alias salescontact
-externalEmailAddress salescontact@pennywiseresort.com
```

Mailboxes   Only User objects can be mailbox-enabled. The Windows PowerShell allows administrators to either create new users with mailboxes or mailbox-enable existing users.

```
[PS] C:\>New-Mailbox -Alias Colin -Database "Mailbox Database"
-Name ColinClayton -OrganizationalUnit Users -FirstName Colin
-LastName Clayton -DisplayName "Colin Clayton" -UserPrincipalName
CClayton@pennywiseresort.com
```

When you create a new user in Active Directory with the New-Mailbox cmdlet, you will be prompted to specify a password. The Enable-Mailbox cmdlet can be used if the user object already exists.

```
[PS] C:\>Enable-Mailbox CClayton@pennywiseresort.com -Database "Mailbox
Database"
```

Once mailboxes exist in the organization, various mailbox tasks get performed on a regular basis. You may need to report on the mailboxes on a specific mailbox database or even all of the mailboxes on a particular server.

```
[PS] C:\>Get-Mailbox -Database "Mailbox Database"
 [PS] C:\>Get-Mailbox -Server servername
```

It is also critical to be able to find the sizes of each mailbox and to understand how many are over their limit. In Exchange Server 2003 and earlier, you could find this information using the graphical administrative tools. Using the Get-MailboxStatistics and Get-MailboxFolderStatistics cmdlets is the quickest way to obtain this information in Exchange Server 2007. The Exchange Management Console doesn't give enough details about mailboxes to help you make storage decisions. Here are some examples of how you can get statistical information about your mailboxes:

```
[PS] C:\>Get-MailboxStatistics -Server PW-EX1
[PS] C:\>Get-MailboxStatistics -Database "Mailbox Database"
[PS] C:\>Get-MailboxFolderStatistics -Identity "John Smith"
[PS] C:\>Get-MailboxFolderStatistics -FolderScope Inbox
```

The combined information you get from the Get-Mailbox, Get-MailboxStatistics, and Get-MailboxFolderStatistics cmdlets can be used to determine if mailboxes need to be moved or distributed. In some cases, it can help you determine if a new storage group and mailbox database is needed.

Distribution Groups You can create three different types of groups to distribute mail: distribution groups, security groups, and dynamic distribution groups. The most common type for distributing e-mail is the distribution group.

```
[PS] C:\>New-DistributionGroup -Name "Sales Team" -OrganizationalUnit
"Pennywiseresort.com/Users" -SAMAccountName "Sales Team" -Type "Distri-
bution"
 [PS] C:\>Enable-DistributionGroup -Identity "Sales Team"
```

Filters When you have to work with a large number of recipients, sometimes you need to narrow down which one you want to display or work with. You can filter objects based on one or more properties. This is especially helpful if you are planning on piping the results to another command. Here are some sample filters:

```
[PS] C:\>Get-Mailbox | Where-Object {$_.department -like "Sales"}
```

The Where-Object cmdlet is used here to filter all the results of the Get-Mailbox command. The $_ is a default variable that represents the data piped to the Where-Object cmdlet. You then specify the property that you want to filter by, preceded by a period. The -like operator is used because it is a "loose" operator that also supports wildcards.

System Management

The creation of new system objects is not as frequent as recipients, but that doesn't mean that server administrators aren't as busy. In fact, there are tasks that must be performed on servers on a regular scheduled basis just in terms of maintenance.

New Storage Groups and Databases

```
[PS] C:\>New-StorageGroup "Sales Mailboxes" -Server PW-EX1
```

Mounting/Dismounting Databases Most manual maintenance tasks performed on a mailbox database will require that the database be taken offline. The good news is that this can be done one database at a time. The following examples show a database being dismounted and then mounted.

```
[PS] C:\>Dismount-Database "Sales Mailboxes"
[PS] C:\>Mount-Database "Sales Mailboxes"
```

Server Status   The Status tool doesn't exist in the Exchange Management Console like it did in the Exchange Server 2003 Exchange System Manager (ESM). However, Microsoft did include a cmdlet that allows us to get the status of servers in the entire organization. The Get-ExchangeServer cmdlet can be used to retrieve either the status of all servers or the status of all servers for a specific domain.

```
[PS] C:\>Get-ExchangeServer -Status | Format-List
```

Unfortunately, this still doesn't tell us if the core Exchange services are running or not. But as you may have already guessed, you can use the Get-Services cmdlet for that.

```
[PS] C:\>Get-Services -Name MSE*
```

Using the MSE* wildcard will only show the MS Exchange services, as shown in the Figure 13-3.

EXCHANGE TASK AUTOMATION

If you go back to the EMC and look at how many steps it takes to actually perform the creation of a new contact or a new user and even just mail-enable or mailbox-enable the object through the GUI, then you will see that the Windows PowerShell cmdlets have actually automated many steps for us.

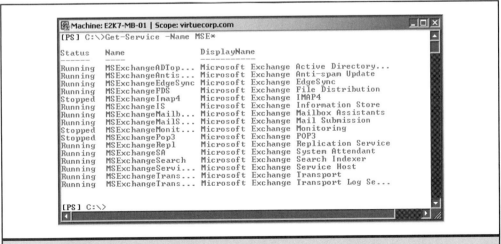

Figure 13-3.   Using Get-Service for Exchange services.

That is so cool. Just by learning the syntax for Windows PowerShell and the Exchange System Manager, we have already learned how to "script" for Exchange Server 2007. How is that for instant gratification? Are you still hungry for more? Fantastic! I was hoping you would say yes! What we have not done yet is actually automate any Exchange tasks.

Basic Automation

At the beginning of this chapter, I asked you to think about the tasks and problems that you perform and face on a regular basis. While I can't name them all, I can predict some of them based on the common issues all Exchange administrators face. I am a strong believer in maintenance. As a consultant, I have seen numerous failed servers and I have worked on bringing those servers back to life. I'm convinced that the servers would have never had the critical failures if they had only been better maintained. Not even *well maintained*—just a little more attention to what was going on in the server would have done the trick.

So why don't administrators know what is happening on their Exchange servers? Most of the time, it is a bandwidth issue—not network bandwidth, but administrators' bandwidth. Even with the potential catastrophes that can ensue from a lack of maintenance, companies will likely continue to ask their administrators to do more without any new hires. There is the ultimate problem statement to solve. The Windows PowerShell does give us an answer to this dilemma. With a little bit of effort, we can reduce the mundane administrative tasks to the execution of a Windows PowerShell command or a script.

Change the Department for an Entire Group of Mailboxes

Let's say that your company decides to do a reorganization with updated department names. You have 2000 users and are not looking forward to the prospect of manually changing everyone's department name in Active Directory. You could use the Exchange Management Shell to knock this out in no time. For each department, you could perform the following:

```
[PS] C:\>Get-User | Where-Object {$_.department -like "IT"} | Set-User
-Department "Business Technology"
```

With a little more work, you could make one script that will change all of the department names for every user.

Checking the Application Event Log

Maybe part of your daily routine is to view the event logs and verify that certain events have occurred or, in some cases, not occurred on your Exchange server. You can use the Get-Eventlog cmdlet to help you perform the mundane procedure and free up some of your valuable time. For example, you could look for a specific Event ID, like 1221, which is generated when online defragmentation completes. This log is unique in that it not only identifies when defragmentaiton completes, but it also indicates how much "white space" exists in each database.

```
[PS] C:\>Get-Eventlog Application | Where-Object {$_.Eventid -eq 1221} |
Format-Table Message,TimeGenerated
```

Or perhaps you just want to find out if any errors were issued by the Extensible Storage Engine (ESE) service.

```
[PS] C:\>Get-Eventlog Application | Where-Object {(($_.Source -like
"*ESE*") -and ($_.EntryType -like "Error"))} | Format-Table Message,
TimeGenerated
```

Use these two examples as building blocks, and you can build a Windows Power-Shell script that can report on all of the events that are important for you to monitor.

Automate Mailbox Creations

In order to automate mailbox creation, there first has to be a source that provides a list of new users. Typically, this will come from a human resources department. As long as you can get this information in the form of a comma separated file (CSV), you can use that file to automate the creation of new mailboxes. The file could look something like this:

```
Name,User Name, Department
Neal Bush, NBush, Consulting,
Jason Judge, JJudge, Executive,
Larry Thompson, LThompson, Sales
Andy Langsam, ALangsam, R&D
```

There are two ways in which you can choose to create the new mailbox. You can choose to use a template account or you can just use the default settings. In the following example, we will use just the default settings. If you want to know more about using templates, see the Microsoft TechNet article "How to Use Templates to Create Recipients" (http://technet.microsoft.com/en-us/library/bb125152.aspx).

```
$Pass = ConvertTo-SecureString "ChangeM3" -asPlainText -Force
Import-CSV "C:\NewMailboxUsers.csv" | ForEach-Object -Process {New-
Mailbox -Name $_.Name -UserPrincipalName "$($_.UserName)@pennywiseresort
.com" -OrganizationalUnit "pennywiseresort.com/Users" -Database "Mailbox
Database" -Password $Pass -ResetPasswordOnNextLogon $true}
```

As we mentioned earlier, when creating new mailboxes, you have to provide a password. When you are trying to automate the creation of mailboxes, you have to find a way to pass a secure string of characters into each new user object. This script accomplishes it with the ConvertTo-SecureString cmdlet. The string is saved as a variable, and then the variable $Pass is called on during the creation of each user. Since every user will end up with the same password, the -ResetPasswordOnNextLogon cmdlet is invoked to force a password change when the user logs on for the first time.

Identify and Move Large Mailboxes

In this exercise, you will create a Windows PowerShell script file that will create a new storage group and mailbox database. Then the script will look for the 10 largest mailboxes in the organization, excluding the system mailboxes. Finally, the mailboxes will be moved to the newly created mailbox database.

1. Open Notepad.
2. Type the following:

```
Write-Host "Creating a New Storage Group"
New-StorageGroup -Name StorageAnnex -Server PW-EX1
Write-Host "New Storage Group Created"
Write-Host "Creating New Mailbox Database"
New-MailboxDatabase -Name SuperSizedMBX -StorageGroup StorageAnnex
Mount-Database SuperSizedMBX
Write-Host "Mailbox Database Created"
Write-Host "Searching for Mailboxes to Move"
Get-MailboxStatistics | where {$_.DisplayName -notlike "System*" }
| sort TotalItemSize -Descending | Select-Object -First 1 | Move-
Mailbox -TargetDatabase "SuperSizedMBX"
Write-Host "Completed Successfully"
```

3. Save the file as C:\toptenoffenders.ps1.
4. Close Notepad.

Configuring PowerShell for Scripts

By default, the security setting in Windows PowerShell may prevent you from running script files. Only the interactive sessions we have been using so far in this chapter will work with Windows PowerShell by default. The ability to run Windows PowerShell script files is controlled by an execution policy. The policies are:

▼ Restricted
■ AllSigned
■ RemoteSigned (default)
▲ Unrestricted

To view the current policy, just type:

```
[PS] C:\>Get-ExecutionPolicy
```

To change the policy to be more or less restrictive, type:

```
[PS] C:\>Set-ExecutionPolicy PolicyName
```

As an additional safety precaution, you have to add one of the following prefixes to even a signed script file in order for PowerShell to execute it (.\ or ./).

Running a Script File

If you download a script from the Internet, then only scripts that are properly signed will be allowed to execute. Since most sample scripts are not signed, there is a good chance you will not be able to run the script. This is a good thing—you will have to view the properties of the file and click the Unblock button or lower the execution policy.

Run TopTenOffenders.ps1:

1. Restore the Exchange Management Shell.

2. Type the following:

   ```
   [PS] C:\>./toptenoffenders.ps1
   ```

3. Type **A** and press ENTER when prompted to accept mailbox moves.

4. Verify the results of the script.

Windows PowerShell Scripting Resources

To continue on your quest to become a better scripter, you will want to bookmark the resources provided in Table 13-4 to help you on your way, all of which were used as references for this chapter.

Resource Name	URL
PowerShell Team Blog	http://blogs.msdn.com/powershell
TechNet Primer for EMS	http://technet.microsoft.com/en-us/library/bb245704.aspx
Viveksharma Blog	www.viveksharma.com/techlog/category/powershell
TechNet Recipient Management Article	http://technet.microsoft.com/en-us/library/bb310752.aspx
ScriptCenter's Windows PowerShell page	www.microsoft.com/technet/scriptcenter/hubs/msh.mspx
Quest Software's PowerGUI	www.powergui.net

Table 13-4.   Windows PowerShell Scripting Resources

SUMMARY

In this chapter, I've given you some basic direction on how to approach scripting, provided a primer on Windows PowerShell, and shown you some specific scripting examples for managing Exchange from within the Exchange Management Shell. I hope this chapter has given you enough information to get yourself started using Windows PowerShell scripts with Exchange. In the next chapter, I'll cover the monitoring of Exchange.

CHAPTER 14

Monitoring Exchange Server 2007

Like any product Microsoft creates, Exchange 2007 is designed to run continuously with minimal downtime. But like any software product on the market, problems will most likely arise (otherwise, you and I wouldn't have a job, right?). Since we all know that we can expect to have troubles with our Exchange servers from time to time, and because most companies now consider their e-mail platform to be a mission-critical application, it would be beneficial for you (not to mention your job security!) to be proactively monitoring your Exchange servers. This chapter will focus on how you can monitor your Exchange environment in an effort to be as proactive as possible in dealing with those problems. I will take a look at several monitoring functionalities that are built into Exchange 2007, as well as Event Viewer. Lastly, I will cover the basics of using Microsoft Operations Manager (MOM) to monitor Exchange 2007.

USING THE EXCHANGE BEST PRACTICES ANALYZER

Monitoring in Exchange 2000 and 2003 involved looking at servers and connections for problems, as well as the notification of those problems. This involved configuring what was to be monitored, how to notify, etc. It wasn't a simple process. In Exchange 2007, this process has been replaced with the Best Practices Analyzer (which was first made available in Exchange 2003). This tool performs a comprehensive scan of the Exchange environment, including Exchange servers, Active Directory, connectors, Exchange storage, and even select third-party software, and then provides a summary report that categorizes its findings so you can determine whether changes need to be made. Let's take a look at the tool and how to utilize it to monitor the health of your Exchange environment.

Before you begin scanning your Exchange and Active Directory environments, you need to be fully aware of the impact on performance a scan will have on your production servers. In many cases, you will want to run an analysis during business hours (particularly the Health Check with Performance Baseline scan—more about that later in the chapter), so it is imperative that you understand what performance hit your servers will take.

The largest hit will be on the server on which you run the Analyzer; this is because it is doing all of the collection, conversion, and storage of data from Exchange and Active Directory to eXtensible Markup Language (XML) files. You really need to keep this in mind, as you will access the Best Practice Analyzer from within the Exchange Management Console, which is conveniently installed on each of your Exchange servers. This server will utilize upwards of 10 megabytes (MB) of random access memory (RAM) for every server it scans, run the processor between 50 and 75 percent utilization, and use up to 2 MB of disk space for XML files. The domain controller you connect to in order to analyze the Active Directory configuration of the Exchange environment will take the next largest hit—up to 50 percent processor utilization while being scanned. Interestingly enough, there will be such a small performance hit on the Exchange servers involved with the scan as to be negligible.

TIP Install the Management Tools on either a separate Windows Server 2003 server or on a Windows XP workstation where you can run the Best Practices Analyzer. With either Windows Server 2003 or XP, you'll need to have .NET Framework 2.0, Microsoft Management Console (MMC) 3.0, and Microsoft Command Shell installed in order to install the Exchange Management Console. Windows Vista will not support the running of the Management Tools until Service Pack 1 (SP1) for Exchange 2007 is released. See Chapter 2 for more information on performing a custom install.

You can open the Best Practices Analyzer by navigating in the Exchange Management Console to the Toolbox node in the console tree, as shown in Figure 14-1, and selecting Open Tool in the action pane.

The Best Practices Analyzer runs as a wizard (see Figure 14-2) that performs two basic functions: performing scans of the Exchange environment and viewing a report of the analysis performed on a given scan. Scans can be performed on one or more Exchange servers, depending on the configuration of your Exchange environment, and can encompass the Exchange configuration within Active Directory, as well as each Exchange server's Internet Information Server (IIS) metabase, registry, and information available via Windows Management Instrumentation (WMI).

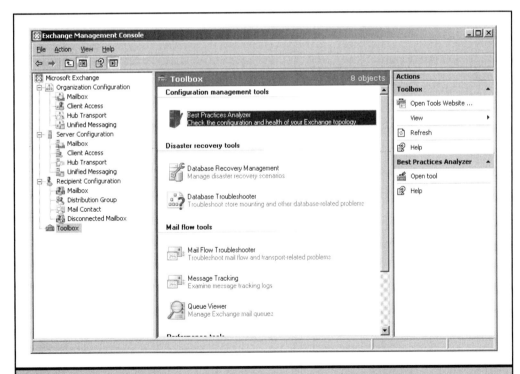

Figure 14-1.   Opening the Best Practices Analyzer.

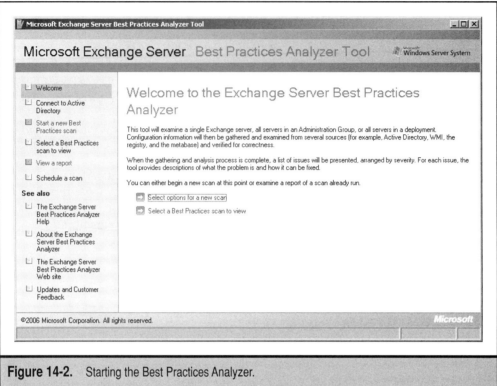

Figure 14-2. Starting the Best Practices Analyzer.

In order to perform a scan, you'll need to be a member of either the Domain Administrators or Builtin\Administrators group, a member of the Local Administrators group on each Exchange server, and be delegated at least view-only permissions within the Exchange organization. Let's start by looking at how to perform a scan of your Exchange environment, and then we'll look at how to read the analysis reports to determine any steps you'll need to take to tweak or fix your Exchange environment.

TIP The Best Practices Analyzer is updated on a regular basis by Microsoft, so look for updates, both in Exchange service packs, as well as in standalone versions.

Performing a Scan

Choosing the Select Options For A New Scan link takes you to the Connect To Active Directory page of the wizard, where you'll specify which domain controller (DC) you wish to connect to in order to perform the scan. If your current account does not meet the requirements I listed previously, you'll need to select the Show Advanced Login Options link to expose fields in which you can specify separate credentials for Active Directory and Exchange (see Figure 14-3). If your account has the proper permissions, simply

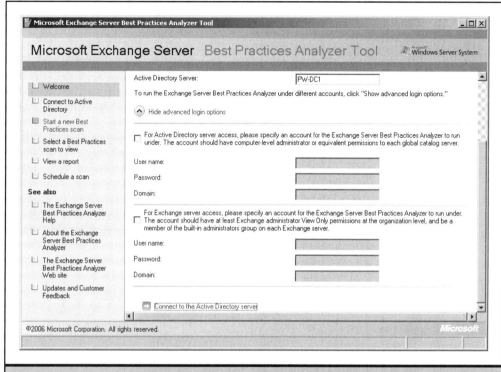

Figure 14-3.   Advanced options for connecting to Active Directory.

specify the DC and click the Connect To The Active Directory Server link. If your account doesn't meet the minimum requirements, specify the appropriate accounts for Active Directory and Exchange, and then click the Connect To The Active Directory Server link.

Once connected to Active Directory, you are presented with the Start A New Best Practices Scan page (see Figure 14-4). Here, you should select the Exchange server(s) you want included in the scan and the type of scan to be performed. Table 14-1 lists the types of scans you can perform and the information collected.

NOTE   Even though the scan options show Administrative Groups (an Exchange 2000/2003 concept), Exchange 2007 does not use Administrative Groups. In Exchange 2007, Administrative Groups have been replaced with Universal Security Groups (USGs) that provide access to the Exchange environment.

When running the Health Check scan, you can also collect performance information for a two-hour duration by selecting the Performance Baseline check box. When running the Permissions Check, Connectivity Test, or Exchange 2007 Readiness scans, there are no options other than to specify the speed of the network (to properly estimate the scan time). Clicking the Start Scanning link begins the scan process.

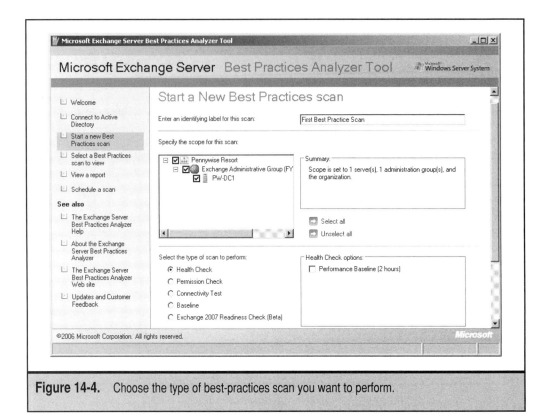

Figure 14-4.   Choose the type of best-practices scan you want to perform.

The Baseline scan has one additional step before it runs: a Baseline Options link replaces the Start Scanning link, as shown in Figure 14-5. Clicking this link yields the Baseline Options page of the wizard, where you can specify a label for the baseline options, as well as a list of over 350 values to compare the current Exchange configuration with, shown in Figure 14-6. You'll also notice that a few values, while selected, are grayed out, as these are just some of the many values that Microsoft has automatically included in the baseline.

Once you click the Start Scanning link for any of the scan types, you'll be shown the Scanning In Progress page of the wizard, which gives you an update on when the scan will be complete. Once complete, select the View A Report Of This Best Practices Scan link to view the report from your scan, shown in Figure 14-7.

You should notice a few things about the report format. First, you can view this report from several views (List, Report, Other). Second, the List report breaks down the scan results into several tabs to make understanding the results a simple task. In my scan, I got, of all things, an error on the Transmission Control Protocol/Internet Protocol (TCP/IP) driver I was using (I had no idea!). Selecting the X icon next to the entry reveals more detail on the issue. Selecting the other tabs may reveal relevant information for each tab's focus.

Scan Type	Description
Health Check	The Health Check scan is a comprehensive scan, encompassing everything from configuration changes to errors and warnings. It is the most appropriate scan type if you are both looking for a general view of the overall health of your Exchange environment and if you are troubleshooting a configuration issue.
Permissions Check	This scan verifies that the appropriate default permissions are in place.
Connectivity Test	This is one of the faster scans, as it scans a limited amount of information on each Exchange server and, more importantly, the network connectivity to each Exchange server. If the Connectivity Test scan fails, you should run a Health Check scan for more detailed information.
Baseline	This scan has many more options for you to choose from that will act as a baseline to compare the current state of your Exchange environment against.
Exchange 2007 Readiness	This scan should be used before moving to Exchange 2007 to determine the steps you'll need to take before you begin your transition.

Table 14-1.   Best-Practice Scan Types

Selecting the Informational Items tab, shown in Figure 14-8, shows you how much detail this report contains by covering over 30 Active Directory–specific and over 40 Exchange-specific pieces of vital information.

Scheduling a Scan

Should you not want to run a scan the moment you launch this tool, you can schedule the scan (see Figure 14-9) to run at a later date using familiar options, such as time, date, and the option to make the scan recur daily, weekly, or monthly. This feature is important when you are interested in determining the health of your Exchange environment without affecting the production use of your Exchange servers. Another example of good use of the scheduling feature is to run multiple connectivity scans throughout the business day to determine if Exchange servers are available.

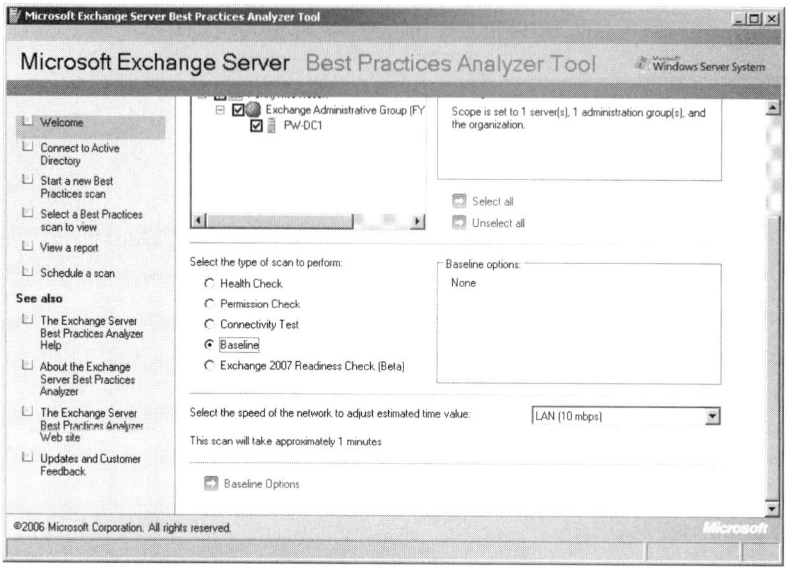

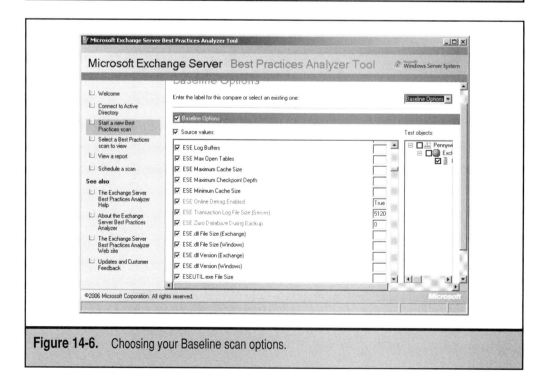

Figure 14-5. Changes you can make when selecting a Baseline scan.

Figure 14-6. Choosing your Baseline scan options.

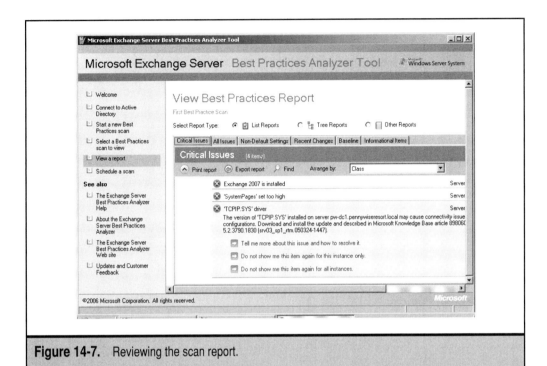

Figure 14-7. Reviewing the scan report.

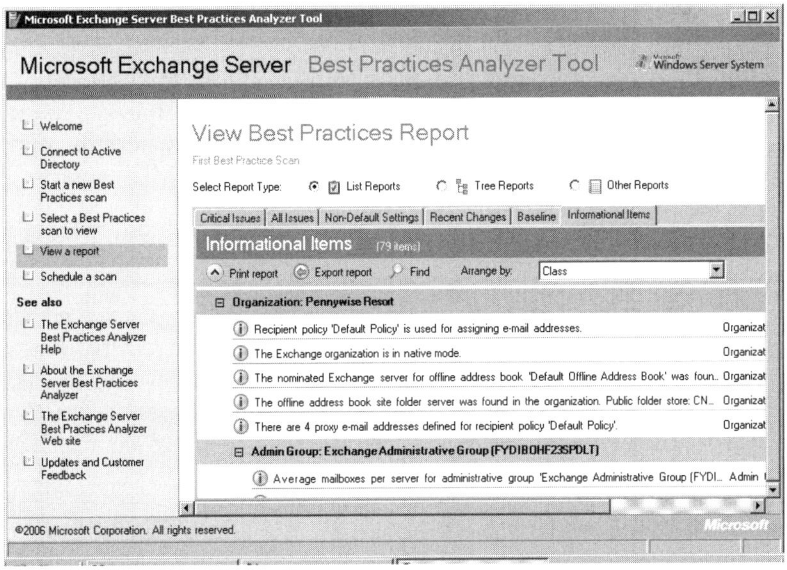

Figure 14-8. Reviewing the environment information.

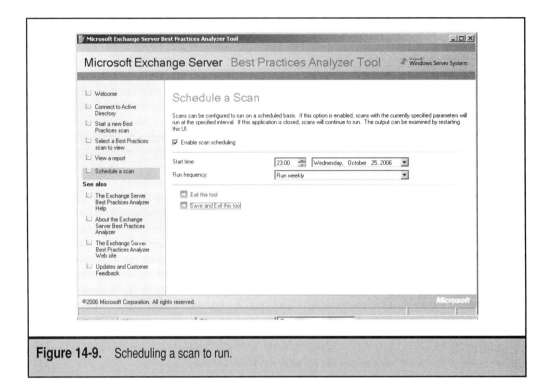

Figure 14-9. Scheduling a scan to run.

Viewing Scan Reports

You are not limited to viewing reports on scans you run in real time; you can view reports from previous scans just as easily. After opening the Best Practices Analyzer, choose the Select A Best Practices Scan To View link to reveal all scans you can view reports from, as shown in Figure 14-10. You can choose to view the report, export it to XML—you can export it to Hypertext Markup Language (HTML) and comma-separated value (CSV) while viewing the report—delete the scan, or give it a more descriptive name than simply date and time.

TIP You may be wondering where you review the performance data you can choose to collect with the Health scan. There is no performance monitor data file to review on your own. Instead, Exchange collects 240 samples at 30-second intervals (thus, the two-hour duration) of the counters specified in the *Troubleshooting Microsoft Exchange Server Performance* whitepaper found on Microsoft's Web site. Rather than review the counters yourself, the data is analyzed, and any irregularities are listed in the report.

One of the best tools within the Best Practices Analyzer is the articles found in the Help file. These articles discuss each of the messages displayed in the scan reports and provide not only insightful information on the topic, but also steps on how to correct issues and

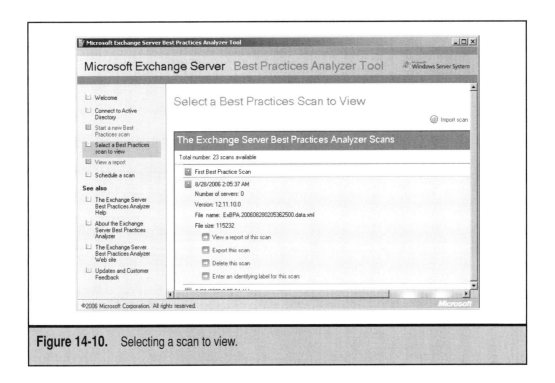

Figure 14-10. Selecting a scan to view.

links to relevant Microsoft Knowledge Base articles. The Help file is, oddly enough, not available from the Help link in the action pane under the Best Practices Analyzer section. Instead, you need to select it from the navigation pane within the Best Practices Analyzer itself under the See Also section. If you browse through the articles under the Microsoft Exchange Server Analyzer – Articles listing, you will begin to gain a sense of just how comprehensive an analysis this tool is performing. There are 350 Exchange issues alone, with eight other categories with entries. As you can see in Figure 14-11, these articles are shared by three Analyzer tools created by Microsoft. The Microsoft Exchange Server Disaster Recovery Analyzer tool is discussed in Chapter 15, and the Microsoft Exchange Server Performance Troubleshooting Analyzer tool is discussed in Chapter 16.

MONITORING EXCHANGE 2007 WITH MOM

Monitoring Exchange with the native tools is reactive in nature and will, therefore, only get you so far in your quest to maintain Exchange service availability—a proactive monitoring approach is necessary to keep systems up and running. Microsoft Operations Manager (MOM) provides not only advanced monitoring of Exchange 2007, but also gives you suggested courses of action to take. In this section, we will focus on the monitoring of Exchange 2007. One quick note: As of the date I wrote this book, Microsoft's

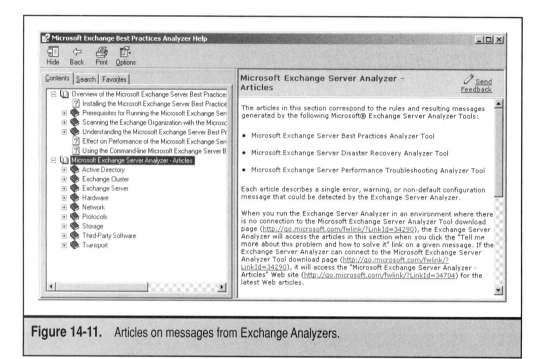

Figure 14-11. Articles on messages from Exchange Analyzers.

pending System Center Operations Manager 2007 (SCOM), which is the new version of MOM, is still in its beta version, and the management pack for Exchange 2007 has not been released for testing, so while I'm going to cover how to monitor Exchange with MOM, you should keep in mind that all of this part of the chapter relates to SCOM.

Monitoring plays an important part in meeting business objectives. Good monitoring directly translates to better server availability and uptime, resulting in more satisfied end users. In addition, if you are in charge of server management, you need to have a snapshot of your system at any given point in time to see its status. One of the powerful features of monitoring with MOM is the reports that are available to you on your Exchange environments. This not only gives you an at-a-glance view of what is going on in your Exchange server environment, it also provides you with a great tool for system capacity planning.

The Importance of Monitoring

Monitoring is all about availability. Monitoring is the act of observing a system in order to detect problems and raise awareness. It allows you to resolve issues before they become problems for users. Monitoring also allows you to pass important information to the correct people, who can then use this information to solve problems. Overall, this works towards reducing the time to resolution when problems occur. Because e-mail is typically mission-critical, it makes sense that any downtime on an e-mail system directly translates to a loss of productivity.

Every piece of marketing material Microsoft has put out on Exchange 2007 always insists that it is a highly reliable platform, so why monitor Exchange 2007 when it is supposed to be a reliable product? First, your Exchange 2007 environment can get complex; no two Exchange 2007 implementations are exactly the same. Next, Exchange 2007, like any other application server, is dynamic. In both cases, monitoring helps determine the current state of the system as changes occur.

Exchange 2007 servers are now monitored based on Exchange server roles, as shown in Figure 14-12. These roles include Mailbox, Client Access, Hub Transport, Edge Transport, and Unified Messaging. Roles-based monitoring gives the ability to streamline the monitoring of Exchange and executing rules (these determine actions to be taken) only when there is a certain role installed on the server. For example, if you don't have a Mailbox Server role on a particular Exchange 2007 server, there is no point in having MOM look for mailbox events in order to execute appropriate rules, since they are not going to be there. Hence, the management pack for Exchange 2007 is fine-tuned for specific roles.

Next, there are several features, and not all features can be monitored in the same way. Traditionally with MOM, monitoring has always been based on alerts, performance

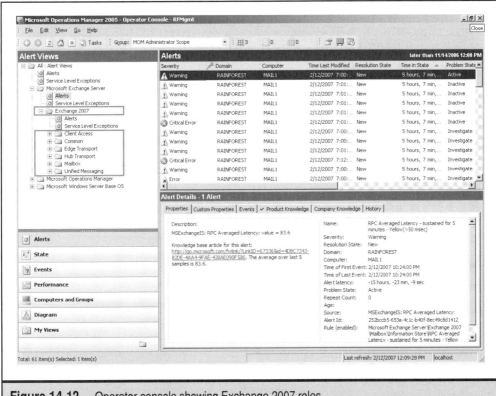

Figure 14-12.   Operator console showing Exchange 2007 roles.

counters, and events. This somehow is not sufficient for Exchange 2007. For example, consider the issue of redundancy. There must be multiple ways of monitoring a feature in Exchange 2007 since systems can be complex. Besides monitoring Exchange using the traditional events and performance counters, in the Exchange 2007 management pack— which defines the set of events and counters to be monitored, as well as the actions that can be taken—you can use synthetic transactions. These are sample transactions run at regular intervals to monitor the latency experienced by Outlook, Outlook Web Access (OWA), Outlook Mobile Access, and Exchange ActiveSync technology. For example, you can generate warning alerts when the latency determined by the synthetic transactions is over a predetermined threshold, allowing administrators to address potential issues before they become a reality.

Some of the new monitoring techniques used by the MOM 2005 management pack for Exchange 2007 are Mailflow, Outlook Web Access, and Transport Queues. Mailflow simulates typical mailflow scenarios that would be transacted by Exchange 2007 users via synthetic transactions. A similar synthetic transaction is executed for Outlook Web Access, simulating a typical usage scenario for monitoring purposes. This directly relates to what a user is experiencing when using the application. This allows the administrators to know what kind of latency users are experiencing without actually logging on to Outlook Web Access. This synthetic transaction also provides for early detection of problems.

Other improvements made to the management pack for Exchange 2007 include the suppression of repetitive and related events. This cuts down on too much information showing up on the MOM console.

Improvements in Monitoring

Let's quickly take a look at what has improved in the monitoring of Exchange from Exchange 2003 to Exchange 2007. Here is a quick list of components in the Exchange 2003 management pack for MOM 2005:

▼   Events

■   Knowledge

■   Performance counters

■   Synthetic transactions through scripts

■   State view

■   Configuration wizard

▲   Exchange Best Practices Analyzer management pack

This list has been improved in all aspects and in some cases, optimized. The following is what's new in monitoring in Exchange 2007:

▼   More synthetic transactions (such as Unified Messaging or Exchange ActiveSync)

■   Integrated with Exchange Management Shell

- Configuration monitoring (using the Best Practices Analyzer)
- Anytime, anywhere, any device knowledge
- Specific rules for specific roles
- ▲ Simplified setup and configuration of the management pack

One of the biggest improvements is the simplified setup and configuration of the Exchange 2007 management pack. Key benefits include the following:

- ▼ Mailbox-role synthetic transactions work out-of-the-box
- No test mailboxes needed
- Client Access –role synthetic transaction configuration has been simplified
- A Simple shell script creates test mailboxes for Client Access
- All relevant services for each role are monitored automatically
- ▲ Advanced configuration takes place in MOM, not the registry

Monitoring Exchange 2007

Monitoring Exchange 2007 can be grouped into the following components:

- ▼ Events
- Performance counters
- State view
- Synthetic transactions
- Configuration monitoring
- ▲ Anytime, anywhere, any device knowledge

Monitoring Exchange 2007: Events

Events are the main building block of MOM monitoring. When Exchange 2007 detects a problem, an event is logged. All relevant error and warning events are monitored by MOM for Exchange 2007, as shown in Figure 14-13. In the management pack for Exchange 2007, there are over 800 different events. All alerts that are raised due to an event that occurs in Exchange are actionable and will include Knowledge Base information.

Monitoring Exchange 2007: Performance

The second building block is the performance-monitoring component. While there are seemingly countless performance counters to monitor Exchange, fundamentally, all performance counters answer the question "Is my server performing well?" If there is a trend or the possibility of the server encountering problems, we want to know about it.

The MOM agent that is installed on the Exchange 2007 server uses rules to monitor performance thresholds. Rules are preconfigured by the people who built the management

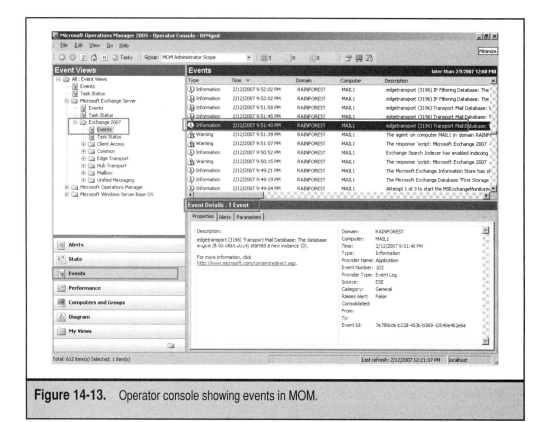

Figure 14-13.   Operator console showing events in MOM.

pack—in this case, it would be the Exchange 2007 team. The following list includes the rules used to answer the question "Is my server performing well?" in simple layman terms:

▼   Are user requests being handled quickly?

■   Are transport queues backing up?

■   Is the number of outstanding Remote Procedure Call (RPC) requests reasonable?

■   Is there a consistently high value indicating a likely resource bottleneck?

■   Is Active Directory responding quickly to requests?

▲   Is there enough free disk space?

Monitoring Exchange 2007: State View

The state view gives you an automatic feel of where you are with your server at any given time. It is definitely good to have the alerts that are continuously generated by MOM, but it is also good to know what the state of the server is at any given time in a single screen, without drilling through alerts, events, and performance counters. State is an auto-updated component and uses simple color codes and shapes to tell you the state of your servers. The following is a list of state components that provide information on the overall state view:

▼   Role-specific services

■   Messaging Application Programming Interface (MAPI) logon

■   Mailflow

■   Client Access Server (CAS) connectivity—OWA, Exchange Active Sync (EAS), Internet Message Access Protocol (IMAP)

■   Unified Messaging connectivity

■   Queues

■   Disk performance

▲   Active Directory access

Note that not every rule in the management pack will affect the state of the Exchange server—just the important ones are considered. Figure 14-14 shows you a good example

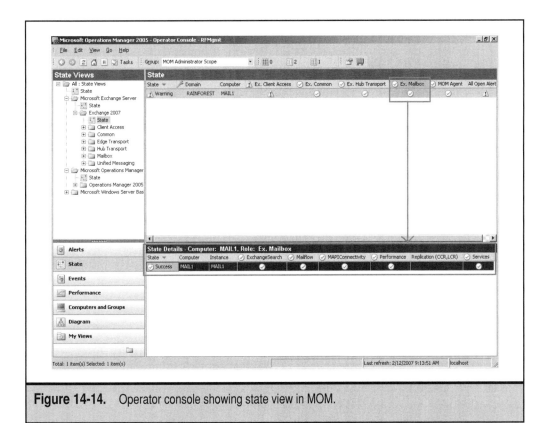

Figure 14-14.   Operator console showing state view in MOM.

of the state view of role-based monitoring. On the top of the details pane, you can see the server MAIL1 from the RAINFOREST domain list of roles. You can see that MAIL1 is a Client Access server, a Hub Transport server, and a Mailbox server. If you select the Ex. Mailbox column, you would see a detailed view of the entire component that makes up the Mailbox role state. This includes ExchangeSearch, MailFlow, MAPIConnectivity, Performance, and Services.

Synthetic Transactions

As mentioned earlier, with MOM 2005 and the Exchange Server 2007 management pack, you can use synthetic transactions to monitor the latency experienced by Outlook, OWA, Outlook Mobile Access, and Exchange ActiveSync technology. Table 14-2 lists the synthetic transactions that can be conducted using monitoring cmdlets and organized by server roles.

Synthetic Transactions: MAPI Connectivity

Let me go through one of these synthetic transactions in detail. In the Exchange 2003 management pack for MOM 2005, Test-MAPIConnectivity was a script-based component.

Server Role	Synthetic Transactions
Mailbox	MAPI Connectivity
	Mailflow
	Exchange Search
Hub Transport	Mailflow
Unified Messaging	Unified Messaging Connectivity
Client Access	OWA Connectivity
	ActiveSync Connectivity
	Outlook Anywhere Connectivity
	Post Office Protocol version 3 (POP3) Connectivity
	IMAP Connectivity
	Outlook Web Services

Table 14-2.   Synthetic Transactions by Server Role

In Exchange 2007, it is fully integrated in the Exchange Management Shell. In Test-MAPIConnectivity for Mailbox servers, technically, what happens is that MOM 2005 tests the length of connectivity between each individual mailbox server and Active Directory that it is talking to. This would allow MOM to test the ability to log on to a mailbox on each database server. This process uses mailboxes that already exist on each database. With performance enhancement and 64-bit architecture, it is possible to run against 50 different mailboxes on the same server in less than one minute!

As for network connectivity from a client to the server, this is monitored by the MOM agent's heartbeat. All this is done with no configuration at all. At the end of Test-MAPI-Connectivity, availability statistics based on the test result is generated.

The following set of figures runs through a Test-MAPIConnectivity usage. Figure 14-15 shows the rule groups organized based on the Exchange server roles. Figure 14-16 shows the Test-MAPI connectivity rule that will execute the Test-MAPIConnectivity cmdlet.

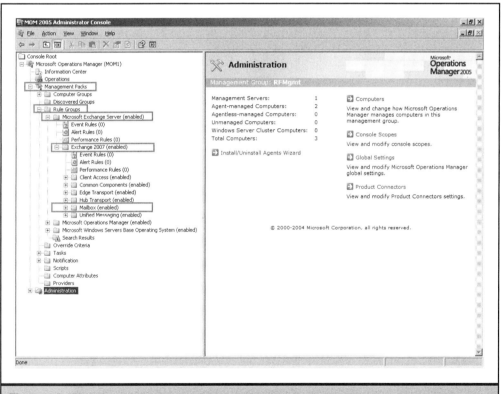

Figure 14-15. Rule groups within the MOM administrator console.

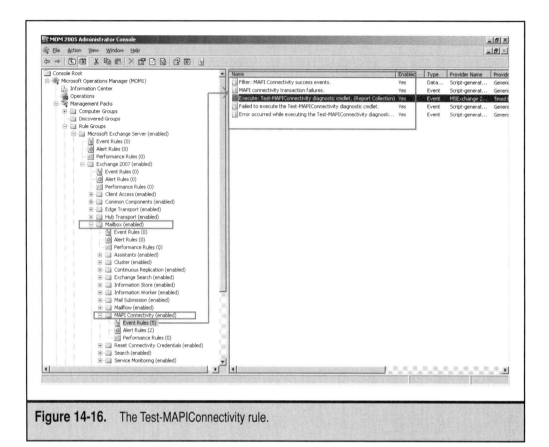

Figure 14-16. The Test-MAPIConnectivity rule.

Figure 14-17 shows the Exchange Management Shell, called by running the Test-MAPIConnectivity rule. The Test-MAPIConnectivity cmdlet runs in five steps:

1. Testing the connectivity when the Information Store service is running. The latency is recorded.

2. Stopping the Information Store service.

3. Retesting the connectivity with the service stopped.

4. Restarting the Information Store service.

5. Retesting the connectivity after the restart and recording the latency.

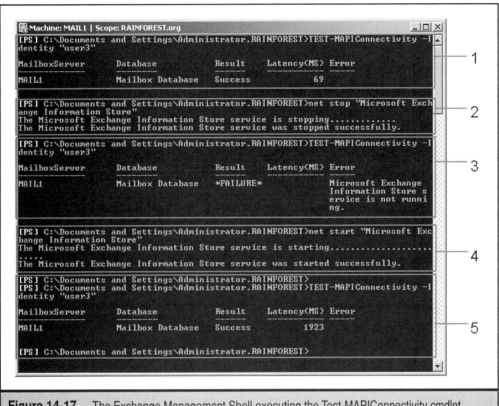

Figure 14-17. The Exchange Management Shell executing the Test-MAPIConnectivity cmdlet.

Synthetic Transactions: Mailflow

The other important synthetic transaction cmdlet is the Mailflow for Mailbox server role. Basically, a test e-mail is sent periodically to test e-mail functionality. There are two rules for this monitoring cmdlet. The first is an internal Mailflow connectivity rule, and the other is the external Mailflow connectivity monitoring rule. The internal rule (top illustration on the next page) shows monitoring mailflow from Mailbox to Hub and back to the same Mailbox server. The external rule (bottom illustration on the next page) shows monitoring mailflow from Mailbox to Hub Transport to another Mailbox server (the dotted lines represent the actual path traveled by the e-mails).

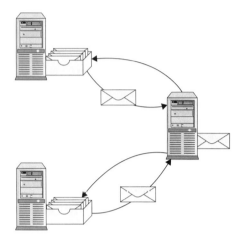

The end result of the Mailflow synthetic transaction includes recording mail delivery latency for reporting purposes. No configuration is required at all for this to work.

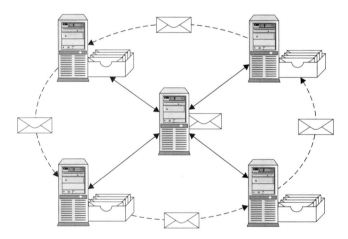

Synthetic Transactions: Client and Devices

It is important to have the capability to monitor all the various clients and devices that connect to Exchange 2007. Hence, the third synthetic transaction I am going to talk about is Monitoring Client Access Server. Fundamentally, there are two components to client-access monitoring: internal monitoring tests on the functionality of each individual server and external monitoring tests on the service as a whole—for example, public Uniform Resource Locator (URL) access.

CAS synthetic transactions require test mailboxes on each Mailbox server. These test mailboxes are created using an Exchange Management Shell script, and the password for each test mailbox is automatically changed every seven days by Exchange 2007; hence, no manual intervention is required from the administrator.

Table 14-3 presents a list of all the synthetic transactions for the CAS. Cmdlets used for executing the synthetic transactions that can be executed from the Exchange Management Shell or from the MOM Administration Console. No matter where you run it from, these cmdlets simulate client activities.

I have mentioned how the configuration of test mailboxes is required for CAS-monitoring cmdlets. The test mailboxes are created using the New-TestCASConnectivity-User cmdlet in the Exchange Management Shell, as shown in Figure 14-18. Figure 14-19 shows the newly created mailbox within the Mailbox node of the Exchange Management Console.

Monitoring: Server Configuration

The Exchange Best Practices Analyzer was mentioned earlier in this chapter. I would like to add that BPA (Best Practices Analyzer) is built into the Exchange 2007 management pack and is executed daily. The BPA in the management pack compares a wide range of server settings against an extensive database of best practices and provides alerts, as shown in Figure 14-20. As you know, these best practices are tested and validated through Microsoft's

Transaction Name	Configuration Needed?	Report
Outlook Web Access	Test mailbox	Yes
Exchange ActiveSync	Test mailbox	Yes
RPC/HTTP	Test mailbox	Yes
POP	Test mailbox	No
IMAP	Test mailbox	No
Outlook Web Services	None	No

Table 14-3. Synthetic Transactions for the Client Access Server Role

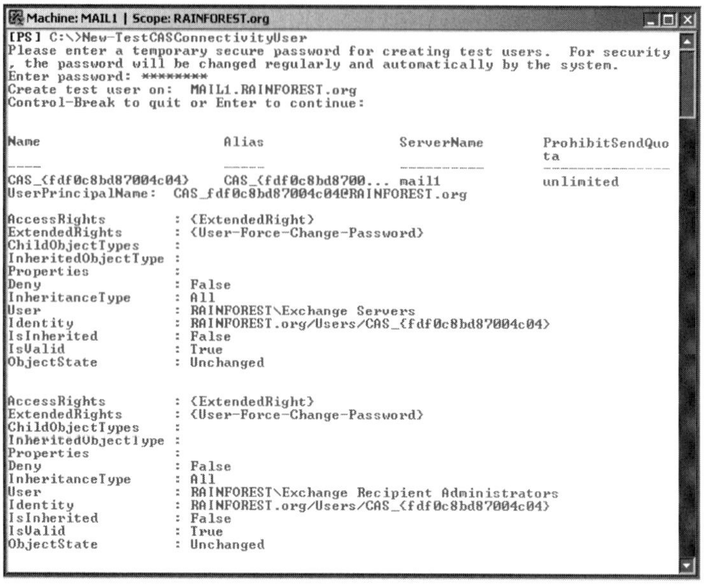

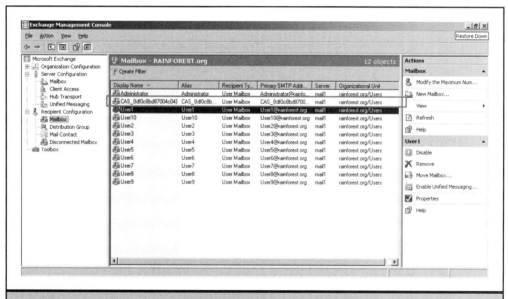

Figure 14-18. Creating test users with the New-TestCASConnectivityUser cmdlet.

Figure 14-19. Viewing the newly created test mailbox.

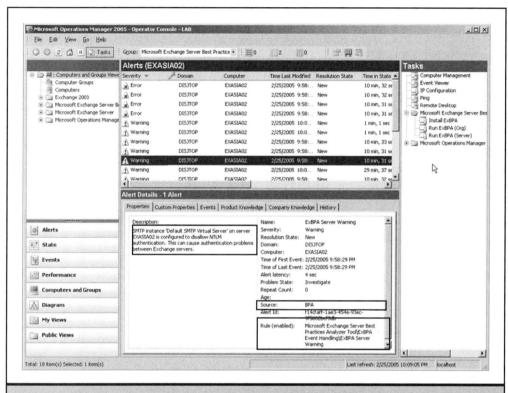

Figure 14-20. The MOM operator console showing a BPA rules-based alert.

own internal network. The biggest benefits of having the BPA in the management pack is that it increases performance, scalability, and uptime for large or small Exchange 2007 deployments and enables IT administrators to stay current with best practices on system management.

Knowledge Base Articles

Usually, once an alert is detected for Exchange 2007, the administrator will go to www .microsoft.com to search for a Knowledge Base article on the alert and related event. MOM 2005 and the management pack for Exchange 2007 make things easier for the administrator by providing a link directly to the relevant Knowledge Base article. Another great advantage is that since Knowledge Base is now on the Web, the information in the Knowledge Base can be updated anytime, without you having to update your management pack's Knowledge Base information. Figure 14-21 shows the URL for the Knowledge Base article provided in the alert information. In addition, you have the option of

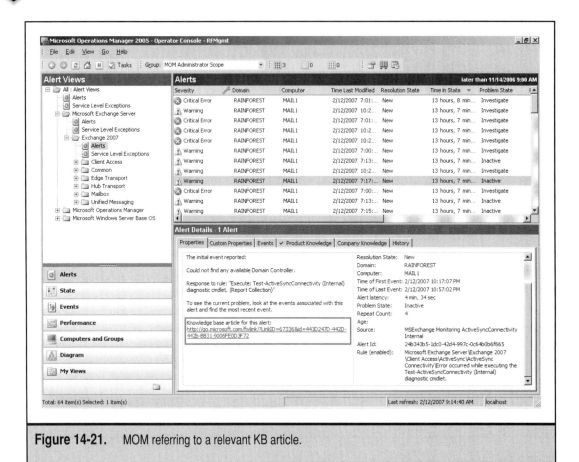

Figure 14-21.   MOM referring to a relevant KB article.

entering your own notes about how you resolve an issue so that your colleagues can take advantage of your previous experience if they see the same issue.

Reporting in MOM 2005 for Exchange 2007

Monitoring is a short-term management tactic, in that it only gives you a view of the current state of your environment; it lacks a bigger picture of what is happening within your environment. Reporting, on the other hand, is a long-term way of looking at management. By long-term, I mean that reporting gives you the opportunity to see what has happened, for example, in the past six months. With this capability, an administrator could use reports to analyze peak traffic or to look into problems where there may be too many mailboxes on one server compared to another.

Reporting is an important part of monitoring. You do not respond immediately to reports—unlike alerts, events, and performance counters—but you can make your system better in the long run. To do that, you need information collected over a period of time, and that is what reports can provide.

In the previous version of the Exchange management pack, reports were basic and were "okay." With the Exchange 2007 management pack, some rather impressive reports are available. In Exchange 2007 management pack reports, all the monitoring cmdlets discussed earlier "feed" data to the various reports for each of the services that are being monitored. Thus, there are top-level summary reports. From there, you could drill down to something specific, like ActiveSync connectivity for mobile device users.

There are some new message hygiene reports. These reports provide the administrator with an overview of how spam is affecting your messaging infrastructure. Edge Transport Servers are very much involved in providing data for these reports. Then there are the performance counter reports, which monitor the performance counters and report on things related to performance.

Let's take a look at some sample reports. Figure 14-22 shows the main top-level page for Exchange 2007 Service Availability Reports from the Exchange 2007 management pack.

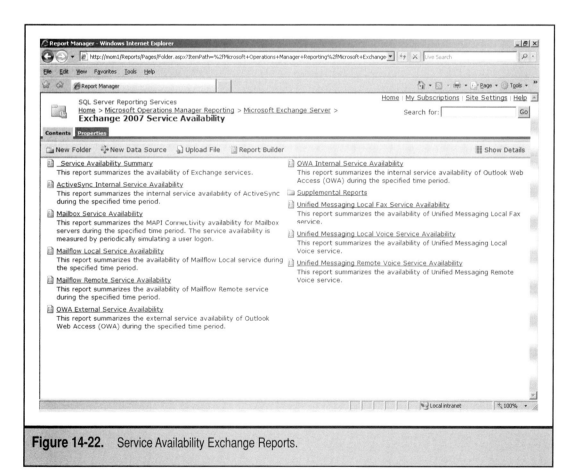

Figure 14-22. Service Availability Exchange Reports.

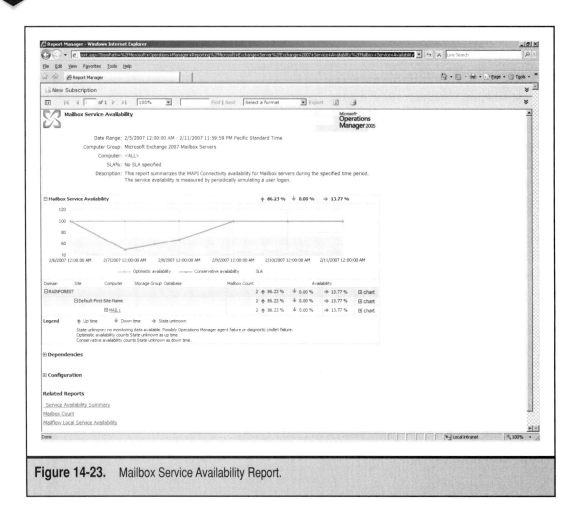

Figure 14-23. Mailbox Service Availability Report.

Figure 14-23 shows the Mailbox Service Availability Report. Figure 14-24 takes it one step further, drilling down on the Mail server name to determine availability down to the database level. If that is not enough, Figure 14-25 shows a chart for the data that you drilled down to.

Summary: Monitoring Exchange 2007 with MOM 2005 SP1

MOM 2005's monitoring philosophy for effective frontline monitoring of Exchange 2007 is to watch the health indicators, including critical events, significant performance counters, and a comprehensive set of synthetic transactions (Exchange 2007 cmdlets).

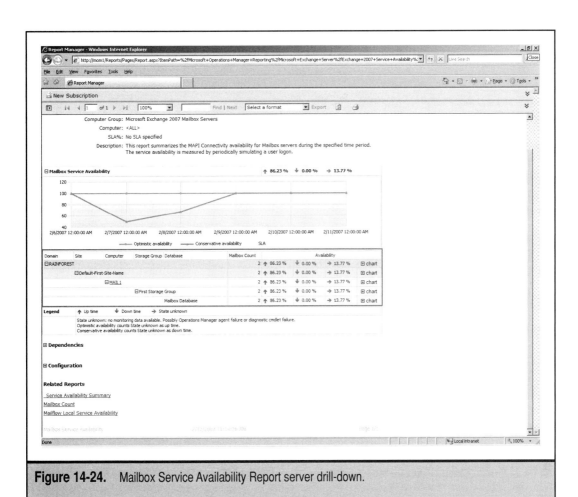

Figure 14-24.   Mailbox Service Availability Report server drill-down.

Monitoring with MOM will help you to understand messaging traffic, what's going on in your Exchange environment, the peak times your Exchange server experiences, and even how attainable your service level agreements for Exchange are.

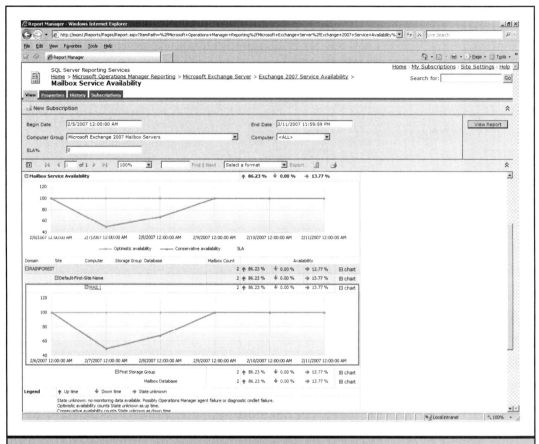

Figure 14-25.   Mailbox Service Availability Report server drill-down chart.

SUMMARY

In this chapter, you learned about the Microsoft tools you can use to monitor your Exchange environment, both those built into Exchange 2007 and those outside of it. All of these tools together will empower your efforts toward keeping your Exchange environment up and running.

In the next chapter, I'll look at not only how to properly back up your Exchange environment, but also how to ensure a good restore. I will also discuss backup terminology and possible errors you may see with the databases when backing up and restoring.

CHAPTER 15

Backup and Recovery

Y ou may or may not be surprised to learn that at one point in time, 24 percent of all calls received by Microsoft Product Support involved the backup or restoration of an Exchange database. This means that there must be a sizable number of Exchange administrators who don't understand databases or how they are backed up and restored.

However, we bet that you would agree that the prospect of having to restore an Exchange database represents one of the most feared administrative duties for any Exchange administrator, including yourself.

As you read through this chapter, you might think that it provides more information than you need, especially as someone who is new to Exchange 2007. Well, the reason why this is a detailed chapter is because we want you to have the information necessary to ensure proper backup and recovery of your Exchange 2007 databases. This is a tricky area and one with which you should be very familiar. Following the principles and suggestions in this chapter will enable you to avoid loss of data and ensure your data's integrity in the event a disaster occurs.

In this chapter, we'll look at several areas. First, I'll explain how to recover the most important data set—the mailbox databases found on your Mailbox servers—by covering some basics on the storage architecture of Exchange and then looking at how the transaction logs are used in both the backup and the restore processes. Then you'll learn how to use the backup program that ships with Windows Server 2003 to perform backups of your Exchange data, followed by learning how to restore the data. Next, I'll discuss advanced techniques to ensure that your data is there after a disaster and, finally, discuss the data sets you'll need to back up in order to recover the various roles beside the Mailbox server role.

NOTE   It is important to understand that your data can be lost, not only due to a disaster, but also because you ran the wrong commands at the wrong time. We will show you when and how to use the recovery commands so that you don't unwittingly create problems for yourself.

DATABASES AND TRANSACTION LOGS

Even though this is an introductory book on Exchange 2007 administration, all of this information is important for you to understand if you are going to do a good job of managing your Exchange databases. Please do not skim this section, because even though it is detailed, it can save you hours of frustration during a disaster.

ESE Databases

The Extensible Storage Engine (ESE) databases in Exchange Server 2007 are comprised of a single *.edb file. (In Exchange 2000 and 2003, there were two files: an *.edb file, which was referred to as the *rich text* file, and the *.stm file, which was referred to as the *streaming* file or the *native content store*. These two have been consolidated back into a single *.edb file.) Even though they are referred to as *files*, they are really databases built on the B-tree structure.

The Exchange EDB Database

The database file is similar to the database that was used in previous versions of Exchange, although there are few modifications to this file in Exchange 2007. It still holds information only in Microsoft Database Encoding Format (MDBEF) and non-MDBEF information must still be converted before being written into the database. Consistent with new ESE standards, information is held in 8-kilobyte (KB) pages (up from 4 KB in previous versions) inside the database. Each page will have a page number, version number, checksum, and other information that aids in ESE's ability to make sure that information is written to and read from the disk in a reliable fashion.

Single-Instance Message Store

Exchange Server 2007 continues to support Single Instance Storage (SIS). What this means is that a message sent to multiple recipients will be stored only once instead of creating one copy per recipient. The goal of this architecture is to ensure that your databases remain as small as reasonably possible.

The way to understand SIS is on a one-message-per-store basis. Please refer to the following illustration while reading this example. If Judy has 20 users, all homed on the same database, to whom she wishes to send a 1-MB message, without SIS, sending that message would consume 22 MB of disk space: 1 MB for each of the 20 recipients, 1 MB for the transaction log, and 1 MB for Judy's Sent Items folder. However, with SIS, only 2 MB of disk space are consumed: 1 MB for the transaction log and 1 MB for the copy stored in the database. Judy and her 20 recipients will get a handle in their inboxes pointing to the one copy of the message.

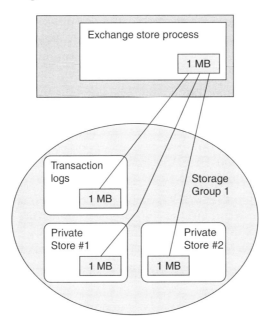

If those 20 recipients are homed on two different databases (10 in each database) in the same storage group, then a total of 3 MB of disk space will be consumed: 1 MB for each database and 1 MB for the transaction logs. Remember that all the databases in a storage group use the same set of transaction logs.

Finally, if those 20 users are homed on two different databases, and each database is homed in a different storage group, then a total of 4 MB of disk space will be needed to send the message: 1 MB for each database and 1 MB for each set of transaction logs.

These scenarios assume that the sender is homed on at least one of the databases that are also home to some of the recipients. If the sender is homed on a different database than any of the recipients, a copy of the sender's message will be retained in the sender's home database and the message will appear under the Sent Items folder in the sender's Outlook interface.

Transaction Logs

Transaction logs are the lifeblood of your Exchange 2007 server. Transaction logs provide the fault tolerance necessary to recover from a disaster. We can't emphasize enough that guarding and managing your transaction logs is one of the most important administrative functions you will perform. So, before we dive into transaction logs, let's lay down several administrative no-no's about managing transaction logs and their corresponding databases:

▼ **Never delete a transaction log.** If you do, you could logically corrupt your databases, but not experience a problem until days or weeks later.

■ **Never run antivirus scanning software on your transaction logs or databases.** Because antivirus software looks for a set of patterns of 1's and 0's, it is possible (and I've seen it happen) that a certain pattern will exist in an innocent log or page of the database. When the antivirus software attempts to fix this "problem," it will corrupt the entries in the transaction logs or the databases.

■ **Never compress your transaction logs or databases.** You will corrupt your databases by doing so and will be forced to recover those databases from tape.

■ **Never move your databases manually.** The transaction logs know where the databases reside on your hard disk, and if you move them manually, they won't be able to find them. Use the methods described in Chapter 6 if you need to move your databases to a new location.

▲ **Never use a controller that has write-back caching enabled, unless you can pull the memory chip off the controller and put it in a new controller.** Information that is written to the controller's memory but not to the disk is always subject to being lost if the controller should malfunction.

Now, in theory, the transaction log could be one giant ever-expanding file that holds transactions for the ESE database; however, this file would grow to the point of running out of disk space, and that would not be a good thing. So Microsoft has divided the transaction activities into multiple files known as *generations*. Each new transaction log is a new generation and is always 1MB in size. (This is a change from previous versions of Exchange, which used 5-MB logs. The change was made to better support the new continuous replication features I'll describe later in this chapter.) Transaction logs are numbered sequentially in hexadecimal format, starting with E0x0000001.log (where "x" is a number assigned by Exchange when the storage group is created) and increments from there. The current generation is always named E0x.log.

NOTE The new version of Exchange can store up to 2 billion log files before the log generation numbering must be reset. You'll probably want to back up before this happens.

When the current generation becomes full, it is renamed to the next hexadecimal number and a new E0x.log file is created. While this is happening, a temporary log file is created to hold transactions that occur while the new E0x.log file is being generated.

Each log file consists of two parts: a header and the data. The header contains vital information for the log file to operate properly, such as the path to the databases that it references. This is why you can't start a database if you manually move it to another location but don't change the header information in the transaction logs.

Since the same set of transaction logs is used to hold transactions for all the databases in a storage group, the job of recovering a database is simplified, because you don't have to go searching for just the right set of transaction logs to recover a database. Moreover, having multiple databases use the same set of transaction logs explains why some databases can be running while you restore another database from tape. The transaction logs can be used to perform multiple types of activities on multiple databases at the same time.

The header of a log file can be dumped using the Eseutil /ml command, as shown in Figure 15-1. The dump shows the generation number of the transaction log, the path to the database it references, and the unique signatures for the transaction log set. The data portion of the log file shows the data and where it was (or will be) inserted into the database on the disk.

How Do Transaction Logs Work?

The main function of transaction logs is to ensure the integrity of changes to the database. Four tests are applied to each change in the database to ensure this integrity. The following list includes the four tests, which are sometimes referred to by the acronym ACID:

▼ **Atomic**   Either all of the operations performed are completed or none of them are completed.

■ **Consistent**   The database must be in a consistent state before and after the changes.

■ **Isolated**   Changes to the database are not visible to the user until all of the operations have been performed and completed.

▲ **Durable**   Changes to the databases must be preserved in the event of a system or database malfunction.

```
C:\Command Prompt                                                    _ □ ×
C:\Program Files\Microsoft\Exchange Server\Mailbox\Second Storage Group>eseutil
/ml e010000001a.log

Extensible Storage Engine Utilities for Microsoft(R) Exchange Server
Version 08.00
Copyright (C) Microsoft Corporation. All Rights Reserved.

Initiating FILE DUMP mode...

        Base name: e01
        Log file: e010000001a.log
        lGeneration: 26 (0x1A)
        Checkpoint: NOT AVAILABLE
        creation time: 10/04/2006 23:45:52
        prev gen time: 10/04/2006 23:45:52
        Format LGVersion: (7.3704.10)
        Engine LGVersion: (7.3704.10)
        Signature: Create time:10/04/2006 22:24:41 Rand:49029852 Computer:
        Env SystemPath: C:\Program Files\Microsoft\Exchange Server\Mailbox\Second
Storage Group\
        Env LogFilePath: C:\Program Files\Microsoft\Exchange Server\Mailbox\Second
 Storage Group\
        Env Log Sec size: 512
        Env (CircLog,Session,Opentbl,VerPage,Cursors,LogBufs,LogFile,Buffers)
        (    off,    502,   25100,  14460,   25100,    2048,   2048,2000000000)
        Using Reserved Log File: false
        Circular Logging Flag (current file): off
        Circular Logging Flag (past files): off
        1 C:\Program Files\Microsoft\Exchange Server\Mailbox\Second Storage Group\
Second Mailbox Database.edb
                dbtime: 29239 (0-29239)
                objidLast: 210
                Signature: Create time:10/04/2006 22:24:42 Rand:49024052 Comput
er:
                MaxDbSize: 0 pages
                Last Attach: (0x1,9,6C)
                Last Consistent: (0x0,0,0)

        Last Lgpos: (0x1a,7FF,0)

Integrity check passed for log file: e010000001a.log

Operation completed successfully in 0.234 seconds.
```

Figure 15-1.   Viewing a transaction log header.

We've used a couple of terms that need to be defined. An *operation* is the smallest unit of change that can be made to a database. A series of operations, when completed, comprise a *transaction*; and a transaction, once written to the transaction log, is said to have been *committed*.

Let's walk though an example of how these concepts work together, and, hopefully, you'll understand the role of transaction logs. Let's assume that John wants to move a piece of e-mail from his inbox to a folder he created called "Important." From John's perspective, this is little more than a drag-and-drop activity; however, from an ESE perspective, this represents a number of important changes to the database:

▼   The message needs to be deleted from the inbox.

■   The message needs to be inserted into the Important folder.

▲   The item number for each folder needs to be updated.

Each change represents an operation. All three operations represent a single transaction. Once these operations have been completed and recorded in the transaction log, the transaction is considered committed. Because these operations are performed in a single transaction, all or none of the operations will be performed. If, during the performance of these operations, the server were to lose power, ESE will remember that this series of operations was not completed. When the store.exe process is started on reboot, ESE will roll back these operations so that the ATOMIC test is passed, since none of the operations were performed.

Notice that in this example we were not concerned about writing this information to the database itself. Instead, our focus was on writing information to the transaction log. This illustrates the *write-ahead* logging architecture of ESE—before we write new information or changes to the ESE database, we first write it to a transaction log. Because we are not constantly writing to the database on disk in real time, but instead use a type of *lazy write* to flush changes from memory to the ESE database at a later time, Exchange Server 2007 operates much faster and more efficiently.

Data Storage in an ESE Database

As we mentioned earlier, data is stored in 8-KB pages inside the ESE database. When a change to a page in the database needs to be performed, and before the page is read into memory, the page number and checksum are verified to ensure that the data is the same as that written to the disk.

Once the page is read into memory, it is considered *clean*. When operations are performed on the data in the page, it is marked as *dirty*. One transaction may require changes to many pages. Dirty pages are not written back to the ESE database in any particular order, so if your server loses power, for example, while the transaction is being written to disk, and some of the pages have been written and some have not, you need not worry. When the store.exe process is started again, those pages that were not yet written to disk from memory will be written from the transaction log to your database and your database will be updated.

When you start the information store service in the Services utility, the majority of the activity is comparing the transactions in the logs to the database, making sure that all such transactions have been flushed to the database, and that the database is in a consistent state. Should there be a failure in this process, you will receive an error message and the database will not be able to start.

There is no single way to know when committed transactions in the log files are written to the database; however, there are some guidelines. Committed transactions in the log file are written to disk when one of the following occurs:

▼   The checkpoint falls too far behind in a previous log file. If the number of committed transactions in the log file reaches a certain threshold, ESE will flush these changes to disk.

■   If the number of free pages in memory becomes too low and affects overall system performance, ESE will flush committed transactions in memory to the disk in an effort to free up pages for system use.

- If another application or service starts and needs additional memory, ESE will flush committed transactions to the disk to free up pages in memory for that application.

- When the store.exe process is shut down, all committed transactions in memory are written to the disk before the process can shut down cleanly.

▲ A full backup is run on the databases with software that is specifically written to flush committed transactions from memory to the database. Examples of such software include Legato, ArcServe, BackupExec, and Windows 2003 Backup.

ESE and Memory Management

Before a page can be loaded into memory that area of memory must first be allocated by ESE for its own use. It would be terribly inefficient to allocate memory in 8-KB blocks on demand. This would slow down Exchange services considerably. Thus, ESE takes care of this by allocating memory for itself in advance of when the memory is needed.

The process that is used by ESE to allocate memory to itself is called *Dynamic Buffer Allocation* (DBA). Many Exchange administrators report that their store.exe process eats up all the available random access memory (RAM) on their Exchange servers. They are surprised to learn that this is by design.

You see, when ESE allocates memory to itself, it takes into consideration the other applications that are running on the same server, as well as its own anticipated needs. It will not allocate memory to the point of hurting the performance of other applications, and it won't consume all available RAM unless it feels that it is necessary to do so. In either event, if another application should start and that application requires memory that is currently being held by ESE, it will release the memory for the other application on demand so that it can run efficiently.

Hence, if you go into Task Manager and see that the store.exe process is consuming two to three times the amount of RAM above the other processes, don't be alarmed. This is by design—your Exchange server is not experiencing a memory leak.

Circular Logging

There needs to be a way to ensure that the transaction logs representing transactions that have been committed to the database are eventually deleted. Usually, the way to manage this process is to allow your backup software to accomplish this activity. When the Exchange databases are backed up properly, but before the process starts, the transactions in the transaction logs are flushed to the database and verified for integrity. Then the backup software purges the unneeded logs.

There might be situations, however, when recovery of information is not important, such as in the case of a client of mine who would receive a ton of feedback e-mail for various television programs they hosted, where the e-mails were so time-sensitive (as some of the feedback e-mails were read on the following evening's show and then no longer needed), they did not care if all of the data in the feedback mailboxes were lost. In this situation, you could consider implementing circular logging.

Circular logging means that ESE will not continue to create new transaction logs, but will recycle its use of logs through the same five log files; thus, when log number five becomes full, instead of creating a sixth log, the first log will be used as the E0x.log and transactions in that log file will be overwritten. Of course, the original transactions are first flushed to the database on the disk before they are overwritten.

Since transactions in the log files are overwritten, you will not be able to utilize the write-ahead features of ESE during a recovery operation. Hence, when circular logging is enabled, you can only recover to the last full backup. Therefore, only enable circular logging when recovery of data is not important.

To enable circular logging, open the Storage Group Properties dialog box (see Figure 15-2), and select the Enable Circular Logging check box.

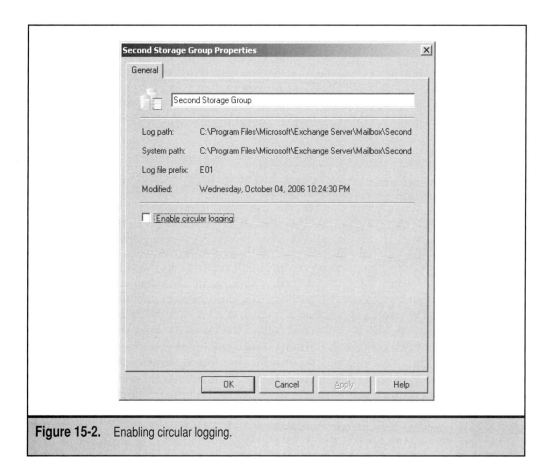

Figure 15-2.   Enabling circular logging.

TRANSACTION LOGS IN BACKUP AND RECOVERY

During the backup process, each page in the database is loaded into RAM in sequential order. After being loaded into RAM, each page will have its checksum recalculated by the backup process. The results of the recalculation of the checksum are compared to the checksum recorded on the page, and, if they match, the page is then copied to tape. If the checksums do not match, this means that the page is most likely corrupted. In this case, the backup process will record an error message in the Event Viewer and stop backing up the database.

While the process of checksumming each page represents significant overhead during the backup process, it also represents a high commitment to quality on the part of Microsoft. They would rather that you knew about a corrupted page—even if that page contained no data—than allow you to back it up and not tell you about it. In addition, the earlier you can catch page-level corruptions in your database, the better your chances of full recovery.

During the recovery process, after you have restored your databases from tape to disk, the log files will be replayed when you start the store.exe process. Replaying the logs constitutes the beginning point of starting the store process and consumes most of the time required to actually start the information store.

Replaying the transaction log files means that for each log record in each transaction log, the corresponding page in the database on disk is read into RAM, and the time stamp on the page read out of the database is compared to the time stamp of the log record that references that page. If the log record has a later time stamp than the time stamp on the page, the page is modified in RAM with the log record information. If the time stamp on the page is equal to or more recent than the time stamp on the log record, the log record is ignored and the process moves to the next log record in the transaction log.

To illustrate this, let's assume a log entry has a time stamp of 40 and the page read from the database has a time stamp of 39. ESE will see this and know that the modification to this page in the transaction log (as represented in the actual log entry) is more recent than the page held in the database, so it will write the log entry to the page in RAM. Later, that page will be flushed to disk to update the actual database on the disk. However, if the page's time stamp was 44, then the log entry would be ignored, because the page in the database has a more recent modification than the log entry, and ESE would move on to the next log record in the transaction log. Therefore, it stands to reason that the more transaction logs that exist when you start the store.exe process, the longer it will take to start the store.exe process.

Modifications to the database that are held in RAM can be manually flushed to the database by one of two actions: performing a full backup of your Exchange databases or performing a graceful shutdown of the store.exe process. Either action will force all the changes in RAM to be written to the database. Transactions are only read out of the transaction logs to the database when the store process is started. Stopping the store.exe process may consume a considerable amount of time, depending on how many transactions in RAM need to be written to the database.

You might have noticed that there is a checkpoint file that accompanies your databases. This file is used to mark which log entries in the transaction logs have been written to the database and which have not. However, the writing of the new information to the database is not done from the transaction logs, but from the pages in RAM. Hence, on an Exchange 2007 server, there are always two copies of each change to the database: the change written to the page (or series of pages) in RAM, and the log record of those changes in the transaction logs.

When a change is made to a page in RAM, that change is recorded to the transaction log, (E0x.log) which has also been loaded into RAM. Then a connection is created between them such that if the change to the page needs to be written to the disk, the log entry will be flushed to the transaction log first. This ensures that in the event of a system crash, we can recover our information.

There is a third element here that we have not mentioned: the version store. As changes are being made to the page in RAM, they are being recorded in the version store. Once the set of changes meets the ACID tests (see "How Do Transaction Logs Work?"), these changes constitute a committed transaction, and it is the entire transaction that is written to the transaction log, and the information is erased from the version store. The version store's purpose is to keep track of operations (changes to the database) that have not been committed to a transaction log in the form of a transaction. Near the end of the time required to start the store process, the version store will be consulted to see if there are any operations that were performed but that didn't constitute a full, committed transaction. If there are such operations in the version store, those operations will be *rolled back*: a message transferred will be untransferred or a counter updated on a folder will be reverted to the former number. This action is called *physical redo, logical undo.*

I've had personal experience with many transactions in the transaction logs not being flushed to disk. One company thought they were getting good backups of their Exchange database until their transaction logs consumed so much disk space that they ran out of space. When they called for help, I was able to help them move their databases and then start the store.exe process. It took 30 minutes for the store process to start because they had 427 transaction logs, containing many entries that had not been written to disk. They were running a popular third-party backup software that indicated the Exchange databases were being successfully backed up when, in fact, they were not. But this illustrates the value of transaction logs. Even if the information is lost in RAM, if it has been written to a transaction log, it can be recovered and written to the database.

BACKING UP EXCHANGE SERVER 2007

It might seem that as long as you have all the files on the disk backed up, you'll be okay. However, when it comes to Exchange 2007, this is not the case. There are more than a few things to which you'll need to pay attention; in this section, we'll outline what some of those things are.

In Exchange 2007 Enterprise Edition, one storage group can hold up to 50 databases. Each database can be either mounted (started) or dismounted (stopped) individually within the storage group. All databases and storage groups run inside the store.exe process, which must be running before any of the databases can be mounted. In addition, you can have concurrent backup and restore procedures running on different databases, regardless of the storage group in which the databases reside.

Fifty Databases?

While you *can* house 50 databases in a single storage group on the Enterprise Edition of Exchange, you should not do so. Microsoft recommends a single database within a storage group. One reason you may want more than one database within a single storage group might be when you have multiple databases with circular logging enabled. Because circular logging would be enabled, no recovery is possible and, therefore, no need for maintaining transaction logs is necessary.

NOTE If circular logging is enabled, you cannot perform differential or incremental backups, because both differential and incremental backups only restore transaction log files to provide the history of changes made to Exchange (and, you'll recall, with circular logging enabled, an extremely limited amount of history is maintained). Only copy and full backups can be performed.

There are different types of backups available for Exchange 2007. Table 15-1 lists these types and their functions.

Type	Copies Database?	Copies Log?	Purges Logs?	Explanation
Full (Normal)	Yes	Yes	Yes	First copies the logs to disk and then purges the logs that are not needed. Backup marker is set on all files backed up.
Incremental	No	Yes	Yes	Backs up log files prior to the checkpoint log file and then deletes them. To restore the database, you'll need the last full backup, plus all the subsequent incremental backups.
Differential	No	Yes	No	Backs up log files prior to the checkpoint log file but does not delete them. To restore the database, you'll need the last full backup and the most recent differential backup. This is the fastest restore process.

Table 15-1. List of Backup Types

Type	Copies Database?	Copies Log?	Purges Logs?	Explanation
Offline	Yes	N/A	N/A	Offline backups mean that the store process has been shut down prior to backing up the database. This means that all the transaction logs have been flushed to the database and that the database is in a consistent state. Therefore, offline backups are always full backups, because the database must be shut down first. No additional transaction log files are needed to complete a restore of an offline backup. Offline backups require manual selection of the database during the backup process.
Copy	Maybe	Maybe	No	Copy backs up any files that have changed since the last full backup. You must specify which files should be copied. In most scenarios, the copy backup will copy the new transaction logs and the databases, since they will have most likely changed since the last full backup. However, if there are no changes, these files will not be backed up. You can manually select which files should be included in a copy backup, and we suggest that you use the copy backup to copy the transaction logs but not the databases.

Table 15-1. List of Backup Types *(Continued)*

During the backup process, it is possible that changes to the database will occur in those parts of the database that have already been backed up. For instance, if there is a 10-gigabyte (GB) database, it is possible that after 7 GB have been backed up, a user will modify a page that resides somewhere in those 7 GB. In order to account for changes in those parts of the database that have already been backed up during the backup process, a *patch* (*.pat) file is created that copies those changes to the file. Once the backup process is completed, the total backed up database is a combination of the database, plus the patch file. These two together will give you the snapshot of your database at that point in time. It is important to note that during a restore process, you could lose information or even corrupt your database by not having the patch file available.

The Exchange 2007 backup process begins with the backup application programming interface (API) telling the store.exe process that a backup is about to begin and what type of backup will be performed. Then the store.exe process informs ESE, and ESE enters backup mode. At this point, the patch file is created for each database in all storage groups. Next, a new log file is created and the current log file is renamed. Then the backup agent requests pages out of the database sequentially, and the checksums are calculated as the page is read. Split pages are written to the patch file.

When the page reading is complete and all the pages have been copied to tape, the remaining log files are copied to tape, along with the patch files. One patch file is created for each database that is being backed up. Unneeded transaction logs are deleted, and the backup set is closed. After this point, ESE returns to normal mode and the backup is considered complete.

PERFORMING EXCHANGE BACKUPS WITH WINDOWS BACKUP UTILITY

The Windows 2003 backup program (ntbackup.exe—referred to as Backup Utility) ships with the Windows 2003 operating system. It is not our intention to explain all the intricacies of this utility but, rather, to demonstrate how this utility is used in conjunction with backing up Exchange databases. For more information on how to use the Backup Utility, please consult the Windows Server Tech Center at http://technet2.microsoft .com/windowsserver/en/default.mspx.

By default, the Backup menu option is located under the System Tools menu, which can be found by navigating from the Start menu to Programs, then to Accessories, and finally to System Tools. After the Backup Utility appears, you can click the Backup tab, as shown in Figure 15-3, which will expand the drives on the local server from which you are working.

You'll notice that near the bottom of this tab is a drop-down box labeled Backup Destination. This is the place where you can choose to back up to tape, disk, or other supported media. It is grayed out in our example because we do not have a tape drive installed on this server. Our examples in this chapter will back up information to disk.

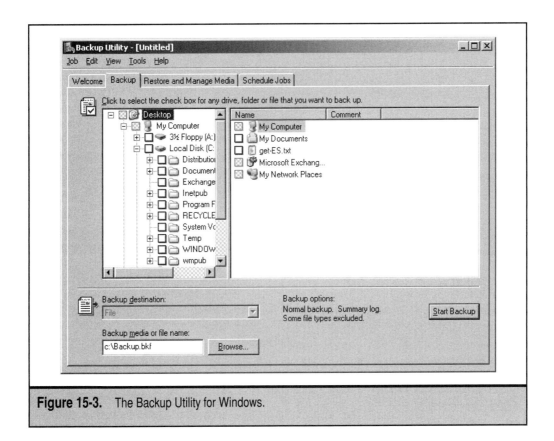

Figure 15-3.   The Backup Utility for Windows.

Referring again to Figure 15-3, you'll also notice that there is a Microsoft Exchange Server object that can be expanded. When expanded, as shown in Figure 15-4, you'll see that all the Exchange 2007 servers in the forest are listed, along with their information stores. If the stores are expanded, you'll find that each storage group can be individually selected for backup.

Once you've made your selections of stores to back up and the media to which they should be copied, then it's time to click the Start Backup button. Once you do this, you'll see that there are more options in the Backup Job Information dialog box (see in Figure 15-5). First, you can choose to either append this backup job to any backup sets that currently exist in your target tape or disk, or you can choose to replace existing backup sets with this new backup set. In our example, I'll choose to overwrite the current backup set and give the new backup set the name "Exchange Full Backup."

If you click the Advanced button, you can modify such settings as whether the backup is an incremental, differential, or normal backup. You can also set the Backup Utility to perform compression on the data being backed up, provided the hardware device is capable of compression.

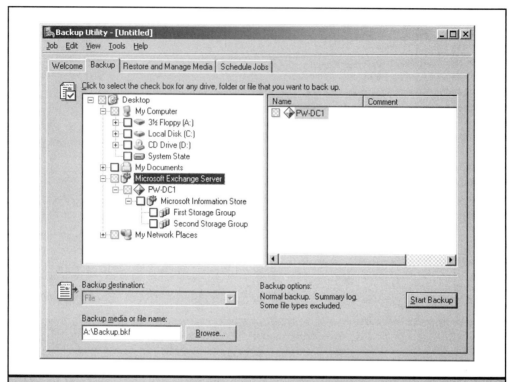

Figure 15-4. Viewing the Exchange selections available in the Backup Utility.

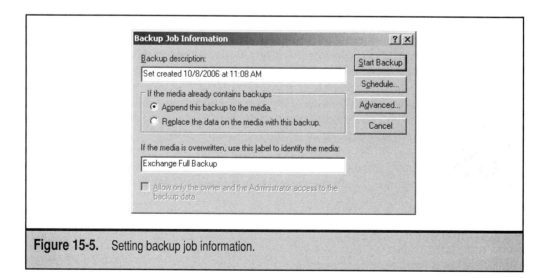

Figure 15-5. Setting backup job information.

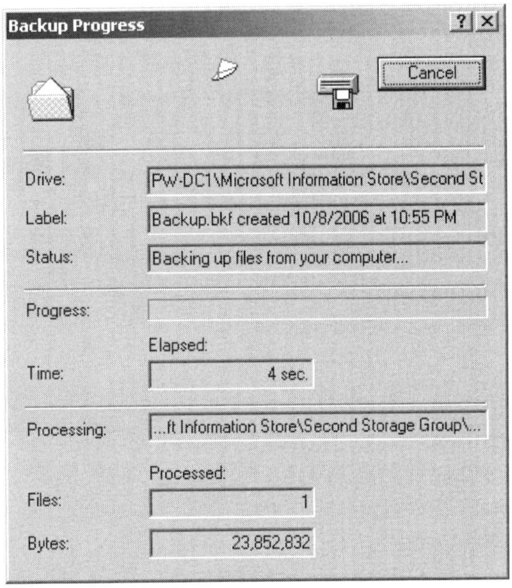

Figure 15-6.   Viewing the backup progress.

Once the backup is started, the Backup Progress display box will appear with information about the elapsed time of the backup, which store it is currently processing, and how many files and bytes have been backed up (see Figure 15-6).

As you can see, performing a standard, basic backup using the Backup Utility is not a difficult activity. However, performing restores is a bit more complicated, so let's take a look at how to use the Backup Utility to restore our data.

PERFORMING EXCHANGE RESTORES WITH WINDOWS BACKUP UTILITY

We'll use the Backup Utility to perform our restores as well. To perform a restore, click the Restore And Managed Media tab. In the left pane, you'll see a listing of the tape drives and files that have been used for backup activities. In Figure 15-7, File is listed as the source location from which to perform a backup; this is because the backup previously performed was done to disk and not to tape.

If we expand the File object in the left pane, shown in Figure 15-8, we can see that under the Exchange Full Backup job, each storage group is listed. If you look around this

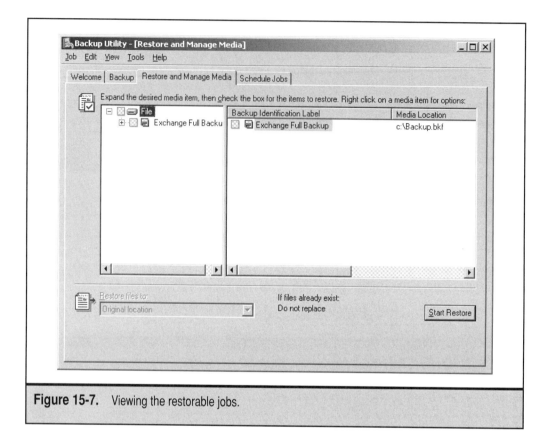

Figure 15-7. Viewing the restorable jobs.

window, you'll notice a few things. First off, each database is listed and is available for restore. Second, you can see that nothing appears in the right pane when selecting either a mailbox or public folder database. In fact, for any database you select, when highlighted, nothing will appear in the right pane. This is because the Backup Utility operates at the store level, not the mailbox level. Restores can only be conducted on the database itself, not on individual mailboxes.

Third, you can see that the log files are also available for restoration. If you've housed both your databases and log files on the same physical drive, then the log files can be restored along with the database.

When the Start Restore button is clicked (after making a restore selection, of course), the Restoring Database Store dialog box appears (see Figure 15-9). Select the server to which you need to restore the database, and then specify the temporary location on that server for the log and patch files.

When you restore an Exchange 2007 database, you have the option to indicate that the restore procedure you are performing is the last restore procedure you will perform before you mount the database. For instance, if you have been running incremental backups,

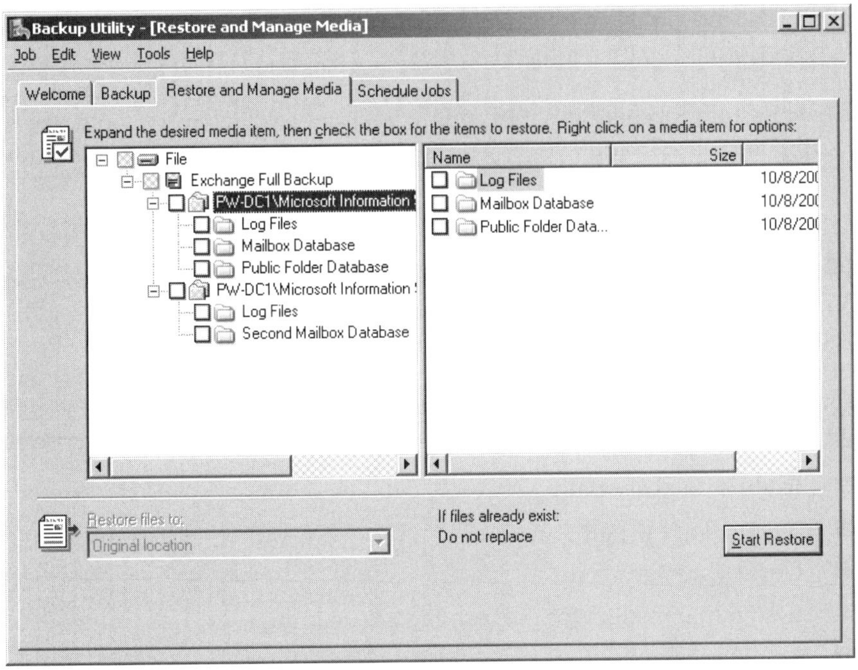

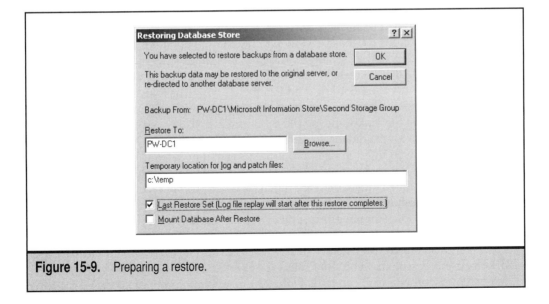

Figure 15-8. Viewing the details of an Exchange backup.

Figure 15-9. Preparing a restore.

you may need to perform several restore operations on the same database before mounting it. To tell the Backup Utility that the current restore operation is the last restore operation that will be performed on this store, select the Last Restore Set check box after you click the Start Restore button.

The Last Restore Set check box determines whether hard recovery should be run after the backup completes. If you select this check box, hard recovery is run automatically

Hard Recovery and the Restore.env File

During the restore process, the backup agent will ask the store process where to place the database based on the database Global Unique Identifier (GUID). The store process will instruct the backup agent to place the database from tape on top of the database on disk. In addition, during the restore process, the restore.env file is created, which holds the following necessary information for the restore process:

▼ Restore database path

■ Restore log file path

■ Correct storage group

■ System parameters for the restore storage group

■ Log file range

▲ Restore time

Remember that when you restore an online backup of an Exchange 2007 database, until the hard recovery process is completed, the database is in an inconsistent state. Bringing the database to a consistent state after a restore procedure is called *hard recovery*. During hard recovery, the ESE replays the log files and patch files to redo operations performed on the database and then to undo any operations that belong to incomplete transactions. Like Exchange 2000/2003, the hard recovery is controlled with the restore.env file that is created in the folder you specify during the restore process in the Temporary Location For Log And Patch Files box. This folder will also contain the log files and patch (.pat) files necessary to complete recovery on the database.

During the log file replay, the log file signature is first checked to ensure that it is the correct log file for the database, the patch file is read, and then each record in the log file(s) is replayed into the database if the time stamp is later than the record in the database. If there are multiple databases in a storage group, only the log records applicable to the failed database(s) are replayed and the other records are ignored.

Concurrent restores can be conducted to databases residing in the same storage group or in multiple storage groups; however, concurrent restores cannot be conducted on the same database. In addition, if you restore multiple databases in a storage group simultaneously, you'll need to restore each backup set to its own temporary log directory and ensure that you *don't* select the Last Backup Set check box so that the hard recovery process isn't run until all the restore operations are conducted.

after the restore procedure finishes, and then the temporary files are removed. At this point, you can mount the database.

If you don't select the Last Restore Set check box, hard recovery is not run. After the database files and temporary files are copied to disk, the restore procedure finishes. You *should not* attempt to mount the database at this point; doing so could cause additional corruption in the database because without the Last Backup Set check box selected, it is assumed that there are more restores or more transaction logs that are needed before recovery is commenced.

The purpose of not selecting the Last Backup Set check box is to allow you to restore a full backup and then restore one or more incremental backups or a differential backup. You only select this check box during the last restore procedure because you do not want hard recovery to run until all the log files to be recovered are in place.

For example, if you are restoring a database from a full backup and two incremental backups, be sure that the Last Backup Set check box is *cleared* when you restore the full and the first incremental backups. Then select the Last Backup Set check box only for the *last* incremental backup.

There may be times when you do not want to run hard recovery immediately after the restore procedure. In addition, you may forget to select the Last Restore Set check box during the last restore procedure. For these reasons, you can manually run hard recovery using the eseutil.exe utility by typing the following command at the command prompt:

```
eseutil /cc <path to directory containing the Restore.env file>
```

For example, if you specified in the Temporary Location For Log And Patch Files box the path of C:\Temp, then the command to run hard recovery would be:

```
eseutil /cc c:\temp
```

TIP Unlike previous versions of Exchange, which required you to run eseutil.exe from the exchsrvr\ bin folder, you can run it from any folder in Exchange 2007.

After you've made your selections in the Restoring Database Store dialog box, you'll click OK and the restoration will begin. The Restore Progress dialog box will appear, informing you as to the progress of the restore procedure. Thereafter, another dialog box will inform you that the restore procedure has completed, and you'll be able to either close the dialog box or print a report detailing the procedure's activities.

To summarize, the flow of events for an Exchange 2007 server is as follows:

1. The database(s) must be dismounted.

2. Verify that the This Database Can Be Overwritten By A Restore check box is selected on the General tab in the database's Properties dialog box.

3. The store process informs ESE that a restore procedure is going to be conducted, and ESE enters restore mode.

4. The backup agent copies the .edb database files from tape (or file, in our example) to their original location by checking the restore.env file for the database path.

5. The backup agent copies the log files and patch file to the temporary folder specified in the Temporary Location For Log And Patch Files input box.

6. If the Last Restore Set check box is selected, ESE checks the log file sequence and warns you if a log is missing or if there are log files from a different file set. (In the event that you cannot supply the missing or correct log files, ESE replays the logs from tape and brings the database to a consistent state; however, information created or modified since the last backup will be lost.) Then the patch file and log files are processed by ESE, unrecorded records are written to the database files, and unfinished transactions are rolled back. If the Last Backup Set check box is not selected, then the database and log and patch files are copied to their original location, and the restore procedure ends.

7. ESE replays any current log files not copied from tape, and unrecorded records are written to the database files.

8. ESE enters normal mode and mounts the database(s).

9. Data is deleted from the temporary directory.

NOTE If you did not verify that the This Database Can Be Overwritten By A Restore check box is selected in the General tab of the database's Properties dialog box, it may take up to 15 minutes for the databases to be mounted after the restore is finished.

WHAT TO BACK UP

So far in this chapter, I've covered the most basic data set to back up—the database and transaction logs. But for each of the server roles, there is far more that needs to be backed up.

Mailbox Server Role

Table 15-2 lists the data sets that need to be backed up for any server with the Mailbox server role.

Data Set	Default Location
Databases, transaction logs	\Mailbox\<Storage Group Name>
Offline address book (OAB)	\ExchangeOAB
Server registry	Via a system state backup

Table 15-2. Backed Up Data Sets for the Mailbox Server Role

Data Set	Default Location
Message queues	\TransportRoles\data\Queue
Message tracking	\TransportRoles\Logs
Registry	Via system state

Table 15-3.   Backed Up Data Sets for the Hub Transport Server Role

Hub Transport Server Role

Table 15-3 lists the data sets that need to be backed up for any server with the Hub Transport server role.

Edge Transport Server Role

Table 15-4 lists the data sets that need to be backed up for any server with the Edge Transport server role.

Client Access Server Role

Table 15-5 lists the data sets that need to be backed up for any server with the Client access server role.

Unified Messaging Server Role

Table 15-6 lists the data sets that need to be backed up for any server with the Unified Messaging server role.

Data Set	Default Location
Active Directory Application Mode (ADAM) data	\TransportRoles\data\Adam
Content filtering	\TransportRoles\data\IpFilter
Message queues	\TransportRoles\data\Queue
Message tracking	\TransportRoles\Logs
Server registry	Via system state

Table 15-4.   Backed Up Data Sets for the Edge Transport Server Role

Data Set	Default Location
Outlook Web Access site	\ClientAccess\Owa
IMAP4/POP3 settings	\ClientAccess
Availability service	\ClientAccess\exchweb\ews
IIS metabase	IIS Metabase
Active\ Sync information	Active Directory, IIS Metabase, \ClientAccess\Sync folder
Registry	Via system state

Table 15-5. Backed Up Data Sets for the Client Access Server Role

ADVANCED BACKUP TECHNIQUES AND CONSIDERATIONS

There are a few techniques to consider, as well as some pitfalls to avoid, when backing up data. This section will outline how to restore a database to an alternate server, as well as how to use the eseutil and isinteg utilities.

Performing a Restore Using Local Continuous Replication

Local Continuous Replication (LCR) is a new feature of Exchange 2007. It allows for a copy of a storage group to be simultaneously maintained on (presumably) a second set of disks on the same server. The main reason to use it as a method of backup is instant access to a completely up-to-date version of a database; in addition, it will serve as your

Data Set	Default Location
Custom audio prompts	\UnifiedMessaging\Prompts
Incoming calls	\UnifiedMessaging\temp
Server configuration	In Active Directory via system state
Registry	Via system state

Table 15-6. Backed Up Data Sets for the Unified Messaging Server Role

first response to a failed database. This will significantly reduce your recovery time, as well as the frequency for full backups of your Exchange databases. Although this sounds pretty good by now, keep in mind that implementing LCR does not provide any kind of true high availability (such as with a clustered environment). In the event of a failure, you won't actually be restoring the failed database; instead, you'll be switching the paths used to define where the logs and databases are.

TIP   You can only enable LCR on a storage group with a single database inside it.

You'll begin by enabling either an existing storage group or a new one for LCR in the Exchange Management Console. I'll demonstrate this using an existing storage group. By selecting a storage group, you'll notice the Enable Local Continuous Replication selection in the action pane. By choosing this, you'll start the Enable Storage Group Local Continuous Replication Wizard, shown in Figure 15-10.

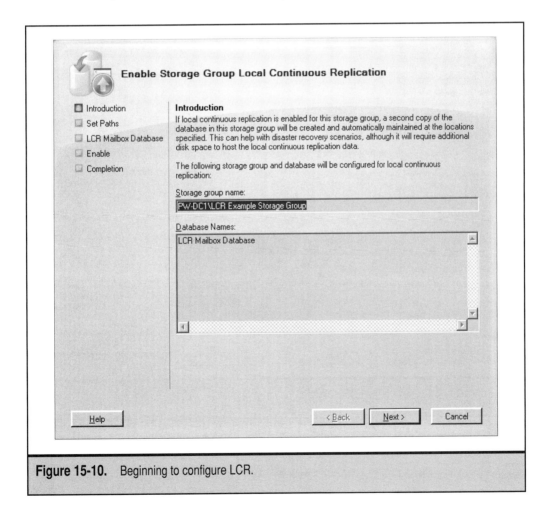

Figure 15-10.   Beginning to configure LCR.

By clicking Next, you can specify the location for the LCR copy of the transaction logs on the Set Paths page of the wizard, shown in Figure 15-11. Click Next to continue.

On the LCR Mailbox Database page, you will specify the paths for the copy of the mailbox database, as shown in Figure 15-12.

The LCR process performs *log shipping*, which automatically copies the transaction logs and commits them to the LCR database, keeping it up to date with the source database. You can check the status of a storage group by looking at its properties on the Local Continuous Replication tab, as shown in Figure 15-13.

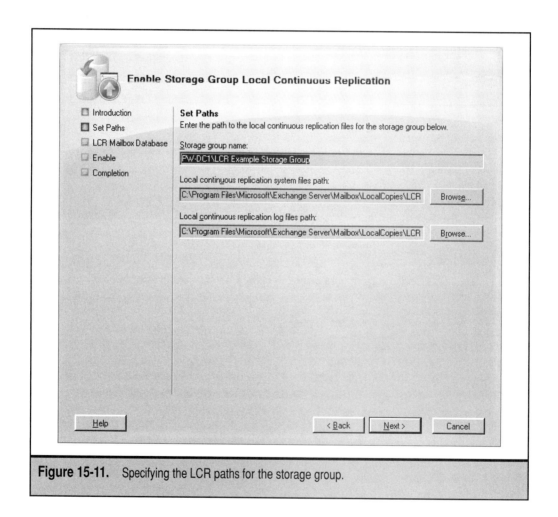

Figure 15-11. Specifying the LCR paths for the storage group.

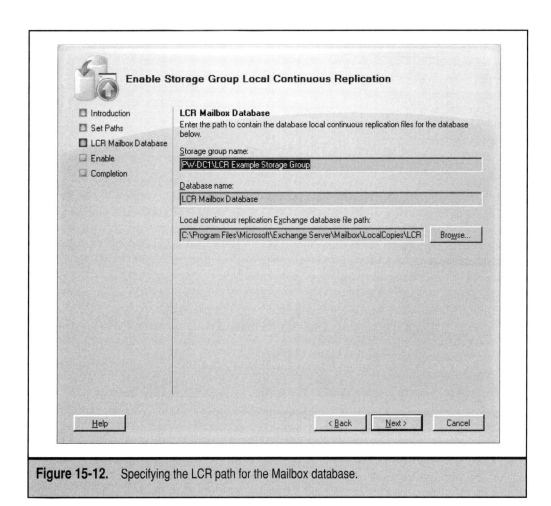

Figure 15-12. Specifying the LCR path for the Mailbox database.

You'll note in Figure 15-14 that Exchange automatically seeds the database, which is the process of initially copying the database over to the LCR path. This is necessary in order for the log shipping to take place.

TIP If, for some reason, the database does not seed, you can use the *Update-StorageGroupCopy* cmdlet. You'll need to first suspend the LCR process with the *Suspend-StorageGroupCopy* cmdlet, followed by the *Resume-StorageGroupCopy* cmdlet once the seeding is complete.

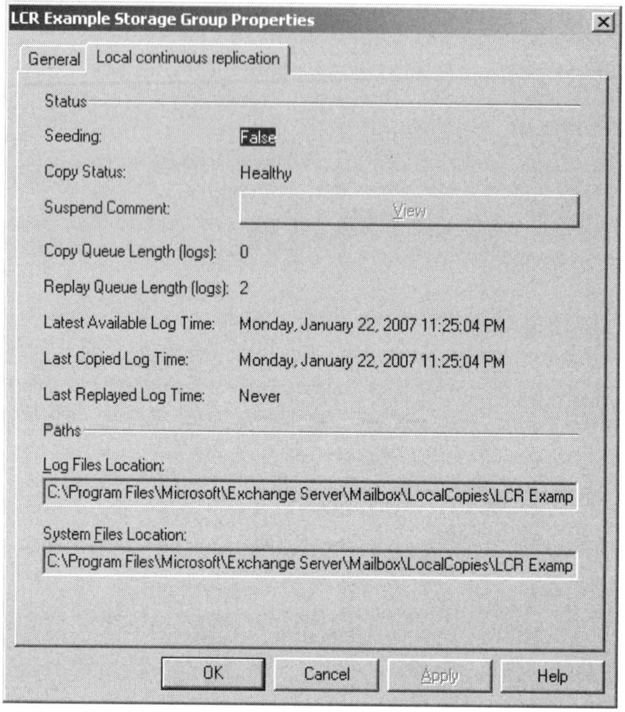

Figure 15-13. Viewing the LCR status.

To switch to the replica database in the event of a failure, you'll need to use the *Restore-StorageGroupCopy* command in the Exchange Management Shell, as shown in Figure 15-15. In the case of my example, I had to dismount the database; in production, you most likely will have lost the database, so it will already be dismounted.

When you run this command, Active Directory is updated with the appropriate paths to the database, logs, and system paths. You'll notice in Figure 15-16 that the database path has changed to the LCR path I specified earlier, and in Figure 15-17, the LCR has been disabled for the storage group.

Restoring to an Alternate Server

Restoring a database to an Exchange server that is different from the one on which you performed the backup enables you to recover individual items from a backup without

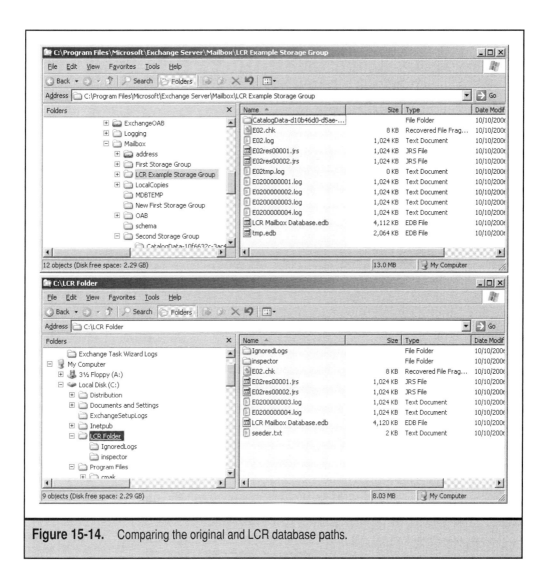

Figure 15-14.   Comparing the original and LCR database paths.

restoring over a server that is in use. Exchange 2007 introduces the concept of *database portability*, which allows you to mount a mailbox database on any Exchange 2007 server within the organization. This means that you can increase the speed by which you recover a failed server by simply moving the services to an existing viable Exchange server.

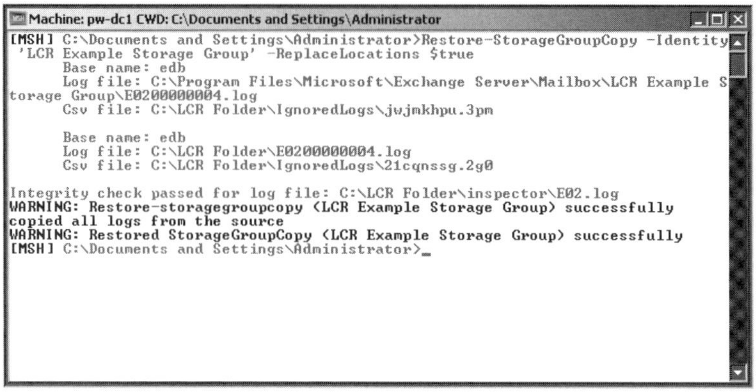

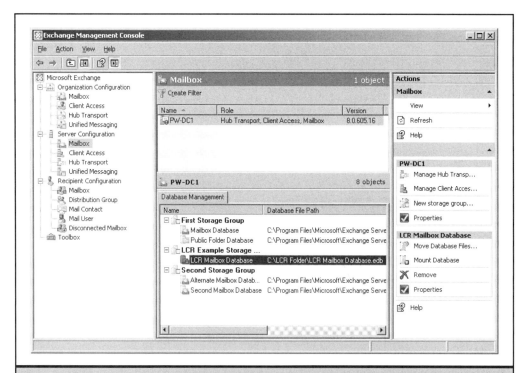

Machine: pw-dc1 CWD: C:\Documents and Settings\Administrator
[MSH] C:\Documents and Settings\Administrator>Restore-StorageGroupCopy -Identity
'LCR Example Storage Group' -ReplaceLocations $true
Base name: edb
Log file: C:\Program Files\Microsoft\Exchange Server\Mailbox\LCR Example S
torage Group\E0200000004.log
Csv file: C:\LCR Folder\IgnoredLogs\jwjmkhpu.3pm
Base name: edb
Log file: C:\LCR Folder\E0200000004.log
Csv file: C:\LCR Folder\IgnoredLogs\21cqnssg.2g0
Integrity check passed for log file: C:\LCR Folder\inspector\E02.log
WARNING: Restore-storagegroupcopy (LCR Example Storage Group) successfully
copied all logs from the source
WARNING: Restored StorageGroupCopy (LCR Example Storage Group) successfully
[MSH] C:\Documents and Settings\Administrator>_

Figure 15-15. Restoring the LCR database.

Exchange Management Console
File Action View Help
Microsoft Exchange
Organization Configuration
Mailbox
Client Access
Hub Transport
Unified Messaging
Server Configuration
Mailbox
Client Access
Hub Transport
Unified Messaging
Recipient Configuration
Mailbox
Distribution Group
Mail Contact
Mail User
Disconnected Mailbox
Toolbox
Mailbox
1 object
Create Filter
Name
Role
Version
PW-DC1
Hub Transport, Client Access, Mailbox
8.0.605.16
PW-DC1
8 objects
Database Management
Name
Database File Path
First Storage Group
Mailbox Database
C:\Program Files\Microsoft\Exchange Serve
Public Folder Database
C:\Program Files\Microsoft\Exchange Serve
LCR Example Storage ...
LCR Mailbox Database
C:\LCR Folder\LCR Mailbox Database.edb
Second Storage Group
Alternate Mailbox Datab...
C:\Program Files\Microsoft\Exchange Serve
Second Mailbox Database
C:\Program Files\Microsoft\Exchange Serve
Actions
Mailbox
View
Refresh
Help
PW-DC1
Manage Hub Transp...
Manage Client Acces...
New storage group...
Properties
LCR Mailbox Database
Move Database Files...
Mount Database
Remove
Properties
Help

Figure 15-16. Verifying the database path after an LCR restore.

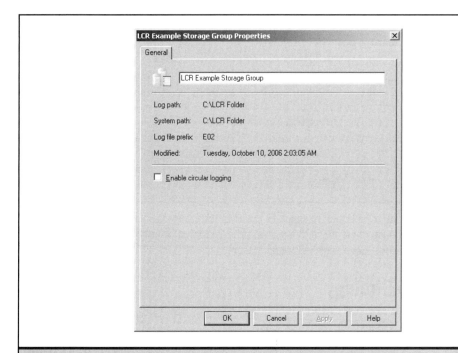

Figure 15-17.   Verifying that LCR has been disabled on the storage group.

 NOTE   Database portability is only available on mailbox databases. Public folder databases cannot take advantage of this feature because of the per-server replication settings that a public folder database (or an individual folder within it) may have.

The first thing you'll need is, of course, another Exchange 2007 server. This can be an existing production server configured with the Mailbox server role or one you install for the purpose of recovery. Once this is out of the way, you'll need to follow these steps:

1. Create a mailbox database with exactly the same name as the original server. (See Chapter 6 for more information on how to do this.)

2. Select the This Database Can Be Overwritten By A Restore check box on the General tab of the mailbox database's Properties dialog box.

3. Perform the restore of the mailbox database, including any incremental or differential backups you need, and remember to select the Last Restore Set check box (or the equivalent in your backup solution).

4. Mount the database.

5. Now the interesting part that makes the database portable. Exchange 2007 utilizes a *move-mailbox* cmdlet in the Exchange Management Shell to modify the configuration of each user account associated with the mailboxes stored on the moved mailbox. The *move-mailbox* cmdlet must be fed the list of mailboxes from the *get-mailboxstatistics* cmdlet. This combination of commands will cause every user account in Active Directory whose mailbox now exists on the alternate server to be updated to reflect that move. So the command you'll need to run is:

```
get-mailboxstatistics -database <NewDatabaseName> | move-mailbox -
configurationonly -targetdatabase <NewDatabaseName>
```

NOTE   Outlook 2007 clients will automatically be updated using the Autodiscover service. Older Outlook clients will need to be updated manually, either via script or using a solution that manages Outlook profiles, such as ScriptLogic's Desktop Authority.

Planning a Backup Strategy

There are three main considerations when choosing a backup and restore strategy. These three elements are as follows:

▼   **Time to restore**   Determine how long a restore should take and then plan accordingly. If your databases are too large to be restored within the desired time, consider creating new databases to host these users.

■   **Capacity to restore**   Make sure that you'll have sufficient hard disk space to complete the restore process. The more transaction logs created between each full backup, the more disk space you'll need to restore the Exchange database.

▲   **Time to backup**   If it takes too long to perform an online backup of your database, consider creating new databases and load-balancing your users across these databases. Then consider running simultaneous backups, increasing the speed of your backup equipment, or both.

The more common methods of performing a backup are outlined in Table 15-7. After selecting which type of backup method meets your needs, have these best practices in place to follow when a disaster strikes:

▼   First restore and then repair. ESE databases are designed to be recovered by restoring the database file and then replaying the transaction logs. Using the repair utilities, such as isinteg.exe or eseutil.exe, may result in some loss of data.

■   Always make copies of your current databases and transaction logs before starting a restore. This will be of use if the restore fails and you need to start over.

Type	Comment
Full Daily Backup	This is a full backup that is performed online each day. Transaction log files are deleted daily, keeping disk space free. However, if a backup set becomes corrupted for some reason, the previous backup set cannot be brought up to the current time because the transaction log files will be missing.
Daily Copy Backup Plus Incremental	A copy backup is the same as a full daily backup, except that the transaction logs are not deleted. An incremental backup, when performed with a copy backup, will save all the transaction log files in the copy process and then will delete those log files by the incremental process. This combination of backup types resolves the problems of a bad backup set for the full daily backup, because the copy backup saves the transaction logs before they are deleted by the incremental process.
Weekly Full Backup Plus Partial Backups	The main benefit of this method is that the backup processes during the week are greatly reduced in time. However, to restore the databases, you'll need enough disk space to hold all the transaction logs that were created since the last full backup. If a differential backup is selected, then the restore time will be faster, because only the full and the last differential backups will be required to restore the database. However, as time passes, there will be a buildup of transaction log files and the backup time will increase as the week progresses.

Table 15-7. Common Backup Methodologies

■   Disable circular logging.

■   Make sure that all the transaction log files are in place before performing a hard recovery and attempting to replay the log files into the database. Replaying log files out of sequence will likely result in your database experiencing further corruption.

▲   Use quality hardware.

If your server fails, there could be one of several database problems:

▼ The contents in memory are lost, and the database file is now in an inconsistent state. This is always a recoverable event (provided you've taken the necessary actions to plan for this).

■ The database file incurs page corruption. This can occur after a power outage, because the spike or brownout will hinder proper writing of information to the disk. This type of problem is dependent on having good backups.

▲ One or more transaction log files have become corrupt. Complete recovery may not be possible if a recent transaction log file is corrupt.

ESE records the state of the database file in its file header. When the database is operating, the state is always marked as inconsistent. It is only marked as consistent when the database is dismounted normally. The database header can be dumped to determine the state of the database.

During a shutdown, ESE reads the checkpoint file to determine which log file(s) need to be flushed to the database on disk. It writes these records to the database on disk, and then the service shuts down. If no checkpoint file exists, ESE starts from the earliest transaction log file that it can find and then attempts to write each record to the database. Those records with a time stamp equal to or older than the record in the database are not written to the database. This is the same routine that is followed when ESE performs a soft recovery. In either case, once the records have been successfully written to the database and the services have shut down, the database should be in a consistent state.

Physical Corruption of the Database

Physical corruption of the database usually occurs at the page level. Since the cause of page-level corruptions is *always* outside of ESE, you should address the causes of page corruption before restoring your Exchange databases. ESE can detect and report page-level corruptions, but ESE is never the cause of these corruptions.

Common causes of page-level corruption include:

▼ **Virus protection software**   Virus protection software watches for certain data patterns in order to detect a virus. It is possible for one of these patterns to appear in an innocent e-mail—especially given the number and type of e-mails being passed today. If the virus software does not recognize the presence of the Exchange server, the software could make changes to the database file that cause physical corruption. Be sure to use virus software that recognizes and works with Exchange Server 2007.

■ **Hard disk controllers**   Sometimes, a controller or device driver cannot keep up with the stress that ESE creates. This can lead to inaccurate read/write errors that, in turn, create page-level corruptions. Be sure you are working with the latest device driver from each hardware manufacturer. If corruption problems persist, replace the firmware or hardware device with a faster, more robust device.

▲ **Bad hard disks** These can easily cause page-level corruptions when a sector goes bad and part of the database is residing on the sector. In this case, the hard disk should be replaced.

ESE uses checksums to detect physical corruption and is proactive in running these. It is important to catch page-level corruptions early, because once a page is corrupted, it cannot be repaired. Early detection can mean that the database can be restored with the transaction logs, and no data will be lost. Once the transaction logs are purged, if the corrupted page is not detected, then you'll probably lose data fixing the problem.

Whenever a page is written from memory to disk, ESE writes a checksum to the page. Then, when the page is read back into memory, the checksum is recalculated and compared to the first checksum written to the page. If they match, the data is assumed to have integrity. If not, ESE will record an event in the Event Viewer. Three things cause ESE to generate errors. First, ESE asked the device driver to write the page to disk, but the device driver malfunctioned or the disk controller malfunctioned and prevented the page from ever being written to the disk. When ESE asks for this page, it's not there, so the checksum fails and an error is generated.

Second, the page was successfully written to the disk, but the device driver or disk controller malfunctioned, causing the contents of the page to change. When the page is read from disk, the checksum fails and an error message is generated.

Third, the page is successfully written to disk, but when ESE requests the page from disk, the device driver or controller malfunctions, causing the wrong page to be returned. Again, the checksums will fail and that will generate an error message in the Event Viewer.

One of the best ways for ESE to detect a page-level corruption is to have an online, full backup performed. During the process, as each page is passed from the database to tape, ESE runs the checksum on each page. If the checksums do not match, the backup process will fail and a 1018 error message will be generated in the Event Viewer. If the online backup finds a page with the first 40 bytes all zeroes, it considers the page uninitialized. However, this may also indicate a page corruption, and a 1019 error will be generated in the Event Viewer.

Troubleshooting Database Recovery

If the recovery of your database isn't successful, you should take a moment to consider some of the more common restore problems that can occur.

First, one of the more common mistakes that administrators make during a restore process is that they have either the wrong transaction log files present or an incomplete set of transaction log files present when hard recovery is attempted. This can occur if a transaction log was renamed, if an incremental backup was not restored, or if the checkpoint file is not removed and files prior to the checkpoint file are skipped during replay.

ESE may respond in a couple of different ways. First, if it finds that a transaction log is missing, ESE will halt and log an error in the Event Viewer. However, if ESE cannot discern that the log file is incorrect or out of order, it will replay the records in the log to the database. When the database is mounted, you might experience additional errors or random freezing of the database.

The way to ensure that you have the correct transaction log files during a restore is to follow these tips:

1. Always copy existing files, including transaction logs, database files, and the checkpoint file, to a neutral location. If the restore doesn't go well, you can use these files to retry the restore.

2. Before performing the restore, preview the transaction log file directory to ensure that there are no gaps in the log file numbers.

3. Never rename a transaction log file.

The point is that you need to ensure you have all the transaction logs in order since the last full backup for all the data to be recovered. For instance, if you experience a system crash on Wednesday at noon and your last full backup was on the previous Friday night, then here is what you'll need to recover to the point of the disaster:

▼ **Database from the full backup tape from Friday**　This will restore all the information in your Exchange database from last Friday.

▲ **All transaction logs from Friday to Wednesday at noon**　This will contain all the information that was entered into the Exchange system between the full backup on Friday night and the system disaster on Wednesday at noon.

NOTE　Before replaying log files, you should move the checkpoint file so that it isn't in the same directory as your transaction logs. If the checkpoint file is present, replay will begin at the location in the log file to which the checkpoint is pointing. Any log files and records previous to the checkpoint file will be ignored because ESE will assume that they have already been written to the database.

Second, one of the more common mistakes Exchange administrators make is running isinteg before restarting the database. Isinteg is a utility that is used when an offline backup is restored to resynchronize the GUIDs between the information store databases and Active Directory. If the GUIDs are not synchronized when the database is started, an error message will be produced instructing you to run the isinteg utility.

However, if this utility is run after the restore of an online backup, the database will become logically corrupt, though no error messages will be generated. It is unnecessary to run this utility after performing an online restore because ESE automatically runs this command when an online restore is performed; hence, you shouldn't run this command unless you are directed to do so by an error message.

Third, a common problem that Exchange administrators run into is that their backup set is bad. Perhaps a single tape in a tape set is missing, or the tape is old and the information was not written to the tape correctly, or the information was never even written to the tape in the first place. If you're running lots of full backups between a few tapes, information could be overwritten on the tape, which would make that backup set useless.

Along the same lines, it is best to use a combination of copy and incremental backup procedures instead of using full daily backups, because full daily backups may leave a transaction log file gap. However, the disadvantage of this method is that duplicate copies of information are saved. In some environments, this could represent several hundred megabytes of information that is duplicated to tape each day.

USING THE TROUBLESHOOTING ASSISTANT

Thus far, I have drilled down and provided you with some of the manual methodology to restore and recover databases. In Exchange 2007, Microsoft has created the Troubleshooting Assistant to help you with some of these very same issues. The Troubleshooting Assistant is accessible from within the Exchange Management Console by first navigating to the Toolbox node of the navigation pane, as shown in Figure 15-18, choosing either Database Recovery Management or Database Troubleshooter, and selecting Open Tool from the action pane. I'll cover the selection of Database Recovery Management, as the Database Troubleshooter results in running one mode of the Troubleshooting Assistant that I will discuss in this section anyway.

Opening either troubleshooting tool will display the Enter Server And User Information page of the Microsoft Exchange Troubleshooting Assistant, shown in Figure 15-19. Here you will need to provide a label for the troubleshooting activity (as one of the options in the Troubleshooting Assistant is to view the results of a previous activity), the name of the Exchange server to troubleshoot, and a domain controller to communicate with (as some of the configuration information used is stored within Active Directory). Optionally, should you need to use alternate credentials, you can click the Show Advanced Logon Options link to provide those details. Once you have filled out the appropriate fields, click Next.

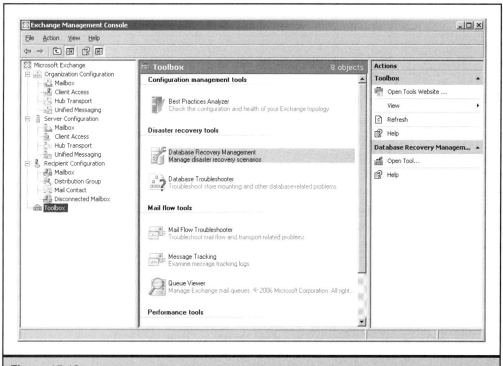

Figure 15-18.   Navigating to the database tools.

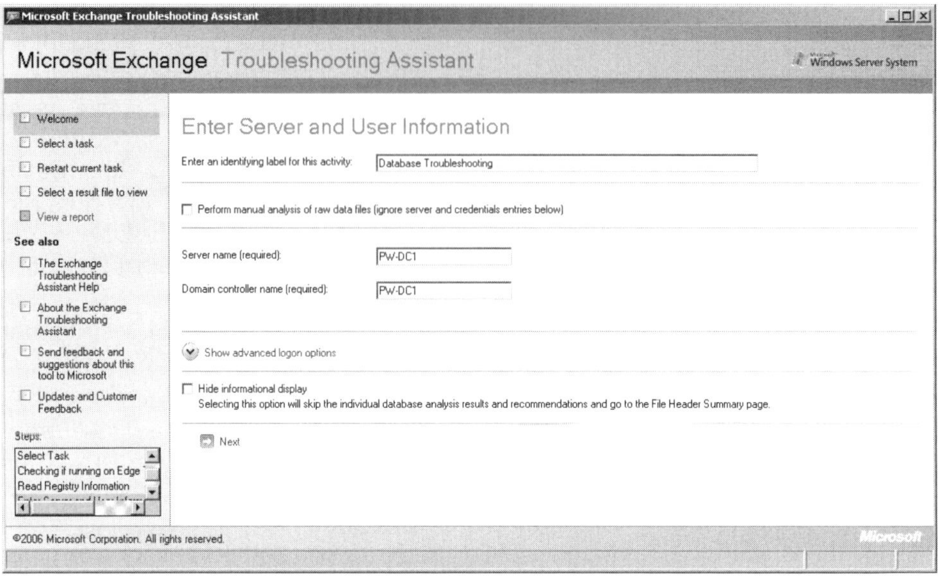

Figure 15-19. Provide server and user information to begin troubleshooting.

After connecting to the specified Exchange server, as well as to Active Directory, you are presented with the five tasks you can use the Troubleshooting Assistant to accomplish, shown in Figure 15-20. Table 15-8 lists the tasks and describes when you would use each of them.

Database Mounting Issues

The first task listed, Verify Database And Transaction Log Files, would be used when a database will not mount. For the purposes of a simple example, I have created a single mailbox database within a storage group (that has no other databases within it) and deleted one of the transaction logs and the checkpoint file. Trying to mount the database normally within the Exchange Management Console results in an error. Upon selecting Verify Database And Transaction Log Files, you are prompted to select the storage group to work with, shown in Figure 15-21, followed by the mailbox database(s) you can verify. Note that mounted databases, while listed by the Troubleshooting Assistant, are not able to be selected, and any dismounted databases are automatically selected for verification.

The Troubleshooting Assistant will analyze the state of the database, the checkpoint file, and the transaction logs, and then provide you with information on the state of the database, along with an appropriate course of action. In my simple example, the database was cleanly dismounted, so while mounting the database is not possible in the state I left the file system in (old transaction logs and no checkpoint file), Exchange suggests

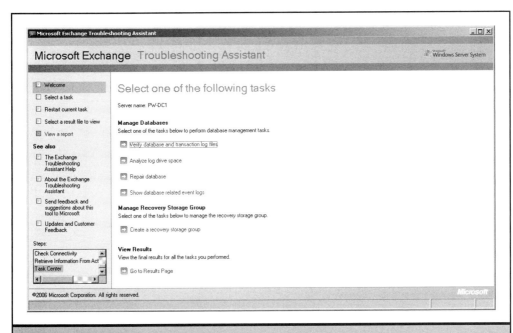

Figure 15-20. Viewing tasks with the Troubleshooting Assistant.

Task	Description
Verify Database And Transaction Log Files	Used to diagnose database mounting issues (you can only diagnose a dismounted database).
Analyze Log Drive Space	Used to check for available disk space and to move transaction logs, if needed, to another disk.
Repair Database	Automates the functions listed in the previous section to repair and defragment databases, as well as to run isinteg.
Show Database Related Event Logs	Scans and filters event logs to show only those log entries that are related to database activity, such as mounting, dismounting, errors, etc.
Create A Recovery Storage Group	Used to create a special storage group for recovery purposes during a restore. This task also has several resultant tasks based on this task being performed first. (I'll cover these later in this section.)

Table 15-8. Troubleshooting Assistant Tasks

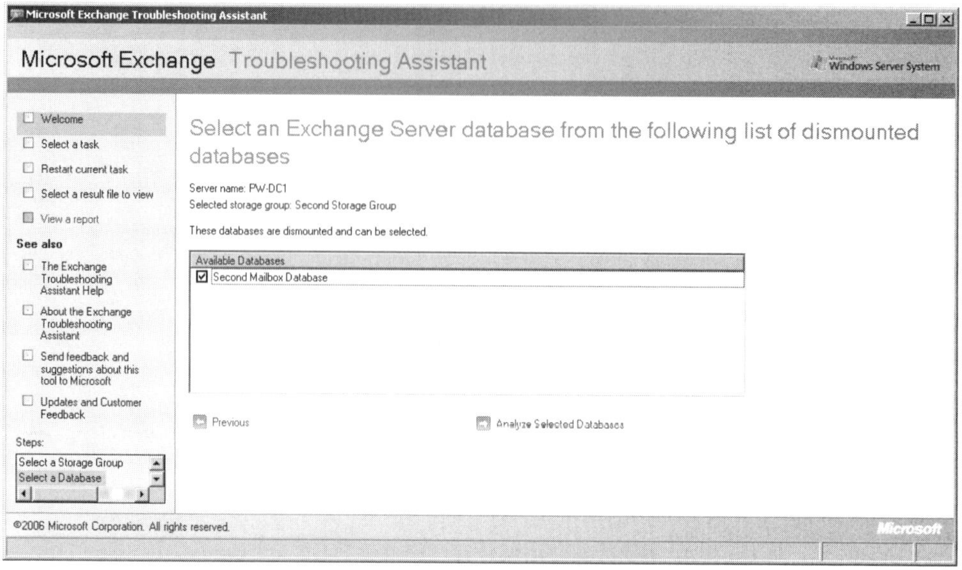

Figure 15-21. Specifying the database to verify.

a course of action via an associated Knowledge Base article, shown in Figure 15-22. In my case, the course of action is to verify the database file and, if in a consistent state, delete the remaining transaction logs. Upon clicking Next, the Troubleshooting Assistant provides you with a set of analysis results to print or review later. Once the transaction files were deleted, per the Knowledge Base article, I was about to mount the database from the Exchange Management Console.

Disk Space Issues

Choosing the Analyze Log Drive Space task results in a simple page informing you of the drive space remaining on the disks hosting the transaction logs. Two of the most useful values on the results page, shown in Figure 15-23, is the average daily log generation rate and estimated days values; these will tell you, based on historical usage of your server, how long you have until you run out of space on the current drives. How sweet is that? Should you choose to, at the bottom of this page, you can select a storage group (and, therefore, a set of transaction logs), select a target path, and move the transaction logs.

Repairing a Database

Selecting the Repair Database task (followed by selecting a storage group and dismounted database), yields a warning page, shown in Figure 15-24, informing you of the need to first perform a file-level backup of the database and transaction logs, as well as ensuring that you have ample disk space (110 percent of the space the current database takes up on the

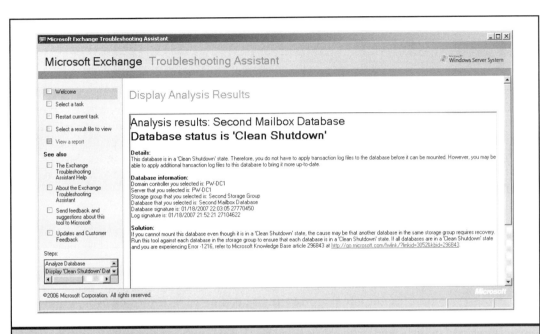

Figure 15-22.   Suggested course of action to repair the database.

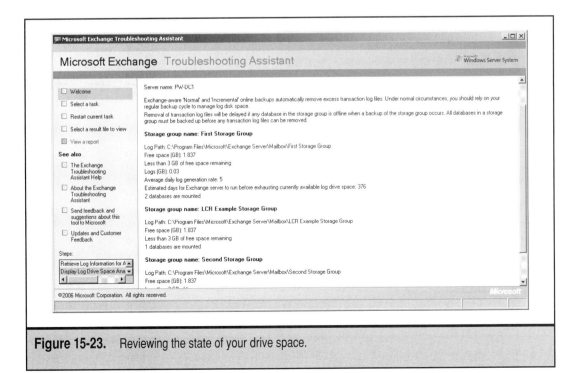

Figure 15-23.   Reviewing the state of your drive space.

same drive). The actual repair will take some time—depending on the size of your database and server hardware, this can still take hours. An isinteg, a repair, and a defragmentation are performed.

Reviewing Database-Related Event Logs

One of the more maddening aspects of troubleshooting a problem via event logs is the need to rummage through the hundreds or thousands of unrelated log entries just to find the one or two entries you need. The Troubleshooting Assistant takes this pain away by filtering out the unrelated entries and displaying only the entries needed to work through your database issues. Selecting the Show Database Related Event Logs task requires that you specify the number of hours the Troubleshooting Assistant should go back and retrieve event log entries from. Figure 15-25 shows an example of the resulting set of events.

Performing a Database Recovery Using the Recovery Storage Group

The Recovery Storage Group is a special storage group first introduced in Exchange 2003. It was created in response to the problem of needing to recover data from within a mailbox database, without the need for completely restoring a mailbox database over the existing one (which would overwrite *everyone's* data, not just the specific mailbox needing recovery). By creating a separate Recovery Storage Group, when a restore takes place, instead of replacing the existing database, the restored database is placed in an alternate location (specified when creating the Recovery Storage Group) so that you can work with the restored database without affecting the production database.

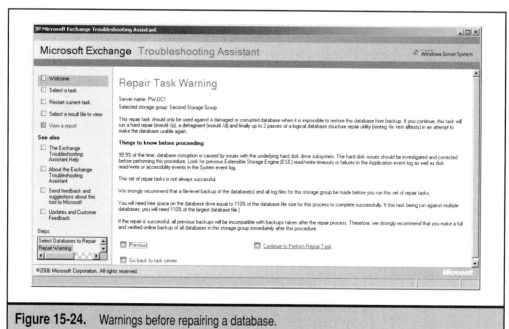

Figure 15-24.   Warnings before repairing a database.

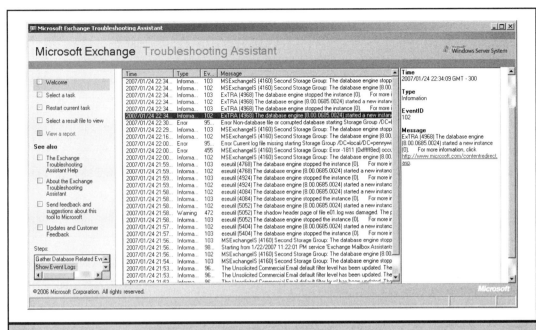

Figure 15-25.   Viewing the database-related events.

Selecting the Create A Recovery Storage Group task requires you to specify a storage group to be linked to the Recovery Storage Group. This "link" is used by Exchange when a restore of the linked database is attempted—instead of restoring to the original location of the database, the alternate location (see Figure 15-26) is used. Note the location of the Recovery Storage Group in Figure 15-27; I'll be showing you this folder in a moment after a quick restore of the database.

TIP   You won't see the Recovery Storage Group in the Exchange Management Console, as it is not a storage group you can work with in the normal manner (creating databases within, etc). It is reserved for when you need to recover a database only. You will manage the mounting, dismounting, and removal of the Recovery Storage Group databases from within the Troubleshooting Assistant.

Now, thus far, the only thing that has been accomplished by the Troubleshooting Assistant is to create the Recovery Storage Group. In Figure 15-28, you'll notice in the lower-left corner that, according to Windows Backup (which represents any Exchange-aware backup you may be using), the restore will be placed in the original location. The idea here is that the Exchange-aware Backup Utility need not know about the Recovery Storage Group. Instead, the placement of restored files is taken care of by Exchange.

Once the restore is complete, the Backup Utility will act as if a normal restore to the original location had occurred. However, if you view the contents of the folder created specifically for the Recovery Storage Group, shown in Figure 15-29, you will see the restored database.

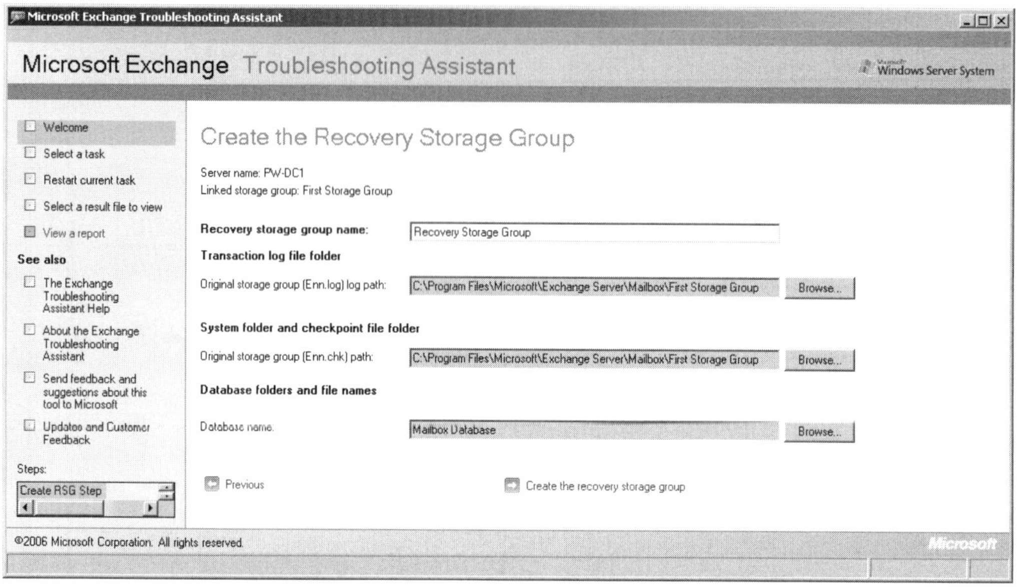

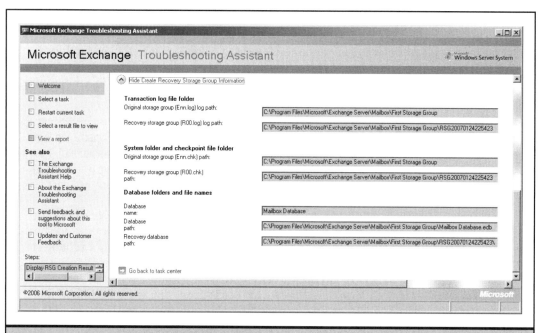

Figure 15-26. Linking the Recovery Storage Group.

Figure 15-27. Results of creating the Recovery Storage Group.

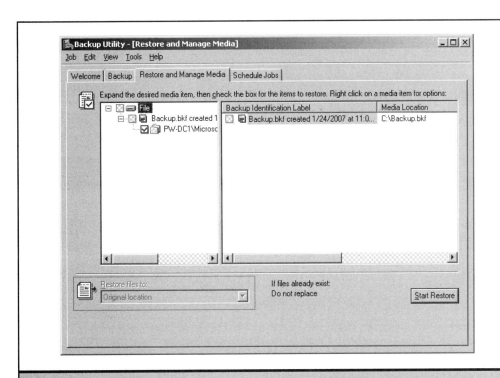

Figure 15-28. Windows Backup is unaware of the Recovery Storage Group.

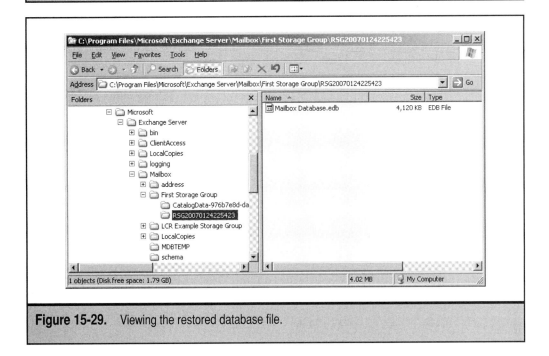

Figure 15-29. Viewing the restored database file.

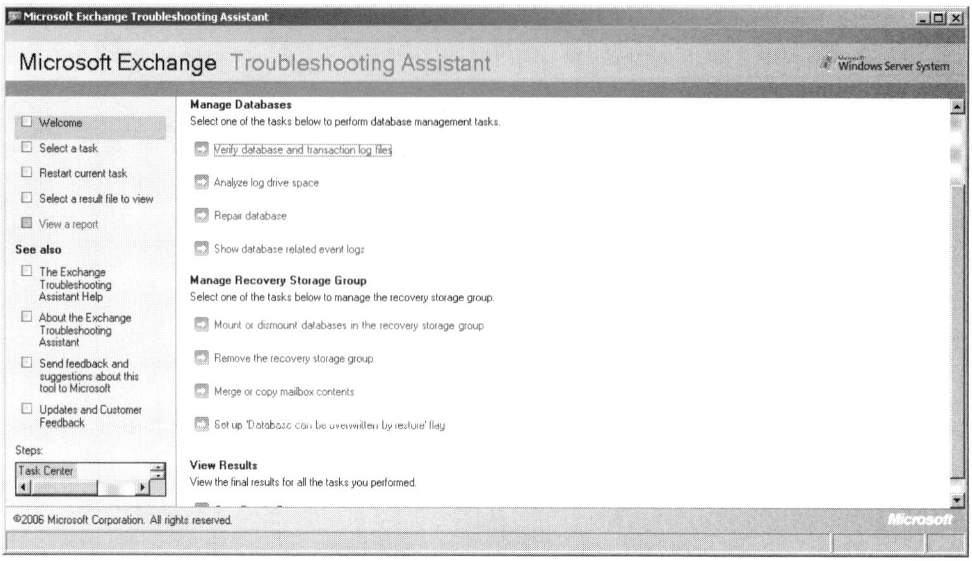

Figure 15-30. Advanced recovery tasks in the Troubleshooting Assistant.

Figure 15-30 shows how the Troubleshooting Assistant tasks have changed slightly to reflect the existence of a database within the Recovery Storage Group. If you are using this process to retrieve information from a specific mailbox, the steps are simple: Select Mount Or Dismount Databases In The Recovery Storage Group, and mount the recently restored database(s). Then use the Merge Or Copy Mailbox Contents task to select the mailboxes to merge or copy. Once you're finished with the recovery database, you can dismount the database and remove the Recovery Storage Group from within the Troubleshooting Assistant.

SUMMARY

Whew! Looks like backing up and restoring Exchange 2007 databases is much more complicated than it appears to be. In this chapter, you learned how to back up and restore an Exchange database using the Windows Backup Utility, the disaster recovery processes that are new to Exchange 2007, and a number of advanced topics, including how to plan your backup strategy and the pitfalls to avoid when restoring a database.

In the next chapter, we'll move our focus away from disaster recovery to Exchange 2007 Server performance tuning.

CHAPTER 16

Performance Tuning Exchange Server 2007

At this point in the book, if you were to read it from front to back and implement your environment with each chapter, you would have a completely functional, well-designed Exchange 2007 organization. Once that's accomplished, the main concern would be the performance of your Exchange servers. Day-to-day performance of Exchange will most likely be considered good (as long as no users call complaining that their e-mail is too slow, right?). However, the question still remains: How well is your Exchange environment running? The Exchange-performance litmus test previously mentioned (no complaints equals good performance) is somewhat of a commentary on the reactive method by which many administrators gauge the performance of Exchange. It would be far more advantageous to actually monitor Exchange's performance.

Performance monitoring of Exchange is not only a good idea, it can also be critical for the maintenance of your environment. Let me ask a few questions about your current Exchange environment to see whether yours will be a success:

▼ When do you project your mailbox store drive will run out of disk space?

■ At what time of day or day of week is your Exchange server's processor busiest?

▲ How many users logged on to Outlook Web Access (OWA) yesterday?

Knowing the answers to these questions won't just help your Exchange server run more efficiently—it can also make the difference between the life and death of an Exchange server. This chapter will first cover some basic information on performance monitoring using the Exchange Server Performance Monitor (the Windows 2003 System Monitor tool prepopulated with Exchange-related data). Then we will look at Exchange-specific counters to monitor, as well as how to make the information gathered work for you. Lastly, we'll look at the new Performance Troubleshooter tool and how it can simplify the process of improving Exchange performance.

PERFORMANCE MONITORING BASICS

Before you can begin monitoring your Exchange servers, you need to know a little about performance monitoring in general. We'll begin by focusing on monitoring Windows 2003 in general. Then we'll see how we can apply what we've learned to monitoring Exchange 2007.

Performance monitoring is the process of collecting performance data for the purpose of analyzing resource usage. There are four basic reasons you will want to monitor the performance of your Exchange server:

▼ To diagnose problems

■ To test configuration changes

■ To identify the effect the server's workload has on its resources

▲ To forecast hardware needs

Monitoring Resources

There are four basic hardware resources you should monitor:

▼ Memory

■ Processor

■ Disk subsystem

▲ Network subsystem

Every server has a finite amount of these resources with which to work—that is, you can itemize exactly how much of each resource the server has—for example, 2 gigabytes (GB) of random access memory (RAM), 500 GB of disk space, a 3-gigahertz (GHz) processor, and so on. With Exchange 2007 (and, therefore, Windows 2003), a delicate balance must be maintained so that you do not overconsume one resource to the detriment of another.

For example, if you are using up too much memory, the server will use the paging file to compensate, causing two repercussions:

▼ Additional disk space may be used if the paging file needs to grow.

▲ Disk performance suffers, because your disk subsystem is spending time away from normal operations to read from and write to the paging file.

This example demonstrates the fact that you need to watch your server's resource usage in order to keep it running at peak performance. In addition to the basic resources, you will probably want to monitor application-specific information (in our case, Exchange 2007) in order to ensure that Exchange 2007 is running at peak performance.

Performance Monitoring Concepts

In order to define what you want to monitor, you need to become familiar with a few concepts: objects, counters, and instances. These concepts will allow you a much deeper level of monitoring granularity. For example, monitoring your server's processor utilization only gives you a bird's-eye view of what your server is doing. Instead, you could look at a specific processor's utilization while running a specific application; then you have a better idea of what your server is actually doing.

Performance Objects

An object can represent any facet of the operating system. Objects like Memory, Physical Disk, and Processor represent hardware on your server. Objects such as Server, Domain Name System (DNS), Browser, and Redirector represent specific services running on the server. Objects such as TCP (Transmission Control Protocol), NNTP (Network News Transfer Protocol), and ICMP (Internet Control Message Protocol) represent specific protocols running on the server. When you install any Microsoft BackOffice product, such as Exchange 2007 Server, additional objects specific to that product are added in order to be monitored.

Performance Counters

A set of counters is predefined for each object. These counters are calculated values measuring some specific aspect of that counter. For instance, the % Processor Time counter of the Processor object would measure what percentage of the time the processor is busy. There are a number of counter types utilized to give you valuable (and not just raw) data.

Instances

A server may have multiple objects of the same type, requiring some method to distinguish between them while monitoring. For example, if your server has multiple processors, and you wanted to see the % Processor Time for only one of those processors, you need to be able to select it to be monitored independently of the other processors. Utilizing instances allow you to accomplish this.

To summarize these three concepts, think of their relationship in this way: You select an object you wish to monitor and choose the counter to report to you a specific measurement about that object. If you need more granularity, use a specific instance of that object.

Maintaining Your Performance Monitoring Focus

What you monitor can depend on what your monitoring focus is. If you are troubleshooting, you will look at different counters than if you are forecasting resource usage. The following table lists the aspects of performance you may want to focus on when monitoring.

Performance Aspect	Monitoring Focus
Usage	Verify resource usage is within acceptable limits
Bottleneck	Look for excessive demand on a certain resource resulting in a possible slowdown of overall performance
Throughput	Ascertain the current performance rate of a specific resource

USING EXCHANGE SERVER PERFORMANCE MONITOR

Windows 2003 provides the System Monitor Microsoft Management Console (MMC) snap-in as a comprehensive performance monitoring tool. System Monitor allows you to both view real-time data and log current data for future viewing. In previous versions of Exchange, you were on your own to not only open the snap-in, but also to determine what counters should be added. With Exchange 2007, these first two steps have been taken care of for you. To open System Monitor (renamed to Exchange Server Performance Monitor, although it is the same as System Monitor), select Toolbox in the console tree within the Exchange Management Console, select the Performance Monitor, and select Open Tool from the action pane. The Exchange Server Performance Monitor, shown in Figure 16-1, appears, with a number of prepopulated counters to begin your performance monitoring.

Table 16-1 lists the default counters and explains why they are important to monitoring the performance of your Exchange server.

What you will notice about the default counters is that, in and of themselves, they do not provide much information about what could be a potential problem. Rather, these counters are very high-level indicators of performance. For example, if you were to look at the RPC Requests counter *and* you knew what a good and bad value was for that counter (by the way, a lower number is worse), the counter itself still wouldn't tell you what this performance issue is; you will need to continue to add more counters to drill down to the core problem. It could be a lack of memory or perhaps a full disk that is causing thrashing (searching for spaces on the disk to store data) which, in turn, is slowing down the Exchange server's ability to process RPC requests. The whole point is that with these basic counters alone, you simply won't know what the issue is. So let me cover some basics on how to create additional counters to monitor.

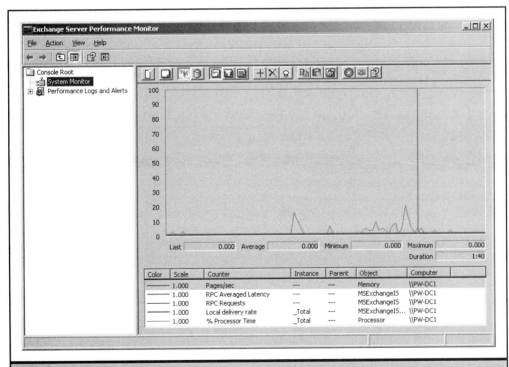

Figure 16-1.   The Exchange Server Performance Monitor.

Object > Counter	Description
Memory > Pages/Sec	The rate at which pages of memory are read from and written to disk. The higher this number, the less often data is available in the server's memory.
MSExchangeIS > RPC Averaged Latency	The average delay in responding to Remote Procedure Call (RPC) requests in the last 1024 milliseconds. This indicates the information store service's overall responsiveness to client requests.
MSExchangeIS > RPC Requests	The number of RPC requests currently being handled by the information store service. Comparing the current number to a baseline value will indicate whether the server is keeping up with client requests quickly enough.
MSExchangeIS Mailbox > Local Delivery Rate	The rate at which messages are delivered to the local mailbox database. Comparing this to a baseline value will determine if the server is delivering messages quickly or not.
Processor > % Processor Time	The percentage of time the processor is busy.

Table 16-1. Default Exchange Performance Counters

In order to have the Exchange Server Performance Monitor (or System Monitor) provide you with any data, you will have to add counters to the chart. You can add counters by right-clicking the chart area and selecting Add Counters, which will open the Add Counters dialog box, shown in Figure 16-2. A number of concepts can be learned about System Monitor just from looking at this dialog box.

The first option is to choose between Use Local Computer Counters and Select Counters From Computer. You can monitor either the server you are logged on to or another computer. Whichever you choose, System Monitor will only display those performance objects that exist on that computer. For example, if you were to run System Monitor on a Windows 2003 member server not running Exchange 2007, the performance objects would not list any Exchange 2007–related objects. However, if you were to choose the Select Counters From Computer option and choose an Exchange 2007 server, the performance objects listed would include Exchange 2007–related objects.

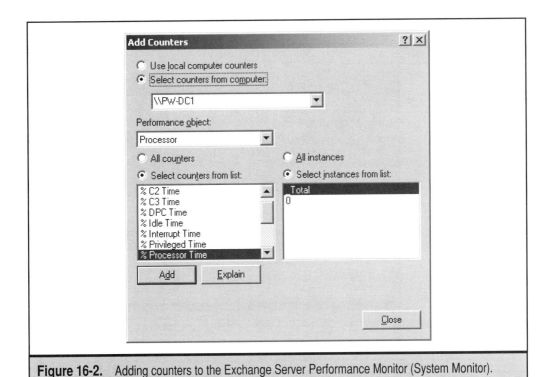

Figure 16-2. Adding counters to the Exchange Server Performance Monitor (System Monitor).

Once you've chosen which computer to monitor, you will want to focus on the objects you want to monitor. Later in this chapter, we will look at not only which generic objects you should use to monitor basic server health (such as memory, processor, disk, and network), but also objects specific to Exchange 2007 functionality. For the purposes of this topic, let's simply choose the Processor object, which is the default object selected when you open the Add Counters dialog box.

Just below the listing of objects in Figure 16-2 is the list of counters to choose from. You do have the option of choosing All Counters. We would not recommend that, however, unless you know what information each counter provides and actually want each and every counter for that object. If you choose All Counters, System Monitor will create an entry on the chart for each one. In some cases, you will end up with a chart that looks like Figure 16-3, which was generated by selecting All Counters under the Process object. It is so confusing that you quickly begin to realize that all of the counters aren't really necessary. Most likely, you will never need to look at all of the counters for a specific object. Each object already has a default counter selected. Microsoft usually selects one counter that provides a general overview of the health or performance of that object.

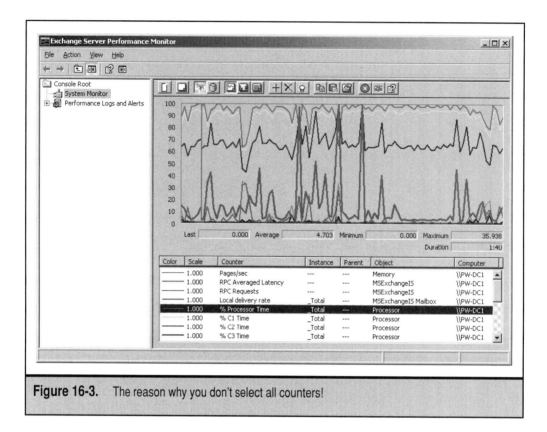

Figure 16-3. The reason why you don't select all counters!

Last, if applicable, you need to select the instance of the object you wish to monitor in the Add Counters dialog box. This could be one of several processors on your computer or, in the case of Exchange 2007, one of many mailbox stores on your server.

MONITORING THE FOUR MAIN RESOURCES IN WINDOWS 2003

We listed the four main resources you should monitor earlier in the chapter:

▼ Memory

■ Processor

■ Disk subsystem

▲ Network subsystem

Let's dig a little deeper into System Monitor by learning how to monitor these resources. We'll cover the preliminary counters you should use, as well as explain why you should use them.

Setting the Foundation: Create a Baseline

If someone were to tell you that their server is constantly running at 75 percent utilization, would you consider that a problem? Your first reaction might be to say yes. However, if you think about it, you really do not know. What if the server is old, and running at 75 percent is considered to be within normal operating parameters? Now that I've got you thinking, it becomes more obvious that the true answer to my initial question is that you really cannot know without a baseline.

A baseline is nothing more than a point of reference for future use. You create a baseline by monitoring certain resources on a server and either documenting or saving the results in a log file. In baselining your server, you really aren't doing anything differently from normal monitoring; you are just going to use the results for a different purpose. I'd suggest that you create your baseline by monitoring your servers during normal business hours, over a period of several days to several weeks, to really get an idea of how a particular resource is being used throughout the workday.

Pay attention to the average value for each counter listed just below the chart you create in System Monitor. The minimum and maximum values could represent as little as a single instance throughout your monitoring period (perhaps hours, days, or weeks), while the average value yields a better idea of how the server is running overall.

Monitoring Memory

The overall reasons for monitoring memory are to see how much is in use, what it is being used for, and how much remains free. Table 16-2 lists some of the counters you will use to monitor memory.

One additional note about memory usage needs to be made: Like its predecessors, in Exchange 2007, the store process will utilize as much memory as the Exchange server has, voluntarily releasing memory to applications as they need it. So don't be alarmed if your Exchange Server's available bytes value is low—this is normal. Keep an eye on the private bytes value to see if you actually have an issue with the amount of memory available.

Monitoring the Processor

The processor is always busy. Even where there is nothing to do, the system gives the processor an idle thread for it to process. When the server is busy processing non-idle threads, questions remain: why is the server so busy, and what is it busy doing? Table 16-3 lists the counters you can use to monitor memory usage.

Object	Counter	Description
Memory	Pages/Sec	This counter shows the number of times per second the server cannot find a page, which is 4 kilobytes (KB) of memory, of information in an application's working set (the application's exclusive area of physical memory) and has to search for that information on the pagefile, which resides on a disk. If this value is constantly above 20, this is an indication that your server does not have enough physical RAM to handle the applications loaded on it.
Memory	Pool Page Bytes	This counter shows the amount of memory assigned to the paged pool, an area of memory for data that can be written to disk when it is not being used. Amounts above 200 MB indicate a problem, except when backups are running.
Memory	Pool Nonpaged Bytes	This counter shows the amount of memory assigned to the nonpaged pool, an area of memory for data that *cannot* be written to disk when it is not being used. Amounts above 100 MB indicate a problem.
Memory	Free System Page Table Entries	This counter shows the number of page table entries not in use by the system. Less than 300 entries indicates a problem.
Process	Private Bytes (_Total)	This counter shows the amount of memory currently in use by running processes that cannot be shared with other processes. If this number has an increasing trend, you may have a process running with a memory leak.
MSExchangeIS	VM Largest Block Size	A healthy server will have at least 200 MB as the largest block of memory free. A lower-sized largest block warrants a closer look at the server's health.

Table 16-2. System Monitor Counters for Monitoring Memory

Object	Counter	Description
Processor	% Processor Time (_Total)	This counter shows the percentage of the time the processor is busy processing non-idle threads. You can also select specific instances of the Processor object to see how busy each processor is in a multi-processor system.
Processor	Interrupts/Sec	This value shows the number of times an interrupt is triggered by a peripheral (such as a disk, mouse, or network card). This will cause a rise in the % Processor Time counter. An increase in this counter when the processor is busy indicates that hardware usage could be the cause.
System	Processor Queue Length	This counter shows the number of threads waiting in a queue for the processor to handle. If this value is consistently above 2, your processor is most likely overburdened.

Table 16-3.   System Monitor Counters for Monitoring the Processor

Monitoring the Disk Subsystem

Windows 2003 allows you to monitor both logical disk counters and physical disk counters. Logical disk counters focus on each logical drive you created on the system, while physical disk counters focus on actual disk usage. Both are enabled by default in Windows 2003. Table 16-4 lists the counters you should use to monitor disk usage.

Because the counters are specific to disk activity, with System Monitor, there is no way to look at Exchange-specific disk activity.

Monitoring the Network Subsystem

System Monitor's ability to monitor the network is limited to counters that inform you of general network information, such as network utilization, throughput, and transmit/receive statistics. If you need to monitor actual network traffic, System Management Server 2003 includes a Network Monitor tool to look at your network traffic packet by packet. However, we will focus on System Monitor in this book. Table 16-5 lists the counters you should use to monitor your network subsystem.

Object	Counter	Description
PhysicalDisk	% Disk Time (_Total)	This counter shows the percentage of the time the disk subsystem is busy. You can also select each disk as a separate instance.
PhysicalDisk	Avg. Disk Queue Length	This counter shows the average number of requests (read or write) that are queued up to be handled by the disk subsystem. Anything over an average value of 2 is considered high and may indicate that the disks are too slow relative to the demands being placed on them.
PhysicalDisk	Avg. Disk Sec/ Transfer	This counter shows the amount of time (in seconds) it takes to complete a single transfer of data.

Table 16-4. System Monitor Counters for Monitoring Disks

Object	Counter	Description
Network Segment	% Network Utilization	This counter shows the percentage of time the network is busy.
Network Interface	Output Queue Length	This counter shows the number of packets sitting in the output queue waiting to be sent. A number above 2 may indicate either that a server is servicing too many clients or that a network interface card (NIC) needs to be upgraded.
Network Segment	Total Frames Received/Sec	This counter shows the rate at which frames of data are being received by that NIC.

Table 16-5. System Monitor Counters for Monitoring the Network

MONITORING EXCHANGE 2007 WITH SYSTEM MONITOR

There are over 60 objects that are either directly or indirectly related to Exchange 2007 (that's double what was available when Exchange 2000 was released!). Each one of those objects has a number of counters associated with it. Microsoft certainly has provided you with enough granularity for monitoring Exchange 2007. It would take a book of its own to cover every object and counter, so we'll focus on a few of the important objects to begin your monitoring of Exchange 2007.

Mailbox Database Counters

Since most of your interaction with Exchange involves sending another user a message, it seems appropriate to take a look at the mailbox database–specific counters. There are so many viable counters with meaningful information you can use to establish a performance baseline or determine performance problems, that this object becomes quite important. Table 16-6 lists the counters that you can use to monitor the mailbox database–specific performance.

Also, note that for each mailbox store counter, you can choose an individual mailbox database in the Instance field (see Figure 16-4). This will allow you to narrow the focus of your monitoring to a subset of your Exchange environment.

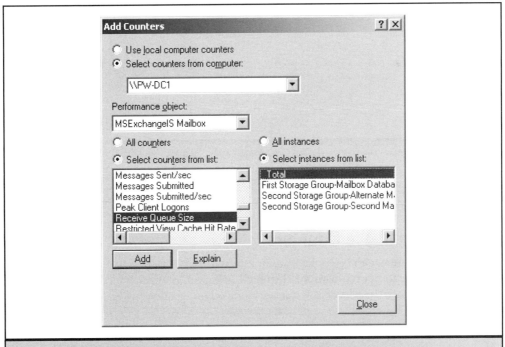

Figure 16-4.   The mailbox databases available in the Instance field.

Object	Counter	Description
MSExchangeIS Mailbox	Average Delivery Time	This counter shows the amount of time (in seconds) it takes for a message to be delivered. This is calculated using the average of the last 10 submissions.
MSExchangeIS Mailbox	Active Client Logons	This counter tells you how many clients are logged on and have performed any actions within the last 10 minutes. The significance of this counter is that you can use this in conjunction with any other counter to see if there is a correlation between the number of users and the performance of Exchange.
MSExchangeIS Mailbox	Receive Queue Size Send Queue Size	These counters show the number of messages in each queue. Compare them against a baseline value to determine whether the Exchange server is overburdened. A high number of messages (relative to your baseline) could mean you need to offload certain Exchange responsibilities, such as OWA, connectors, or public folder store access to other Exchange servers.

Table 16-6. System Monitor Counters for Monitoring Mailbox Databases

Public Folder Database Counters

Public folder counters can be broken down into two distinct areas: client usage of public folders and public folder replication. The client usage counters will most likely be used to determine how busy the server is while servicing client requests to access public folders, as well as to see if performance degradation exists as you increase the number of users. The replication counters will most likely be useful in troubleshooting replication performance issues. Table 16-7 lists some of the counters you will use to monitor client access to public folders, and Table 16-8 lists some of the counters dealing with public folder replication.

Like the mailbox database counters, you can select an individual public folder database to monitor in the Instance field under each of these counters.

Object	Counter	Description
MSExchangeIS Public	Active Client Logons	This counter tells you how many clients are logged on and if they have performed any actions within the last 10 minutes.
MSExchangeIS Public	Folder Opens/ Sec	This counter shows the rate at which public folders are opened. An increase above your baseline would indicate larger numbers of users traversing the tree structure.
MSExchangeIS Public	Receive Queue Size	This counter tells you how many messages are waiting to be delivered to the appropriate public folder. If this number exceeds your baseline, your server could have too many responsibilities within the Exchange organization.
MSExchangeIS Public	Single Instance Ratio	This counter shows the average number of references to a message within the public folder store. You want this value to be as low as possible. Exchange tries to store a message only once within its databases and use pointers to the same data if multiple instances of the message need to exist.

Table 16-7. System Monitor Counters for Monitoring Public Folder Access

Object	Counter	Description
MSExchangeIS Public	Replication Folder Changes Sent Replication Folder Changes Received	These counters tell you how many changes have been sent to and received from other servers since startup. You need to monitor how quickly the number increases, rather than look for a threshold value.
MSExchangeIS Public	Replication Receive Queue Size	This counter shows the number of replication messages waiting to be processed.
MSExchangeIS Public	Replication Backfill Requests Sent Replication Backfill Requests Received	These counters tell you how many replication backfill messages have been sent or received. An increase above your baseline would indicate a possible connectivity problem to that server's public-folder replication partners. Backfill requests should only occur if normal replication is not functional. A server that has not replicated in a long time due to connectivity problems, once finally connected to another public folder replication partner, will send a backfill request to ensure that all public folder changes are replicated.
MSExchangeIS Public	Single Instance Ratio	This counter shows the average number of references to a message within the public folder store. You want this value to be as low as possible. Exchange tries to store a message only once within its databases and uses pointers to the same data if multiple instances of the message need to exist.

Table 16-8.   System Monitor Counters for Monitoring Public Folder Replication

USING THE EXCHANGE SERVER PERFORMANCE TROUBLESHOOTING ANALYZER

Now that I've covered some of the monitoring basics with System Monitor, let's take a look at a tool that automates the monitoring of Exchange for specific problems. The Exchange Server Performance Troubleshooting Analyzer had its debut with Exchange 2003. The goal of the tool is to allow you to simply select the issue you are having, and the tool will analyze your Exchange environment for any related problems and notify you of its findings. Let's take a look at how the tool works and the types of performance problems it analyzes.

You can open the Performance Troubleshooting Analyzer by navigating in the Exchange Management Console to the Toolbox node in the console tree, as shown in Figure 16-5 and selecting Open Tool in the action pane.

Figure 16-5. Opening the Performance Troubleshooting Analyzer.

The Performance Troubleshooting Analyzer runs as a wizard and assists in determining the source of a problem you specify by collecting information on the Exchange environment and performance data and reporting on findings related to the initial problem. The initial page of the wizard, shown in Figure 16-6, gives you the option of selecting what the problem is that your Exchange environment appears to be experiencing.

In my example, I've chosen to troubleshoot a problem of users seeing RPC cancel request pop-up messages. There are currently two issues you can choose from. While a good sign that Exchange 2007 is a solid messaging platform, your problem may not be listed here. As new common Exchange performance issues arise, Microsoft will add other problems within the tool.

The next step is to establish a connection with Exchange and Active Directory by specifying which Exchange server and which domain controller to connect with, as shown in

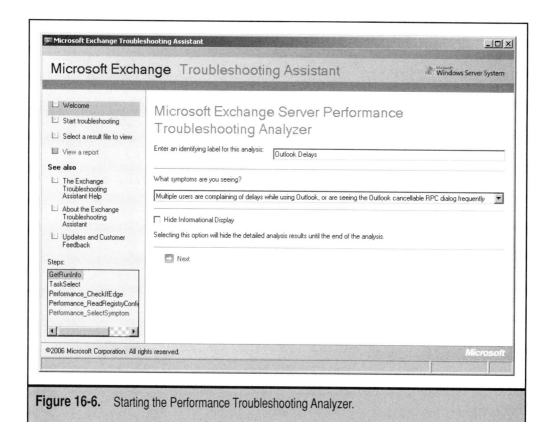

Figure 16-6. Starting the Performance Troubleshooting Analyzer.

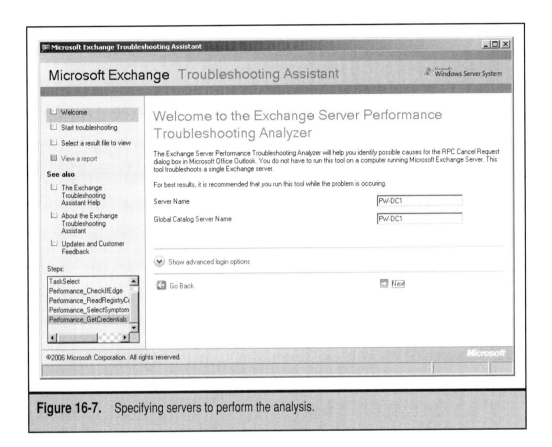

Figure 16-7. Specifying servers to perform the analysis.

Figure 16-7. Credentials can be specified by selecting the Show Advanced Login Options link if the account you're currently using doesn't have the appropriate permissions to perform the analysis.

An extensive connectivity test is performed, with the results displayed in Figure 16-8. Any issues connecting with Active Directory, as well as the general configuration of the Exchange environment, will be listed here and must be corrected before continuing with the analysis.

If your environment passes the connectivity test, clicking Next will take you to the Configure Data Collection page of the wizard (see Figure 16-9). Here you will specify whether to collect performance data, run an analysis on performance data, or both.

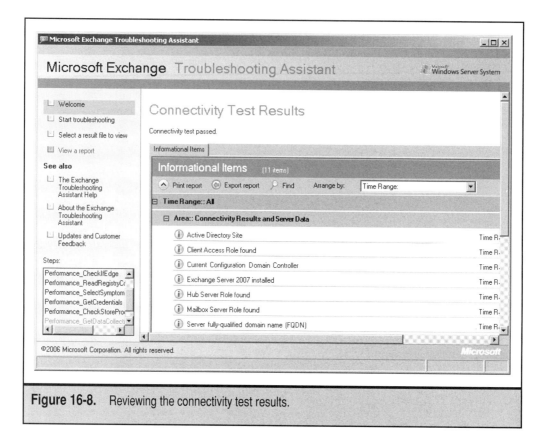

Figure 16-8. Reviewing the connectivity test results.

Once you click Next, the wizard proceeds to collect the needed performance data for the duration you specified on the previous page. Once this is done, the actual analysis begins, with a report being automatically generated showing both critical issues and all other non-critical issues. You can export your report to Hypertext Markup Language (HTML), comma-separated value (CSV) and eXtensible Markup Language (XML) formats.

The normal causes of the RPC Cancel Request dialog box are sometimes as simple an issue as of not enough server memory to appropriately respond to client requests, but can be as complex as issues like Global Catalog server placement, accessing a public folder server from another Active Directory site, or connectivity issues related to your physical network topology between clients and the Exchange server.

Like the Best Practice Analyzer, which I covered in Chapter 14, the Performance Troubleshooting Analyzer will tell you both what is wrong with your environment and the steps you can take to fix the problem.

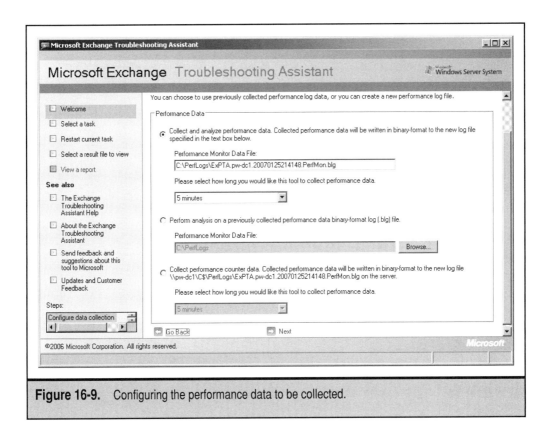

Figure 16-9. Configuring the performance data to be collected.

SUMMARY

In this chapter, we looked at the basics of monitoring Windows 2003 and Exchange 2007. We saw how to monitor the four basic resources using standard counters provided by Windows 2003 and how to monitor specific aspects of Exchange 2007 using System Monitor. Lastly, we took a look at the Exchange Server Performance Troubleshooting Analyzer tool and how it can be used to troubleshoot common Exchange performance problems. In the next chapter, we will take a look at how compliance standards affect Exchange and the steps you can take to make your Exchange environment compliant.

CHAPTER 17

Exchange and Regulatory Compliance

I read the other day that e-mail has surpassed the use of the telephone as the primary method of business communication. With e-mail becoming a more productive means of communicating, nearly all important conversations take place within your Exchange environment. Now you may have read the title of this chapter and have no regulations imposed on your business. However, I would encourage you to read the chapter just the same; this chapter is not only about the regulations that require the retention of e-mail, but also about the built-in technologies. Exchange has to keep a record of messages that have passed through its environment. Some day, even those organizations that have no applicable regulations may have a need to pull old messages due to a lawsuit or in the case of a data leak via e-mail.

In this chapter, I will cover the general needs that compliance standards mandate with regards to message retention. Then I will go over how Exchange can be configured to meet those needs, as well as touch on some third-party solutions that will assist in the process.

COMPLIANCE STANDARDS AND EXCHANGE

Many governments have imposed regulations that require organizations in specific industries to protect sensitive data. For example, the Healthcare Insurance Portability and Accountability Act (HIPAA) seeks to protect patient information. The problem is that nearly all of these regulatory standards are vague, at best, in their execution. Match that with the fact that the protected information may or may not be within your Exchange environment. So, if a particular regulation applies to your company, you are left basically *over-protecting* your company just to be on the side of caution, which means you need to involve your Exchange system.

Now, at this point, you should be asking yourself, "Wait a minute—what does protecting sensitive data have to do with e-mail?" Beyond the security aspect of locking down access to systems that manage sensitive information, e-mail comes into play when attempting to *prove* that the sensitive data was not inappropriately made available via e-mail. So now you see how Exchange (unfortunately) comes into the picture. Table 17-1 lists just a few of the standards today that have an application to Exchange.

The bottom line is that if any of these apply to you, you'll need to retain not just pertinent messages, but in some cases, *every* message to prove that no pertinent message was purposely deleted. Exchange 2007 natively has several features that assist with message archival and retention (which is the term you'll hear used in the industry). In addition, Microsoft provides some online services that assist with compliance standards. Let's begin by looking at what you can do with Exchange out of the box.

Regulation	Jurisdiction	Sector Affected	Effect on Exchange
Sarbanes-Oxley Act (SOX)	United States companies (including multinational) listed on U.S. stock exchanges	Any publicly traded company, as well as private companies in the financial and accounting sectors	Any correspondence related to an audit or review of a company's financial records must be retained for five years.
Securities and Exchange Commission (SEC) Rule 17-A4	United States	Financial	All communications must be preserved for seven years, with the first two being easily accessible.
HIPAA	United States	Healthcare	Be able to prove that transmission of healthcare information is safeguarded.
Basel II Capital Accord	European Union	Banking/financial	Operational risk needs to be identified. This means an audit of electronic messaging may be required.
Freedom of Information Act (FOIA)	United States and other countries	Government	Gives public access to any documents and communication outside of that which is not in the best interest of the general public.

Table 17-1.   A Few Compliance Standards that Apply to Exchange

JOURNALING

The first Exchange technology you can use to assist with compliance is *journaling*. Journaling is the process of recording messages that are sent and received within an Exchange organization. In Exchange 2007, there are two flavors of journaling:

▼ Standard journaling enables the recording of messages on a per-mailbox–database basis. All messages sent to and from a given mailbox database will be also sent to a specified recipient.

▲ Premium journaling is only available to Microsoft customers with an Enterprise Client Access License (CAL). With premium journaling, rules can be established with far more granularity, covering individual mailboxes or groups of mailboxes.

In both cases, Exchange uses a Journaling Agent. The agent's role is to look at the journaling configuration, watch for messages that meet the criteria established by the rules, and make copies of the messages that apply. The only difference between the two journaling types is the level of management granularity that you have. To determine if the Journaling Agent is installed and running on your Exchange server running the Mailbox server role, you'll need to use the Exchange Management Shell and run the following command:

```
Get-TransportAgent
```

The output is shown in Figure 17-1. Note the value of *true* in the Enabled column for the Journaling Agent.

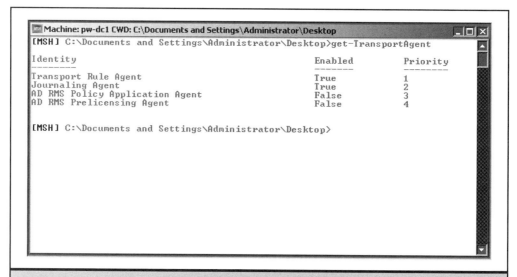

Figure 17-1. Verifying that the Journaling Agent is started.

If, for some reason, the Journaling Agent is not enabled, you can use the following command to enable it:

```
Enable-TransportAgent -Identity "Journaling agent"
```

Let's take a look at how to configure journaling by beginning with the standard mode and then covering the premium mode.

Configuring Standard Journaling

You enable standard journaling by configuring each mailbox database individually. To begin, you'll need to navigate within the Exchange Management Console to the Mailbox node under Server Configuration in the console tree. Select the mailbox database you wish to configure in the results pane, and select Properties from the action pane, as shown in Figure 17-2.

On the General tab, you will need to select the Journal Recipient check box, click the Browse button, and select a recipient, as shown in Figure 17-3.

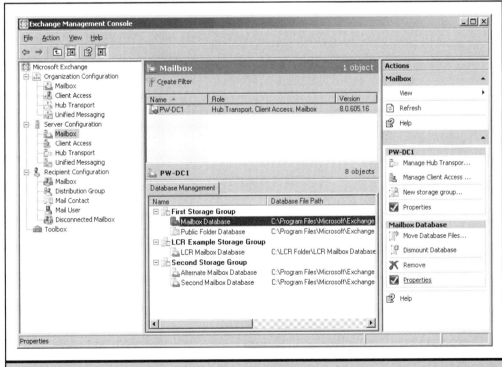

Figure 17-2.   Opening the mailbox database properties.

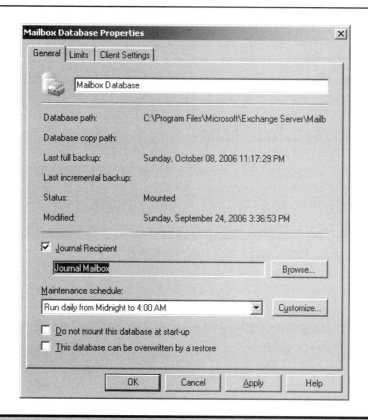

Figure 17-3.   Specifying a Journal recipient.

Management Shell Corner

You can enable journaling on a mailbox database using the following command:

```
Set-MailboxDatabase "Mailbox Database" -JournalRecipient "Journal Mailbox"
```

Once a journal recipient is specified, any messages that are sent to or received by a mailbox within a database configured for journaling will be copied to the journal recipient. Figure 17-4 shows the creation of a message by a user whose mailbox database is configured for journaling.

When I open the mailbox of the journal recipient (see Figure 17-5), you will notice not just a copy of the message, as in previous versions of Exchange, but also a special type of message called a journal report. I'll cover journal reports in more depth later in the chapter. For now, know that the journal report lists information about the message, along with an attachment of that message.

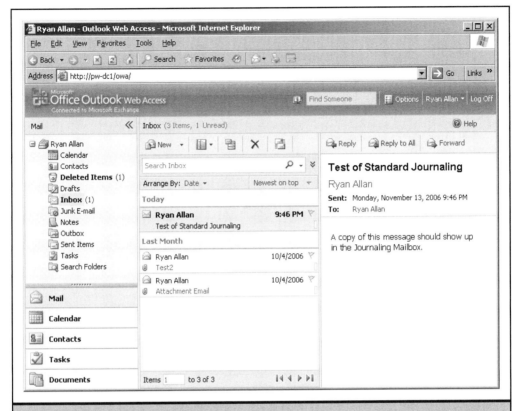

Figure 17-4.   Creating a message in a journaled mailbox.

Journal Recipients

You should notice that when you browse to select the journal recipient, you can see mailboxes, distribution groups, and contacts. The most common selection is a single mailbox. If you were to choose a distribution group, keep in mind that a copy of *every* message will be going to the members of that distribution group. If you select a contact or a distribution group that contains a contact, keep in mind that copies of your company's messages are going outside your organization, potentially beyond the constraints of the security and management you have in place. In each of these cases, you should first consult your legal counsel, as the very reason you are most likely running journaling is for legal reasons, whether reactively to meet government regulations that exist or proactively to protect the data and assets within your organization. A single mailbox is recommended as the journaling recipient because it has the best chance of remaining under tight security. Access to a mailbox designated as the journaling recipient needs to be a part of a documented plan of who has access and the proper procedure to access data.

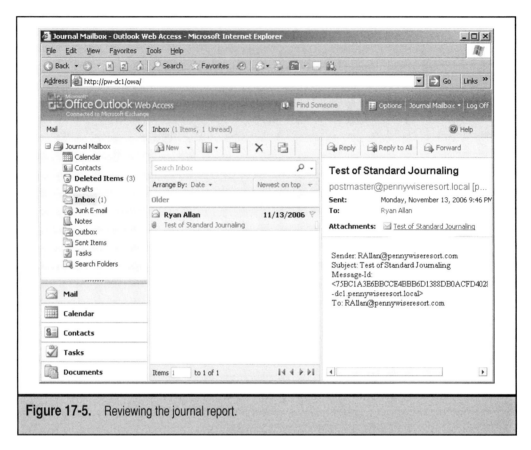

Figure 17-5. Reviewing the journal report.

Opening the attachment (see Figure 17-6) yields a copy of the original message for you to review.

Configuring Premium Journaling

The problem with standard journaling is that every message within a mailbox database, regardless of content, is copied to the journal recipient. This means that unnecessary messages (like jokes, inquiries about lunch plans, etc.) are also processed and copied by the Journaling Agent to the designated recipient. This is the very reason why premium journaling is another option. It is a far more advanced offering, designed to allow you a greater lever of management and reporting.

Premium journaling is only available to those customers that purchase the Exchange Enterprise CAL. It differentiates itself from standard journaling by first allowing journaling at a much deeper level than per-mailbox database. Premium journaling can be enabled for an individual recipient or distribution group. Secondly, you have three journaling scopes to establish what kind of messages you want to journal. Table 17-2 describes the journal scopes available and the types of messages that will be copied by the Journaling Agent.

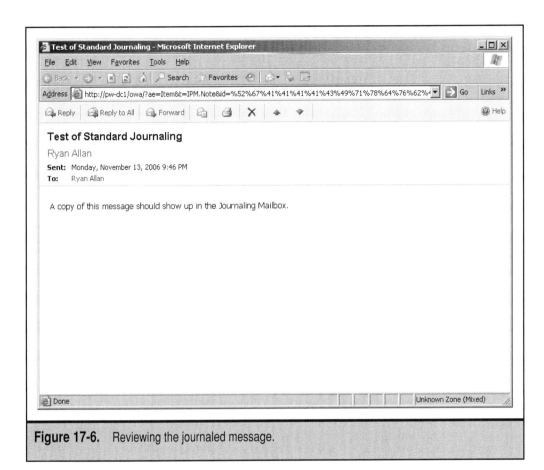

Figure 17-6.   Reviewing the journaled message.

Scope	Description
Internal	Journaling only captures those messages sent from and to internal mailboxes
External	Journaling only captures those messages that are sent from or to external e-mail addresses
Global	Journaling captures messages that are sent from or to both internal and external recipients

Table 17-2.   Premium Journaling Scopes

Lastly, premium journaling supports the replication of journal rules. Unlike standard journaling, which only establishes the per-mailbox–database journaling rule on the mailbox server hosting the mailbox database, premium journaling runs on Hub Transport servers, so all premium journaling rules are stored within Active Directory and are, therefore, accessible to all Hub Transport servers. This means that any journaling rule you establish will run on all Hub Transport servers.

When configuring premium journaling, you first need to ensure that the Journaling Agent is enabled. See the previous section "Journaling" for information on how to do this. Next, you will configure the individual journal rules within the Exchange Management Console. Navigate to the Hub Transport node under Organization Configuration in the console tree, and select the Journaling tab in the results pane, as shown in Figure 17-7.

Click the New Journaling link in the action pane to start the New Journaling Rule Wizard, shown in Figure 17-8. Provide a name for the rule, and specify the e-mail address of the recipient that will receive copies of all messages meeting the criteria within this rule. Next, specify a scope for your rule. If you stop here and click Next, the rule will

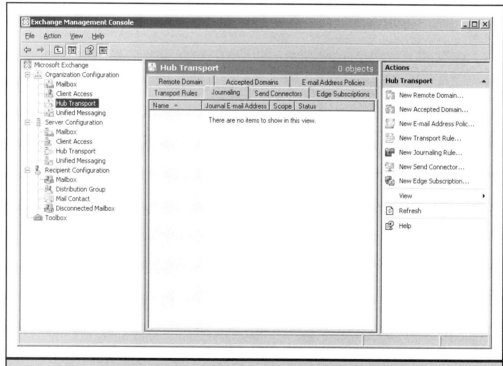

Figure 17-7. Managing journaling rules.

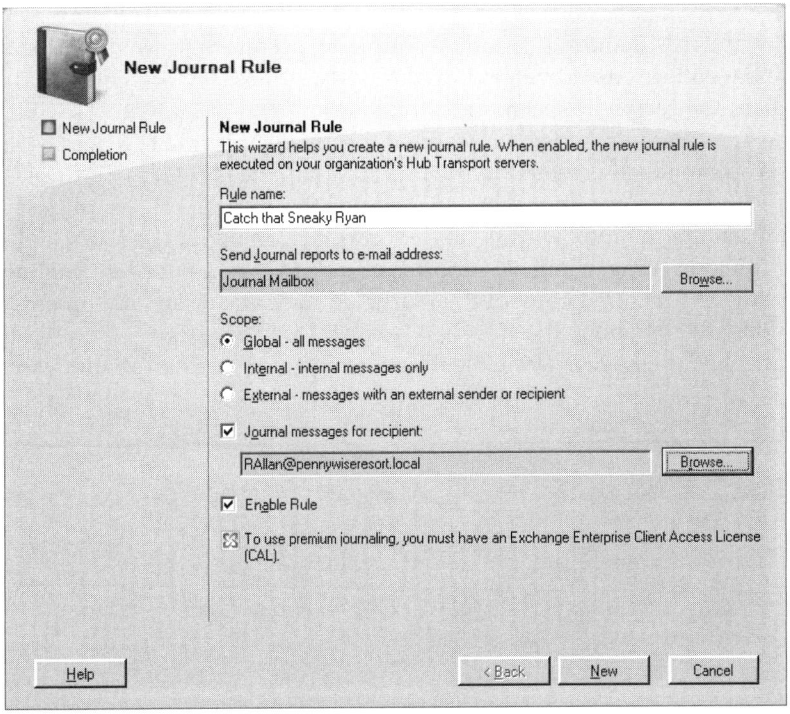

Figure 17-8. Creating a new journaling rule.

apply to all recipients and to all messages within the scope of the rule. If you need to monitor specific mailboxes, use the Journal E-mail For Recipient field to specify which individual mailbox or distribution group (theoretically, multiple mailboxes) will be monitored for journaling. Once done, click Next and click Finish.

Management Shell Corner

To create a journaling rule, you can run the following command:

```
new-journalRule -Name:'Watch that Sneaky Ryan' -JournalEmailAddres
s:'pennywiseresort.local/Users/Journal Mailbox' -Scope:'Global' -
Enabled:$true -Recipient:'RAllan@pennywiseresort.com'
```

Journal Reports

Figures 17-9 and 17-10 show a simple example of premium journaling, including one concept we haven't discussed yet—journal reports. A message is created in the mailbox of Ryan Allan, the recipient specified in the journaling rule I created (see Figure 17-6). Because the message falls under the scope of the journaling rule I created earlier, a journal report is automatically created in the Journal Mailbox, shown in Figure 17-10.

Unlike standard journaling, where a copy of the message is simply placed in the specified journaling mailbox with no added information about the journaled messages, with premium journaling, a journal report is placed in the specified journaling mailbox. Besides saving an unaltered copy of the journaled message as an attachment, the report itself provides details about the message as well to ensure that as much information about the attached message is available. For example, you normally cannot see if anyone

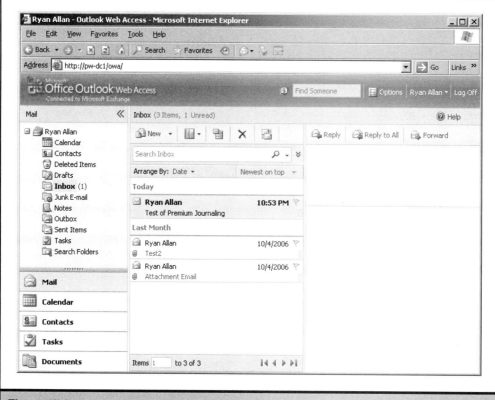

Figure 17-9.   Creating a message to be journaled.

is added as a blind carbon copy (BCC) recipient, but any BCC recipients are listed in the journal report. Figure 17-10 shows an example of a simple journal report consisting of a message sender, subject, ID, and recipients. Table 17-3 lists the various pieces of information that can be part of a journal report.

Figure 17-11 shows a message being created with a more intricate recipient configuration. In this message, Jack Brown is an internal mailbox with a Forward To configured to copy the message to another internal mailbox; Maggie Rose is an external SMTP recipient; the Premium Journaling Test DG contains one internal mailbox; and Nicholas John is another internal mailbox. In total, there are six recipients (Jack, Jack's forward to, Maggie, Ryan, the Test DG, and Nicholas). This is reflected in Figure 17-12, where not just one journal report is displayed, but six, each one detailing the recipients who received the message.

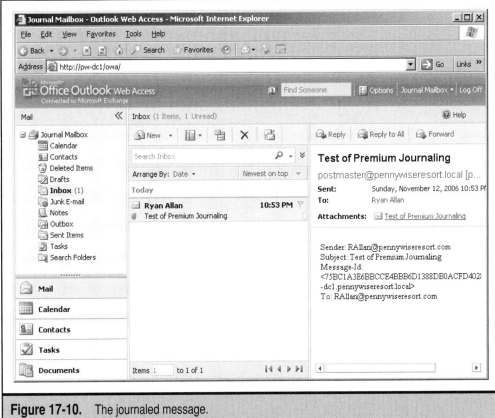

Figure 17-10.   The journaled message.

Report Field Name	Description
Sender	Lists the Simple Mail Transfer Protocol (SMTP) address of the originator of the message. Even if the sender is internal to the Exchange organization, an SMTP address is always shown to properly identify the unique sender.
On-Behalf-Of	Lists the SMTP address of the mailbox the messages appear from if the Send On Behalf Of feature is used.
Subject	Lists the message subject value.
Message ID	Lists the internal Exchange message ID used by Exchange to track the message.
To	Lists the SMTP addresses of all recipients specified in the To field within the message. This includes recipients directly specified in the original message, recipients indirectly specified by membership within a distribution group, and recipients that receive a copy of the message by means of the Forward To delivery option feature within Exchange.
Cc	Lists the SMTP addresses of all recipients specified in the Cc field within the message. The same recipient inclusions as the To field apply here.
Bcc	Lists the SMTP addresses of all recipients specified in the Bcc field within the message. The same recipient inclusions as the To field apply here.
Expanded	Lists the SMTP addresses of the distribution groups used in the To, Cc, and Bcc fields described earlier. This field is displayed as a sub-field to each of the To, Cc, and Bcc fields, as appropriate.
Forwarded	Like the Expanded field, this is a sub-field of To, Cc, and Bcc. It lists the SMTP addresses of recipients that receive a copy of the message as a result of the Forward To delivery option.
Recipient	Lists any SMTP addresses of recipients outside of your Exchange organization.

Table 17-3. All Fields for a Journal Report

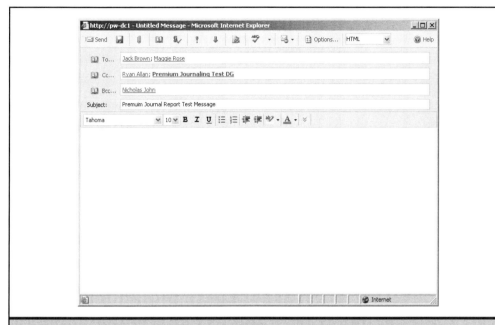

Figure 17-11.   A test of premium journaling's journal reports.

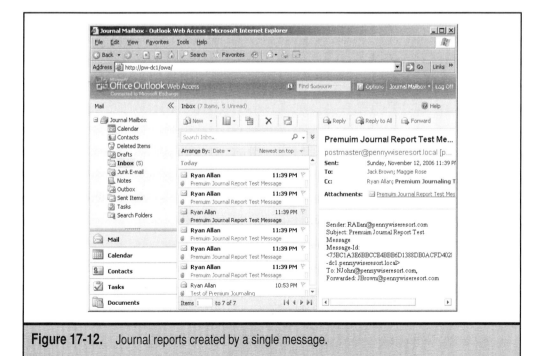

Figure 17-12.   Journal reports created by a single message.

MESSAGE CLASSIFICATION

In cases of both standard and premium journaling, the level of management granularity only goes as low as the database and mailbox, respectively. And even then, that only helps determine which messages are stored for later retrieval. But when the need for searching messages arises due to compliance or legal issues, being able to isolate pertinent and related messages can be helpful. Exchange 2007 provides a new feature that works in conjunction with both Outlook 2007 and Exchange 2007–based Outlook Web Access that will allow identification of the purpose of messages using *message classifications*.

Classifying messages is the process of tagging messages with metadata that can be used to proactively categorize them for later use. For example, classifications could be used to mark messages that are attorney-client privileged or messages that are related to a specific project. This is a highly flexible technology that can improve your ability to quickly find messages. Figure 17-13 shows a simple example of a classified message marked with the Company Internal message classification.

Creating Message Classifications

By default, Exchange 2007 creates four message classifications: *A/C Privileged* (that is, Attorney/Client), *Attachment Removed*, *Company Confidential*, and *Company Internal*.

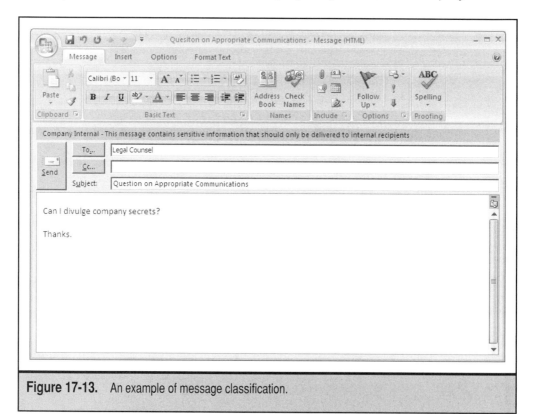

Figure 17-13.   An example of message classification.

To create new message classifications, you will need to utilize the *New-MessageClassification* cmdlet in Exchange Management Shell. A simple execution of this command would be as follows:

```
New-MessageClassification -Name <name> -DisplayName <display name>
-SenderDescription "Description of the message classification"
```

So if you wanted to create a message classification for messages related to a pending lawsuit over spilt milk, you would run the following command:

```
New-MessageClassification -Name SpiltMilk -DisplayName "Spilt Milk Lawsuit"
-SenderDescription "Messages related to the lawsuit over spilt milk"
```

Figure 17-14 shows the output of the command.

Figure 17-14. Creating a new message classification.

Configuring Outlook Clients for Message Classifications

Outlook 2007 supports message classification, but to preserve the security of messages and their relevance to sensitive topics, message classification must be enabled on a per-client basis. The process involves the creation of a message-classification definitions file on the server side and the configuration of the Outlook client. Each Exchange user that is using message classifications may not need to utilize (or truly be kept from doing so) every one. So you will need to create the classification definition file, classifications.xml, manually within the Exchange Management Shell using the following command:

```
"<name of classification>" | Get-MessageClassification | .\Export-Out-
lookClassification.msh > path\classifications.xml
```

Let's suppose you want to create a classifications.xml file for the Company Internal and Spilt Milk message classifications. You'll need to run the following cmdlet:

```
"Company Internal", "Spilt Milk Lawsuit" | Get-MessageClassification |
.\Export-OutlookClassification.msh > c:\export\classifications.xml
```

Figure 17-15 shows the output of the command (which is just another command prompt) and the output of the file. Notice that in order to get the power shell script (Export-OutlookClassifications.msh) to work, you'll need to be in the Scripts folder under your Exchange installation folder.

The next step is to make a few registry changes on the Outlook client. You'll first need to create the following registry key:

```
HKEY_CURRENT_USER\Software\Microsoft\Office\12.0\Common\Policy
```

Next, you'll need to create three registry values, listed in Table 17-4.

Once configured, the client's registry should look like that shown in Figure 17-16.

The final step is to place the classifications.xml file in the location specified in the AdminClassificationPath entry in the registry. You can accomplish this, as well as make

Value Name	Value Type	Value Data
AdminClassificationPath	REG_SZ	<path to classifications.xml>
EnableClassifications	REG_DWORD	1
TrustClassifications	REG_DWORD	1

Table 17-4.   Registry Entries to Enable Message Classifications

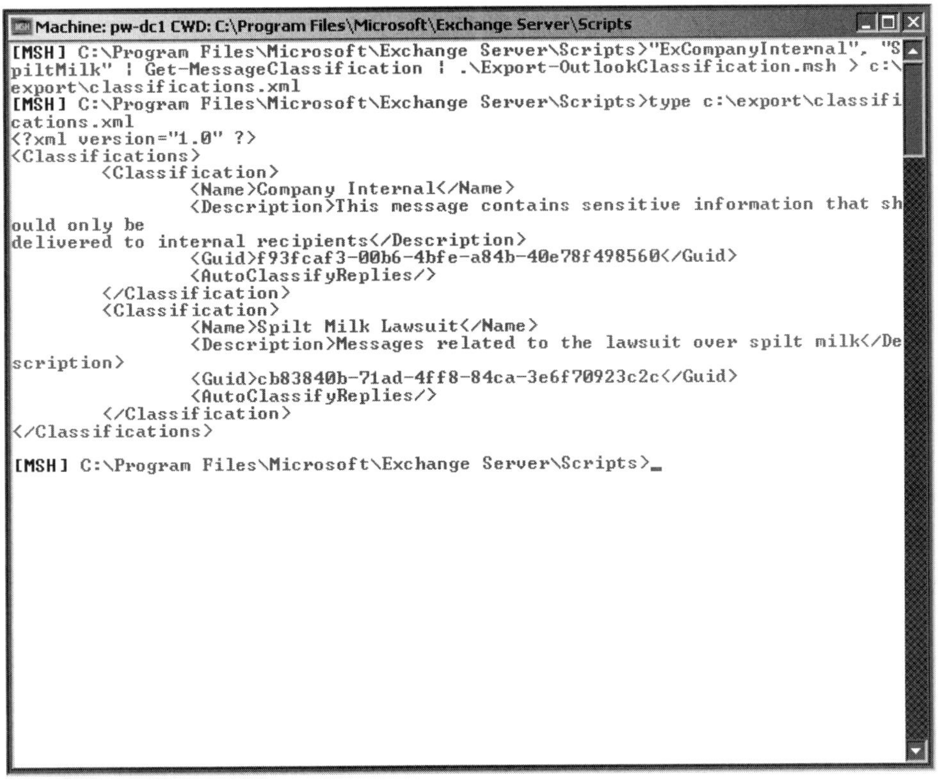

```
Machine: pw-dc1 CWD: C:\Program Files\Microsoft\Exchange Server\Scripts
[MSH] C:\Program Files\Microsoft\Exchange Server\Scripts>"ExCompanyInternal", "S
piltMilk" | Get-MessageClassification | .\Export-OutlookClassification.msh > c:\
export\classifications.xml
[MSH] C:\Program Files\Microsoft\Exchange Server\Scripts>type c:\export\classifi
cations.xml
<?xml version="1.0" ?>
<Classifications>
        <Classification>
                <Name>Company Internal</Name>
                <Description>This message contains sensitive information that sh
ould only be
delivered to internal recipients</Description>
                <Guid>f93fcaf3-00b6-4bfe-a84b-40e78f498560</Guid>
                <AutoClassifyReplies/>
        </Classification>
        <Classification>
                <Name>Spilt Milk Lawsuit</Name>
                <Description>Messages related to the lawsuit over spilt milk</De
scription>
                <Guid>cb83840b-71ad-4ff8-84ca-3e6f70923c2c</Guid>
                <AutoClassifyReplies/>
        </Classification>
</Classifications>

[MSH] C:\Program Files\Microsoft\Exchange Server\Scripts>_
```

Figure 17-15. Creating the classifications.xml file.

the registry changes, with solutions like ScriptLogic's Desktop Authority, which can not only copy the XML file and make the registry setting changes centrally, but can also easily distinguish one group of users from another to ensure that the proper XML file is pushed to the client's desktop.

Using Message Classifications

Once the client has been properly configured, Outlook clients can immediately take advantage of the message classifications for documentation purposes. Figure 17-17 shows the two configured message classifications available for selection upon creating a new message within Outlook 2007.

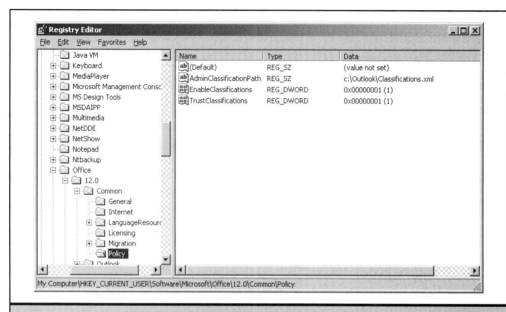

Figure 17-16. Registry settings to enable message classification.

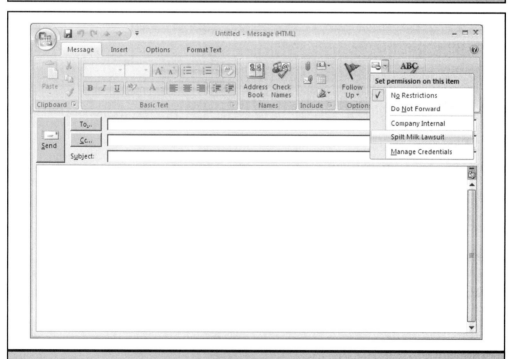

Figure 17-17. Specifying a message classification within Outlook 2007.

You'll be relieved to know that Outlook Web Access requires no special configuration to enable message classifications. However, all classifications are available, as shown in Figure 17-18.

Once a message has been classified, the classification metadata is made a part of the message and cannot be removed. Figure 17-19 shows what the message looks like on the receiving end.

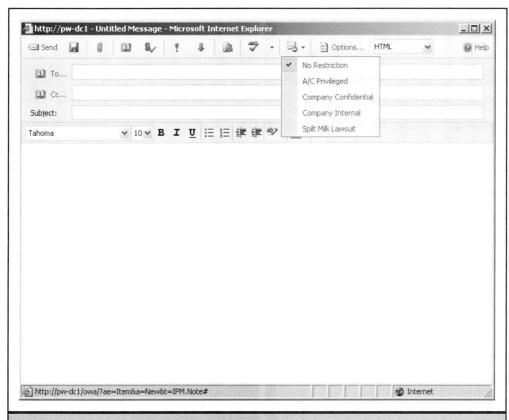

Figure 17-18.   Specifying message classifications within Outlook Web Access.

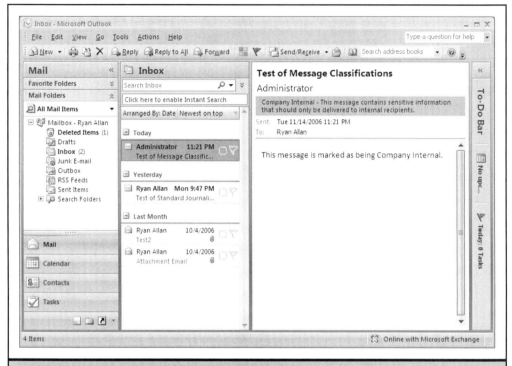

Figure 17-19. Receiving a message with classification applied.

Using Transport Rules to Enhance Message Classification

While message classifications can be used for simple documentation purposes, they can also be used in conjunction with transport rules to restrict message transmission, add text to subject and message bodies, send copies of classified messages to a journal-type mailbox, and more. Figure 17-20 shows a simple transport rule that is configured to prepend a phrase to the subject of any message with the classification of *SpiltMilk* (denoted as "marked with SpiltMilk").

More advanced rules can be created to enforce that specific individuals be a recipient in a classified message. This is a great way of helping to enforce your company's compliance policies while also documenting message purposes.

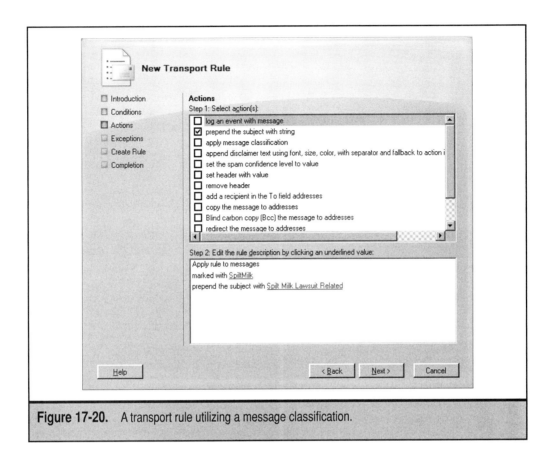

Figure 17-20.   A transport rule utilizing a message classification.

CONCLUSION

In this chapter, I provided an overview of standards that require the retention of messages and discussed how to utilize built-in Exchange technologies to meet these requirements. In addition, I covered how to implement message classification to better document messages and their content.

This is the last chapter of the book. I hope you learned quite a bit about Exchange 2007 and can take some of the information presented here and put it to good use. If you would like to get even more information on Exchange 2007, there is a ton of information in the Help file. Also, Microsoft has created a special TechNet "TechCenter" just for Exchange—you can find the Exchange TechCenter at http://www.microsoft.com/technet/prodtechnol/exchange/default.mspx.

INDEX

F

G

 H

 I

N

 O

Q

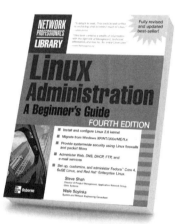